3 0250 01315 1456

D0720133

94

Internet Cryptography

Richard E. Smith

ADDISON-WESLEY

An Imprint of Addison Wesley Longman, Inc.

Reading, Massachusetts · Harlow, England · Menlo Park, California
Berkeley, California · Don Mills, Ontario · Sydney
Bonn · Amsterdam · Tokyo · Mexico City

For more information, please contact:

    Corporate & Professional Publishing Group
    Addison Wesley Longman, Inc.
    One Jacob Way
    Reading, Massachusetts 01867

Smith, Richard E., 1952-
    Internet cryptography / Richard E. Smith.
        p. cm.
    Includes bibliographical references and index.
    ISBN 0-201-92480-3
    1. Internet (Computer network)—Security measures.   2. Data encryption (Computer science)   I. Title.
    TK5102.94.S65   1997
    005.8'2—dc21   97-13773
                                            CIP

0-201-92480-3

1 2 3 4 5 6 7 8 9
First printing July 1997

To

Kelsey Chandler Smith,

Alexander Ives Smith,
and
Lesley Ann Atwood, MD,

this book is dedicated,
since it would not exist without
their love and encouragement.

Contents

Chapter 11 Secured Electronic Mail   267

Preface

This book is about delivering data safely across unsafe territory. The features that give the Internet its vitality also make it unsafe, like the streets of a major city. People do not walk carelessly in a vital, teeming city. Likewise, a careful person approaches the Internet with caution. Business data that crosses the public Internet can be forged, modified, or stolen. The Internet's technology and style don't fit well in the traditional mold of common carrier communications, so traditional security techniques don't fit well either.

Cryptography has emerged as the only alternative to protect Internet data, and it does the job well. Modern crypto techniques have evolved from the secret codes of decades past, brilliantly augmented with a deep knowledge of modern mathematics. New cryptographic products and technologies have been developed particularly for Internet applications. This book describes the principal techniques used in today's products, how they work, and how to use them. While we must talk about people "cracking" codes, we will spend far more time looking at system configurations and operating procedures. Configuration and operating errors have often been the bane of crypto system security. Mathematical details alone don't ensure the security of practical crypto systems. Even the most capable products can be defeated by carelessness.

Effective use of crypto systems requires a clear understanding of what your security objectives are and how they depend on important system properties. This book applies cryptographic techniques to particular Internet security goals like site protection, message secrecy, or transaction security. These goals are lined up against today's off-the-shelf products to show which are best suited to meet particular business and security objectives.

Who This Book is For

This book is intended for people who know very little about cryptography but need to make technical decisions about cryptographic security. Many people face this situation when they need to transmit business data safely over the Internet. This often includes people responsible for the data, like business analysts and managers, as well as those who must install and maintain the protections, like information systems administrators and managers. These people are the book's primary audience. Cryptographic concepts are explained using diagrams to illustrate component relationships and data flows. At every step we examine the relationship between the security measures and the vulnerabilities they address. This will guide readers in safely applying cryptographic techniques.

This book requires no prior knowledge of cryptography or related mathematics. Descriptions of low-level crypto mechanisms focus on presenting the concepts instead of the details. Programmers and product developers must look elsewhere for implementation details, and each chapter ends with a list of appropriate references. However, developers will still find a few useful insights here, like why crypto experts are so picky about mathematical arcana like random number generators ("No, it's a *pseudo*random number generator!") or why their theoretically unbreakable system is vulnerable to attack.

This book also contains some general tutorial material about the Internet Protocol (IP) and its cousins, but it is best if readers already have a general familiarity with computers, networking, and the Internet. In particular, it helps if readers already understand the notion of message and packet formatting—in other words, your information must be embedded in other information for the network to deliver it correctly.

How this Book is Organized

We start with cryptographic basics, apply them to product evaluation, and then look at example deployment to achieve various business and security objectives. When we understand the risks against which various security measures might protect, we can reasonably trade off between conflicting techniques. Each chapter ends with a list of references that may provide you with deeper explanations when needed. If your particular problem cannot be solved with available products, the references can provide the technical details for implementing custom solutions.

This book is organized around a small number of basic security objectives that are addressed by a few basic Internet cryptographic technologies. The objective of extending one's internal site via the Internet is illustrated with link encryption and network encryption using the IP Security Protocol (IPSEC). The objective of transaction security is illustrated using Secure Socket Layer (SSL) as applied to the World Wide Web. Message-based security is illustrated using Pretty Good Privacy (PGP) and Privacy Enhanced Mail (PEM).

Chapter Summary

The book's contents fall roughly into three parts, starting with low-level but simple techniques and working upward to high-level, complex crypto systems.

- **Introduction and traditional crypto (Chapters 1, 2, 3, and 4)**
  These chapters contain general introductory material and cover traditional crypto techniques. The Introduction provides a cross-reference of security goals against the crypto techniques presented in the book. Traditional crypto includes link encryption and the handling of secret crypto keys.

- **Network encryption with IPSEC protocols (Chapters 5, 6, 7, and 8)**
  These chapters describe the IPSEC protocol suite that protects data passing between pairs of hosts on the Internet. These protocols were originally developed for the upcoming IP version 6, but many vendors are incorporating them into existing IP products, like routers and firewalls.

- **Public key crypto and protocols for transactions (Chapters 9, 10, 11, and 12)**
  These chapters describe public key crypto techniques and their application in World Wide Web and e-mail protocols. The Web security discussion centers on the SSL protocol and related client/server software. The e-mail discussion examines the techniques of PGP and PEM. Public key certificates are discussed in the final chapter.

A Typical Chapter

Most chapters follow the same general organization. A typical chapter introduces a security service and a particular cryptographic mechanism underlying that service. Chapter information is usually organized in these general sections:

- **Security objectives**
  This section contains a list of objectives you wish to achieve in protecting your information. The product and deployment examples in the chapter are chosen to achieve these objectives.

- **Basic issues**
  This section contains an overview of important problems associated with the cryptographic services and mechanisms presented in the chapter.

- **Technology**
  There are one or more of these sections, each presenting a technical concept underlying the products introduced. These sections always include a prioritized list of requirements for securely applying the technology.

- **Product example**
  There are one or more of these sections to introduce products used in the deployment examples. These sections always include a prioritized list of requirements for assessing potential product choices.

- **Deployment example**

  There are one or more of these examples to illustrate different ways of achieving the chapter's stated security objectives. These sections always include a prioritized list of requirements for assessing a particular deployment.

- **For further information**

  This section contains an annotated list of references for more in-depth information on a subject. The chapters' lists identify the author and title of the work; the bibliography at the end of this book contains the complete citation.

Crypto Today and Tomorrow

The crypto mechanisms and products appearing in this book were chosen because they illustrate what people can buy off the shelf and use today. Simple, commercially available solutions are given preference over more sophisticated techniques that require extensive vendor support or custom engineering. Naturally this limits the discussion to a fraction of what the technologies can do. However, it is risky to speculate about the behavior of nonexistent products. Countless implementation details will affect their practical effectiveness, so it's pointless to speculate about how they *might* best work.

This book does not try to predict which future technologies will succeed or fail as easy-to-use products. An elaborate cryptographic infrastructure for safely sharing keys among computer users worldwide has been on the drawing boards for more than a dozen years; the enabling technology and its relatively modest success in off-the-shelf products is described in Chapter 12. Likewise, the chapters on IP security focus on today's products and not on the draft standards for tomorrow. The future is left to future books.

Comments and Questions

Send comments and questions via Internet e-mail to internet-crypto@aw.com. While I tried to focus on techniques that have been used successfully, many of the techniques have not seen extensive use. I'd value any "war stories" or "been there; done that" evaluations based on personal experience. I regret that I can't guarantee a personal reply to every e-mail I receive, but I will try to respond.

Up-to-date information about this book will be maintained on the Addison Wesley Longman web site (http://www.aw.com/cp/rsmith/). This page will include links to the Web pages noted in this book, plus an indication of pages that have gone offline. There will also be pointers to any corrections or errata.

Acknowledgments

A few times in my career I've been fortunate enough to work with a world-class technical team. This book would not exist but for the mentoring and shared experiences of my colleagues at Secure Computing Corporation. There is something indescribable about working with a team that set the standard for a particular technology. We did it for secure computers and I'm honored to have played a part in it.

There isn't space to recognize everyone individually at Secure Computing who contributed to the journey that led to this book, but I'll note a team and a person. Technical discussions with the IPSEC product development team were particularly valuable while developing this book's midsection and provided important insights into practical uses of certificate systems. The one individual that did the most to start me down the path leading to this book is W. Earl Boebert, our former Chief Scientist. He didn't set out to make me into a "cryppie"; instead, he encouraged me to think deeply and thoroughly about security problems, and led me to places where I had to do just that. Security isn't mysterious. It just looks that way to casual onlookers because it requires so much clear, careful thought.

A vital contributor to this book is the Internet itself and the spirit of open discussion it inevitably encourages. I expect to learn a good deal more about cryptography in the future and many of the lessons will come from Internet discussions. The Internet may be an unreliable source of facts, but it's flush with people who are gleefully prepared to dispute any opinions you might have, even if they have none of their own. I've found an ample number of people to provide knowledgeable discussions on the sci.crypt newsgroup, and the mailing lists ssl-talk (contact majordomo@netscape.com) and cypherpunks (contact majordomo@toad.com).

I would also like to thank Renee Frank of the Public Affairs Office of the National Security Agency, and Jack E. Ingram, Curator and Historian at the National Cryptologic Museum, for photos and research assistance. I must also thank Marcus Ranum of V-One Corporation, Toni Santillan of Cylink Corporation, and Roberta Bowersox of IRE for providing additional photographs.

The rough drafts for this book were all developed using a 1990 version of MORE, the first and last professional-quality outlining and document development program. It appears that the vendor, Symantec, no longer supports it. Fortunately the 1990 release has been robust enough to survive major revisions to the Macintosh OS without serious "bit rot." The remaining drafts and diagrams of this book were produced using FrameMaker, now owned by Adobe.

I tend to look at book writing as a variant of computer programming, and the only "debugging" I get is when some brave soul is willing to read and critique some part of the book. My benefactors include some people named "Anonymous" as well as Steve Bellovin, Mary Budge, Peter Galvin, Chris Kostick, Gene Leonard, John Linn, Joanne Luciano, Tom Markham, Radia Perlman, Jeff Pomeroy, and Ted Stockwell, with a special thank you to Phil Rogaway. I also have to give special thanks to Marcus Ranum, whose suggestions and recommendations have followed the book from the beginning. It seems as if Marcus has always understood exactly what this book was trying to achieve and I hope it hits somewhere near the mark we both seem to share. As any software developer will tell you, debugging won't find all the bugs, so the remaining flaws are all mine.

This book was constructed through an incremental process of writing and reviewing that is the essence of book writing for Addison Wesley Longman's Computer and Engineering Publishing Group. It probably costs more to write a book this way, and it might not appeal to every writer, but it appeals to me. I feel blessed. Carol Long, my editor, has consistently held the same vision of this book that I held and has helped keep things focused at her end as well as at mine. I must also thank Mary Harrington and Melissa Lima at Addison Wesley Longman for their crucial help in the process.

I also thank my family, friends, and neighbors for good-naturedly putting up with the self-centered obsession that goes with writing a book in what we charmingly refer to as my "spare time." The Balsams Hotel in Dixville Notch, New Hampshire, provided unmatched comfort while I labored on final revisions. As usual, I also need to thank Nancy's Cafe in Hastings, Minnesota, for their hospitality and fine breakfasts.

1

Introduction

He that will not apply new remedies must expect new evils.

—Francis Bacon

IN THIS CHAPTER

This chapter introduces basic concepts of cryptography (or *crypto*), of internetworking, and the application of crypto products to fulfill particular needs. The following topics are described:

- The basic problem we are trying to solve

- The basic terms and concepts of crypto, and the basic problem: poor use

- The basic terms and concepts for networking and the Internet

- How to identify and establish your security goals

- How to choose cryptographic products to fulfill your communications goals

- The legal issues surrounding crypto today

1.1 The Basic Problem

Most people associate safety and security with physical protection: stout walls, locked doors, alarms, and guards. This is also true for computers. The safety of a computer's data relies heavily on the physical security of the computer itself. This is a problem in our "wired" world. Computer data often travels from one computer to another, leaving the safety of its protected physical surroundings.

Once the data is out of your hands it can fall into the hands of people with bad intentions. If it suits them, they could modify or forge your data, either for amusement or for their own benefit. Cryptography can reformat and transform your data, making it safer on its trip between computers. The technology is based on the essentials of secret codes, augmented by modern mathematics that protect your data in powerful ways.

We can illustrate the problem with Alice and Bob, imaginary people who are often used to explain crypto systems. In this example, Alice's job is to tell Bob to pay some money to someone outside their company. In the good old days, Alice would write a memo or tell Bob in person at the home office. But Alice's job takes her on the road now and she often must send instructions to Bob. Electronic mail (or *e-mail*) is her medium of choice, since it doesn't involve phone tag and Bob never listens to his voice mail. Bob is never able to contact Alice because she travels so much.

Figure 1-1 shows what happens. Alice, in the branch office, composes a message for Bob, instructing him to "PAY $100." This is sent out of the branch office over a network, received at the home office, and delivered to Bob's desk for action. They use the Simple Mail Transfer Protocol (SMTP), the standard internet e-mail

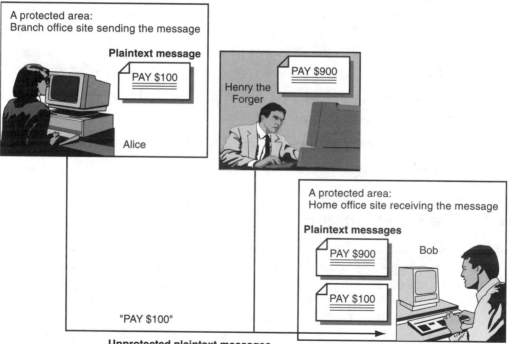

Figure 1-1: PLAINTEXT MESSAGES ARE EASY TO USE BUT RISKY. Alice sends a payment request to Bob. Henry the Forger will receive payments if Alice tells Bob to pay him, so Henry forges a payment request of his own. There is no way for Bob to tell the difference between legitimate payment requests from Alice and bogus payment requests from Henry.

protocol. It has proven highly reliable in practice, especially when delivering e-mail directly from one host (Alice's) to another (Bob's).

Unfortunately, Alice's electronic messages are incredibly easy to modify and forge. Bob really has no way of distinguishing a genuine message from Alice from a forgery. In Figure 1-1, Henry the Forger personally profits from this by giving Bob a forged message. When Bob receives an e-mail message that says it's from Alice, there is no way to tell whether or not it was really constructed by some third person who, like Henry the Forger, might actually receive the money being paid. Standard Internet e-mail is so easy to forge that its forgery is almost a rite of passage for novice administrators and clever users. In some cases people write longer, more personal messages simply to convince the recipient that the message is authentic. This does make it a bit harder for the forger. However, someone could still intercept the long, authentic, personal message and change the $100 to some larger amount. Bob would have no way of knowing that the message has been changed.

Communications would be relatively safe if Bob, Alice, and the computing equipment they use are all physically protected. They can physically lock the forgers and other hostile outsiders away from their computing systems (keyboards, CPUs, mainframes, and the network wiring them together). But full physical protection also defeats Alice's objective, which is to give instructions to Bob while she is away from the home office. Using dial-up phone lines is somewhat safer, but Alice is uncomfortable with persistent reports of kids tapping phones and penetrating central office switches. Such attacks were reported in 1990 and 1992 on phone systems in Denver, Atlanta, and New Jersey; similar attacks were attributed to a fellow named Kevin Mitnick in the 1980s. Besides, dial-up access doesn't meet all of Alice's communications needs and she faces much more serious risks when she uses the Internet. Alice knows that her best strategy is to try to make passable forgeries so expensive that the benefits aren't worth the effort. She can't afford to protect against every conceivable attack, but she needs to make it harder for attacks to succeed. If the attacks are difficult enough, Henry the Forger and his associates will look elsewhere for a victim.

Crypto techniques give Alice the right balance of communications capabilities and security protection. These techniques mark, transform, and reformat the messages to protect them from disclosure, change, or both. Alice uses secret codes (or *encryption*) to disguise the message contents. This traditional technique has been used for thousands of years, although modern codes reflect a truly modern mathematical sophistication. Alice can also use a completely modern crypto mechanism, the *digital signature*, to protect her messages from forgery. Like the trick of incorporating personal information into messages, the digital signature reliably identifies the message's author. Unlike the personal message example, the digital signature clearly and reliably tells the recipient if the contents of the message were modified after the author composed it.

1.2   Essentials of Crypto

Crypto is a collection of techniques that transform data in ways that are hard to mimic or reverse by someone who isn't in on the secret. Traditionally, crypto was used simply to disguise the contents of messages, and this gives enough protection in some cases. Here is what happens after Alice and Bob agree that all messages shall be encrypted.

In Figure 1-2 Alice takes her *plaintext* message ("PAY $100") and uses the crypto device to *encrypt* it. This operation produces a scrambled version of the message ("y9_nba%d") that leaves no hint about what it says. The scrambled message is called the *ciphertext*. Alice then sends the ciphertext to Bob across the Internet or whatever other communications medium she uses. If anyone intercepts the message, they encounter the text "y9_nba%d" instead of "PAY $100." In most cases an eavesdropper won't know if the message is a "PAY" message, a meeting reminder, or a valentine. No one can read the message easily unless they have exactly the same crypto system set up in exactly the same way.

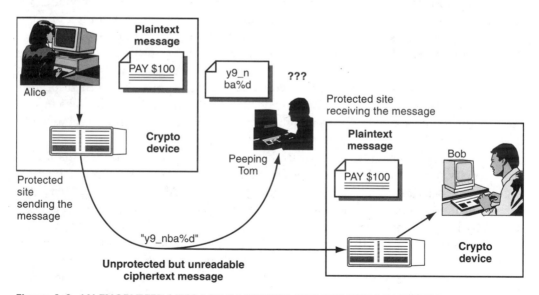

Figure 1-2: AN ENCRYPTED MESSAGE CAN RESIST ATTACKS WHILE IN TRANSIT. Peeping Tom intercepts a copy of Alice's message to Bob. Since it is encrypted he cannot tell what the message is about. Since he can't decipher it he doesn't know how to exploit it for his own benefit.

The crucial element in setting up the crypto equipment is the *crypto key*, a special piece of data that directs the crypto device to encrypt a message in a distinctive way. In traditional crypto systems the key is a randomly chosen number on which Alice and Bob agree beforehand. They can read and send encrypted messages to each other as long as they have installed the same keys in their respective crypto devices. Anyone who eavesdrops on their traffic will only find unreadable gibberish. Eavesdroppers can read nothing, even if they use exactly the same crypto equipment, since the transformation between plaintext and ciphertext depends on having the right key (Figure 1-3). Bob and Alice will have to arrange somehow to establish and share a crypto key, but the resulting security should make that extra step worthwhile.

With the crypto devices and keys in place, Bob is no longer fooled by Henry the Forger's messages. Alice and Bob now send all of their messages through their crypto devices, so Henry's forged messages go through there, too. When Bob decrypts a forged message, the crypto device treats it as ciphertext, and scrambles it into some unpredictable and unreadable data.

Bob and Alice use the crypto device to encrypt their messages, which hides the messages from prying eyes. In fact, they rely on crypto techniques to assure themselves of three specific things about their messages:

1. Bob and Alice are reasonably sure their messages can't be read by anyone else, since nobody else has the crypto key. In more formal terms, they rely on

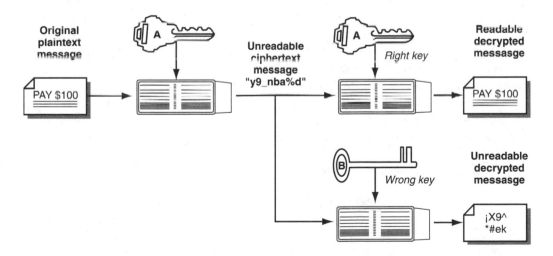

Original plaintext message

Unreadable ciphertext message "y9_nba%d"

Right key

Readable decrypted messasge

PAY $100

PAY $100

Wrong key

Unreadable decrypted messasge

¡X9^ *#ek

Figure 1-3: YOU NEED THE CORRECT CRYPTO DEVICE AND KEY TO DECRYPT THE MESSAGE.
Peeping Tom cannot read the encrypted message even if he buys exactly the same crypto device. With the wrong crypto key, the messages are still unreadable.

the *confidentiality* of the messages. Even if others use the same crypto device, they cannot read messages between Bob and Alice because Bob and Alice did not share their crypto key with anyone else.

2. Bob is reasonably sure that incoming messages are from Alice, since Alice is the only other person with the crypto key. In more formal terms, Bob relies on the *authenticity* of the messages. Bob worries less about forgeries because a forged message shouldn't decrypt properly.

3. Bob knows that readable incoming messages have not been created or modified by anyone except Alice. In more formal terms, Bob relies on the *integrity* of the messages. A forger can't tell what a message says and therefore can't modify its contents reliably. Random changes to a message will probably render it unreadable.

This example illustrates the principal properties that crypto techniques ensure: confidentiality, authenticity, and integrity. However, notice that none of these properties is referred to in an absolute sense. Bob and Alice are *reasonably* sure, not certain, of message properties. A forger can't modify a message *reliably*. The encryption they use can keep the message contents secret, but it does not necessarily make it hard to modify or forge. Whenever we examine a particular crypto device or application we will also review the security objectives it can reliably achieve. In a low-risk environment, simple encryption might be enough to deter attacks.

Another problem with relying on simple encryption is that not everyone can use their computers the way Bob and Alice are using theirs. For example, people who really use the Internet can't run all their messages through a crypto device. Lots of information on the Internet is in plaintext and must bypass the crypto if it is to be read. However, we run extra risks if some messages must always be processed by crypto and some don't. What if a message bypasses the crypto when it shouldn't have? Bob could receive a forgery that bypasses the crypto and tricks him, or he could send out secret information in plaintext that should have been encrypted. This is a real problem and it is very difficult to handle correctly.

1.2.1 Crypto is Hard to Use

Popular imagination traditionally associates crypto with diplomats, soldiers, and spies. In fact, crypto techniques have been used for centuries to protect business and commercial messages. With the evolution of computer communications, strong crypto techniques were developed for commercial purposes as well as for protecting government messaging. Initially, these techniques were only used by institutions that had a lot at risk and were willing to invest a lot in protection.

While the history of crypto holds many stories of weak codes overcome by clever adversaries, it is also has many stories about strong codes overcome by improper use. Though many stories are of wars and armies, the lessons apply to the private and commercial worlds, too.

All modern histories of World War II credit various Allied victories to code-breaking: cracking enemy codes. The U.S. Navy's successful surprise attack on the Japanese in the Battle of Midway is credited largely to decrypted Japanese radio messages. The U.S. Navy also cracked the Japanese convoy code and waged a devastating submarine campaign against their convoys. In the Atlantic, the Allies used knowledge of German codes to track their submarines.

However, this was not a one-sided success. Thanks to what some have called "sloppy" behavior by Allied coding clerks, the Germans were equally effective in reading dispatches sent to Allied convoys. Thus, the German submarines played same the game in the Atlantic that the U.S. Navy played in the Pacific.

The Navy appreciated both the value of code breaking and their own vulnerability to it. A classified dispatch was distributed in late 1943 to alert communications personnel to the risk and to repeat various rules for correct operation. While the rules of the 1940s for secure radio communication are hardly relevant, the rationale behind them still holds true:

```
The principles of communications security cannot be
overstressed, for such security is vital to the success of
operations. Errors which seem minor in themselves may, when
accumulated, offer to the enemy an entering wedge for the
eventual compromise of a system. The object of this memorandum is
to enlist your cooperation in protecting our cipher systems and
hence our national security. (See Pekelney in Appendix B.)
```

Confidentiality was crucial to the achievement of the Navy's objectives, and they relied on communications security measures to provide it. They also realized that subtle mistakes, especially when repeated, could provide an "entering wedge" for cracking the system. All crypto systems are vulnerable to the entering wedge—the careless mistakes that give adversaries the opening they need to crack your system.

1.2.2 Balancing Crypto Use with Your Objectives

It is not enough simply to purchase and install a system that contains some crypto somewhere. It has to be the right crypto for your problem and, most importantly, *it must be used* and used correctly. Consider the story of the Russian Army going to battle in Tannenberg.

On the eve of World War I, the Russian Army realized that they needed secret codes to protect radio messages sent during battle. They developed the codes and managed to distribute them just as war was declared. Unfortunately, two separate armies marched into Germany without setting up the codes to allow the armies to talk reliably.

A German army marched out to meet them. The German army was well matched to fight either Russian host, but vastly outnumbered if it met them simultaneously. The Germans attacked the northernmost army first, inflicting damage on the Russians before being driven back. Then the Russian northern army sent a radio dispatch to the southern army, revealing their timetable for moving slowly westward after the retreating Germans. This dispatch had to be sent without coding because the two armies had not coordinated their codes. The Germans overheard the dispatch and knew they had time to attack the southern Russian army. During the German attack the Russians continued to send plaintext radio messages, reporting status and ordering attacks. The Germans exploited this knowledge to defeat the Russians.

The lesson is not "the Russians should have used codes." The lesson is "they had codes they could not use." They had a goal (invade Germany) and they had the tools (the army, the radios, and the codes). But because the tools weren't used properly, they could not achieve their goal. Crypto is useless if used incorrectly.

At its root, however, the Russians' behavior holds another lesson that is fundamental to all security measures: security is always subordinate to a specific goal. The Russians took a risk when they marched to battle unprepared to use their codes. They had a goal, and to achieve it they knew they had to march and they had to use their radios. They took a data security risk and the result was a disaster. But they may have fared no better if they had delayed their march and made their crypto systems work first. For all we know the delay may have spoiled some other part of their preparations or given the Germans an opportunity to stop their invasion sooner. If the Russians had marched and enforced radio silence since they couldn't use the codes, they still risked defeat.

1.3   Essentials of Networking and the Internet

To protect network traffic you must insert crypto mechanisms into the networking system somewhere. Networking allows you to connect two or more host computers. The hosts may be desktop systems, mainframes, servers of various sorts, or portable laptops. There are usually other devices involved, like routers, bridges, and modems, depending on the type of network used.

An important distinction to understand in networking is that between *packets* and *messages* (Figure 1-4). When speaking of data traveling across a network, a *message* is generally a complete data item of some kind that a user sends to some destination. For example, Alice's "PAY $100" is a message. A *packet* is a single block

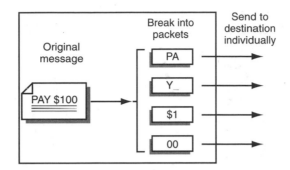

Figure 1-4: EACH MESSAGE IS CONVERTED INTO PACKETS FOR DELIVERY ACROSS THE INTERNET. The networking software accepts the message as a stream of data and transmits it as a sequence of individual blocks called *packets*. The packets are reassembled into messages on receipt at the destination.

of data that the network carries from one point to another. The size of individual packets depends on the specific networks carrying the packet. Some network technologies or devices can carry large blocks of data while others are restricted to smaller sizes. Modern networking systems automatically disassemble each message into packets for transmission and then reassemble the packets back into messages at the other end.

1.3.1   Protocol Layers and Network Products

The intent of computer networking is to allow a large variety of computers to intercommunicate. Experience has shown that there is no single, universal solution to networking. Components need to be selected and customized according to local needs and particular applications. This has yielded the modern *network protocol stack*, a suite of hardware and software that organizes the networking components as discrete, identifiable layers.

The notion of protocol layering is based on the engineering concept of interchangeable parts and modularity. A collection of communications protocols are well designed if you can essentially substitute one component for another at a given layer in the stack in order to construct what you need. Theoreticians have defined the *Open System Interconnection (OSI) Reference Model*, an idealized set of communications protocols organized into seven distinct layers (Figure 1-5). However if you buy your networking software off the shelf, there are only three distinct components you are likely to encounter: application software, network protocol software, and peripheral devices. Crypto mechanisms are generally integrated into one of these three components or installed at one of the interfaces between them (Figure 1-6).

The *application* is the software package that actually performs a particular, useful service, like e-mail or access to information. Networking software at the

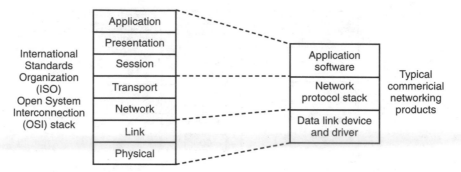

Figure 1-5: COMMERCIAL NETWORK PRODUCTS GENERALLY PACKAGED IN THREE LAYERS.
Network architects recognize seven distinct layers of networking activity, but commercial packages generally fall into one of three categories: applications, network protocol "stacks," and peripheral devices. Commercial crypto products generally appear within or between one of these three components.

application level is easily installed on desktop workstations and usually follows the same procedures as installing any other type of application software. Installing server software may be a bit more complex and usually also requires the development of whatever materials the server is to provide (Web pages, for example). Here are examples of typical network application packages:

- Electronic mail: Eudora, CCMail, MSMail, X.400

- World Wide Web: Netscape, Spyglass, Mosaic, CERN

- File Transfer: File Transfer Protocol (FTP), FTAM

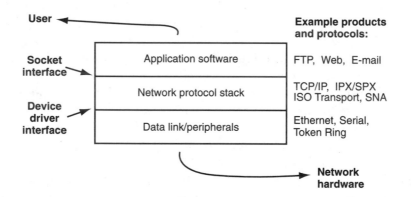

Figure 1-6: COMMERCIAL NETWORKING SOFTWARE USUALLY COMES IN THREE SEPARATE COMPONENTS. The application software interoperates with standard network software through the socket interface, and the network software interoperates with data link devices through the device driver interface.

The application software has preprogrammed hooks inside it to communicate with the host computer's networking software. The interface between the application and the network is usually called the *socket interface*. The application uses this interface to identify the networking service being provided or used and to establish connections with other, identified hosts on the network.

The *network protocol stack* refers to the software that implements the socket interface on a particular host computer. The network software provides the glue between diverse networking applications and a comparably diverse variety of data links. Network software is usually a special software package that is installed into the host computer's operating system. While some systems can operate with two or more different network protocols, most do not because of the extra storage and processing costs. In addition, there may be incompatibilities between network packages that prevent them from sharing the same host computer. Here are some typical network protocol choices:

- Transmission Control Protocol with the Internet Protocol (TCP/IP)
- OSI transport and network protocols
- Novell Netware IPX/SPX
- IBM's System Network Architecture (SNA)

In practice, the protocols used by most of these network layers have established ways to interoperate with TCP/IP, the Internet's network layer protocols.

The *data link* refers to the interface hardware you use to connect to your network. You generally select the link layer to match the network to which you are connecting. A local area network (LAN) connection must generally match the rest of the networking hardware used at your site. A remote or wide area network (WAN) connection must generally connect to a modem or a special-purpose digital connection established by your WAN service provider. The network protocol software communicates with the data link via a *device driver* installed in the system. To install a particular data link into a host system you need both hardware and software. The hardware consists of an interface device to connect the host physically to the network. The software consists of a device driver to allow the host's network software to talk to the device. Typical link layers are:

- Modems connected to telephone lines
- Frame relay, asynchronous transfer mode (ATM)
- Integrated Services Digital Network (ISDN)
- Ethernet
- Fiber Distributed Data Interface (FDDI)

1.3.2 Internet Technology

The Internet emerged from the development of packet-switched networking, funded primarily by the Advanced Research Projects Agency (ARPA) of the U.S. Department of Defense in the late 1970s. By then the growth of computer networks had spawned numerous techniques to interconnect computers, but few managed to interoperate effectively. The Internet Protocol (IP) was developed to solve this problem. IP provides the simplest packet networking service possible—a service that practically all networking techniques can support. This service is combined with a procedure for automatically forwarding packets between networks when a packet's destination address is not on the current network.

As shown in Figure 1-7, we can interconnect a large variety of hosts using IP. When a message is going between two hosts on the same network, it goes directly from the creating host to the destination host. If the message is intended for a host on a different network, it travels via a host on the network boundary. These boundary hosts are generally called *routers*. Routers may be commercial devices designed

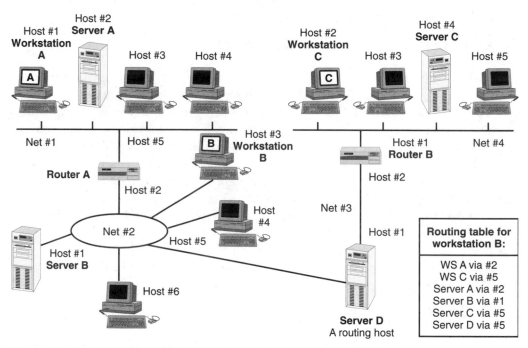

Figure 1-7: AUTOMATIC INTERNET ROUTING CONNECTS NETWORKS. Traffic can travel between any host on any network. Every host has a *routing table*—a list of addresses for traffic it sends. Workstation B uses the table shown here. If the destination is not on a directly attached network, the packet is sent to a router or routing host that relays it to the next closer network. Traffic from Workstation B to Server C is automatically sent through Server D (a *routing host*) and Router B to reach Server C's network.

to connect different networks or they may be conventional hosts connected to two or more networks. The router looks at the packet and determines to which network the packet should be sent and the host's address on that network. This process occurs several times if the data must traverse several networks to reach its destination. Host computers on early packet networks used IP and the rest of the TCP/IP family to connect their local networks to national and international long-haul networks, which led to the modern Internet.

As shown in Figure 1-8, IP introduces another component to the protocol stack. It inserts an extra "internet" layer below the usual transport activities. The transport software provides the socket interface to application software as usual. The internet software provides the interface to the device driver and is also responsible for routing packets between networks. When a host receives a packet, the packet is either directed at one of the host's applications or it uses the host as a router, and "hops" through the router on the way to its real destination. In the latter case, the internet software receives the packet from the device driver, figures out the network on which the packet belongs, and passes it back to the appropriate device driver for delivery. Only packets destined for a local application on the host will be passed upward to the host's transport software.

Internetwork routing relies on the format of IP addresses. A complete IP address contains two parts: a network address followed by a host address. Workstation B's address in Figure 1-7 could be represented as 2.0.0.3, where the 2 represents the network number and the 3 is the host number on that network; numbers in between are used for either hosts or networks, depending on the address format assigned to that network. Hosts connected to two or more networks have separate addresses for each interface. Server D can be addressed either as 3.0.0.1 or 2.0.0.5.

The network address identifies a specific network among all those on the Internet. Network addresses on the Internet are assigned by the Internet Address and Numbering Authority (IANA). The host address identifies an individual host on a

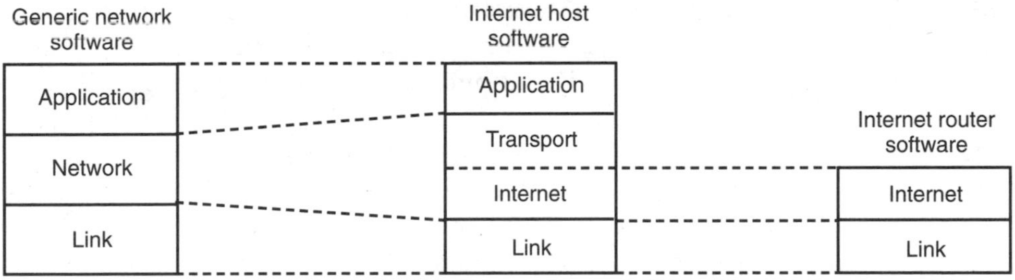

Figure 1-8: INTERNET SOFTWARE PACKAGING ALTERNATIVES. Internet protocol stacks always carry an extra component to route packets based on their internet address. This component is separate from the transport software that provides the socket interface to application programs. Devices that simply route packets between networks don't need the transport software.

specific network. Host numbers are assigned locally by the manager of the individual networks. Each host with internet software has a routing table that associates IP addresses with network destinations that can be reached from that host. The internet software passes data to different data links according to the following situations:

1. If the network address in a packet matches one of the host's data links, then the packet goes to that data link. The data link translates the host address into a physical network address and transmits the data to the destination host.

2. If the network address in a packet does not identify a network connected to the host, the routing table provides the IP address of another host that will route the packet. The network address of this other host determines which data link receives the packet and the host address to which the packet is sent.

Each host that receives an IP packet repeats the routing process until the packet arrives at the destination host. The path a packet follows through the Internet usually depends on the current connections and load being carried by Internet networks and the routers connecting them. There are several routing protocols that automatically reroute traffic when a particular router or communications trunk is too busy. TCP/IP applications can not normally tell what route the data took through the network.

1.3.3   Internet Protocols in Your Host

TCP/IP network software is similar to other network software when you install it in a host. The software is installed as part of the operating system, residing "underneath" your application software. It provides a socket interface to applications and uses a device driver interface to interact with network interfaces. The distinction between its transport and internet forwarding activities aren't visible as distinct components when you install the software. In fact, the only time you are likely to encounter a distinction is if you implement a basic internet router and omit the transport mechanisms entirely.

However, the distinction between internet and transport is very important when you look at the format of internet data packets. As shown in Figure 1-9, there is a distinct field in the packet for each layer of protocol software, starting with the data link and proceeding up to the application. When an application sends some data through the network, it places its own header on the message and passes it through the socket interface to the network stack. The transport and internet headers are added by the network stack according to the packet's destination. The data

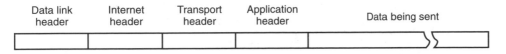

Figure 1-9: **PROTOCOL HEADERS ARE PREFIXED TO DATA SENT ACROSS THE NETWORK.**
Each header provides any data necessary for that protocol layer to handle correctly the data you
send. Application headers are not always required; it depends on the application being used.

link header is added by the data link layer based on routing information from the
internet software.

Unlike Novell and other popular networking systems, internet-style networking is largely decentralized. Users do not log in to a single, central server to access a
variety of services. Instead, there are independent servers for each type of service.
These individual servers may reside on different hosts and they rarely cooperate.
Most servers provide their services indiscriminately to any user that sends them a
request. If a server needs to enforce access control on its services, then it usually
performs its own authentication operation.

A host usually runs several different internet services and protocols simultaneously. Different application software packages provide different internet services.
The protocols use *port numbers* in the transport header to indicate which software
is to handle the packet when it is received. Standard server software generally uses
preassigned port numbers. When client software on a host seeks service from
another host, it opens a connection to the server software residing on that host. To
do so it sends a packet to that host containing the port number of the application
server desired. Packets going from client to server put the server host's address in
the internet header and the server's port number in the transport header.

Data follows different paths through the networking software according to
addresses and port numbers in the data packet (Figure 1-10). A packet arriving at a
network interface will travel "upward" until it reaches the internet software. Then
its path depends on the address in its internet header. If the internet address is for
a different host, the software will forward the packet to its next hop as indicated in
the local routing table.

If the header contains the address of this host, it is passed upward to the transport software, which extracts the port number from the transport header and sends
the packet onward according to the port number. Many port numbers are assigned
to particular application protocols. Port number 25 is always used in e-mail packets, for example. The transport software uses the port number to direct the packet
to the correct application package.

Data produced by an application moves "downward" through the protocol stack
until it reaches the internet software. Then the packet is treated like any internet
packet and is routed according to its IP address. The routing process chooses which

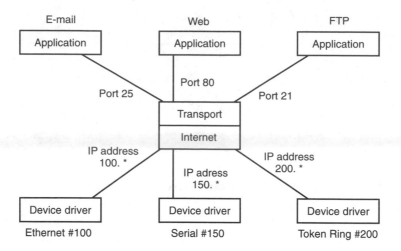

Figure 1-10: INTERNET PORT NUMBERING AND NETWORK NUMBERING. The network number at the front of an IP address identifies the network to receive an outgoing packet. The port number in an incoming IP packet identifies the application that will receive and process that packet.

data link to use. Each host contains separate data link software for each of its networks.

THE INTERNET, INTERNET PROTOCOLS, INTERNETS, AND INTRANETS

It is useful to keep these concepts separate. The *Internet* (capitalized) or *global Internet* is the internationally connected network of computer networks with addresses that are administered by the IANA. The *internet protocol suite* is the set of protocols used by the Internet, principally those protocols that interoperate with TCP/IP networking protocols. An *internet* (lowercase) is a set of interconnected networks that use the Internet protocol suite but might not necessarily be connected to the Internet itself. In typical use, an *intranet* is a private internet that is not fully connected to the global Internet. Private organizations often set up intranets because the Internet protocols are useful and widely available, but using the protocol does not obligate anyone to connect to the global Internet.

1.3.4   The Internet Security Problem

The modern Internet first appeared in the early 1980s when a set of research-oriented enterprise networks were connected to a group of WANs using TCP/IP protocols. This step was something of an experiment, since packet-switched networks themselves were still considered somewhat experimental. Despite official skepticism about packet switching, many organizations had been using those networks to do real work for several years. However, this experimental flavor encouraged a good deal of openness and resource sharing, and tended to penalize network users that tried to modulate or control the traffic flow between their hosts and the Internet.

This permissiveness remained until about 1989. The first shoe, a big one, dropped in late 1988 when the "Internet Worm" penetrated several thousand hosts on the Internet, grinding them to a halt. The Worm was a program written by a Cornell graduate student with some experience in computer security and it was supposed to exercise quietly several security holes in various Internet services. The Worm would search for computers over the Internet, install itself at the computers it found, and then repeat the process. The Worm's installation process exploited security bugs in the e-mail service and the "finger" information service. Unfortunately, the Worm was anything but quiet. The Worm included special procedures to limit the number of times it infested a single computer, but these procedures failed to work. Hosts ended up running so many copies of the Worm that they had no resources left to do anything else. The Worm caused so much mayhem that the U. S. government took several steps to encourage improvements in computer and network security.

One step was to establish organizations to track computer security problems and distribute reports of security fixes. One of these was the Computer Emergency Response Team (CERT), which operates out of the Software Engineering Institute at Carnegie Mellon University. CERT collects reports of computer security incidents, publishes periodic reports on them, and publishes advisories when computer security problems have been found and fixed. Similar organizations were also started to support the needs of various government agencies: The Computer Incident Advisory Capability (CIAC) was started by the Department of Energy, and the defense community also established watchdog groups. Similar teams were started in other countries, and the Forum of Incident Response Teams (FIRST) was also established to promote cooperation between these groups worldwide.

The year 1989 saw the publication of *The Cuckoo's Egg* by Cliff Stoll, then a graduate student in the astronomy department of the University of California at Berkeley. Stoll was managing a host system on the Internet when he stumbled across someone using his host to attack other hosts, particularly U.S. government sites. Stoll found himself tracking the intruder through a tangle of different Internet hosts across the continent and across the ocean. The intruder was eventually identified as a West German trying to sell information to foreign intelligence agencies. Stoll's lesson was that a determined attacker with a little training could easily penetrate typical Internet hosts.

An uninformed observer might suggest that such penetrations are a problem for the affected hosts, but won't affect the rest of the Internet population. Unfortunately, this is not true. Many of the penetrated hosts were, in fact, routing hosts.

They carried data for countless Internet users in addition to those connected to that particular host. We can see what that might mean by looking back at Figure 1-7. If someone penetrates Server D they can snoop on or interfere with any traffic between Net #4 and any other hosts on the other two networks.

The explosive growth of the Internet has made this particularly troublesome. The Internet grew dramatically because anyone can connect to it, and because anyone connected to it can connect others to it as well. Each site that connected to the Internet could, if they wished, become an Internet Service Provider (ISP) to other sites. Anyone with a small computer and Internet software could connect to the Internet as a fully capable host and even offer Internet service to others. While this has yielded explosive growth, it has also eliminated any trust that could be placed in the underlying network. Anyone that carries Internet traffic can monitor or interfere with that traffic. Even high school students have become ISPs, with banks of modems in their basements or under their beds. While many of them may be reputable and strive to provide proper service, the Internet will send its traffic through the good and bad alike.

Unfortunately, security problems are not the sole province of low-budget ISPs. In 1994 CERT reported that a major Internet routing host and service provider had been penetrated. The attackers had installed monitoring software that collected passwords as people logged in to other hosts across the Internet. In the first half of 1995 CERT reported more than 140 similar incidents in other routing hosts. In another incident, an attacker penetrated another ISP's host and copied more than 10,000 credit card numbers. Attackers had also developed a technique by which they could "hijack" an active connection between two IP hosts, allowing the hijacker to masquerade as one of the connection's endpoints. For example, if someone was logged in to a host, the hijacker could steal the logged-in connection and masquerade as the legitimate user.

In practice, the Internet has become a giant version of the childrens' game of "telephone." That is the game where children sit in a row and one child whispers a message to her neighbor, who then whispers the same message to his neighbor, and so on. In theory, each message will get through without error, but often a prankster will undetectably modify the message when whispering it to his neighbor. The Internet continues to work reasonably well because there are few pranksters in proportion to the amount of traffic. However, anyone transmitting valuable information is at risk and is, therefore, a target.

The essential problem is that you can make no assumptions about data you send or receive over the Internet. Data you send could be modified by a subverted routing host before it arrives at its destination. The data could be stolen and rerouted to a different destination, never arriving where it should. Data you receive could be completely forged or simply modified in transit. If your data is important and there is a real risk of someone interfering with it, then you need crypto protections on it.

1.3.5   An Internet Rogue's Gallery

In order to make discussions of attacks as clear as possible, we will look at them in terms of four separate mechanisms, and associate each with a name. We have already met Henry the Forger and Peeping Tom and we will now also meet Play-It-Again Sam and Bailey the Switcher. Below is a description of each attacker's style, what they require, and the difficulties they typically face.

- **Henry the Forger**

  Henry has the easiest job. All he has to do is construct internet data messages and send them to his intended victim. This is easy to do as long as he has an internet host that can send packets to his victim. Most of the time he simply has to arrange the proper collection of bits according to the protocol specifications and the victim can't tell his forgery from a legitimate packet. This is especially true for protocols that don't require a response like e-mail or "datagram"-oriented protocols like the Network File Service. Things are a bit harder if a particular forgery requires a bidirectional connection. Then he needs to be sure that the victim's packets are routed back to him and not to the legitimate destination. This can be difficult to arrange for short routes through a well-managed network, but can become a crime of opportunity as traffic winds its way across the global Internet.

- **Peeping Tom**

  Password sniffing is Tom's classic pastime. He has a harder job than Henry because he must have access to his victim's traffic. This means he must penetrate or already control a routing host or a network that carries his victim's messages. This is not an impossible task, since password-sniffing incidents appear regularly in CERT's periodic reports. Once Tom has access to the victim's traffic, he simply watches for useful information: passwords or other access codes, negotiable company secrets, or any other sensitive information. Standard Internet protocols give no protection against Peeping Tom.

- **Play-It-Again Sam**

  Play-It-Again Sam combines the peeping of Tom with Henry's forging. Sam intercepts messages of value or significance and simply replays them to the recipients. For example, he might intercept one of Alice's "PAY $100" messages to Bob and replay it a few times, yielding multiple unintended payments. While Henry might do as well with his forgeries, Sam's little specialty poses special risks to crypto systems.

- **Bailey the Switcher**

Bailey has the hardest job of all. She intercepts messages, makes careful changes to them, and then sends them along. For example, she might intercept a message from Alice and change the amount from $100 to $900 before forwarding it to Bob. In many cases she must change messages "on the fly," within tight time constraints. Many protocols have timing requirements, and her trick messages must arrive in time for them to be accepted by the victim. In some cases Bailey can construct a "programmed attack" that modifies the messages automatically. Despite the difficulty of such attacks, an easy-to-use programmed attack could make Bailey's threat a real and serious one.

The essential security measure is always physical security. Don't let untrustworthy people touch your important computing systems. Put the systems inside a protected area and keep unauthorized people out. Most organizations do this naturally. They don't let strangers wander about their offices looking at memoranda lying about, so they don't let strangers come in and play with their computers, either. The office walls become a *security perimeter* and the safety of your information depends on the security of that area. None of these rogues must reside on inside systems.

Furthermore, valuable business activities should have security measures in place that resist attacks by all four of these attackers. Casual or experimental use rarely risks attack. Even if it is attacked, the potential losses are relatively small. However, any one of these attacks can be mounted against a suitably valuable target unless appropriate protection is in place.

1.4   Setting Realistic Security Objectives

There seems to be something special about computers that makes people expect perfection of them. Perhaps it is because the hardware must achieve such breathtaking reliability. A typical desktop computer executes millions of instructions a second, day after day, almost flawlessly. Others might be seduced by the spare perfection inside the computer's own world. You can indeed create a perfect, if small, virtual world inside a computer. However, the model worlds inside a computer, or shared among networks of them, are not the real world. We can't achieve perfect security outside the computer simply because we might achieve an illusion of perfect security inside.

HOW CAN I ACHIEVE PERFECT COMPUTER SECURITY?

The most practical and effective computer security is physical. Lock up the computer and every peripheral device, including remote workstations and terminals, and take whatever physical measures are necessary to keep outsiders away. Use physical wiring for everything. Use no wireless networking devices. Allow no external connections, not even through security devices like firewalls. Marcus Ranum, a noted pioneer of Internet firewalls, likes to speak of his perfect "A1" firewall—a pair of wire cutters carefully applied to all external connections.

Naturally, this state of affairs does not really yield perfection. Every survey ever performed on computer crime and abuse cites "insiders" as major players. If you successfully block outsiders from reaching your computer, you don't eliminate the threat of abuse; you just restrict the likely abusers to insiders. For some organizations this is enough security. However, most people today expect modern computers to communicate with one another. Many workers just can't do their jobs effectively without networked access to printers, e-mail, disk farms, shared databases, and so on. The practical needs of the workers make simple physical security impractical.

HOW MUCH SECURITY IS ENOUGH?

We install security because we have a valuable, worthwhile activity going on and we need to protect it from attack or disruption. As a practical matter, there should be a "break-even" point between the value of the activity and the cost of effective security. Sometimes an activity loses all of its value because of attacks. For example, a series of thefts could "clean out" the entire inventory of a retail store. In other cases an activity under attack might remain profitable even without security. For example, traditional cellular phones are identified over the airwaves by a serial number for billing purposes; thieves can intercept these serial numbers and build them into other phones. Calls made by these "cloned" phones will all be billed to the original phone with that serial number. Cellular phone companies continue to flourish despite this abuse.

In some cases there are legal requirements to protect the secrecy or integrity of data: employee confidentiality, medical records of patients, and data affecting company stock prices are a few examples. There are also cases when you might be contractually obligated to protect other peoples' information, and you might face legal action if you fail to do so. Explicit requirements should always be followed, but in practice they are rare outside of the military and some financial environments.

The level of risk and level of security is almost always a business decision. Look carefully at the potential risks. What happens to your business if an attacker crashes your site or steals its contents? If the site performs commercial transactions, look at how big a risk you might face from bogus transactions. What is the most you might lose, and how can you spot potential fraud? Every retail store owner accepts losses as part of the cost of doing business, and their security expenditures try to balance fewer losses against security costs and inconvenience. If you cannot offer a service with the right balance of profit and safety, then it doesn't make business sense.

HOW MUCH CRYPTO IS ENOUGH?

How much crypto is enough? The short answer is: Enough to make attacks too expensive to be practical. The traditional competitors in crypto have been governments: one hides its secrets while the other tries to penetrate them. With political and military objectives at stake the threat has few limits. The traditional mantra of the U.S. National Security Agency (NSA) has been: "Never underestimate the time, money, and effort an adversary will spend to read your traffic." At the other end of the scale we have casual e-mail between acquaintances. Who would bother to read or manipulate the plaintext of such messages, much less take the effort to penetrate an encrypted version? Crypto requires special facilities, and it takes extra time and effort to apply crypto protections correctly. It is simply an expensive bother when it isn't really needed. The risk for commercial traffic falls somewhere between these extremes, and so does its practical application.

The practical sections of this book describe various types of crypto products and ways to deploy them. Each of these sections also provides a prioritized list of security requirements. It is unlikely that you will find perfectly integrated products that meet all the listed requirements. It is also unlikely that you'll achieve all of your system's operating objectives and at the same time fulfill the appropriate deployment requirements. This is because security is almost always a trade-off. You will always take some risks to make a system operate effectively.

Since you must compromise on the listed requirements, the next problem is to decide how to make sensible compromises. This is the reason the requirements are in priority order. The most important requirements are always given first, so those are the ones that warrant most of your attention. However, be sure to review every requirement that applies to your system and try to understand the risk you take if you don't comply with it.

1.5   Appropriate Communications Security

This section examines the problem of defining your communications security goals and how to achieve them. First we review the problem of identifying your real needs for communications security and examine a list of goals you can achieve with crypto technology. Then we briefly review the different types of crypto technologies described in this book and present a table associating goals with products.

The first step in selecting security measures is to identify what you need to achieve. Security is always a burden, so you must start by identifying your true goals and why the burden of security helps you to achieve them. Realistic security is a three-part balance between your goals, the security threat against those goals, and the costs of security measures. In some cases a goal can't be achieved because the benefits are too uncertain given the risk and associated security costs. If the threat is minor, then weak security measures may be justified. If a security failure could be costly, then weak security measures can lead to disaster.

In the Internet arena, the threat is real and continues to evolve. Unlike threats to dial-in modems, geographic distances (and related long-distance rates) are never a deterrent. It is as easy to attack a machine on the other side of the globe as it is to attack one down the street. Attackers used to simply "sniff" passwords and reuse them. Now they locate active, authenticated connections and "hijack" them, taking over all their privileges along with the data stream. The public information access that bred the original Internet is rarely threatened by such antics, but business and commercial activities are.

1.5.1   Communications Security Goals

This review of security goals assumes that you need to communicate business or commercial data, and that the data transmissions may on occasion be part of a valuable transaction. In other words, you need to protect communications between a group of people and you will be using internet protocols. The basic goal in protecting communications will be to provide reasonable assurance that outsiders can't read or modify your messages. All other things being equal, we will assume that an occasional but rare lapse in security measures is acceptable—a single message "leaked" once in a while through an operating error or a really persistent code-breaker, or perhaps a rare, successful forgery. We shall note any alternatives for achieving higher security as we continue to review goals.

The following is a summary of communications security goals and trade-offs to consider when planning to apply crypto or any other network security measure. You should pursue a particular security goal when you believe there is an active threat against that goal. For example, you probably don't need crypto security to distribute free information reliably over the Internet. However, there are credible threats against vendors who distribute information in exchange for payment. Look at your Internet application and decide if someone will benefit by tricking it somehow. If such behavior is a threat to your objectives, look for security measures to protect your interests.

- **Economy in both procurement costs and ease of use**
  This is the principal trade-off for most organizations. Expensive, hard-to-use solutions are unrealistic for many organizations. However, some organizations will accept higher costs for better security.

- **Easy communication with multiple hosts**
  This is the usual case today: Each host in the organization needs to communicate with a growing community of other hosts. This generally implies that each host is connected to at least one LAN.

- **Generic Internet access**
  Some users' job duties routinely require reference information from the World Wide Web and unprotected e-mail exchanges with other members of the general Internet community. This is another important trade-off. The Internet provides a wealth of information and communication opportunities, but it also brings a broadly based, international threat directly to your desktop.

- **Vending products to outsiders over the Internet**
  Current and potential customers need to access your host, browse for desired products, and safely close a sale. Both buyer and seller want to identify the other participant reliably and protect the transaction from outside interference. However, there is no way to know beforehand if visitors are new or potential customers, or if they are intending to attack your site.

- **Strong secrecy**
  Confidentiality is important to most organizations, but to some it is really crucial. In such instances, leaking a single message can seriously compromise the organization's goals and cause damage from which it is very difficult to recover. Strong secrecy is very expensive to achieve.

- **Strong authentication of messages**
  The organization needs to associate messages with particular individuals or authorized agents, and do so very reliably. The organization faces serious loss or damage if important messages are forged.

Every one of these objectives may be beneficial for some business activity or other. However, it is impossible to achieve all of these objectives simultaneously in a single application. If you need to achieve conflicting goals you may need to allocate separate networks to them. Focus on immediate operational needs first. Security can be costly, so first deal with immediate risks and operational needs.

1.5.2   Internet Crypto Techniques

The following is a summary of the crypto techniques described in this book. Each resides in a different place within the system's software elements (Figure 1-11). Each technique is covered in one or more chapters, starting at the bottom of the system and working upward. Table 1-1 shows which communications security goals are addressed by the different solutions presented in the book, and indicates the solutions discussed in each chapter.

- **Point-to-point link encryption**
  This produces a fully isolated connection between a pair of computers by applying crypto to the data link. It yields the highest security by being the most restrictive in physical and electronic access. It is not necessarily an "internet" solution since it doesn't need to use TCP/IP software. It is the simplest design, but the most expensive to implement and extend.

- **IP link encryption**
  This produces a highly secure, extensible TCP/IP network by applying crypto to the data link and by restricting physical access to hosts on the network. This architecture blocks communication with untrusted hosts and sites. Sites use point-to-point interconnections and apply encryption to all traffic on those interconnections.

- **A virtual private network (VPN) constructed with IP Security Protocol (IPSEC) routers**
  This is a VPN that uses the Internet to carry traffic between trusted sites. Crypto is applied at the Internet layer using IPSEC. This approach uses

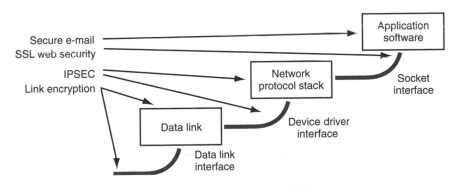

Figure 1-11: INSTALLING INTERNET CRYPTO TECHNIQUES WITHIN A COMPUTER SYSTEM. The different techniques are installed within or between the existing network software components. The simplest techniques reside at the bottom; more complex ones reside in higher level software components.

Table 1-1: Relationship between communication security goals and crypto products

Product	Chapter	Communication Security Goals					
		Economical	Multi host	Internet Access	Vending	Secrecy	Authentication
Point-to-point link encryption	3					√√	√√
IP link encryption	3	√	√√			√√	
IPSEC router VPN	6	√√	√√			√	
IPSEC firewall VPN	8	√√	√√	√√			
Web service with SSL	10	√√	√√	√√	√√		√
E-mail with PGP	11	√	√√	√√	√		√√
E-mail with PEM	11		√√	√√	√		√√

√√ = a technique strongly supports a given goal; √ = partial support.

encrypting routers and does not provide the sites with access to untrusted Internet sites.

- **A VPN constructed with IPSEC firewalls**
  This is a different approach to the VPN that uses encrypting firewalls instead of encrypting routers. Crypto is still applied at the Internet layer using IPSEC. The firewalls encrypt all traffic between trusted sites and also provide controlled access to untrusted hosts. Strong firewall access control is necessary to reduce the risk of attacks on the crypto mechanisms as well as attacks on hosts within the trusted sites.

- **World Wide Web Service with the Secure Socket Layer (SSL) Protocol**
  This applies crypto services using the SSL protocol. The protocol is integrated into application software packages for Web clients and servers. This protects selected data transfers between the Web client and server.

- **E-mail with Pretty Good Privacy (PGP)**
  This applies a variety of crypto protections to e-mail using the PGP encryption package for e-mail. An important feature of this package is that independent individuals or groups can create their own cryptographic credentials that attest to the authenticity of electronic files they create.

- **E-mail with Privacy Enhanced Mail (PEM)**
  This applies a variety of crypto protections to e-mail using the PEM proto-col. Although there are technical differences in the way the PGP and PEM apply similar protections, the most important difference is how PEM's cryp-tographic credentials are handled. PEM uses a hierarchical system for cre-ating credentials. Individuals cannot produce credentials themselves. This increases security assurance in some ways, but also increases administra-tive costs.

1.6   Legal Restrictions

decrypt() may blow up if given ill-formed ciphertext. This is normal in a technology that some people class as a munition.

—Earl Boebert, source code comment

The Allies during World War II achieved several dramatic military successes that they attributed to codebreaking. They came to see their adversaries' weak codes as their ally in war and strong codes as a threat. This view became law in the United States through the International Traffic in Arms Regulations and its U. S. Munitions List. The List identified all devices and technologies that were consid-ered weapons of war and forbade export of such things without special licenses from the state department. The List included cryptography.

Many countries, particularly those allied with the United States, have taken similar steps or at least cooperate with U.S. government attempts to restrict crypto exports. Several countries, particularly those suffering from totalitarian traditions or local unrest, have taken the further step of legally restricting crypto use by its citizens. A 1997 review of crypto laws in forty major countries found restrictions on crypto use in approximately a dozen countries. In some cases the restriction only applies to radio transmissions or is regulated by the local telecommunications pro-vider. In a few cases the restrictions aren't codified in law and can arise unexpect-edly. A cellular phone company in Pakistan found itself shut down because the phones used an encryption mechanism that the local government couldn't crack.

The United States has also seen political moves to restrict private crypto use. The U.S. Federal Bureau of Investigation (FBI) has an established tradition of investigating crimes by tapping phone lines, and encrypted telephones make such taps difficult or impossible to use. The FBI has taken the lead within the govern-ment in promoting legislation to support wiretapping and to restrict private crypto use. Telecommunications legislation promoted by the FBI was passed in the early

1990s that requires phone companies to maintain wiretapping facilities in their equipment. Legislation was also promoted by the FBI to restrict private cryptography use, but no such laws have been passed. Many observers are skeptical about such legislation. Some question why the tiny number of wiretaps approved each year (a few hundred at most) justify laws inhibiting the growth of electronic commerce, which holds the promise of enormous economic and productivity benefits. Others find it extremely likely that laws restricting private crypto use would be found unconstitutional if challenged in court.

The problems are complex and the "last word" has not been heard on either the laws or the technologies. In 1996 the National Research Council (NRC) published a comprehensive study of cryptography and public policy. The study reviewed both the federal government's need to regulate crypto and the private sector's need to apply it to emerging problems of data protection. The study concluded the following:

1. There should be no restriction on crypto products within the United States. The study noted both technical and constitutional issues that made restrictions unwise.

2. Export controls should be relaxed but not eliminated. The study noted that export controls don't completely prevent the spread of strong, capable crypto, but they do make it harder for adversaries to acquire and use it.

3. Crypto policy should be driven less by internal government discussion and more by public discussion. Traditionally, crypto policy was dictated by government agencies and justified by references to military secrets, removing the discussion from public discourse. The study concluded that this approach is no longer justified.

4. Growing crypto use represents "new technical realities" for law enforcement and national security organizations. Those organizations must take explicit steps to adjust, and not expect to maintain the technological status quo.

While the NRC's recommendations may affect future discussions of legislative and executive policy, there is no guarantee that they will actually manifest themselves in future laws or regulations. It seems unlikely that legal restrictions on crypto will increase in the future, but it is safe to assume that existing restrictions will remain in force.

In early 1997 the U.S. government revised its export rules for commercial products containing crypto. The principal change was the establishment of "bulk licenses" that allow U.S. vendors to sell licensed crypto products to almost any customer in almost any country. While the revised rules dramatically changed the situation for crypto product vendors, they did not yield an immediate increase in the range of exportable U.S. crypto products. The principal beneficiary of the new rules are vendors of "mass market" products with relatively limited crypto capabilities. Under the new rules, bulk licenses were made easy to acquire for such products. Many U.S. software products include limited and often weak mechanisms for protecting data, and such products used to be very difficult to export. The bulk licenses are granted to acceptable products after they pass a one-time review by the U.S. Department of Commerce.

The 1997 rules also loosened up the export restrictions on stronger crypto in exchange for the promise of a "back door" for government eavesdropping. The export of "mass market" crypto products was loosened since law enforcement and intelligence agencies could penetrate their weaker crypto mechanisms when needed. Stronger crypto measures make such access too difficult or even impossible in many cases, so special measures are required before such systems are allowed to be exported. The new rules require the presence of an approved *key escrow* system before a product with strong crypto can receive a bulk export license. Key escrow is a technique that allows approved government agencies to recover the crypto keys being used and thus read the messages being sent. The technical details are introduced in Section 3.5. Crypto systems that incorporate an approved key escrow facility may be granted bulk export licenses, but the licenses must be renewed periodically.

The 1997 rules also allow bulk licenses for exporting products that use the U.S. Data Encryption Standard (DES) as long as the product vendor is involved in the key escrow program. In particular, the vendor must be actively developing future crypto products that support an approved key escrow mechanism. These bulk licenses are also reviewed periodically and could be revoked if the vendor fails to make acceptable progress in developing their key escrow system. The rules established a two-year period ending in 1998, during which DES-based crypto products can be exported without a key escrow system, but only if the vendor is also developing products that include key escrow. So far, three licenses have been issued to vendors that are actively developing key escrow products.

Export is also being allowed for software to protect financial information. So far, one such license has been issued for a system that applies strong encryption only to financial data. Such licenses are issued on a case-by-case basis following a detailed review of the product in question.

Traditionally, the U.S. government has allowed the export of strong crypto products when it unconditionally benefits U.S. interests. In particular, U.S. companies have always been able to get approval to export crypto systems for their own use or for use by their foreign subsidiaries. The government has also traditionally allowed the export of strong crypto products when the customer is a foreign bank or other financial institution. The rationale has been that the integrity of the world financial system is important enough to justify the risk of misuse. Furthermore, the United States holds a dominating position in the world financial system and it is likely that crypto will protect numerous transactions that directly or indirectly involve U.S. business interests. Unfortunately, this special case did not show up in the revised 1997 rules. It may be possible to acquire individual export licenses in these cases, but such licenses will probably be assessed on a case-by-case basis, and may require several weeks to be issued.

In short, the legal climate identifies crypto systems as either lightweight or strong. Lightweight systems are afforded little or no restriction beyond what is necessary to ensure that the crypto facilities are in fact relatively weak. Lightweight crypto can be exported from the United States and is sometimes tolerated in countries that restrict private crypto use. Strong crypto systems earn the largest share of legal restrictions. The NRC report suggested that DES should fall in the lightweight category, but the 1997 rules put it in its own "medium-strength" category. DES falls at the boundary between systems that can be attacked in practice and those that can't, so legal restrictions are ambiguous.

The specifics of what makes a system "strong" or "lightweight" are discussed in later sections about crypto algorithms (Section 2.3), secret key exchange (Section 4.5), and public key exchange (Section 9.3). Keep in mind that lightweight crypto has a number of reasonable applications, just as cheap safes and door locks provide protection for some applications. We achieve security by making the cost of an attack greater than the promised gain, and even weak crypto can serve this purpose.

1.7   For Further Information

- **Kahn, *The Codebreakers: The Story of Secret Writing***
  The classic history on cryptography, spanning the centuries, and perhaps the first book to speak openly of the NSA. There is a good deal of technical detail on classic code techniques and the basics of cryptanalysis. It is showing its age with respect to events in the last half of the twentieth century. This is the place to go to find out about Tannenberg or other historic crypto users like Mary, Queen of Scots.

- **Comer, *Internetworking with TCP/IP, Volume 1: Principles, Protocols, and Architecture.***
  A good text describing the TCP/IP backbone protocols.

- **Stevens, *TCP/IP Illustrated, Volume 1: The Protocols***
  A thoroughly illustrated, detailed exposition of the basic TCP/IP backbone protocols.

- **Stoll, *The Cuckoo's Egg***
  A fascinating, personal journal of Stoll tracking an intruder in Berkeley's computer across the continent and eventually across the ocean. A sobering tale of countless computers being exploited by an overseas attacker.

- **Computer Emergency Response Team, *CERT Advisories***
  ftp://info.cert.org/pubs/advisories/
  The standard source of information about computer security flaws and fixes. Most Unix and Internet product vendors participate in CERT.

- **Cheswick and Bellovin, *Firewalls and Internet Security: Repelling the Wily Hacker***
  A comprehensive, in-depth look at Internet security problems and security measures, covering both theory and practice. Key security problems are marked with "bombs" and, like any realistic book, addressed from a standpoint of risk management.

- **Koops, *Crypto Law Survey***
  http://cwis.kub.nl/~frw/people/koops/lawsurvy.htm
  A survey of crypto laws in forty countries, covering import and export controls as well as laws that either promote or restrict private crypto use by citizens. The survey includes pointers to other legal reports and surveys.

- **National Research Council, *Cryptography's Role in Securing the Information Society***
  A comprehensive study of federal cryptographic policy in the United States. Reviews the commercial need for cryptography, existing legal restrictions, and national security and law enforcement concerns with cryptography, and makes balanced recommendations based on its findings. Unfortunately, the report's specific coverage of U.S. export rules is already obsolete.

2

Encryption Basics

It may well be doubted whether human ingenuity can construct an enigma of the kind which human ingenuity may not, by proper application, resolve.

—Edgar Allen Poe, *The Gold Bug*

IN THIS CHAPTER

This chapter presents basic concepts and terminology for constructing and for attacking encryption systems, plus recommendations on choosing an appropriate encryption technique. The following topics are described:

- Types of ciphers, algorithms, and modes

- How encryption systems fail

- How to recognize adequate crypto: algorithms and modes

2.1 Encryption Building Blocks

A modern crypto device has several essential elements that determine how it works. First is the *crypto algorithm*, which specifies the mathematical transformation that is performed on data to encrypt or decrypt it. Some algorithms are for *stream ciphers*, which encrypt a digital data stream a bit at a time. The best known algorithms, however, are for *block ciphers*, which transform data in fixed-size blocks, one block at a time. When block ciphers are applied to data streams, the *cipher mode* defines how the algorithm is applied block by block to the data stream.

A crypto algorithm is a procedure that takes the plaintext data and transforms it into ciphertext in a reversible way. A good algorithm produces ciphertext that yields as few clues as possible about either the key or the plaintext that produced it. The word *algorithm* is a mathematical term often associated with computer science. It indicates that the transformation between plaintext and ciphertext can be described in purely symbolic terms involving the transformation of sets of mathematical symbols. In practice, most people work with crypto algorithms as digital circuits or software packages. If a particular device, package, or product claims to implement a particular crypto algorithm faithfully, then any weaknesses in the algorithm are also present in the device. The algorithm's strengths should also be present in the device, assuming they haven't been weakened by some other feature of the device's construction. Often, but not always, devices that implement the same algorithm can decrypt each others' ciphertext, assuming that matching keys are used.

An important distinction between crypto algorithms is whether they are *secret key* or *public key* algorithms. The algorithms we introduce in this chapter are all secret key algorithms, but it is worthwhile to summarize the distinction. A secret key algorithm is symmetric; that is, it uses the same key for encryption and decryption. The security of a secret key algorithm rests with keeping the key itself completely secret from outsiders (hence the term "secret" key). Public key algorithms use different keys for encryption and decryption. One key, the *private key*, must be kept secret by its owner and in general is never shared with anyone else. The other key, the *public key*, may be shared with anyone. In fact, the two keys are mathematically related. Data encrypted with the private key may be decrypted with the corresponding public key, and vice versa. While the technique is very powerful, it cannot fully replace more traditional secret key algorithms. Typical products combine both public key and secret key techniques in order to benefit from the particular strengths of each. We will examine the important, practical uses of public key algorithms in later chapters.

2.1.1 Stream Ciphers

Stream cipher algorithms are designed to accept a crypto key and a stream of plaintext to produce a stream of ciphertext (Figure 2-1). The classic digital stream cipher is the *Vernam cipher*, developed in the early twentieth century for encrypting teletype traffic. The original Vernam cipher used a crypto key stored on a very long loop of paper tape. Each bit of plaintext in the data stream would pick up the next bit from the crypto key paper tape, and the ciphertext was produced by adding the plaintext bit and the crypto key bit, discarding the carry. This "add" operation is the same as the *exclusive-or* logical operation, which we will see again in later sections.

In practice, simple Vernam ciphers turn out to be easy to break. An attacker can mathematically combine ciphertext messages in pairs to factor out the key stream and produce a message that is easier to crack . If the attacker solves one message, extracting its plaintext from the ciphertext, that plaintext can be used to deduce the key stream. Once the key stream is recovered, the attacker can decipher all of the other messages protected with that key stream.

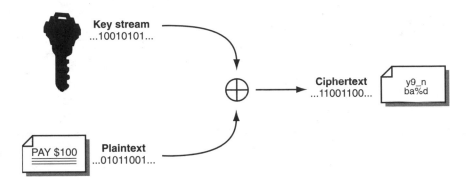

Figure 2-1: STREAM CIPHERS ARE DESIGNED TO ENCRYPT A STREAM OF DATA. The simplest stream cipher is called the *Vernam cipher*. A bit from the key is added, with the carry discarded, to a bit from the plaintext to yield one bit of cipher text (this operation is also called *exclusive-or*). This is called a *one time pad* if a truly random key bit is used to encrypt each bit of plaintext. Different stream ciphers use different keying approaches. Some use a variable-length key stream and others use a key with a fixed size.

This brief glimpse into codebreaking illustrates how details of code weaknesses are important when constructing effective crypto systems. We cannot avoid mistakes unless we review the weaknesses of previous and current techniques. Knowledge of codebreaking techniques provides guidance in identifying features of a strong code.

Despite its weakness in simple applications, the Vernam remains an important cipher. It is weak when we use repeating keys, but it can be very effective when the key stream varies constantly. This approach is often used in modern stream ciphers. Such ciphers consist of two parts: a procedure to generate a sequence of bits that outsiders can't guess and a Vernam cipher using that sequence as its key.

We can also take the original, randomly generated Vernam key to its logical extreme and use a fresh, randomly generated crypto key bit for every bit of every message we send. This yields a special cipher called a *one time pad*. An important result from information theory is that it is impossible to extract the plaintext from a one time pad's ciphertext if the key stream is truly random and is never reused. The "hot line" connecting world leaders in Moscow and Washington, DC, used one time pad encryption in the past and probably still uses it today. However, a one time pad does not protect against all types of attacks; we will look at a feasible attack against it in Section 3.2.3.

Today, very few stream ciphers are used in commercial systems. The most well known is RC4 ("Rivest Cipher #4"), developed by Ron Rivest of RSA Data Security.

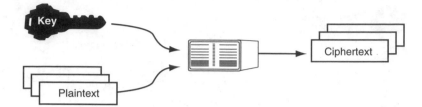

Figure 2-2: BLOCK CIPHERS ENCRYPT DATA IN FIXED-SIZE BLOCKS. To encrypt a stream of data, the data must be broken into block-size pieces and each block encrypted individually. When decrypted in the right order, the encrypted blocks will yield the original plaintext message.

RC4 is widely used in part because the U.S. government allows it to be exported if the associated software uses an acceptably short secret key.

2.1.2   Block Ciphers

Block ciphers are designed to take data blocks of a particular size, encrypt them with a key of a particular size, and yield a block of ciphertext of a particular size (Figure 2-2). Today's practical block ciphers all generate a ciphertext block that is the same size as the plaintext block. Table 2-1 lists some block ciphers and their properties. DES may be the best known block cipher. It has been a U.S. national standard for twenty years and is still widely used. Its posture as a national standard makes DES particularly appealing to many users, since this shows the U.S. government endorses it for protecting private and commercial data.

Block ciphers are analyzed and tested for their ability to encrypt data blocks of their given block size. A reasonable cipher should generate a ciphertext that has as few discernible properties as possible. A statistical analysis of ciphertext generated by the block cipher algorithm should find that individual data bits as well as patterns of bits appear completely random. Nonrandom patterns are the first thing for

Table 2-1: Properties of some secret key block cipher algorithms

Secret Key Block Ciphers	Data Block Size (bits)	Crypto Key Size (bits)	In Use?
DES	64	56	Yes
International data encryption algorithm (IDEA)	64	128	Yes
Modular multiplication block cipher (MMB)	128	128	No
Cellular automata cipher CA-1.1	384	1088	No
SKIPJACK	64	80	Yes

which a code breaker looks as they usually provide the entering wedge needed to crack a code.

Patterns in the ciphertext become a problem when we apply block ciphers to streams of data. If we encrypt the same block twice with the same crypto key, we will get the same ciphertext. Figure 2-3 gives an example of this. The "encrypt" operation encrypts blocks of four characters each. When encrypting the message "FIVE BY FIVE," the word FIVE appears twice, both times landing on the boundary of an encrypted block. This yields ciphertext "vFa3" both times, and produces a repeating pattern in the ciphertext.

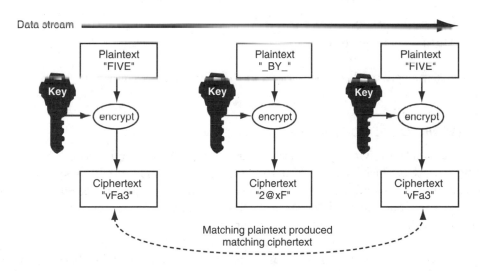

Figure 2-3: ENCRYPTING A STREAM BLOCK BY BLOCK CAN YIELD PATTERNS IN THE CIPHERTEXT. This mode of encrypting a data stream with a block cipher is also called *electronic code book mode.* Identical plaintext blocks will be encrypted into identical ciphertext blocks when the same key is used. This makes the messages more vulnerable to attack by producing visible patterns that attackers can exploit.

Reasonable amounts of plaintext in general and computer communications data in particular will always yield repeated sequences like this. If we encrypt a data stream block by block, patterns in the plaintext will produce statistically significant patterns in the ciphertext. These patterns can give a codebreaker the entering wedge needed for an attack. Another possibly worse problem in commercial applications is that an attacker with some knowledge of message contents can substitute encrypted blocks from one message for those in another (a "cut-and-paste" attack). For example, the attacker could cut and paste fields between bank deposit and withdrawal messages to forge a beneficial message without ever really cracking the crypto keys.

The term *cipher mode* refers to a set of techniques used to apply a block cipher to a data stream. Several modes have been developed to disguise repeated plaintext blocks and otherwise improve the security of block ciphers. Each mode defines a method of combining the plaintext, crypto key, and encrypted ciphertext in a special way to generate the stream of ciphertext actually transmitted to the recipient. The published standards for DES include specifications for standard modes to use with it. In theory there could be countless different ways of combining and feeding back the inputs and outputs of a cipher. In practice, four basic modes are used:

- Electronic code book (ECB)
- Cipher block chaining (CBC)
- Cipher feedback (CFB)
- Output feedback (OFB)

These modes are described briefly in the following sections.

ELECTRONIC CODE BOOK MODE

ECB mode is the trivial case illustrated in Figure 2-3. The cipher is simply applied to the plaintext block by block. It is the most efficient mode. It can be sped up using parallel hardware and, unlike other modes, does not require an extra data word for seeding a feedback loop. However, a block of padding may be needed to guarantee that full blocks are provided for encryption and decryption.

As noted earlier, however, ECB has security problems that limit its usability. Patterns in the plaintext can yield patterns in the ciphertext. It is also easy to modify a ciphertext message by adding, removing, or switching encrypted blocks.

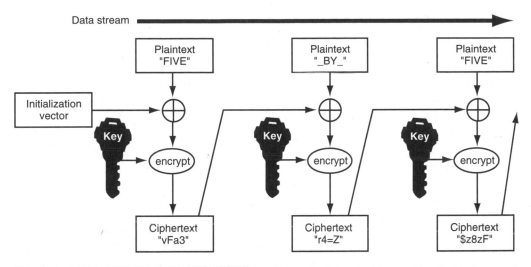

Figure 2-4: ENCRYPTION WITH CBC MODE. Each block of plaintext is combined with the previous block of ciphertext before it is encrypted. The first block is combined with the initialization vector. Unlike straight ECB mode, repeated words in the plaintext produce a different ciphertext each time they are encrypted. This makes it more difficult to crack the encryption.

CIPHER BLOCK CHAINING

CBC mode hides patterns in the plaintext by systematically combining each plaintext block with a ciphertext block before actually encrypting it. The two blocks are combined bit by bit using the exclusive-or operation. Instead of directly encrypting the plaintext data, the block cipher encrypts the plaintext data after it is combined with random-looking ciphertext (Figure 2-4).

In order to guarantee that there is always some random-looking ciphertext to apply to the actual plaintext, the process is started with a block of random bits called the *initialization vector* (IV). Two messages will never yield the same ciphertext, even if the plaintexts are identical, as long as the IV is different for each message. When used in networking messages, most CBC implementations add the IV to the beginning of the message in plaintext.

A shortcoming of CBC in networking applications is that encrypted messages may be as many as two blocks longer than the same message in ECB mode. One block is added to transmit the IV to the recipient. Proper decryption depends on the IV to start the feedback process. The other block contains padding so that a full block is always encrypted and decrypted. Some applications only transmit the IV in an initial packet and depend on the recipient to keep track of the last block decrypted. This can affect the efficiency of decryption since it prevents the recipient from immediately decrypting packets that arrive out of order.

CBC is a popular mode because it has reasonably good security properties. Patterns in the plaintext are hidden as intended. Furthermore, the interrelationship between data blocks caused by the chaining can make it difficult to modify structured messages in a useful fashion.

However, there are risks of "cut-and-paste" attacks against free-form messages like e-mail. For example, Bailey the Switcher can take a sequence of blocks from a different message encrypted with the same key and insert them into another message. The CBC process will generate a block of garbage text where the data was inserted and then decrypt the rest of the message correctly. A message will also decrypt properly if Bailey truncates it at the beginning or end.

CIPHER FEEDBACK

CFB mode is similar to CBC in that it "feeds" the ciphertext block back through the block cipher. However, CFB is different because the block cipher doesn't directly encrypt the plaintext. Instead, the block cipher is used to generate a constantly changing "key" that encrypts the plaintext with a Vernam cipher. In other words, blocks of ciphertext are exclusive-or'ed with successive blocks of data generated by the block cipher to generate the ciphertext (Figure 2-5). This mode is also called ciphertext auto key (CTAK) in military systems.

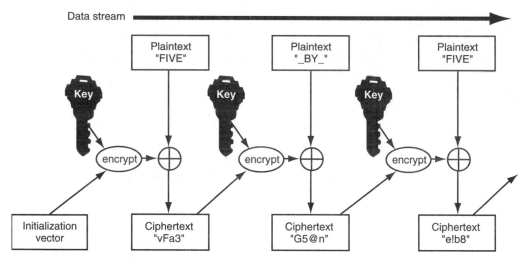

Figure 2-5: ENCRYPTION WITH CFB MODE. This mode doesn't use the block cipher algorithm to encrypt the data; it uses the cipher to generate a temporary key. The plaintext is encrypted by exclusive-or'ing it with the temporary key. The temporary key is generated by encrypting the previous ciphertext block (or the IV for the first block) with the block cipher. Unlike CBC, this can be adapted to encrypt partial data blocks without requiring padding.

A particular benefit of CFB is that it isn't limited to the cipher's block size: the mode can be adapted to work with smaller blocks down to individual bits. A problem with CBC is that it must operate on full blocks of plaintext, though message lengths rarely occur in exact block lengths. This makes CFB more efficient in terms of message sizes for handling encrypted network traffic. Like CBC, however, CFB messages do require a random Initialization Vector value.

The resulting ciphertext has comparable security properties with CBC. Attackers can try to cut and paste new messages from older ones encrypted with the same key. Such messages will produce a small amount of garbage in the plaintext at the spot where the pasting occurred, and will decrypt cleanly after that.

OUTPUT FEEDBACK

OFB mode is similar to CFB but slightly simpler. It uses the block cipher all by itself to generate the Vernam keys (Figure 2-6). Unlike the other two modes, the key stream does not depend on the data stream at all. Neither plaintext nor ciphertext is fed back to affect the encryption process. In this mode the block cipher has nothing to do with processing the message; it is only used to generate the keys. This is also referred to as *autokey mode* in military applications (Figure 2-7).

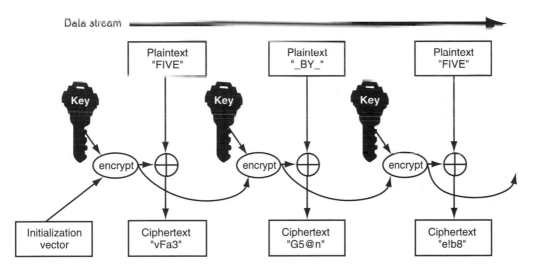

Figure 2-6: ENCRYPTION WITH OFB MODE. This mode uses the block cipher algorithm to generate a key stream independent of the data being encrypted. The plaintext is encrypted by exclusive-or'ing it with the key stream. The key stream is generated with the block cipher, starting by encrypting the IV and then encrypting the previous block of the key stream to produce the next block. Like CFB, this can be adapted to encrypt partial data blocks without requiring padding.

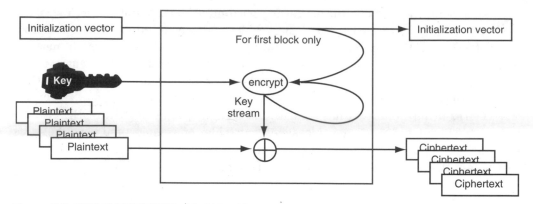

Figure 2-7: IMPLEMENTATION OF OFB MODE: AUTOKEY ENCRYPTION. This is the process shown in Figure 2-6, rearranged for simplicity. The plaintext is encrypted with a Vernam cipher. The key stream for the Vernam cipher is generated entirely by the block cipher as controlled by the crypto key. A random IV is used to seed the key generation process. This technique is called *autokey encryption* because it automatically generates new key values for the Vernam cipher.

Like CFB, the length of the plaintext does not have to fit exactly on block boundaries. Each message requires an IV, so transmitted ciphertext must include an extra data block containing the IV. An efficiency benefit to OFB is that the key stream may be computed before data is ready to be sent or before it is received, since the key stream relies only on the key and the IV.

While OFB ciphertext has better security properties than ECB, it has shortcomings compared with the other modes. In particular, there is a direct relationship between bits in the plaintext and bits in the ciphertext, so a message containing known plaintext is vulnerable to change. A "rewrite" attack of this type can be undetectable and never leaves garbage in the decrypted plaintext. This attack is fully discussed in Section 3.2.3.

While it is possible to construct other, more esoteric modes for special purposes, the best choice will almost always be one of these four modes. The shortcomings noted for some modes are not relevant to all applications. Operational and error handling properties can make otherwise attractive modes a bad choice for some applications. Section 2.3.3 discusses the selection of modes and crypto algorithms.

2.2   How Crypto Systems Fail

Networking systems fail to protect messages because people are motivated to attack them. Typical data communications protocols are designed to deal with random errors: TCP/IP delivers data reliably even when a broad range of accidents and failures occur. But these protocols aren't designed to stand up against conscious attempts to fool them.

Unlike generic communications protocols, crypto systems are designed to stand up against attack. When crypto systems do fail, we can identify weaknesses as falling into either of two categories: in the cipher itself or in the operating environment. The cipher itself is the mechanism by which a given message is transformed from plaintext into ciphertext. The environment in which the code is used includes the rules for handling plaintext, the distribution of keys, the roles of people involved, and the physical protections given to the various elements.

A very trivial example illustrates the basic concept of a "weak" code. Consider the codes used for cryptograms published as puzzles in newspapers. Typically, cryptograms use a very simple encryption technique that can be cracked by applying some basic rules. Here is a classic:

$$\begin{array}{r} \text{SEND} \\ + \text{MORE} \\ \hline \text{MONEY} \end{array}$$

We can tell that the solution requires a substitution of letters for digits by the way the problem is presented. We can immediately identify the letter standing for one digit based on the rules of arithmetic: M must stand for 1. Systematic trial and error quickly yields the rest of the code. This is perhaps the easiest example there is of *cryptanalysis*—the systematic breaking of encrypted messages and coding systems.

Simple ciphers like those used in cryptograms are usually a form of the *Caesar cipher*, named for the Roman emperor who used it. History does not tell us how long, simple, Caesarlike ciphers were effective in protecting important secrets. We do find the earliest recorded discussion of code-breaking techniques in an Arabian encyclopedia of the thirteenth century. Those techniques were soon put to use in Italy, France, and other European countries. Most countries used codes, but the more successful ones also worked at breaking codes.

Ever since the fourteenth century we have found the strongest codes emerging from teams that understand how to break codes as well as build them. It is no coincidence that the NSA is responsible for both creating and cracking encryption systems. By knowing the tools available to crack a code, they know the properties needed to make a code harder to crack. Sophisticated crypto designers and users recognize that you must understand a system's weaknesses before you can rely on the system's strengths.

Cracking a code involves either an attack on the code itself or on the way the code is used. Given the strength of modern codes, the real risk today is in how they are actually used. However, it is still important to select an appropriately strong alternative from the number available in today's marketplace.

The essential objective in choosing a strong code, or a strong crypto system for that matter, is to look at the *work factor* it presents an attacker. The work factor is an estimate of how hard the attacker must work in order to bypass the protections and achieve some valuable goal. Stronger systems present a larger work factor while weaker systems are easier to overcome. Ideally the work factor should be large enough to make the costs of an attack greater than the potential benefits to the attacker.

2.2.1   Cryptanalysis and Modern Codes

By the start of the twentieth century, cryptanalysis had become quite sophisticated. Caesar ciphers had become newspaper puzzles, and popular books showed how to crack simple codes by counting the frequency of letters in the ciphertext. In English, the letters E, T, and A are most common. In a Caesar-encrypted message written in typical English, whatever letters appear most often most likely correspond to the letters E, T, and A.

Meanwhile, the protection of serious secrets used more sophisticated techniques. The principal goal had evolved from simply disguising messages to systematic attempts to suppress any relationship between the ciphertext and the words and letters of the original plaintext. Basic tricks like counting letters were defeated by using multiple alphabets, then by using a continually changing relationship between the plaintext letter and the alphabet to use. Such techniques reached their zenith with *rotor machines*, which automatically translated a plaintext letter into a ciphertext letter according to its location in the message and the sequence of letters preceding it. The resulting stream cipher was so bewilderingly complex that encryption and decryption had to be mechanized. While the technique was unpopular in newspaper cryptograms, it was extremely popular with governments and diplomats.

In 1925 the American cryptographer William Friedman took the first steps toward cryptanalysis of rotor machines. By the time World War II arrived, rotor machines were widely used for military and diplomatic traffic (Figure 2-8). Friedman's evolving techniques had borne fruit, and not only in America. Work by Polish cryptanalysts led to British successes against German cipher machines in the now-famous code breaking establishment at Bletchley Park.

Military histories of World War II are filled with stories of how the Allies broke this German code or that Japanese code, and similar stories circulate about how the Axis powers exploited weaknesses in Allied codes. Many details of wartime successes were in fact kept secret for decades. This allowed those "in the know" to continue reading the ciphertext of less sophisticated rivals. Automated techniques pioneered at Bletchley Park were transferred to the evolving technology of elec-

Figure 2-8: ROTOR-BASED CRYPTO MACHINE FROM WORLD WAR II. This rotor machine, called the *SIGABA*, was used by the U.S. military during World War II. The rotors are the numbered wheels on the top of the device. They established the crypto key. Operators would type in messages and the result would be printed on paper tape. Photo courtesy of the National Cryptographic Museum.

tronic computers. This fueled computer development, which in turn yielded dramatic advances in codebreaking.

Eventually the effectiveness of computer-based codebreaking became public knowledge and sophisticated customers sought better codes. Banks and other commercial organizations had come to rely heavily on fast communications and the integrity of the messages they sent. Modern and more efficient communications techniques tended to sacrifice speed for security and did not always provide enough protection. Most sophisticated crypto knowledge was closely held by governments, so private organizations and mathematicians evolved their own techniques for strong cryptography. In practice, these techniques have proven very effective.

The basic strength of modern crypto lies in a large body of mathematical work arguing that certain computations are inevitably more difficult to reverse than they were to perform in the first place. For example, if two prime numbers have been multiplied together to produce a third number (225389, for example), it is very difficult to start with that number and compute which two primes produced it. Crypto designers start with these mathematical tools and apply known cryptanalytic techniques against the crypto algorithm as its design evolves. This reduces the risk of weaknesses in the algorithm design that would admit systematic "short cuts" for cracking it.

The mathematical foundations of different block ciphers, stream ciphers, and of the various public key techniques are generally quite different. In practice, weaknesses in one crypto algorithm have never pointed to a general weakness in all algorithms. The notion of finding a general shortcut makes terrific fiction and was, in fact, the premise behind the 1992 movie *Sneakers*. Like perpetual motion or teleportation, it is fertile ground for fiction and entertaining speculation. However, a large amount of mathematical analysis makes it very unlikely that such shortcuts exist.

The basic mathematical result sought when analyzing a modern code is evidence that there is no shortcut for deriving the plaintext or the key associated with some ciphertext. This result means that a cryptanalytic attack must generally take a "brute force" approach that tries all possible keys in search of the right one. This approach is actually practical if there are a small number of keys and the cryptanalysts have a fast computer. There can never be a defense against such an attack, so modern crypto design seeks to make brute force attacks as time-consuming as possible. Thus, a mathematically sound code is more secure if it has a longer key rather than a shorter one.

2.2.2   Brute Force Cracking of Secret Keys

Cryptanalysis has long relied on the lengthy, patient application of trial and error in order to crack a code. The advent of electronic computing dramatically enhanced that process. It is no coincidence that the NSA played a pivotal role in funding American computer system development in its early decades. A practical result today is that anyone with a workstation can crack ciphertext encrypted with a short key. For example, many commercial applications like spreadsheets and word processors provide password protection for their documents, using encryption to provide the protection and the password as the key. Since users often forget such passwords, clever software developers have produced utility programs to recover passwords, often using brute force. The techniques are very efficient. The developer of one such package admitted that the software includes artificial delays to make the cracking activity appear to take longer than it really does. Fortunately, access control in such situations is most often intended just

Table 2-2: Brute force attacks on shorter key lengths

Type of Key	No. of Bits	No. of Keys	Time to Test One[a]	No. of Parallel Tests	Average Search Time
3-digit luggage lock	10	1,000	2 sec	1	17 min
4-digit cash card PIN	14	10,000	60 sec	1	3.5 d
Short text password	28	81,450,625	50 μsec	1	34 min
Netscape export crypto	40	1,099,511,627,776	50 μsec	1	10 mo
Netscape export crypto	40	1,099,511,627,776	50 μsec	50	6 d
Long text password	56	6,634,204,312,890,620	50 μsec	1	5,274 yr
DES key	56	72,057,594,037,927,900	50 μsec	1	57,280 yr
DES key	56	72,057,594,037,927,900	0.02 μsec	57,600	3.5 hr

[a] One microsecond (μsec) is a millionth of a second (0.000001 second).
PIN=personal identification number.

to keep honest people from making mistakes. Such files are not generally shared with truly untrusted recipients.

Brute force cracking works by trying all possible values for the key until the right one is found. Once it succeeds, the attacker can read the message that was encrypted with that key, along with any other messages encrypted with that key. The principal defense against brute force cracking is to produce as long a list of legal keys as possible. As the list gets longer, so does the amount of work it could take to guess the right key.

Table 2-2 illustrates how this works. The first columns indicate the type of key and its size. From that we compute the number of possible keys, which appears in the next column. The number of possible keys depends on whether the key is comprised of digits, characters, or pure binary data. The fourth column tells how long it takes to try a single key. The first example is a luggage lock—a simple mechanical lock with three wheels marked with digits. The lock opens when the right combination is dialed. The time to test one key corresponds to the time needed to switch the combination to a new setting and see if the lock opens. The rightmost column shows, on average, how long it should take to find the right key value using this "brute force" search. Even though the luggage lock has a thousand possible combinations, the average time to find the right one is less than a half hour. A lucky person might find it quicker, but no search will take more than twice as long.

The example in the second row is a four-digit personal identification number (PIN) on a typical cash card. The time to test a cash card PIN reflects the time needed to stick the card into a cash machine, key in the PIN, and wait for the machine to reject the card if the PIN guessed is incorrect. Since there are more combinations and each test takes longer, the attacker must keep trying, on average for three and one-half days. One can only hope that the bank would call the police if someone kept trying successive PIN values constantly for hours on end.

The rest of the table illustrates computer-based key searches. Passwords on traditional Unix systems are vulnerable to brute force attack because the password file is readable by all users. The secrecy of passwords on such systems is supposed to be preserved by encrypting them. It has become a popular pastime for attackers to capture a site's Unix password file and try to guess passwords. As indicated in Table 2-2, attackers can easily recover shorter passwords, but longer passwords generally resist attack.

The Netscape and DES examples illustrate the value of teamwork in brute force cryptanalysis. The fifth column from the left in Table 2-2 indicates the number of keys being tested simultaneously in different attacks. The Netscape examples refer to the encryption used on "secure" World Wide Web accesses by the Netscape Navigator. The Navigator's encryption software uses a reasonably long key, but most copies only keep 40 bits of the key secret (this was a compromise to acquire permission to export it). Table 2-2 also shows that a single workstation requires an average of 10 months of work to recover the 40 bits. The next row illustrates what happens if 50 workstations are all applied to the problem simultaneously. The average time is reduced to slightly more than six days.

Brute force cracking of a Netscape 40-bit key was demonstrated by a pair of French graduate students in the summer of 1995. They started with a sample World Wide Web transaction that someone else had encrypted with Netscape Navigator's 40-bit encryption. For computing power they used an office filled with workstations left idle during the August vacation in France. It took them slightly longer than a week to crack their particular example—a couple days longer than the predicted average time using 50 workstations. Contrast this with the average time of 10 months required by a single workstation. Fifty workstations are not that difficult to acquire for the right price. An especially rich and impatient attacker could acquire more or faster workstations and decrease the attack time accordingly.

DES has been used by the banking industry, including the U.S. Federal Reserve System (which has primary authority over American currency), ever since its introduction in 1975. Table 2-2 shows how well a 56-bit key resists brute force attack by typical workstations. The workstation would certainly be a pile of rust and sand by the end of the 57,000 years needed, on average, to extract a DES key. On the other hand, optimized hardware combined with massively parallel computation could change this equation.

The DES example shown in the bottom row is a theoretical one taken from a 1994 proposal by Michael Wiener of Bell-Northern Research. Weiner worked out the design for a device based on available technology that would perform brute force searches for DES keys. He estimated that a minimal version of the machine would cost $100,000 and could brute force crack a DES key in thirty-five hours. One

Table 2-3: Brute force attacks on longer key lengths

The average search time assumes that the $1 million cracking engine can try approximately 3 trillion keys per second.

Algorithm	No. of Bits	No. of Keys	Average Search Time with a $1 Million Cracking Engine
DES	56	10^{16}	3.5 h
SKIPJACK	80	10^{24}	6,655 yr
Triple DES with 2 keys	112	10^{33}	30,000,000,000,000 yr
IDEA, RC4/128	128	10^{38}	2,000,000,000,000,000,000 yr

million dollars would produce a proportionally larger machine that cracks DES encryption in three and one-half hours. Given that progress has not stopped in digital circuit fabrication, the cost and speed of brute force cracking will only improve as time goes on.

Some sources have questioned whether Weiner's cracking engine represents a realistic project, largely on issues of component cost and scalability. The history of technology shows that Weiner's proposal is precisely the sort of engineering artifact that is likely to become more feasible as technology matures. Costs for digital devices have dropped by a significant percentage every year for decades, and performance has similarly improved. Weiner's proposed million-dollar design will probably remain an expensive, special-purpose device that appeals to government intelligence agencies or to shady divisions of other large, well-funded organizations. Although more pedestrian attackers are unlikely to achieve its performance, we shall use it as a benchmark for brute force cryptanalytic power. Weiner's engine can test almost 3 trillion keys per second. Table 2-3 illustrates how the longer keys of more modern crypto algorithms stand up to a device like the Weiner cracking engine.

Some suggest that there actually may be a fundamental limit to brute force cracking. The basics of thermodynamics can be used to estimate the minimum amount of energy needed to perform a single-bit transition, and this can be used to estimate the amount of brute force cracking that can be performed by a given amount of energy. The crypto policy report issued by the NRC estimates that it would take the total energy output of the sun over its estimated lifetime to crack a single 250-bit key. If we set our sights lower and harness the sun's energy for a year, then we are limited to cracking one 192-bit key per year. In practice, of course, the number would be far less. Testing a single key requires far more than a single-bit transition. Furthermore, the Earth receives only a fraction of the sun's radiation, and most of that energy is spent on weather, photosynthesis, and other such pursuits.

2.2.3 Attacks on Improper Crypto Use

The random cipher key sequence—the "gamma" in KGB slang—is only used once and is often called the "one time pad." For a cipher clerk, using the same cipher key twice is a serious offense.

—Major Victor Sheymov, KGB (retired), *Tower of Secrets*

The finest technical cryptographic system in the world will not protect a message against carelessness or incompetence. And, more often that we might wish, a powerful technical concept will be weakened by poor implementation or improper use. This is a fundamental lesson of cryptographic history. Clever techniques are no substitute for overall correctness and proper use.

A classic example of improper crypto use occurred during and shortly after World War II. At that time the Soviet Union was using one time pads to encrypt all sensitive messages transmitted from their offices all over the world to Moscow. As noted in Section 2.1.1, one time pads are theoretically unbreakable if properly used. However, if the cipher keys are reused, the one time pad becomes a Vernam cipher with a repeating key and is vulnerable to cryptanalysis.

The encrypted Soviet messages were intercepted by operators in the United States and in other countries. If the pads had been used correctly, all attempts to decrypt the intercepted messages would have failed. Unfortunately, those responsible for Soviet cipher security had not yet learned the lesson that Major Sheymov noted. Early in World War II the Soviets ran short of cipher keys as they tried to keep up with rapidly growing demand. In fact, the difficulty of generating and distributing enough keying material remains the fundamental problem with the practical use of one time pads.

The Soviets resolved their dilemma by making copies of the keys they had and distributing the duplicate keys to different offices. Thus, a typical Soviet office might never reuse a one time pad itself; but, in fact, the same pad would be reused by a different office elsewhere. For example, the pad used by the KGB for sending messages from New York to Moscow might also be used by the Soviet trade mission in Mexico City to encrypt their traffic. This approach seemed reasonably safe, assuming a cryptanalyst doesn't happen to look at the Mexico City trade messages at the same time as the KGB messages from New York.

In fact, something of that nature happened early in World War II. Despite the discouraging prospects of attacking one time pads, cryptanalysts working for the

U.S. Army's Signal Intelligence Service began a project, code named VENONA, to try to decipher them. The team eventually cracked hundreds of messages about Soviet espionage in the United States, revealing for the first time the extent of these activities. In all, the messages referred to 200 different individuals spying in the U.S. on the Soviet's behalf. Several messages referred to Julius and Ethel Rosenberg, who were eventually convicted of espionage and executed for passing atomic bomb secrets to the Soviets. Other messages reported on the activities of atomic spy Klaus Fuchs and U.S. State Department official Alger Hiss. Also appearing was Greg Silvermaster, the only U.S. citizen ever to be inducted into the KGB Hall of Fame. Dozens of agents mentioned in the messages have never been identified.

The Soviets revised their crypto procedures in the late 1940s, eliminating the use of duplicate pads. Although the VENONA work was highly classified and not widely discussed even among senior government officials, agents working on the Soviets' behalf probably passed them some information about it by 1945. The Soviets probably didn't learn the full extent of the project until 1949, when it was described to Kim Philby, a senior member of the British intelligence community. Philby was also an agent for the KGB.

The cryptographic lesson of VENONA is that strong measures must be used correctly or the effort is wasted. The Soviets protected their most treasured secrets with a one time pad, theoretically the best crypto protection possible. Improper use gave American codebreakers the entering wedge they needed.

However, cryptanalysis is not the only way to read a secret messages. Remember that the message itself, unprotected, is often available to the patient spy or eavesdropper. People of a mathematical persuasion might want to call this "cheating," but we must keep the eavesdropper's basic objective in mind. If there is a way for an attacker to read the message, the attacker will use it.

2.3   Choosing Between Strong and Weak Crypto

Mystery; Finesse—how they pervert the understanding!

—Jane Austen, *Emma*

The advice anyone would desire at this point is an ordered list of the technologies known to be the strongest. Unfortunately, it is difficult to choose reliably that way. Not all crypto products support all strong algorithms or modes, or provide comfortably long key lengths. Also, there is no way to predict which of today's stronger alternatives is least likely to contain an unexpected flaw. We can speak more reliably about which techniques contain identified problems or shortcomings and what those problems are. Then when faced with a product containing a particular problem, we can decide if the risk is acceptable for our application.

In any case, prudent planners will anticipate how their system can migrate to a different crypto mechanism and key length in the future. No security technology remains effective forever. The decreasing effectiveness of DES echoes similar declines in past crypto systems—the effectiveness wanes gradually. Cautious users generally can see ahead of time that their security is eroding and have the opportunity to migrate to newer techniques. More immediate threats come from architectural and operational risks, which are the focus of the rest of this book.

2.3.1   Properties of Good Crypto Algorithms

This section summarizes some basic rules for evaluating and selecting strong crypto algorithms, and how they relate to a list of available modern algorithms. Here are the algorithms we will discuss:

- DES
- Triple DES (3DES)
- IDEA
- RC4
- SKIPJACK

Preferred algorithms generally have the following properties to some degree. How specific algorithms stack up against these properties will be discussed in the next section.

- **No reliance on algorithm secrecy**

  While it may, in some cases, increase the attacker's work factor to keep as much secret as possible, keeping a crypto algorithm secret can be a double-edged sword. If we don't know how the algorithm works we can't tell if it has some easy-to-exploit flaw. For example, a product's "secret" or "proprietary" algorithm might simply be a Vernam cipher with ciphertext that is good enough to trick casual observers but is easily attacked by a competent code breaker.

  Good crypto algorithms rely exclusively on the keys to protect the data. Revealing the algorithm should not significantly improve an attacker's likelihood of success.

- **Explicitly designed for encryption**
  The algorithm should have been designed in the first place to resist cryptanalysis. This is not always true of algorithms used for encryption. For example, some products use simple random number generators to produce a Vernam cipher key stream. Simple notions of statistical randomness do not guarantee strength against cryptanalysis. Occasionally a product or protocol will use a hash algorithm like Message Digest #5 (MD5) with a secret key to yield a Vernam key stream. This is not what the MD5 algorithm was designed to do, and without a serious analysis there is no reason to assume such a key stream will resist cryptanalysis.

- **Available for analysis**
  Ideally, the algorithm has been published and subjected to scrutiny by the public cryptographic community. The longer mathematicians and cryptanalysts have to look at the algorithm, the more likely they will find its weaknesses. DES has stood the test of time and is likely to be used for many years to come in some form or other.

  It is less satisfactory when the developer offers the algorithm for analysis under various confidentiality and nondisclosure arrangements. Fewer experts review it under such conditions, and the time and circumstances tend to limit the depth of the review. Too often the experts are brought in as a marketing gimmick, so the resources available for the review are dictated by appearances. The review will rarely continue beyond the point where some positive, if superficial, report can be produced.

- **Subject to analysis**
  Have recognized cryptanalysts published results regarding the algorithm's strength? Ideally, recognized experts should be openly discussing the algorithm and publishing analyses in refereed professional journals that ensure the work is reviewed by other experts. This almost never occurs except in cases when the algorithm itself has been published.

  In weaker cases the algorithm may have been reviewed by recognized experts in cryptanalysis who have published opinions regarding its strength against vulnerabilities recognized in similar codes. Unfortunately, this approach suffers from the "marketing gimmick" problems noted in the previous case. It is always important to judge the experts rendering the opinion: Are they within their scope of expertise?

- **No practical weaknesses**
  The analyses performed should show that there are no serious weaknesses in the algorithm that an attacker can easily exploit. Custom-built algorithms embedded in commercial software tend to have serious weaknesses, as noted

in an earlier section. If a commercial package claims to encrypt data and does not use a recognized algorithm, do not presume that it protects against any motivated attacker.

There are a few other criteria worth considering. These do not directly apply to the algorithm but instead apply to the organization responsible for the algorithm— its experience, motivation, and how it portrays the algorithm.

It is probably unwise to use any algorithm with the smell of snake oil. Avoid products touted with inconsistent and misleading verbiage. For example, a product was released that called itself a "one time pad" though additional product details made it clear that it was in no sense a one time pad. By mislabeling the product the vendor ran the risk of confusing customers into misapplying it. When stripped of marketing hype, the underlying product may in fact have been capable and effective, but misleading terminology makes its effectiveness harder to establish.

It is uncomfortably appealing to prefer algorithms created by or closely associated with recognized cryptographic experts on the basis of their professional prestige. The relatively young commercial cryptographic industry has never experienced a major mistake by a recognized expert. The newer creations of experienced masters have tended to reflect the creator's depth of knowledge and skill. However, some of these experts have had a long career and earlier creations naturally do not always reflect the sophistication of later work. So one must always look beyond the authors' names when evaluating a crypto algorithm.

An interesting political problem in the United States is the NSA's combined role of intercepting electronic data traffic and of protecting such traffic from interception. On the one hand the NSA's historic depth in cryptography would argue that it should be the premier producer of crypto systems. The organization can easily trace its roots back to William Friedman's work in the 1920s. But the NSA's tradition of secrecy fueled the development of a completely separate discipline of cryptography: Today's "public" crypto community incorporates members of the academic and commercial communities with their own particular interests and needs.

The gulf between these communities combined with the obvious conflict in the NSA's goals, has led many members of the public cryptographic community to avoid NSA products and technologies. There have been rumors for decades that recommendations by the NSA had unnecessarily weakened the DES algorithm. Other rumors have hinted at a secret "back door" inserted in the algorithm by the NSA to simplify cracking its ciphertext. Decades of public scrutiny have failed to find any such weakness. In fact, recent public advances in cryptanalysis showed that some questionable NSA recommendations actually made DES stronger or more efficient. In any case, the conflict of goals is very real. The NSA tradition of secrecy does not allow the public scrutiny of its technology, which would help dispel doubts.

2.3.2   Crypto Algorithms to Consider

The following paragraphs review crypto algorithms you are likely to encounter in products intending to provide strong crypto protection. If a candidate product or system contains a different algorithm than one of these, check the references given at the end of this chapter for guidance. If the algorithm stacks up poorly against the criteria noted earlier in this section, then do not use it for protecting valuable messages or information.

- **Data Encryption Standard**
  DES has the benefit of being a known quantity with familiar strengths and weaknesses. In typical applications it is unlikely to be vulnerable to any attack short of brute force. In the late 1980s the public cryptanalysis community developed the technique of *differential cryptanalysis*, which proved to be effective against DES under a narrow and impractical set of conditions (specifically, the existence of an enormous amount of specially constructed plaintext with corresponding ciphertext). While the attack is very interesting to mathematicians, it does not affect DES security in typical applications. The most often cited problem of DES today is its relatively short 56-bit key length.

  Many users are drawn to DES because it is a U.S. government standard. This provides justification for its use, which other crypto algorithms lack. This status is scheduled to be reviewed in 1998, at which point the algorithm could be retired or at least see revisions in its recommended applicability.

- **Triple DES**
  3DES is a technique by which the DES algorithm is applied three times to each plaintext block (Figure 2-9). Typical approaches use two conventional

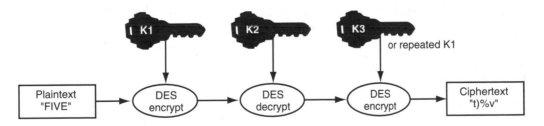

Figure 2-9: ENCRYPTION WITH TRIPLE DES. This technique applies the DES algorithm to the plaintext three times, potentially using a different 56-bit DES key each time. Typical applications use a 112-bit key constructed of a pair of 56-bit keys, K1 and K2, with K1 being reused for the final encrypt operation. A triple DES device can interoperate with conventional DES encryption by using an identical key value for K1, K2, and K3. This is because the second step is a decrypt operation; using the same key in all three steps yields the same result as encrypting only once with that key.

DES keys, yielding a length of 112 bits. Some applications use three different keys, yielding a total key size of 168 bits, which is truly enormous for a symmetric cipher. The earlier discussion of thermodynamic limitations on brute force cracking would suggest that a 168-bit key size will never be obsolete.

- **International Data Encryption Algorithm (IDEA)**
IDEA is a block cipher that appeared in 1990. Xuejia Lai and James Massey developed IDEA at the Swiss Federal Institute of Technology. IDEA is more efficient to implement in software than DES or 3DES, and its 128-bit key makes it more attractive than conventional DES. IDEA may be used with the usual block cipher modes.

    As of this writing there are few rigorous mathematical analyses of IDEA, but many unsuccessful attempts to apply known cryptanalytic techniques. The developers present evidence that the algorithm's underlying mechanism resists differential cryptanalysis better than DES. Other analyses have found that simpler forms of IDEA's algorithm are vulnerable to certain attacks, but that the weaknesses are eliminated as the full details of the algorithm are applied. Many experts are optimistic about IDEA and its likelihood to stand the test of time.

- **Rivest Cipher #4**
RC4 is a stream cipher marketed by RSA Data Security. Although its key size can vary, it is often used with a 128-bit key. Originally the cipher was protected as a trade secret, only to be "leaked" to the crypto community via the Internet. The cipher was developed by Ron Rivest, a highly respected crypto designer, and the vendor claims that the algorithm is immune to differential cryptanalysis and other well-known techniques. Independent reviews since the code was leaked have found much to admire and little to question in its design.

    The most commonly cited problem is its use with short key lengths. The U.S. government allows it to be exported when it uses secret key lengths of 40 bits or less. Thus, typical implementations use a very short key length and suffer from a corresponding vulnerability to brute force cracking.

- **SKIPJACK**
SKIPJACK is a block encryption algorithm developed by the NSA. It encrypts 64 bit blocks using an 80-bit key. The usual block cipher modes may be used with it to encrypt streams. It is provided in prepackaged encryption chip sets and in the Fortezza crypto card, a PC card containing a crypto processor and storage for keying material.

    The SKIPJACK algorithm is classified, which dramatically limits how much is publicly known about its essential cryptographic properties. A published report on the SKIPJACK algorithm claims it has a variety of important properties, including resistance to differential cryptanalysis and other short-cut attacks. The report also claims that the algorithm's effectiveness does not depend on it being kept secret, and that the algorithm is kept secret to protect the NSA's design techniques.

According to the report's claims, the algorithm is at least as resistant to attack as the best commercial algorithms. The NSA is promoting SKIPJACK to protect military communications in the Defense Message System (DMS) and to protect classified information in some cases. This reflects a measure of confidence that is consistent with the SKIPJACK report.

The crypto algorithm is but one element in the security of a crypto system. Its choice, however, establishes much of the system's strength or vulnerability when faced with a sophisticated attack.

2.3.3   Selecting a Block Cipher Mode

If you are using a block cipher, its resistance to attack also depends somewhat on whether you are using the right crypto mode with it. Here are some possible data communications applications and suggested modes to support them. Unfortunately, all of these modes produce ciphertext that can be manipulated in one way or another. If message authenticity is crucial, then the crypto system should apply separate integrity protection. This will be discussed in more detail as specific techniques and products are examined.

- **Arbitrary communications protocols with arbitrary data: CBC, CFB**
  If, for example, you are applying a block cipher to raw internet packets containing arbitrary data, CBC mode and CFB mode are the best choices. Repeated plaintext data will be effectively obscured. The constantly changing encryption keys in these modes will defeat differential cryptanalysis attacks even if the attacker is able to generate chosen plaintext. There is a risk of cut-and-paste attacks, but they will probably leave residual garbage in decrypted messages.

- **Protocols with crypto integrity protection: CBC, CFB, OFB**
  If the protocol incorporates crypto integrity protection, then OFB may be added to the list of acceptable modes. Messages protected by OFB are especially vulnerable to being modified by an attacker who knows the message's plaintext contents, and, unlike cut-and-paste attacks in other modes, the modifications leave no trace.

- **Small amounts of truly random data: ECB**
  If the information being encrypted is truly random, then ECB mode may be safely used. For example, ECB can be used to encrypt randomly generated keying material that is being sent across the network. ECB should never be used to encrypt information that could have been supplied by an attacker, since this could support a chosen plaintext cryptanalytic attack. The other three modes could also be used safely in this situation. They are not recommended simply for efficiency reasons.

2.3.4   Identifying a Safe Key Length

Like the choices of algorithm and block mode, your choices for key length are going to be controlled by what is available in products you can use. The likely range of keys for symmetric ciphers will be between 40 and 128 bits, although you may also encounter 168-bit 3DES implementations. The important decision often will be whether or not appropriate products have sufficient key lengths to protect your information.

The following is a list of questions associated with the sensitivity of your data. Each "yes" answer to one of these questions indicates that a longer crypto key is preferred over a shorter one.

1. Will a single key be used to protect a large number of different messages and transactions? For example, some systems will generate and use a different crypto key for every session or transaction while others will reuse the same key for some period of time. The more a single key is used, the longer it should be.

2. Can an attacker do serious damage by recovering and using the crypto key? In the worst case military and intelligence scenario, people can die. If this is the case, then the key should be very long and the rest of the system be of very high quality.

3. Is any of the information in a message treated as strictly confidential by the owners, subject to costly abuse, and rarely disclosed except in these messages? For example, a bank might assign a confidential account number to the account holder that for various reasons is difficult to change. Reusable passwords that grant access to important databases or other computing resources are another example. Personal credit card numbers are not, since they are released to any merchant that accepts the card to pay for a purchase.

4. Does the key prevent unauthorized people from manipulating valuable assets, causing payment for them, or arranging their shipment? The greater

the value of assets protected by an individual key, the longer that key should be. For example, if the key protects a credit card sale that could be of a very high dollar value, then the key should be longer rather than shorter.

If we start with a 40-bit crypto key we can probably feel safe as long as each question is answered "no." Each question that yields a "yes" answer indicates that a longer key should be used. As more "yes" answers appear, an even longer key is appropriate until we reach the vicinity of the 112-bit 3DES and 128-bit IDEA keys.

Key size selection is also affected by the particular crypto solution being used; that is, how the crypto is being used to protect network traffic and how it integrates into various protocols. This will be discussed in more detail as each crypto solution is examined in subsequent chapters.

LEGAL RESTRICTIONS ON ALGORITHMS AND KEY LENGTHS

As noted in Section 1.6, U.S. export regulations treat crypto products differently according to their relative strength. Particular algorithms with particular key lengths are treated differently according to these rules.

- **Lightweight crypto**
  Algorithms: RC4 and Rivest Cipher #2 (RC2, a block cipher)
  Key length: 40 bits
  Products using lightweight crypto may be granted bulk export licenses.

- **Medium-Strength crypto**
  Algorithm: DES
  Key length: 56 bits
  Products using medium-strength crypto may be granted bulk export licenses if the vendor is actively developing products that support key escrow. These licenses must be renewed periodically and it is not clear whether they will be renewed indefinitely under the current rules.

There are two peculiar wrinkles to these rules. First, a product can get a bulk license if it can be convincingly shown that encryption is only applied to financial information and cannot be applied to other data. The second wrinkle is that the number of bits only refers to the number kept secret and not to the actual number used in the crypto algorithm. In other words, a longer crypto key can be used as long as no more than 40 bits of the key are kept secret from an eavesdropper. It is generally assumed that this feature is provided so that law enforcement and intelligence agencies can eavesdrop on messages protected by lightweight crypto systems.

2.3.5   Levels of Risk for Different Applications

An essential element in choosing between different crypto or security solutions is the level of risk faced by the application. If the application faces a high risk, then more complicated, expensive security measures are justified. If the application faces a low risk, then it makes sense to take shortcuts and use lower cost, less comprehensive solutions. The following is a review of different levels of risk that different applications might face and a summary of what makes one application riskier than another.

- **Low-risk application**

  These are applications for which the risks to the enterprise are relatively small. If the application is somehow disrupted or the system supporting it is penetrated, the enterprise can easily afford the trouble and inconvenience of restoring the system and recovering from the temporary outage.

  Typical examples would be lower volume Web sites used primarily for advertising and public relations, or e-mail service that supports informal communications among colleagues and customers as a convenient alternative to the telephone.

  Low-risk applications can usually achieve adequate protection with typical commercial software and a reasonable amount of care in setting it up. These applications do not tend to draw attackers' attention so they do not have to defend against serious attack attempts.

- **Medium-risk application**

  These are applications for which the enterprise faces quantifiable monetary losses on the order of shoplifting losses in retail environments. Some degree of loss is expected and tolerable, but serious losses could injure the enterprise. Occasional but rare service outages can be tolerated by the customer community, though such outages will cause customer inconvenience that is best avoided.

  Typical examples would be Web sites that support relatively small commercial transactions or that provide customer service to an active user population. Another example would be a bank that allows customers to transfer money between their own accounts, but doesn't allow transactions that deliver money to others.

  Medium-risk applications are attractive targets of attack and should take serious steps to protect themselves from attack. There should be someone responsible for tracking Internet security problems and ensuring that site protections are all up to date.

- **High-risk application**

  These are applications for which a security failure could cause serious losses, either monetary losses or embarrassing headlines. Recent examples include the penetration of Citibank customer accounts and vandalism of Web sites at the U.S. Department of Justice and the Central Intelligence Agency. Bank customers always represent an obvious target for embezzlement, and large government agencies represent obvious targets for publicity stunts.

  High-risk applications attract sophisticated attackers and must naturally take their security very seriously. Unfortunately, there is very little off-the-shelf security technology to protect high-risk applications from sophisticated attacks. Traditionally such applications resided within mainframe systems with which few attackers were familiar. Today, however, newer applications tend to reside on more widely available commercial systems. Security on these systems is usually built for the larger, medium-risk market.

  Enterprises with high-risk applications must pay serious attention to security engineering as part of application development and deployment. Some high-risk applications might be able to treat security as an independent part of the overall system structure, but that can be risky. Once the system is deployed, security must be reviewed periodically to ensure that existing security measures are still adequate.

- **Critical application**

  These are applications for which failure could cause loss of life or some other major disaster. Traditionally, such applications were primarily in military environments, though commercial examples are becoming more common. The growing automation of utilities like power and transportation increase the risk that someone might be tempted to penetrate and damage a critical system seriously.

  As with safety planning, critical applications must integrate security planning and mechanisms into the basic system architecture and design. It probably cannot be added on after the fact and provide the protections needed. As with any application facing a real threat, security must be reviewed periodically to ensure that existing security measures are still adequate.

2.4 For Further Information

- **Schneier, *Applied Cryptography: Protocol, Algorithms, and Source Code in C***
  The book is a necessity for anyone constructing a crypto device. The book provides descriptions of all crucial cryptographic techniques and points to the original sources as well.

- **Anderson, "Why Cryptosystems Fail"**
  A classic paper giving several real-world examples of commercial crypto applications defeated by means other than cracking the codes.

- **Weiner, "Efficient DES Key Search"**
  This is the complete description of how to build the Weiner cracking engine for DES.

- **Pekelney, *Electronic Cipher Machine (ECM) Mark II***
  http://www.maritime.org/ecm2.shtml
  This is a Web page describing the ECM Mark II, otherwise known as SIGABA, otherwise known as CSP-889 shown in Figure 2-8. This was the primary high-level U.S. cipher system from 1941 until approximately 1959. The Web site includes a copy of the U.S. Navy memo on crypto security cited in Section 1.2.1.

- **National Security Agency, *The VENONA Translations***
  http://www.nsa.org:8080/museum/venona
  This site contains historical reports about the VENONA project along with copies of the declassified messages the project decrypted and translated.

- **Brickell, Denning, Kent, Maher, and Tuchman, *SKIPJACK Review Interim Report: The SKIPJACK Algorithm***
  http://www.cosc.georgetown.edu/~denning/crypto/clipper/ SKIPJACK.txt
  This is the interim and apparently the only report produced by the outside reviewers of the SKIPJACK crypto algorithm. The reviewers were very impressed, and the report claims that a good deal of technical effort went into testing the resistance of SKIPJACK to cryptanalytic attacks.

Link Encryption

Everything should be made as simple as possible, but no simpler.

—Albert Einstein

IN THIS CHAPTER

Our first crypto technique is *link encryption*, the classic method of applying crypto to digital communications. Designed to hide secrets, link encryption can also protect data against forgery if used properly. Link encryption is a simple concept that can fit transparently into existing communications applications. The following topics are discussed:

- Security objectives achieved by link encryption
- In line encryptor hardware that implements link encryption
- Point-to-point deployment example
- IP-routed deployment example
- Key recovery and escrowed encryption

Link encryption may not be the best choice for most applications, but it is the simplest, so we look at it first.

3.1 Security Objectives

Like any security measure, link encryption should only be used if it matches your security objectives. It is the traditional choice when you need complete separation between insiders and outsiders. Link encryption makes it easy for insiders to share data and almost impossible for outsiders to do so. Protection is transparent, except for the strong boundary between inside and outside. Here are specific security objectives you can achieve with link encryption.

- **Maintain confidentiality on an isolated set of computers.**
  Your computers contain very sensitive data. You need to exchange data with other sensitive sites and keep the risk of leakage as low as possible.

- **Communications with outsiders is unwanted and to be blocked.**
  You do not want to exchange data with unauthorized sites, and you want to prevent it from happening through accident, carelessness, or overt attempt.

- **Hide data traffic as much as possible.**
  You really need to shield everything possible about the data you send, including details of message sources and destinations, and other communications control information. You assume that "insiders" will not leak the information you are trying to protect.

- **Safety and familiarity is more important than cost.**
  You wish to use a well-established technique that is simple to understand. You are willing to pay a premium even though the technique may be more difficult to operate.

Here is a final security objective, listed separately because it is not unconditionally provided by "pure" link encryption:

- **Protect data transfers from forgery by outsiders.**
  You need to protect data from tampering while in transit between authorized sites. You need assurance that the contents of an incoming message were in fact produced by a host at an authorized site.

Link encryption yields a highly reliable design from a security standpoint. If you have established a strong security perimeter within your organization, link encryption gives you a proven technique for maintaining it. If you strictly control the flow of physical documents in and out of the security perimeter, link encryption can provide complementary protection to electronic documents. You can build an environment with encryptors on every data link traversing the boundary. All readable electronic documents will reside inside the perimeter and the encryptors will protect any electronic data that leaves. This technique has been used for decades to protect the most sensitive military traffic, and to provide secure links between banking organizations.

Since link encryption is the oldest approach to data security, it has also developed a long history of failures from operational and technical flaws. In its simplest form, link encryption does not reliably protect against forged traffic. It blocks outside access so thoroughly that users will sometimes use dial-up links to secretly punch holes in its defense. And, like all crypto measures, it is vulnerable to risks from improper key management.

3.2   Product Example: In-line Encryptor

An in-line encryptor is the building block for link encryption. It is a hardware device with two data ports: one always handles plaintext and the other always handles ciphertext. When plaintext data arrives on the plaintext port, the encryptor transforms the data into ciphertext and transmits it out the ciphertext port. Data is likewise transformed from ciphertext to plaintext after arriving on the ciphertext port. A pair of encryptors will pass data between one another only if the crypto keys have been set up correctly between them.

A modern in-line encryptor can be a relatively small device with two network data link connections and a power supply connection (Figure 3-1). Some in-line encryptors are packaged as encrypting modems so that one data port is a connection for a communications line, like a telephone jack. Some devices will have a facility for manually installing or specifying a secret key, while others may permit keying via the data link connections.

Figure 3-1: IN-LINE ENCRYPTION DEVICE. This is a commercial in-line encryption device—the IRE Model HS Remote Encryptor. It is small enough for convenient desktop use. Photo courtesy of Information Resources Engineering, Inc.

In-line encryption can be applied to any data link technology. It is possible to construct encryptors to handle asynchronous or synchronous serial lines. The data being encrypted can be structured as packets and the encryption embedded in a network bridge device.

Be sure to check the encryptor's operating speed against your data link requirements. Crypto can be slow, so choose products and design systems accordingly. So-called "hardware" implementations of some algorithms may in fact be slower than "software" implementations of newer algorithms.

3.2.1   Red/Black Separation

Rule 1 of cryptanalysis: check for plaintext.

—Robert Morris, NSA (retired)

Separate plaintext and ciphertext ports reflect a well-respected principle of good crypto design: *red/black separation*. The term is taken from a military tradition in which red data refers to plaintext and black data refers to ciphertext. The principle is that a well-designed crypto device will keep the two separated as much as possible (Figure 3-2). In high-end military systems this is taken to the logical extreme.

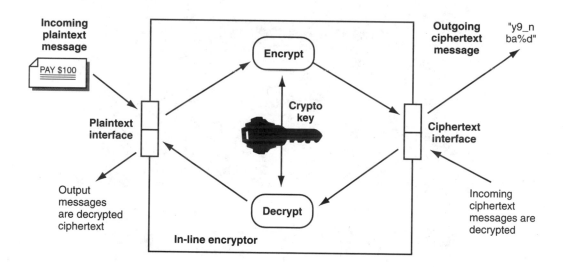

Figure 3-2: INSIDE AN IN-LINE ENCRYPTOR. There are two separate interfaces: one for plaintext and one for ciphertext. Data entering through the plaintext interface is always encrypted and sent out the ciphertext interface, and vice versa. The safest encryptors provide no way to "bypass" the encryption; crypto is applied to everything passing through it.

Every part of a circuit is specifically identified according to whether it carries plaintext or ciphertext. Some devices have multiple power supplies to service the plaintext and ciphertext circuits separately.

There is a Cold War story about a clever bit of tunneling performed under the Berlin Wall. The target was a telephone conduit under the pavements of East Berlin. The eavesdroppers were pleased when they tapped in to the cable and detected encrypted Soviet message traffic. According to the story, the code itself was never cracked and never needed to be. The Soviet's encryption equipment had a flaw in its red/black separation. The plaintext of each encrypted message was also sent across the cable as unintended "random noise."

While Cold War attacks and security measures may be overkill for commercial applications, the lesson is clear: If you keep plaintext and ciphertext separate, you are less likely to mix up the two. If you transfer plaintext and ciphertext through the same network interface, you run a much greater risk of sending plaintext data in the wrong direction. This mistake is much harder to make if the networks are kept completely separate and plugged into separate ports on the encryptor.

3.2.2   Crypto Algorithm and Keying

Since the in-line encryptor processes a stream of data, we must either use a stream cipher or a block cipher with an appropriate streaming mode. In practice, a stream cipher is an unlikely choice. The only stream cipher with a significant commercial reputation is RC4, and in-line encryptors using it are rarely encountered. Most commercial devices were produced for the banking industry and implement the DES algorithm in some form. SKIPJACK-based encryptors have also appeared that use the Fortezza crypto module to perform the encryption operations; some of these systems incorporate a "key recovery" facility that is described in Section 3.5. Other acceptable block algorithms might be used in newer products. (Consult Section 2.3 to evaluate other choices.)

Block ciphers will require a mode in order to process the data stream. The CBC mode is widely used in this application, though CFB also would be a reasonable choice.

As noted earlier in Section 2.2.2, DES with a traditional, shorter 56-bit key is vulnerable to attack by a sufficiently motivated adversary. If you are hiding trade secrets from an aggressive foreign government, or commercial transactions that are particularly vulnerable to forgery, you may want a product with a longer key. Triple DES implementations would be a good choice.

An active link will carry a lot of traffic. Since keys become easier and more attractive to crack as more data is encrypted with them, the preferred device should have a way of rapidly switching keys. Many devices implement automatic key generation or exchange facilities. Devices used in the banking industry often follow American National Standards Institute (ANSI) standards for key exchange. Key handling protocols and capabilities are introduced in Section 4.5.

3.2.3   Encryptor Vulnerabilities

As with any security device, it is easier to choose the right one after considering the problems, from which they may suffer. This section reviews the following vulnerabilities:

- Replay attacks
- Rewrite attacks
- Covert signaling attacks

REPLAY ATTACKS

Many people assume that encrypted data is self-validating, since a message that decrypts sensibly can only be generated by a matching encryptor with the appropriate keys. The problem is that outsiders will have access to lots of encrypted data, and thus to data that "decrypts sensibly." If an outsider captures some external data traffic and retransmits it, the encryptor might simply decrypt it a second time and deliver it like any other data it successfully decrypts. This can be a problem if an outsider can recognize and intercept an encrypted message of personal value.

Figure 3-3 shows Alice sending a payment order to Bob. Payment orders are only visible as ciphertext outside their respective sites. This payment order hap-

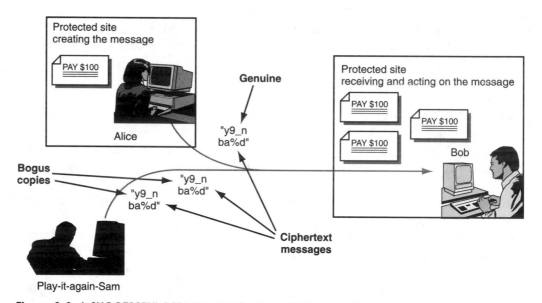

Figure 3-3: A SUCCESSFUL REPLAY ATTACK BY PLAY-IT-AGAIN SAM. Sam made a copy of a legitimate, encrypted message originally written by Alice. He gets money each time the message is sent, so he retransmits a few copies of it, without decrypting or otherwise changing it. Bob treats the copies as legitimate, since they were encrypted with the correct crypto key.

pens to benefit an outsider named Play-It-Again Sam. Somehow or other (and these things are much easier to arrange than we might like) Sam heard about the payment order and intercepted an encrypted copy of it. If Sam simply retransmits the encrypted message a few more times, Bob will receive additional payment orders to process. The encryption will not detect the forgery itself.

An interesting property of this attack is that it depends on the attacker knowing the contents of a particular message. Such attacks are called *known plaintext attacks*. It is always easier to attack crypto protections if the attacker has plaintext messages that match up with intercepted ciphertext.

This type of attack is thwarted by embedding extra information in the data so that duplicate transmissions are detected. For example, the plaintext message could include a message number, and the recipient could discard any messages with a duplicate number. Connection protocols like the internet TCP protocol provide some degree of replay protection.

REWRITE ATTACKS

A rewrite attack is another known plaintext attack that forges messages. Certain crypto algorithms are vulnerable to it, depending on the technical aspects of how the plaintext and key are combined to produce the ciphertext. Simple mechanisms that use binary addition and rely primarily on hard-to-guess keys are especially vulnerable. For example, *one time pads* are vulnerable to this attack. This is important because people often make too much out of the theoretical security properties of one time pads. A true one time pad is *unconditionally secure*, a mathematical property indicating that brute force decryption is ineffective against it. In other words, attackers cannot extract the contents of a message if they do not already know it. However, a message is vulnerable to modification if the attackers know its contents and intercept it in transit.

This type of attack is illustrated in Figure 3-4. Again, Alice is sending a payment message to Bob. This time an outsider called Bailey the Switcher has found out about the message transmission and seeks to benefit by manipulating the message. If Bailey knows the exact contents of the message, she can combine it with the desired message to identify which bits in the encrypted message need to be changed. This works easily when there is a direct relationship between each bit in the plaintext and the corresponding bit in the ciphertext. If you change a bit in one, the same bit will change in the other. In Figure 3-4, Bailey changes a single bit in the letter "a" of the ciphertext, turning it into the letter "i." This produces a corresponding 1-bit change in the plaintext, replacing the value $100 with the value $900.

As with replay, this attack is often thwarted by adding extra information in the data being sent. Here are some approaches that a good product might use to defend against these attacks:

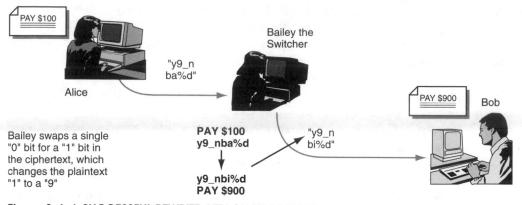

Figure 3-4: A SUCCESSFUL REWRITE ATTACK BY BAILEY THE SWITCHER . Bailey gets a percentage each time Bob processes a PAY message, so she decides to increase her income. She intercepts the ciphertext message and, without decrypting it, changes the dollar amount by swapping bits in the ciphertext. When Bob decrypts it, the ciphertext changes Bailey made will directly modify the plaintext.

1. **Block mode algorithm using CBC or CFB modes.** Avoid products using other modes, straight block ciphers, or Vernam techniques unless the product provides some other protection against rewrite attacks. Some alternatives are noted here. However, keep in mind that crude rewrite attacks are still possible even with CBC or CFB.

2. **Special packet format with random data.** If the underlying network is implemented using packets, the product can reformat the data into a special packet that defends against rewrite attacks. One approach would be to insert a random number into each packet, include it in the packet checksum, and encrypt the resulting packet. An attacker would not be able to predict the random number and thus could not reliably modify the packet.

3. **Special packet format containing a *crypto checksum* based on keyed data** (Section 5.3). This is a variant of the previous technique that is used in the IPSEC protocols described in Chapter 5. Another more expensive alternative is to use a *digital signature* to protect the data from modification (see Chapter 11).

COVERT SIGNALING ATTACKS

This last type of attack simply illustrates that link encryption's strong boundary does not unconditionally keep secrets inside. There will always be a way to leak information if there is a process inside that tries to do so. Generally this is not a problem in commercial settings since the need for confidentiality rarely justifies extreme security measures.

The technique is sometimes called an INFOSEC attack since it combines an attack on the site's crypto protection with an attack on its internal computers. The attack consists of inserting a subverted program into a host on the plaintext side of an encryptor. The program collects sensitive data and then transmits it to a program outside the security boundary by generating distinctive patterns in the stream of ciphertext messages. The actual techniques will depend on the system being attacked, but there will always be a way to send signals according to the formal dicta of information theory.

We only need to pay attention to this threat because it establishes a limit as to how much privacy protection crypto can give us. There have been no reported or even rumored instances of such an attack being used against a commercial target. For most applications this remains, at most, a theoretical risk. For most attackers it will be less costly and more reliable to try to locate and copy the physical plaintext than to use this technique.

3.2.4   Product Security Requirements

Here is an ordered list of basic security requirements for a high-security in-line encryptor. Remember that this is not the whole list. You will encounter more requirements when we look at how you will deploy the encryptors.

1. **Separate network connections for plaintext and ciphertext.** Keeping these connections physically separate is the most reliable approach. It is much too easy to mishandle plaintext and send it to the wrong recipient if both are sent through the same network connection. If you are spending the extra money and administrative overhead to do link encryption, be sure you buy equipment that is most likely to do it correctly.

2. **Crypto key length.** The device must provide a key size consistent with the sensitivity of the information you send across the data link. Review the questions in Section 2.3.4 if you need guidance on establishing your key size requirement.

3. **Crypto key changing.** The best devices will provide mechanisms to change the crypto key automatically and periodically or whenever a connection is established. This is preferred since it reduces the amount of ciphertext an attacker sees that is encrypted with a given key. Review the examples in Chapter 4 against the capabilities of candidate in-line encryptors.

4. **Crypto algorithm.** This, plus the key, determines how well your data is protected after it leaves your site. Your best choice is a respected algorithm like DES or one of the others noted in Section 2.3.2.

5. **Compliance with crypto hardware standards.** The U.S. government published Federal Information Processing Standard (FIPS) 140-1, which provides specifications for cryptographic modules used to protect digital communications.

6. **Replay and rewrite attack protection.** Is it likely that an attacker can identify a packet with predictable contents and cause you damage by modifying or replaying it? The answer depends on your traffic. Choose a product that defends against rewrite attacks if you're unwilling to predict what protocols your network might use.

3.3   Deployment Example: Point-to-Point Encryption

This first deployment example does not necessarily involve Internet protocols. Point-to-point encryption can be applied to any protocol, standardized or custom, that passes between a pair of hosts over an untrustworthy data link. This deployment technique directly supports all the link encryption security objectives: strong isolation, traffic hiding, and simple design. It is also subject to every in-line encryptor vulnerability listed in the previous section.

In its simplest and most secure form, each connection to another external host uses a separate data link and in-line encryptor. Each host, secure within its own physical site, passes its data through an in-line encryptor before reaching the modem or bridge that connects to another host somewhere in the outside world. Each pair of hosts arranges to use identical encryptors and the same cryptographic keys.

Figure 3-5 shows the hardware arrangement. Each host's data link is connected to the plaintext port of the in-line encryptor. The ciphertext port of the encryptor is then connected to the modem or bridge connecting to the outside data link. The host has no connections outside the site's physical boundary except through an encryptor. This ensures that outsiders can't access the hosts, since outsiders don't have the right crypto keys. Existing workstation software is unaffected by the link encryptors, as shown in Figure 3-6.

This technique has long been a favorite in high-security military applications. It disguises the data contents most completely. More importantly, it gives users the least opportunity to accidentally (or intentionally) leak data.

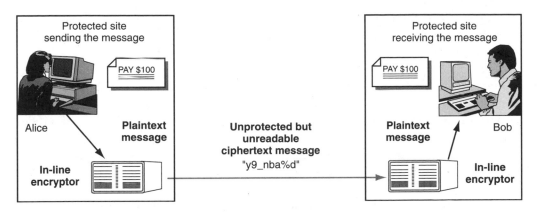

Figure 3-5: HARDWARE ARRANGEMENT FOR LINK ENCRYPTION. Bob and Alice protect their information by keeping it inside the protected site in which they work. Messages only leave a site by traveling through an in-line encryptor. The workstation, encryptor, and the external network connection being used all reside within the protected perimeter of the site. Only encrypted data leaves the site.

3.3.1   Point-to-Point Practical Limitations

Point-to-point encryption has a brute force simplicity that makes it an appealing solution from a security standpoint. However, it has certain properties that make it hard to use in every application. First, system users have no choice regarding encryption. You can either link to a host using encryption or you can't communicate at all. Second, it can be difficult to establish a link to a new host. These facts make point-to-point encryption a bad choice for some sites.

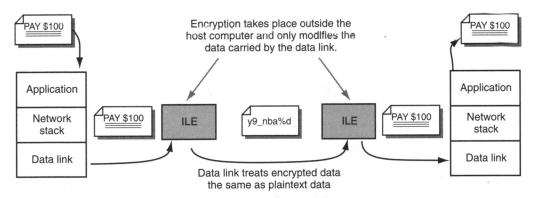

Figure 3-6: IN-LINE ENCRYPTORS DO NOT AFFECT EXISTING, INSTALLED SOFTWARE. Link encryption can operate completely outside the view of workstation software, retaining compatibility with existing applications. Changes can be restricted to hardware at the LAN level.

Encryption will never be free, nor will it soon be available to every possible destination. Not all data benefits from encryption. Information of a public nature is best sent in plaintext if only because plaintext requires fewer computing cycles. This reduces the response time needed to retrieve the information. If a host only connects to other hosts via encryption, then there are hosts with which it will never be able to communicate. Any mandatory encryption arrangement is a double-edged sword. It protects from hostile outsiders, but also blocks access to beneficial outsiders.

Another problem is that point-to-point encryption scales very poorly. There is no prevailing industry standard for an in-line encryptor, so you will probably need to purchase more equipment each time you establish a secure link to another host. You must coordinate equipment, algorithms, and keys with every host with which you ever need to communicate, even if new equipment doesn't need to be purchased. This rapidly becomes extremely complex and expensive even if the number of hosts increases slowly.

3.3.2   Physical Protection and Control

Physical protection is the application of red/black separation to your host computers and the information they contain. All security begins with physical protection. To ensure the security provided by the crypto services, the devices using and providing the services must be physically protected. In addition, it is important to protect the integrity of the software on your hosts. Software on your host computer can send messages and perform computerized actions on your behalf. Subverted software can do so, too, and not necessarily with your knowledge or consent.

The first step is to control the physical integrity of your hosts. Typical organizations keep computers in offices and rarely give visitors or guests access to those computers. Provide additional physical security when it makes sense. For example, careful organizations place the payroll department in a separate office area with controlled access. The area is locked when the office is normally closed. This blocks physical access to those machines and reduces the risk of direct misuse.

Another physical security measure is to ensure that every external data link goes through an encryptor. A fully secure point-to-point network will not have any dial-up modems except those that go through an encryptor. In practice many organizations are finding this to be a difficult restriction with which to live, because modern networking has left the point-to-point approach far behind. We shall discuss that problem in the next section.

It is very important to protect your in-line encryptors from physical access by outsiders. Physical access gives them several opportunities to impair your security. Physical access might give them a way to extract crypto keys, allowing them to masquerade as a legitimate host when talking to your other hosts. An even easier trick is simply to disable the encryption by rewiring the network connections or by manipulating the encryptor somehow. A similar trick was played on an Army unit several years ago while it was deployed overseas for several months. The soldiers had trouble keeping their encrypted radios working and used local technicians to repair them. On returning home, engineers found that the local technicians had essentially disabled the radios' encryption.

A final physical security measure is to control the integrity of the software on your hosts. Virus checkers are the state of the art for most desktop systems, but they will not catch a customized attack on your own hosts. If you manage money or resources that are valuable enough to others, they could someday send you a program that generates messages or other transactions to their benefit without your knowledge or participation. This might not look at all like a virus. It might just look like a legitimate application program. The most effective defense is to compute checksums on all critical, unchanging files like executable binaries, and to validate the checksums regularly. In higher risk environments, cryptographic checksums should be used. This will catch any changes to executable code even if the change doesn't match the pattern of a known virus. Another important defense is to only accept software that clearly comes from a trustworthy source. But remember that no source is unconditionally trustworthy. In the past, major vendors have occasionally distributed viruses with their software.

3.3.3   Deployment Security Requirements

The following requirements for deploying point-to-point link encryptors are listed in priority order with the most important requirements given first.

1. **Appropriate link encryptors.** Select link encryptors after reviewing them against the product security requirements specified in Section 3.2.4.

2. **Physical isolation of hosts and encryptors.** Physical security measures must block outsiders from physical access to the hosts that handle encrypted traffic. The encryptors themselves must also be protected. Physical access gives outsiders several ways to bypass or subvert the crypto protections.

3. **Software integrity control.** Take steps to ensure that hosts on your network only execute software that is trustworthy and is known to do its job correctly. Regularly scan your hosts for viruses or other potential infestations of subverted software. Virus checkers provide some protection but the best defense is to maintain and verify checksums on all critical files.

3.4   Deployment Example: IP-routed Configuration

Naturally, link encryption can also be applied to links carrying IP traffic. This yields a much more flexible and capable networking environment. In the IP tradition, individual site LANs connect to intrasite data links, and the intrasite data is passed through the in-line encryptors. Outsiders still see nothing but encrypted traffic.

As shown in Figure 3-7, almost all of the packet gets encrypted when link encryption is applied. The data link header is left in the clear so that the low-level network can process the packet. All remaining protocol headers are encrypted and will not be processed until after the packet is received and decrypted. If we follow the packet flow in Figure 3-8, we see that encryption is applied after the message passes through the router. On arrival at the destination site, the IP routing data is encrypted, but it is still decrypted before it arrives in the router.

An important difference between this deployment and the previous (point-to-point) one is that the encrypted traffic carries data from a much larger networking population. The larger population modifies the security properties of the solution somewhat. A benefit of the point-to-point case was that a user at one end point knew with high certainty that messages were created by the authorized user of the workstation at the other end point. The benefit of connecting additional hosts may be offset by the reduced certainty of the origination of individual messages. If the network's protections are properly in place we can at least say that messages originate from people with authorized physical access to the network.

This different architecture yields special security considerations at the site and the network level. At the site level we would handle the hosts and in-line encryptors differently than we did in the point-to-point case. Host security is less critical, but the encryptor security becomes more critical as each one carries more traffic than before. At the network level we must confront risks produced by a larger host population and the use of a specific and capable protocol suite. Site and network issues present special challenges to the link encryption security objectives set forth at the beginning of the chapter.

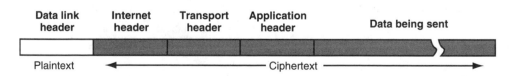

Figure 3-7: BASIC PACKET FORMAT USED BY IN-LINE ENCRYPTORS. Only the data link control information is sent in plaintext. All other header and user data is encrypted.

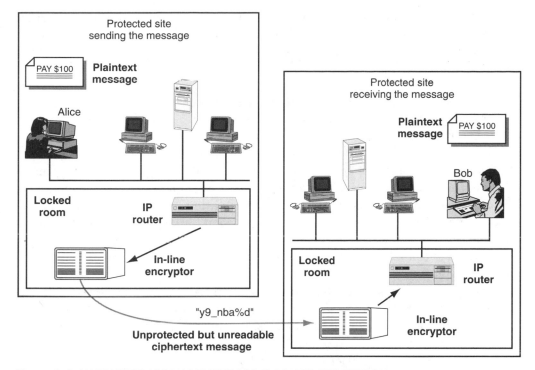

Figure 3-8: HARDWARE ARRANGEMENT FOR IP ROUTER ENCRYPTION. The site's perimeter protects the hosts from unauthorized access. The encryptors, routers, and external connections reside in a locked room to protect them from unnecessary access since they are critical to site security.

3.4.1   Site Protection

As with the point-to-point deployment, site security implements a form of red/black separation with the "red" part inside your protected perimeter and the "black" part along the external communications lines that carry your encrypted traffic. Unlike the point-to-point case, however, here we will treat hosts differently from the in-line encryptors. The hosts still need the degree of protection appropriate to keep outsiders from accessing them. The in-line encryptors, however, now need more protection.

Figure 3-8 illustrates the different levels of protection. The hosts are within the protected boundary of the site. The in-line encryptors are, too, except that they are further protected from unnecessary physical access.

The integrity of the protected network depends on the hosts themselves being protected from unauthorized access. They need to be within the site's physical, protected perimeter. Workstations should not be installed in areas frequented by outsiders or where unauthorized people could use them without appropriate supervision. In most cases it is sufficient to protect them the same as other important organizational papers and assets are protected. Naturally, if hosts on the network are able to manipulate valuable assets, access control must be consistent with the risk of such assets being misused.

In this deployment the in-line encryptors and the routers connected to them are given extra protection. Ideally both devices are kept in a locked room and provide the only link between outside communications lines and the internal LAN wiring. This reflects the extra responsibility each in-line encryptor now carries. Instead of protecting communications between a pair of hosts, it now protects messages for a large number of hosts. Thus, compromise of the encryptor's keying material or of its physical integrity would risk a larger amount of organizational traffic. Furthermore, there is no benefit to giving workstation users access to the encryptor, its physical connections, or its keys. This prevents accidental or intentional acts that might disclose the keys or cause message traffic to bypass the encryption. The locked room becomes the point in your site at which red/black separation is implemented and enforced.

This arrangement reflects an important distinction that is not present in the point-to-point case. We protect the hosts for the information and control they represent, and not because they hold crypto keys. We protect the in-line encryptors with additional measures because they establish the red/black separation and individual workstation users are no longer responsible for it.

3.4.2 Networkwide Security

What we have constructed here with our in-line encryptors and internet routers is a private internet, with many of the strengths and weaknesses of the public Internet. The principal difference is that we have some control over the population of individuals that can physically access it. Beyond that, however, it is an internet and we face the associated problems in networkwide security.

The first problem this raises is that of accountability. The internet protocol mechanisms that associate messages with individuals are weak and unreliable. Even though a single individual might be associated with a specific host, the host's IP address is not always constant. Some installations assign them temporarily. Even when IP addresses are permanently assigned, a capable person can forge identities at practically every level of the protocol stack. This is made worse by the natural extensibility of the internet architecture. Any site can add a router and extend the network further. Thus we encounter another problem: It is hard to constrain the network's extent, and each new portion has the same capabilities as existing portions. The extreme case of the extensibility problem is that any host on the network is the potential site for a back door that lets the rest of the world into the protected network.

CHASING BACKDOOR CONNECTIONS

The internet protocols are designed to be persistent and inclusive. They will route data to any directly or indirectly connected device the protocols can reach. A router will forward a packet solely on the speculative belief built into its routing algorithm that, even if it doesn't recognize a packet's destination address itself, another router somewhere will know how to route the packet. Unauthorized connections to other networks can exist, and if they do they can communicate with any destination inside your network.

As we noted earlier, any host on the network can route traffic between networks if it in fact connects two networks. And so, any site on the network can provide a connection to additional sites and networks. This makes the network very easy to extend but very hard to control. This can reduce the certainty you have regarding the security properties of your network.

Each time a new host is connected to the protected network, it is crucial to ensure that it complies with the network's security requirements. It must implement the appropriate set of physical security measures you need to protect it from unauthorized people. You may also need to verify that it does not contain software that could attack other hosts on the network or otherwise subvert the network's security. Perhaps most importantly, the new host must not provide connections to other hosts. Extension of the network should be controlled to ensure compliance with security requirements.

This approach has traditionally been used to construct classified networks used by the U.S. military. No computer equipment is ever allowed to handle classified information, whether networked or not, until it has been *accredited* to do so by a senior officer at the site with final authority for site security. Usually accreditation is granted after a review of the host computer's physical security and the computing system intended to be used for the classified work. There are special standards regarding the amount of physical protection required for information with different degrees of classification, ranging from strong locks and reinforced walls for secret information to complete vault-like enclosures for sensitive intelligence data.

When a network of computers must handle classified information, every component of the network must be equally protected: hosts, wires, hubs, routers, and so on. If data links must leave the protected area, then they generally use in-line encryption devices produced especially by the NSA to protect classified information. Other sites are connected only after accreditors of the affected sites agree that adequate security is provided by both sites and by the encrypted link. Connections to classified networks that link multiple sites are managed by a militarywide agency that establishes security and accreditation requirements.

Few commercial organizations would require or benefit from that level of security management and control. Many do, however, need to isolate their sensitive enterprise network from the outside, so they share a continual dread with the military networks: the unexpected backdoor connection with inadequate security.

This problem was best illustrated in the 1985 movie *WarGames*, in which a high school kid inadvertently found a way to dial in to the computer systems that defended the country against a nuclear missile attack. He found this back door by programming his home computer's modem to dial every telephone number in a given area. Whenever a computer answered the phone, the number would be saved for later investigation. This technique is now known as *war dialing*. Many telephone companies have since implemented techniques to detect war dialing, but the technique still poses a threat.

The other side of the threat is the undesired back door. War dialing would not be so much of a threat if we were certain that dial-in access always went to security-conscious hosts. Unfortunately, the plunging cost of modems has spoiled this assumption. Many workstation vendors routinely include a modem with the computer systems they sell, along with convenient software to use it. Many people find it very tempting simply to connect an extra wire from the back of their computer to their office phone. This produces the worst kind of back door if the modem accepts dial-in connections, but it can also be dangerous when dialing out. We trace that problem back to the protocol stack and the IP layer.

As described in Section 1.3.2, the IP layer of a TCP/IP protocol stack typically does one of two things with packets: it transfers packets between the network and the host's application software or it forwards packets received on one network connection via another. This second process is often called *IP forwarding*. If a host computer contains two or more network connections (for example, a LAN interface and a modem) then it may be possible for the IP software to transfer packets between them. This risky behavior is not what most workstation users intend. Some vendors have recognized this risk and have produced TCP/IP packages that do not support IP forwarding between different interfaces. Others make forwarding a configuration option, allowing individual hosts to enable it if the user desires.

Dial-up IP connections combined with IP forwarding produce a difficult network management problem, and the solutions can be difficult to achieve. The military networks rely heavily on punitive sanctions. It is a federal crime to leak classified information and, by definition, every bit of data on a typical classified computer system is considered classified information. Thus, violations of security measures can lead to a vacation behind bars. Few commercial organizations can produce similar deterrents.

Commercial organizations rely primarily on proactive measures like education and physical protections, and use various detection techniques to locate violators. One large, multinational corporation established a rule that no packets on their corporate network may contain an external network address; any external addresses thus indicate that an external Internet connection has been made. The networking administrators detect "leaks" approximately once a month from all sources. Experts in IP routing also suggest that leaks can be controlled by tuning the routers to reject external packets traveling in the wrong direction with respect to an approved, external connection. See Chapter 8 on firewalls, regarding the management and use of controlled connections to untrusted hosts.

A technique used by many sites is to eliminate vigorously all desktop modems. Many organizations have already converted their internal phone system from traditional, modem-friendly analog lines to digital systems. Connecting a modem to a digital phone is at least ineffective and possibly damaging to the modem. Few individuals will be motivated enough to purchase converters, particularly when the connections are forbidden. Some sites also adopt the attackers' tools, using war dialers to seek dial-in modems within the organizations' incoming telephone lines.

3.4.3   Deployment Security Requirements

The following requirements for deploying IP-routed link encryptors are listed in priority order with the most important requirements given first.

1. **Appropriate link encryptors.** Select link encryptors after reviewing them against the product security requirements specified in Section 3.2.4.

2. **Physical protection of hosts.** Physical security measures must block outsiders from physical access to the hosts that handle sensitive data. Physical access may allow outsiders to type in their own transactions, or worse, install subverted code.

3. **Physical isolation of routers and encryptors.** Physical security measures must prevent physical access to network security devices by everyone except operators and administrators who need access to do their job. Routers as well as in-line encryptors must be treated as network security devices and protected accordingly.

4. **No access paths to untrusted hosts or sites.** This reflects the security objectives listed at the beginning of this chapter. If you need the strong isolation that link encryption can provide, then access to untrusted hosts is a risk factor you should avoid. If untrusted host access is a requirement, skip ahead to Chapter 8 on firewalls.

5. **Active measures against backdoor connections.** The general approach is to characterize potential techniques used by back doors and then try to detect any that might exist. Some sites use "war dialers" and scan the organization's telephone banks for modem tones where there shouldn't be any. Another approach is to control the IP addresses used on your network and to enforce address-based access rules on internal routers. Packets with addresses from outside the network can then be detected and blocked.

3.5   Key Recovery and Escrowed Encryption

Key recovery is a mechanism by which the keys that encrypt the data traveling between two users can be recovered by someone else, probably without the others' awareness. The mechanism is generally intended to allow eavesdropping by a third party. *Escrowed encryption* is the system by which secret keys are stored for the purpose of key recovery. The secret keys are held in escrow until an authorized entity requests access to one. The entity then uses the escrowed key to recover the actual key used to encrypt a particular message.

This mechanism has no practical benefit in typical commercial applications, since data is encrypted only temporarily for the journey between sites. However, the U.S. government has been promoting this technology as a prerequisite for granting export licenses on cryptographic systems. Key recovery is seen as a way by which U.S. law enforcement and intelligence agencies will be able to eavesdrop on encrypted communications when so permitted by U.S. laws. Without such a facility these agencies would not be able to decipher intercepted messages if the crypto measures are correctly applied.

Several approaches to key recovery have been proposed and implemented. The Escrowed Encryption Standard (EES), established by the U.S. government in 1994, is used in the CLIPPER and CAPSTONE chips. CLIPPER is designed for use in encrypted telephones for the commercial market, and CAPSTONE is designed for messaging applications like e-mail. Both use the SKIPJACK block cipher algorithm. The chips are designed to support the typical range of crypto functions yet also provide a secure but reliable "back door" for decrypting any data they encrypt. The EES defines how this back door is supposed to work.

The key recovery process is illustrated in Figure 3-9. As an example, let us assume that Alice is using CAPSTONE encryption for her e-mail and the FBI needs to wiretap Alice's communications. They begin by collecting ciphertext that Alice sends to other people. Using the family key built into all devices they decrypt the law enforcement access field (LEAF) from an intercepted message. The LEAF contains a device identifier that identifies the specific CAPSTONE chip that Alice is using to encrypt her messages.

Next, the FBI approaches the escrow agencies that hold Alice's keys. These agencies are organizations that keep copies of the keys belonging to CLIPPER and CAPSTONE chips, indexed by device identifier. The lists of keys are produced when the chips are manufactured and are kept under strict security. The agencies are not to release keys except to authorized officials with appropriate legal documents that authorize the wiretapping. The FBI provides the appropriate documents along with the device identifier for Alice's CAPSTONE chip.

Once the FBI has received the escrowed keys for Alice's device, they can decrypt the session key stored in the LEAF. The session key is the particular key

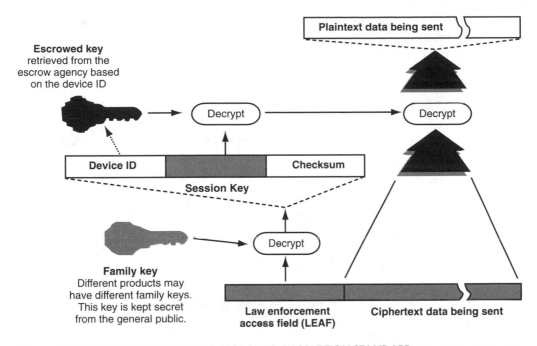

Figure 3-9: KEY RECOVERY WITH THE ESCROWED ENCRYPTION STANDARD. To recover the contents of a message, we fetch the family key for the product and use it to decrypt the LEAF carried with the ciphertext data. We extract the device ID and contact the escrow agents that hold the keys for that device. If the paperwork is in order, the escrow agents give us the escrowed key for that device. We use that key to decrypt the session key stored in the LEAF. The session key will decrypt the ciphertext data.

used to encrypt the data in the message that carried the LEAF. Different messages may be encrypted with different secret keys, so each message must carry its own LEAF. Regardless of what key is used for a particular message, a copy of it will always be stored in the LEAF and transmitted with the message. This restriction is enforced by the CLIPPER and CAPSTONE chips. They will not decrypt a ciphertext message correctly unless the LEAF is present. The FBI can then read all of Alice's messages as long as they have the family key and the escrowed key for Alice's particular chip.

Although key recovery serves no practical benefit, the mechanism's presence might be tolerated by users if it brings along no serious drawbacks. Here are some of the problems associated with the key escrow and recovery facilities implemented in the CLIPPER and CAPSTONE chips:

- **Increased product costs**
  It is far more expensive to manufacture escrowed crypto devices because of increased security requirements. Conventional crypto devices do not have

secret information built into them. Security during manufacturing is solely concerned with guaranteeing correctness of implementation. The escrowed keys in escrowed crypto devices must be generated, installed, and delivered to escrow agencies under extremely tight security. Proposed government standards for manufacturing escrowed devices suggest security measures comparable to those that protect the government's most sensitive intelligence information. Such measures are always very expensive. These costs will be passed on to the users of crypto devices, dramatically increasing product costs.

- **Increased product complexity**
  Developers have a fairly broad latitude when incorporating conventional crypto mechanisms into a system. When using escrowed encryption, however, they are restricted to the interface provided by the CLIPPER or CAPSTONE chips. This produces unexpected design constraints, increasing development costs.
  Once the chips are integrated into the design, the developers must still take care to handle the LEAF correctly when formatting and transmitting messages. Errors in LEAF handling will render a message unreadable, reducing the product's reliability.

- **Financial support of escrow agencies**
  Escrow agencies must comply with stringent and costly operating procedures. They must protect the keys against the most sophisticated attacks, since theft of the escrowed keys would be an incredible prize. The agencies must also follow strict rules for accepting and releasing escrowed keys in order to fulfill their obligations and maintain their credibility as escrow agents. These activities will be expensive and, in an environment of shrinking government budgets, costs will eventually be passed on to crypto users.

Technological purists might also point out that carrying the session key in every message is an unnecessary risk no matter how thoroughly it is encrypted. In practice, the risk to users of someone cracking session keys in this manner is probably far smaller than other security risks over which users have more control, like the handling of plaintext within their workstations.

Despite the costs, some systems will need to incorporate escrowed encryption and key recovery. In such cases it is important to recognize up front that the system will be more complex and costs will be higher. Many applications might achieve better security by using weaker crypto that doesn't require escrow and key recovery. Resources can then be applied to operating convenience, which sometimes yields the biggest payback in improved security.

3.6   For Further Information

- **Voydock and Kent, "Security Mechanisms in High-Level Network Protocols"**
  The classic paper on attacking network messages that are "protected" by encryption.

- **Department of Commerce, Federal Information Processing Standards, "FIPS-140-1: Security Requirements for Cryptographic Modules"**
  The standard for cryptographic hardware devices.

- **Department of Commerce, Federal Information Processing Standards, "FIPS-185: Escrowed Encryption Standard"**
  The official standard for escrowed encryption as used by CLIPPER, CAP-STONE, and Fortezza. The requirements for escrowed encryption continue to evolve, but this is still the only published standard.

Chapter

4

Managing Secret Keys

To keep your secret is wisdom; to expect others to keep it is folly.

—Samuel Johnson

IN THIS CHAPTER

This chapter discusses the crypto keys themselves—the secrets that protect all others. In particular, we examine the production and handling of secret keys for conventional symmetric ciphers. All crypto systems, even public key systems, depend on some keys that must be kept secret. The following topics are discussed:

- Security objectives and basic issues associated with secret keys
- Technology for generating random, hard-to-guess crypto keys
- How to generate and handle secret keys
- The basics of automatic key exchange and key distribution centers
- Summary of steps for maintaining keys and system security

4.1 Security Objectives

The underlying security goal is to provide cryptographic services to authorized people and devices, and to prevent the same services from being successfully used by unauthorized people or devices. In the world of secret key cryptography this is achieved solely by protecting the secret crypto keys. This leads to the following objectives:

- **Everyone authorized to exchange data gets a key.**
  If we want someone to participate in data exchange, then we must produce a key for them and be sure that they receive it.

- **Keys are transmitted reliably to recipient devices.**
  Each crypto key must be installed reliably into the device that performs the encryption. If the wrong key value is installed, the recipient won't be able to communicate.

- **Keys are protected from disclosure.**
  The key must be distributed to authorized recipients and *only* to authorized recipients. There should be as little risk as possible of the key being given to the wrong person or shared with anyone except when absolutely necessary. Ideally, keys should be installed automatically into machines and people should never have to see the key's actual value.

- **Keys are hard to guess.**
  There should be no practical way for an attacker to guess the crypto key. Otherwise, physical protection of the crypto key is wasted. The more random a key, the harder it is to guess. The more data you encrypt with a single key, the easier it can become for an attacker to guess it.

Organizations rarely handle information that demands the level of secrecy required for crypto keys. The combination to a safe is similar, since it is information given to very, very few people. Secret keys protecting an Internet site may be even more sensitive than a safe combination. The attacker usually needs to "break and enter" to exploit a discovered safe combination, while the secret key can be exploited from across the globe.

4.2   Basic Issues in Secret Key Management

Here are some basic issues in secret key management. They play a major role in the effectiveness of various technical solutions and in formulating the requirements that should be met when producing and distributing crypto keys.

- **The data isn't secret unless the key is secret.**
  This is the essential feature of all commercial crypto systems. Since you are using commercial devices, your worst enemy could also go out and buy a copy of the same device. If they have your crypto keys too, then they can do anything with the ciphertext that you can. On the other hand, if you are using a properly constructed device and you keep your keys secret, your adversaries have a very tough problem.

- **The more random your key, the harder it will be to guess.**
  Attackers will have the hardest time guessing your key if they can make no assumptions about its form or contents. On the other hand, if you take short-cuts to generate your keys, like using a poor random number generator or like limiting them to alphanumeric characters or readable words, then you give attackers an edge. Compare the 56-bit long text password with the 56-bit DES key in Table 2-2. There are ten times as many binary DES keys as there are text strings with the same number of bits.

- **Randomness really does not come easily, especially to computers.**
  Despite occasional bouts of apparent unpredictability, computers really are deterministic machines. They are designed and built to act the same way every time, and variations you might see really aren't very extreme. Even though most contain procedures called *random number generators*, they have a very hard time generating really unpredictable keys. Attackers can and have used this essential predictability to guess keys efficiently.

- **The more a key is used, the easier it is to crack.**
  This is an ancient lesson from cryptanalysis and explains why every cautious user of codes—from Mary, Queen of Scots, to you today—will periodically modify his or her code. In modern systems we do this by changing the key. If we fail to do so, the similarities in messages sent time and time again will eventually permit that entering wedge for which the patient code breaker waits.

The first step in key management is to produce some keys to manage. This requires high-quality random numbers.

4.3   Technology: Random Key Generation

A practical and secure crypto system needs keys that cannot be guessed. There should be no way for an outsider to predict what keys are being used, or even to guess approximately which keys might be used. If attackers can even approximately duplicate your key generation process, they can use it to look for your keys. If they only have to try a few thousand or even several million possibilities, you have lost most of your protection. It takes more than 57,000 years to search for a random 56-bit DES key on a typical workstation. If the attackers can focus on the few million keys your key generator is most likely to produce, they can try all the possibilities in less than one minute.

A good key generator will produce keys that cannot be guessed even if attackers know how the generator works. To do this it must generate numbers that are practically impossible to predict. Computers by themselves are poor sources of unpredictable numbers; they are essentially deterministic machines that are designed to be predictable. Mathematicians have produced many procedures called *pseudorandom number generators* (PRNGs), which generate hard-to-predict sequences of numbers. But these procedures contain no magic; they are still mathematical procedures that yield consistent results from consistent inputs. For true randomness you must *seed* these procedures with an initial value. Then the PRNG will yield an acceptably random sequence of numbers suitable for crypto keys (Figure 4-1).

This two-step process is important because a practical and secure crypto system needs a lot of good, random keys. A good system replaces keys often. If only a little ciphertext is encrypted with each key, then attackers have less to gain by trying to break individual messages. If a lot of ciphertext is encrypted with a single key, then the key becomes a more attractive target. Good random key generation is at the heart of every strong crypto system.

4.3.1   Random Seeding

Anyone who considers arithmetical methods of producing random numbers is, of course, in a state of sin.

—John von Neumann

A good PRNG is not enough by itself to produce effective keys. The generation process must be seeded by a random number that is sufficiently hard to guess. In traditional random number applications, seeding is not much of a problem. The seed

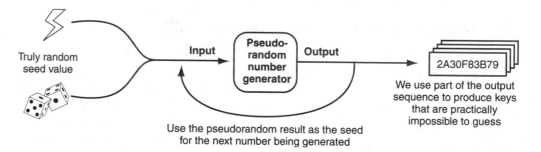

Figure 4-1: GOOD KEYS COME FROM A RANDOM SEED AND A GOOD PSEUDORANDOM NUMBER GENERATOR. The two-part process is needed when generating many separate keys, and most applications require more than one piece of random data. The PRNG produces a sequence of numbers that is practically impossible to predict. The random seed value starts the sequence at an unpredictable point so that others can't repeat it. If they could repeat it, they could reproduce all of the same keys.

simply needs to be different each time the application is run. In crypto applications the seed itself must be hard to guess. If attackers can make a close guess of the seed, then they can probably guess what keys were generated by using the same PRNG. This happened to early versions of Netscape Navigator software.

Netscape Navigator, the well-known software package for browsing the World Wide Web, has probably placed state-of-the-art crypto on more desktops than any other package. The Navigator introduced the SSL protocol for encrypting data being passed on a TCP connection. Netscape applied SSL to the protection of Web accesses for commercial purposes. Security depended on the Navigator generating a random session key that it shared with an SSL server host.

In late 1995 several graduate students took the time to reverse engineer the Navigator software in order to determine how the random keys were generated. The PRNG was acceptable, but the seeding process was not. The Navigator would sample a small number of varying quantities within the system, including the system clock, and construct the random seed from those values. The students studied this process closely and discovered that under certain circumstances they could generate seed values very close to the one the Navigator would use. This allowed them to write an attack program that could rapidly guess the key Netscape would use to encrypt an SSL connection. Their program would calculate all the likely seed values, and this yielded a relatively small number of possible keys to try. The seeding process was greatly improved in later versions of the Navigator in order to protect against this type of attack.

We need a random technique to generate a random seed value so we can generate a series of random numbers. But if we have this random seeding technique, why not just use it for generating all of the keys? In practice, this does not work. The techniques for producing seeds tend to be slow, inefficient, and in some cases inconvenient. So we do the slow and difficult step once and let the PRNG do the rest. In practice there are three computer-based approaches for producing truly random data:

1. Monitor hardware that generates random data.

2. Collect random data from user interaction.

3. Collect hard-to-predict data from inside the computer.

Hardware-based random number generation is the best though most costly approach. The generator is usually an electronic circuit that is sensitive to some random physical event, like diode noise or cosmic ray bombardment, and converts the event into an unpredictable sequence of bits. Such circuits will most likely generate enough random bits to make a PRNG unnecessary. However, they rarely appear in systems or even in peripheral boards. Their rarity makes it expensive to add them to a system.

User interaction is a very good source of random data, though it can be inconvenient. People are notoriously bad at doing exactly the same thing twice, and random data can be collected by tracking interactive human behavior. For example, the PGP e-mail package (see Chapter 11) collects keystrokes from the user and measures the time between keystrokes to produce a random seed value. PGP collects several hundred random bits in less than a minute of typing. A less efficient but random method is to require the user to enter a random number. When faced with such a task, you should use a table of random digits, dice, or a deck of cards, and generate an appropriately long number one digit at a time.

A random value can also be constructed from a variety of varying quantities within the computer system itself. The random number is constructed by sampling the selected quantities, extracting the low-order bits from them, and concatenating the bits into an appropriately large number. The sampled quantities could include the system clock, the number of files in the file system, the number of free or used disk blocks, the amount of memory in use, the amount of system queue space in use, and so on. Only the low-order bits may be used, since the quantity becomes predictable as higher order bits are used. Also, the randomness depends on selecting values that are largely independent of one another. Recent versions of the Netscape Navigator are reputed to use hundreds of internal variables to construct the random seed used with SSL.

4.3.2   Pseudorandom Number Generators

Mathematicians have developed a large body of work on random numbers that has served the study of statistics, operations research, and simulation. Public research in cryptography has also contributed to the study. Most people have an intuitive grasp of what a random number should be. Its value should be somehow unpredictable, like rolling dice. A series of random numbers will probably but not necessarily be different. In practice, mathematicians have found that good random numbers are hard to generate; the subject has yielded a good deal of sophisticated research. Cryptographic applications place the heaviest requirements on PRNGs.

In *The Art of Computer Programming*, the classic computer science reference on statistical random numbers, Don Knuth describes two important properties of the sequence of numbers produced by a good PRNG:

1. Statistically the numbers should reflect the desired distribution of values. For cryptographic purposes we want a *uniform* distribution; that is, there should be an equal chance that a given number falls anywhere within the range of numbers being generated.

2. The sequence should not repeat itself.

In a somewhat whimsical experiment, Knuth once attempted to create a good PRNG by writing a program with a behavior that appeared unpredictably random. The program computed numeric values, extracted bits from these intermediate results, and used the extracted bits to select the next transformation to perform. The procedure would yield a random number after skipping through the procedure a varying number of times. The experiment was a failure. Usually the procedure produced a repeating sequence of a few thousand values, but in some cases it would get stuck and continually emit a single constant value. If Knuth were using this procedure to generate crypto keys, adversaries would have a simple task indeed.

The lesson is that a good PRNG demands a careful design. Apparently random program behavior does not yield random results. Knuth also noted that intuition was a poor guide. Attempts to make a procedure's output "more random" would often produce the opposite result.

While Knuth's lesson regarding the value of careful design is important for us, his well-designed techniques are not. There is a very important difference between random sequences that are *statistically* random and those that are *cryptographically* random. Knuth provides a good deal of information about the construction and validation of statistically random PRNGs, and about linear congruential generators in particular. Unfortunately, while the output of linear congruential generators may have good statistical properties, they have poor cryptographic properties.

Statistical PRNGs must be *unbiased*. The set of generated numbers must reflect the desired statistical distribution. This is not good enough for key generation. Cryptographically strong PRNGs must also be *unpredictable*. This requires two properties that are not as important to statistical PRNGs:

1. There should be no obvious mathematical relationship between numbers in the sequence, like common multiples, ordering of values, or patterns of values.

2. Any given key may be generated as part of a variety of different key sequences.

The second requirement illustrates a particularly important property. The problem with PRNGs is that they produce *sequences* of numbers and, being mathematical procedures, they tend to want to produce the same sequences over and over. Since keys could fall into attackers' hands we must plan for the threat: Can an attacker reconstruct all of the recently generated keys if a single key is captured?

Crypto algorithms often play a central role in constructing cryptographically random sequences. For many years, banks have generated sequences of random key values using the DES algorithm. The technique is illustrated in Figure 4-2. The technique yields keys that are hard to predict and unlikely to repeat. They are hard

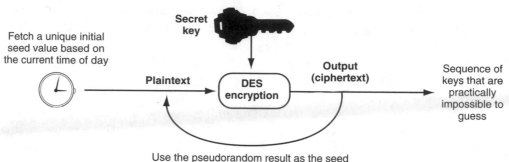

Figure 4-2: BANKERS' KEY GENERATION USING DES WITH A SECRET KEY AND A UNIQUE SEED VALUE. This technique appears in the banker's key distribution standard ANSI X9.17. The new keys are unpredictable because they depend on a random, secret key value. The clock input ensures that new keys are different.

to predict because they are generated using a random, secret key as a seed. They are unlikely to repeat because keys are generated by encrypting a constantly changing time-of-day clock value. Even if attackers managed to recover a single secret key, it tells them nothing about other keys. They would need the secret seed key, which the banker has no real need to keep.

A similar DES-based approach using an autokey mode is shown in Figure 4-3. Several PRNGs are described by Schneier in *Applied Cryptography* and are based either directly or indirectly on well-known crypto algorithms like RSA (a public key crypto system developed by [and named after] Rivist, Shamir, and Adelman).

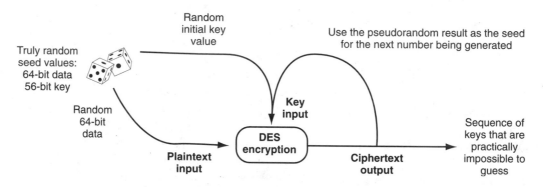

Figure 4-3: USING DES IN AUTOKEY MODE TO PRODUCE GOOD RANDOM NUMBERS. Instead of using a clock, we use additional random seed data as input. Note that the output is fed back into the key input (with adjustments for DES key format requirements) instead of the data input.

4.3.3 Technical Security Requirements

A safe and effective random key generator should be effective even if your adversaries know how it works. Thus they won't be able to predict your keys even if they reverse engineer the key generation procedure.

1. **The entire key should be constructed of random data.** If you use 16 bits of randomness to produce an 80-bit key, the attacker will never need to try more than 65,536 keys (2^{16}) to find the one you chose. The extra 64 bits in the key are wasted.

2. **Generate keys from an unpredictable seed.** Ideally, use a hardware random number generator that is based on physically random events. A bad choice is a seed based entirely on the time of day. The output must be impossible to predict in practice. The number of bits of randomness in the seed determine the randomness of the keys you generate.

3. **Use a cryptographically secure PRNG.** This is important if you must generate several keys from a single random seed value. Not only must the output meet traditional statistical tests for randomness, but the sequence of generated numbers must be unpredictable. The PRNGs provided in typical commercial software are, at best, statistically random.

4.4 Deployment Example: Manual Key Distribution

Every strong, modern crypto system depends on some keying data that must be hand delivered to each participating device. The system is then secure only as long as that secret data was not compromised during shipment and as long as the device is protected from physical tampering by unauthorized people. This is obvious in basic secret key systems: The secret key itself must be delivered (Figure 4-4).

But the principle continues to hold as systems become more complex. All techniques for "automatic keying" are really methods of automatic rekeying and they depend on a previously established key to produce or protect the newly generated keys. Even public key systems work this way. Each distinctive user, device, or site must have its distinctive private keying material that is mathematically associated with its openly distributed public key. That private key must be protected as effectively as any secret key, or security is lost.

Another important aspect of secret key assignment is pairwise keying. Each key should only be used by a pair of users. In the past it has been relatively common to share a single key among several devices. However this suffers from two shortcomings. The first is that it increases the amount of data that is encrypted with the single key. The second problem is that key changing becomes a logistical

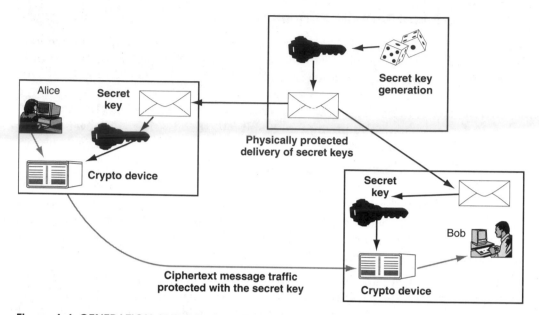

Figure 4-4: GENERATION AND DELIVERY OF A SECRET KEY. This is the classic approach to allow Bob and Alice to communicate using secret key crypto. Their company generates keys that allow authorized employees to intercommunicate, and carefully delivers the keys to the authorized employees. The company sends an identical key to Bob and Alice under tight security.

nightmare. If all sites use the same key, then the key can only be changed if all sites are able to do so at the same time. This becomes nearly impossible as the number of sites increases. This is particularly painful in battlefield conditions if a key is captured by the enemy.

Once we have a method for generating keys, we must generate them, assign their individual use, and produce copies of them for delivery to authorized recipients. Secret keys are also used in some commercial systems that provide "strong authentication" (also called *one-time password* systems). In such cases the system administrators must also occasionally distribute secret keys to authorized individuals. Delivering and installing these keys presents the same set of problems as distributing secret crypto keys, so some examples will be drawn from authentication systems.

4.4.1   Preparing Secret Keys for Delivery

Secret key delivery can happen in a variety of ways, depending on the hardware and software being rekeyed. The techniques generally fall into three categories: paper, writable media, and hardware docking.

PAPER DISTRIBUTION

Paper distribution is a very common low-tech method with strengths and weaknesses that should be familiar. All organizations have the equipment necessary to generate and distribute keys on paper. A key distribution message might not even look like a security- or even a computer-related message. However, keys on paper require people to read the key value—a disclosure best avoided if possible. There are also risks of keys being transcribed incorrectly when being entered into equipment. Section 4.4.3 suggests methods of securely generating keys on paper.

DISKETTES OR OTHER WRITABLE MEDIA

Writable media has the benefit that administrators won't need to see the key's value at either end. However, keys are also very easy to copy in such a situation, especially if standard media are being used. It also takes a carefully constructed set of procedures to write the correct keys onto the correct diskettes and not accidentally send the wrong key to the wrong destination.

Some systems use special media like *datakeys* or magnetic cards for loading keys. This makes casual copying more difficult and can make personalized keying material easier to carry. The STU III encrypted telephone, used by the U.S. government, keeps personalized keying material on a datakey that is often worn on a small chain.

DOCKING APPROACH

The docking approach is specific to particular hardware products. Key loading can only take place by physically attaching the crypto device to a keying device. The keys are then loaded directly from one device to another. This has the benefit that keys are only handled by the devices that must handle them. No copies of the keys need to exist outside of the keyed devices.

Several authentication systems use small card-sized calculators to generate one-time passwords. Certain models produced by Secure Computing, Digital Pathways, and CryptoCard allow keys to be loaded through a special connection.

Paralon Technologies manufactures in-line encryptors that use a direct docking connection to install secret keying material. Some encryptor models must be individually docked with other encryptors with which they are to communicate; other models must be docked with a special programming station. In both cases the docking procedure exchanges identification data and shared secrets that are later used to establish per-session secret keys. This is an interesting technique since this particular key exchange can't occur when the devices are connected to normal communications equipment. It can only happen when two devices are directly connected.

The Fortezza crypto card used by the U.S. Department of Defense is a PC card that performs encryption and other crypto services. The initial keying material can only be loaded into the card by a specially programmed workstation that has the special access codes needed to update keys on the card.

The next two sections don't generally apply to docking devices; however, the packaging and delivery discussions in Section 4.4.4 will often apply.

4.4.2   Batch Generation of Keys

More often than not we will find ourselves distributing several keys at once, possibly even a large number. This often occurs when a new crypto system is deployed and numerous new devices must be keyed. Interactive keying techniques can be cumbersome and labor intensive if the number of keys is especially large. This can lead to shortcuts, mistakes, and attendant security breaches. If the equipment you are keying will accept manually entered keys from paper or from electronic files, you may prefer to implement your own keying procedures.

The key generation process has several important objectives:

* Generate random, hard-to-guess keys.

* Arrange key handling so that people don't have to look at the keys. Don't show keys to administrators or even the end users unless absolutely necessary, such as when keys must be typed into a device.

* Allow separation of duty so that you don't have to give someone access to every part of the system. For example, the best people to produce and package the keys are people who never have physical access to crypto devices. Key splitting is another technique for this and is described in Section 4.4.5.

The following is the outline of a procedure for generating and delivering secret keys. While some commercial products may include tools to support this procedure, you may need to construct part of it yourself. Much of this can be constructed with a basic spreadsheet or database manager and a mail merge package.

1. Identify the types of keys to be generated and the authorized recipients of them.

2. Generate an appropriate set of high-quality secret keys.

3. Assign the individual keys to the authorized recipients in your database.

4. Generate the keys in a form that limits their risk of unnecessary disclosure.

Before we start, let us briefly consider physical security. Although experiences with computer crashes may lead people to think otherwise, computer data is very persistent. Information tends to stay around even when you really want to be rid of it. In the case of secret keys, it is vital to the security of your system that the keys only leave the system via the distribution method discussed here. You do not want the keys to sneak out through a discarded diskette or printer ribbon, or a deleted but unwiped disk block. Step 1 can be set up and performed on any computer you want, but *do not* perform any of the other steps on a computer that might be shared with an untrustworthy person. Furthermore, if you must write keys onto removable diskettes or system backups, treat that media as if it will forever hold your keys. Because it just might. The safest bet is to dedicate a separate computer to key management and not do anything else with it.

In the following example, we assume you are using a database manager to generate the keys. Table 4-1 suggests a database record format to use. The USAGE field identifies the particular key being generated. Be sure it is the right size for describing the key. There are two each of the SERIAL, CUSTODIAN, and LOCATION fields, since each key is sent to two devices. The SERIAL fields contain a unique serial number for each copy of the key being distributed. This gives us a way to refer to the key without having to refer to the key's actual value. The CUSTODIAN fields identify the individuals responsible for receiving and installing the key. These and the LOCATION fields are used for delivering copies of the key. There is only one KEY field, and it contains the actual crypto key value. If your site has special needs, you might want to include other data items like employee identification

Table 4-1: Database format for the key distribution database

Field Name	ASCII Data Type	Length (bytes)	Notes
USAGE	Text	50	Must be descriptive to the recipients
SERIAL1	Integer	5	Make large enough for the batch size
CUSTODIAN1	Text	50	The person to be trusted with the key
LOCATION1	Text	250	Unambiguously identifies the destination
SERIAL2	Integer	5	Make large enough for the batch size
CUSTODIAN2	Text	50	The person to be trusted with the key
LOCATION2	Text	250	Unambiguously identifies the destination
KEY	Text	30	Length depends on the key size and format

numbers or device serial numbers. However, it is most important to keep matters simple, since this reduces the risk of accidentally leaking the keys.

Now that we have defined the database layout, we need to define a data entry screen and enter the initial data items. We want to start by identifying the keys we will generate, who will receive them, and the recipients' delivery information, like address, office, or mail stop. Figure 4-5 shows a possible screen layout for entering this information. There is no screen entry for SERIAL since we can configure most database systems to generate such numbers automatically and ensure that they are unique. We also omit the KEY field since we will deal with that later. This database is a less risky object with the keys omitted. For now we can concentrate on ensuring that we have identified the right individuals, collected their addresses, and correctly identified the keying materials they should receive. By using a standard database package and omitting the keys, we can perform the task in a less secure environment and even delegate the data entry task to an assistant.

While the data is being entered we can turn to the problem of generating the appropriate set of high-quality keys. The most convenient and least satisfying approach is to use the PRNG built into your database manager. This PRNG is almost certainly built to provide statistically random numbers, not cryptographically random ones. If clever attackers figure out that you use a relatively weak technique to generate keys, they can exploit this knowledge to crack them. The safest approach is to locate or construct a program to generate a list of high-quality keys for you.

If you must construct the key generator yourself, your safest bet is to construct one based on the discussions in Section 4.3. The generator should write the keys into a data file in the appropriate text form for distribution (i.e., decimal, hexadecimal, or whatever form the destination system requires), one line per key. If the key requires some sort of checksum or parity, be sure that is generated with the key. Do *not* look at the contents of this file.

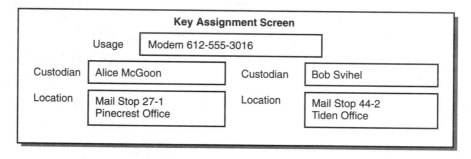

Figure 4-5: SAMPLE SCREEN FOR ENTERING KEY ASSIGNMENT DATA. The screen identifies the usage of each key to be generated and assigns the key to two specific individuals as its custodians. Each assigned custodian is identified by name and delivery address.

Once you have generated the keys and constructed the database of key recipients, you must assign keys to recipients. Do this by merging the file of randomly generated keys into the spreadsheet or database file. If the key file is properly formatted, the application program should be able to import it directly. The merging technique will depend on the particulars of the application being used. The result should be that each row or database record contains a field with a key value filled in.

Now that the database is complete, you can generate the keys for distribution. Recommendations for generating and handling paper keys are given in Section 4.4.3. The following are some general recommendations for generating and distributing keys on diskettes. The basic concept is to produce a custom database procedure that creates the key files and writes them to labeled diskettes. You can do this with the following procedure:

1. Configure the database to write diskette labels. Each label should contain the key serial number, the custodian's name and address, and the key usage data.

2. Print the labels, two per database entry. You may need to print them in two batches: one for CUSTODIAN1 and a separate batch for CUSTODIAN2, depending on your database manager.

3. Label the diskettes that are to receive the keys.

4. Create another database procedure for writing the keys onto the diskettes. This procedure should follow these steps:

   a. Prompt the user for the diskette by key serial number.

   b. Once the diskette is inserted, write the key file onto the diskette. The format will depend on the equipment being keyed.

   c. Eject the diskette.

   d. Repeat the process until all keys have been written.

5. Package the diskettes for delivery to the custodians named on the diskette labels.

This procedure has some important operational benefits. Nobody ever actually has to look at a crypto key. The keys never exist except in the database and on the diskette. Accuracy is improved over manual keys since we skip the error-prone manual entry step.

However, there are a couple of drawbacks. The operator must be careful to match the serial number on the diskette label with the one for which the system has asked, otherwise keys will go to the wrong devices and will probably prevent them from working. More importantly, however, is that the key diskettes are a serious security risk. It is probably best to destroy the diskette after the key has been loaded into the device. It is not enough simply to delete or even reformat the diskette, since there are utility programs that can recover deleted and even reformatted data. It is not really safe even to keep the key diskettes with the keyed device, since they could be surreptitiously copied.

4.4.3 Printing Keys on Paper

Printing keys on paper is the classic low-tech approach to key distribution. It represents a minimal essential function for any system, since there are often situations when more sophisticated mechanisms can't be used. It is always important to have a secure and effective set of procedures for producing and distributing keys on paper.

We shall start with a technique for printing keys in a manner that reduces the risk of disclosure. Figure 4-6 illustrates the approach. We use the key database produced in Section 4.4.2 to generate a mail merge report in which each key is printed on a separate page of paper. The custodian name and location from the database entry are centered in the top third of the page. The key is printed in the middle third. Identifying information about the key and its usage are printed on the bottom third of the page.

The printer itself also deserves some security attention. The printer should have a trustworthy staff member present and collecting the keys as they are printed. No other printer users should have the opportunity to look accidentally or intentionally at the printed keys. If you are using a printer with a ribbon, remember that the ribbon picks up an image of what is printed. You might need to lock it up and destroy it eventually to protect the keys.

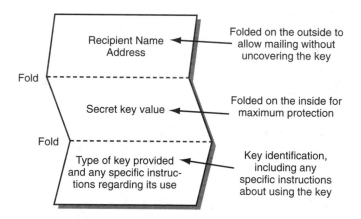

Figure 4-6: PRINTING A SECRET KEY FOR PAPER DELIVERY. The objective is to make the printing and delivery process as safe and simple as possible. Folding prevents accidental key disclosure while allowing typical database software to print keys in a straightforward manner.

You may also want to print the keys on special paper. This will lend an extra degree of authenticity to the keys being distributed if the paper cannot be used for any other purpose. Here are four paper properties to consider:

1. **Opaque paper.** This is almost a requirement, since otherwise the folding might not quite shield the key from observation.

2. **Distinctive paper.** If this paper is never used for other purposes, it lends authenticity to the key distribution as well as gives extra warning that this is special information.

3. **Colored paper.** An appropriate color will make it very difficult to produce a readable copy of a key using an office copier.

4. **Dissolving paper.** Unwoven paper can be thoroughly destroyed by dissolving it in water. This would be appropriate for very high-security situations.

After printing out all the keys, fold the paper into thirds. The recipient's name and address should be on an outer fold and the key itself on an inner fold. Ideally this should be performed by a trustworthy clerical employee with no other duties or access permissions to crypto equipment. Once folded, the paper should at least be stapled to prevent it from accidently unfolding and disclosing the key.

4.4.4 Key Packaging and Delivery

Regardless of the medium that holds the keys, they must be delivered somehow. This usually entails a third-party delivery service or some other entity that would not otherwise be trusted with your crypto keys. The choice of delivery method depends on numerous factors, including perceived security, cost, convenience, and schedule. There is no third-party delivery method with security that is sufficient for all purposes. Registered mail and bonded couriers are no guarantee, particularly as keys travel longer distances.

Appropriate measures depend on the threat of loss you face and the resources of potential attackers. If they stand to benefit dramatically, then they can afford to invest in a significant effort. Situations that require the most security should use key splitting (Section 4.4.5) and deliver the separate portions via clearly independent delivery services.

We must protect keys from intentional, undetected disclosure during shipment. This is generally done by sealing the key inside an envelope. Window envelopes may be sufficient for distributing keys via interoffice mail in a low-risk environment. They are less appropriate for external delivery. Postal regulations prohibit window envelopes in international mail.

Keys that are mailed or otherwise shipped as parcels should be delivered in a fully opaque envelope with the recipient's name and address on the outside. The address may be manually copied from the outside of the folded key printouts or printed separately from the same database, minus the actual keys. Then, a trustworthy clerical employee stuffs the key printouts into the envelopes with matching addresses and seals the envelopes. Additional protection can also be provided by sealing the package with delaminating tape (that is, tape with an embedded pattern that comes apart if the tape is disturbed). This increases the likelihood that tampering with the keys will be detected.

4.4.5   Key Splitting for Safer Delivery

For most organizations the physical delivery of keys is going to be a weak link in the process. The keys must be sent via the postal service, a parcel delivery service, or some other third-party delivery enterprise. Unfortunately, the art and craft of resealing envelopes and of extracting paper from sealed envelopes is centuries old. If the crypto system is protecting particularly valuable information you may wish to take additional steps to protect keys while in transit. One approach is to send two keys instead of one, and to construct the working key by combining both keys. This is called *key splitting* and it increases the keys' protection since the attackers must now intercept a variety of deliveries instead of just one.

The process of key splitting is shown in Figure 4-7. Instead of generating a single crypto key you must generate two. The second key is used to encrypt the actual key one-time-pad style. Then the encrypted first key is sent via one delivery technique and the second key is sent via a different delivery technique.

Splitting attempts to thwart an attacker who has access to parcels in transit, possibly a subverted employee of a delivery service. By producing two different keys we require the attacker to locate and intercept undetectably two different parcels in order to capture the key successfully. Once the keys are split, the level of security is established by the level of difference in the delivery processes. The simplest and least secure technique is to send both key parcels via the same service in two separate transactions. For example, the parcels could be sent through the mail in separate envelopes, possibly on different days. More cautious distributors might send one key through the postal service via registered mail and the other by fax.

A much worse technique would be to take the key and literally split it in half, sending half of the bits in one parcel and the other half in the other. If attackers intercept a parcel, they can use the half key to reduce the number of keys dramatically that they must search to crack your encryption. For example, if you are sending 56-bit DES keys in two parcels of 28 bits each, the attackers only have to recover the other 28 bits. This will be easy to do with an exhaustive search, since 28

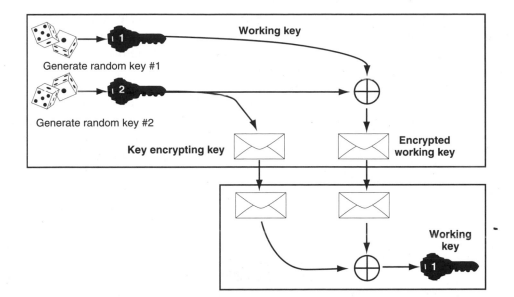

Figure 4-7: EXTRA PROTECTION BY "SPLITTING" A KEY ACROSS TWO SEPARATE DELIVERIES. This technique protects the working key from disclosure by splitting it in two. The process computes two separate, random data patterns that must be combined to yield the working key. Neither of these "splits" gives any useful information by itself about the key's real value. An attacker needs both splits to reconstruct the key.

bits represents perhaps a quarter billion keys to test and requires, at most, a few hours on a good workstation computer.

KEY SPLITTING FOR ESCROWED ENCRYPTION

Section 3.5 discussed the Escrowed Encryption Standard (EES), which is designed to allow authorized people to intercept and decrypt others' ciphertext messages. EES key handling is a practical example of key splitting. Each crypto device that complies with the EES has a unique device identifier and secret key embedded in it. The secret key is used to implement the "back door" that allows ciphertext to be decoded. An important part of the process is to store the device identifiers and secret keys with escrow agents that protect the keys' secrecy and only release the keys under strictly enforced conditions.

In order to increase the security of escrowed keys, the EES requires that each key be split among two separate escrow agents. Legal requests to release the keys for a particular device must be submitted to the escrow agents separately and processed separately. This reduces the risk of keys being improperly released since any error or other failure would have to affect both escrow agents independently.

The key splits for escrowed encryption are generated and installed into the crypto devices during manufacturing. A device serial number and two random keys are generated for each crypto device under very tight security. Each batch of partially completed crypto devices and the keys are taken to a highly secure manufacturing site, currently at Mykotronx Corporation in California. In the presence of independent observers, the device identifiers and pairs of split keys are programmed into the new devices. The programming equipment writes the working key into the device by combining the two split keys with an exclusive-or operation as shown at the bottom of Figure 4-7. The programming equipment also writes the keys' device identifier into the device. The separate lists of split keys are kept separate at all times.

When programming is finished, the lists of split keys are sent to the escrow agents under tight security. If the FBI, for example, needs to tap a device with a key that is escrowed in this fashion, the FBI applies to the escrow agents for the appropriate keys. The "back door" to the encrypted data is activated by combining the split keys retrieved from the two separate escrow agents.

4.4.6 Deployment Security Requirements

Here is an ordered list of security requirements for manual keying:

1. **Generate the keys randomly.** True randomness means that adversaries have no way of guessing your keys. See Section 4.3 for requirements on random key generation.

2. **Protect the key generation process from "leaks."** Use a computer that is not accessible by untrustworthy people while actually generating the keys. Be sure to protect any devices while they are writing out the keys and to destroy any media that might contain copies of the crypto keys. The only copies of the keys should be those explicitly produced by the key generation process. All other copies must be purged to prevent accidental disclosure.

3. **Keep the key's value separate from its address.** Peoples' memories are unpredictable. It's easier on everyone if you don't make people unnecessarily aware of key values, even trusted people. If the value is kept separate from the address, then clerical people can process the keys for delivery without actually seeing the key values.

4. **Protect the keys during shipment.** Use a trustworthy delivery service and package the information so that the contents are unreadable and tampering is obvious. It is usually easier to assess the integrity of a delivery ser-

vice within a given country than when borders are crossed. Key splitting may be necessary if delivery services are of questionable trust.

5. **Require positive acknowledgment before new keys are used.** Have a procedure by which recipients notify one another that the key has arrived and can be used.

6. **Have a procedure to handle compromised keys.** If a key arrives and appears to have been tampered with, do not use it. Have a clear procedure in place to identify and report tampering.

7. **Minimize disclosure of keys.** Appropriate processes and procedures should avoid ever disclosing actual key values to users and administrators. This is an objective for which to strive. Keys should be generated and placed on distribution media without having to be examined by operators, administrators, or clerical personnel. Keys should be installed automatically without human intervention at the destination.

8. **Keys should have internal integrity checksums.** DES keys were originally designed to carry check bits. If a key was incorrectly transcribed, the check values would detect the error. While this is valuable for detecting media errors when keys are moved from one storage device to another, they are even more important for detecting manual transcription errors. Any device that accepts manually entered keying should require keys with internal integrity checks and should validate the key's integrity after it is entered.

9. **Generate and distribute key splits if higher security is needed.** If your keys protect you from a very serious threat, then you should take extra measures to prevent interception of your keys. Delivering key splits via different paths will give attackers a much higher work factor, reducing the risk of interception.

4.5 Technology: Automatic Rekeying

A fundamental rule of key management is that an individual key should not be overused, since it becomes easier to guess a key as it is used more and more often. However, manual rekeying is inconvenient and even risky. If one device already has a key that allows it to exchange encrypted data with another device, then the two could just as easily exchange crypto keys to use. This is the principle behind automatic rekeying.

In part, automatic rekeying is motivated by the sheer complexity of manual key distribution, especially as organizations grow. ANSI X9.17, the banking industry's standard for exchanging DES keys, was developed because it had become impractical to update keys manually, particularly as networks grew from dozens to hundreds of sites.

In one celebrated case, a bank spent a year carefully planning for a single, rapid, worldwide key change. It was a disaster. Keys were lost. Some were stolen by carriers who thought the "Registered" letters between banks might contain money. It took the bank two additional years to complete the key change. Other banks concluded that without an automated updating procedure it was more risky to change keys than to continue using existing ones.

The banking community developed ANSI X9.17 to help solve this problem. Although X9.17 was originally developed for messages sent by mail or telex, the basic concepts also apply to more automated applications, like Internet protocols. The process involves two different types of keys:

1. **Key encrypting keys (KEKs).** These keys are used to encrypt data keys. When two devices need to communicate, one of them generates a random data key and sends it to the other device encrypted with their shared KEK. The KEKs are manually distributed to devices.

2. **Data keys or session keys.** These are the keys used to encrypt and decrypt regular messages with another device. The device that created a particular key transmits it to the other device encrypted with their shared KEK.

This arrangement allows the devices to use a given data key only as long as it seems reasonable and prudent. When a data key has been used long enough, the two devices can establish a new one to use. Devices connected to dial-up modems tend to negotiate a new key every time a new connection is made. Devices on the Internet are essentially connected continuously and must establish their own rules.

4.5.1   ANSI X9.17 Point-to-Point Rekeying

Figure 4-8 illustrates the essentials of the X9.17 key exchange procedure. Alice's site wishes to start sending data to Bob. Alice generates a random number to use as the data key. She DES encrypts the data key with her KEK and sends it to Bob, including information identifying the key as coming from her. Bob uses his copy of the KEK (the same one Alice used) to decrypt and validate the key Alice sent. Once the key is validated, Bob sends an acknowledgment to Alice, so that she knows the key will be used. Then both Bob and Alice install that key in their respective crypto devices.

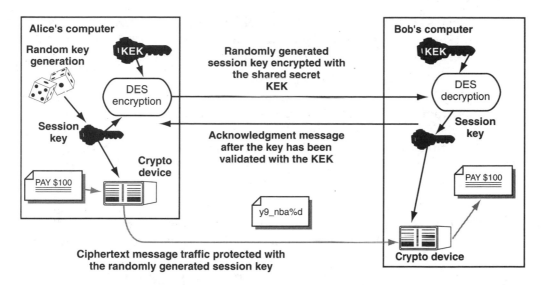

Figure 4-8: ANSI X9.17 KEY EXCHANGE. Bob and Alice share a KEK. When Alice needs to send a message to Bob, she generates a random session key and sends it to Bob, encrypted with their shared KEK. Then she encrypts her message with the session key and sends that to Bob. On receipt, Bob decrypts the session key and then the message.

SECURITY ISSUES IN AUTOMATIC REKEYING

An essential objective of automatic rekeying is to limit the damage if an attacker does manage to acquire a crypto key. If you are rekeying regularly, then the attacker can, at most, only read the traffic encrypted while that one key was being used. However, this is not simply a matter of encrypting a new key and exchanging it with the other station. X9.17 incorporates several features that prevent various attacks and we shall briefly examine them.

We shall assume that there are two hosts—A and B—for which A periodically establishes a new data key for both to use. For the following example we shall assume that attackers at some point managed to deduce the data key being used between A and B:

- **Deduce and use a single key.**
  If the attackers managed to deduce a single key, they could masquerade as A to B or B to A until one of the hosts decided to perform a rekey operation. An effective countermeasure to this is to negotiate a new key every time the two hosts begin communicating after a lengthy pause or after some significant amount of traffic has been exchanged. This approach is widely used and is typically referred to as *per-session keying*. Each time a new communications

session is started between the two hosts, they negotiate a fresh data key. The attackers would not be able to resume the masquerade after the rekey takes place, unless they manage to capture the new data key, too.

- **Capture and decrypt the rekey operation.**
  If A and B agreed to use the current data key to encrypt the next data key they wanted to use, efficient attackers can track those key changes and decrypt them as they happen. This is why X9.17 uses a separate key, the KEK, to encrypt new keys. The attackers are unlikely to see enough data encrypted with the KEK to crack it reliably. It is never used to encrypt anything except information in rekey messages.

- **Masquerade as A to B at will.**
  This can happen if rekey messages are encrypted with a separate KEK, but the messages contain little information in addition to the encrypted key itself. If the attackers managed to intercept the rekey message that established the one data key they have acquired, they do not need to encrypt it to use it. They can simply replay it to B and masquerade as A. When B receives the replayed message, B will start using the attackers' known data key. Then the attackers can exchange traffic with B, leaving B to believe it is really exchanging traffic with A.
  X9.17 rekey messages include a counter field that is incremented every time a new key is established. Both hosts maintain the count and use it to identify duplicate rekey messages. A repeated count value would generally cause the message to be discarded as invalid. Some hosts also include key expiration dates in the rekey message. This would make the intercepted key worthless in any case after the date had passed.

LEGAL RESTRICTIONS ON AUTOMATIC REKEYING

U.S. government export regulations have special rules for rekeying protocols based on secret key or public key techniques. Products using secret key techniques like ANSI X9.17 are treated most leniently when the KEK is limited to 64 bits or less. Such products are considered lightweight crypto and are eligible for the least restrictive export licenses. Unfortunately, products that fully comply with ANSI X9.17 are not automatically eligible for such licenses, since they would support 112-bit keys.

4.5.2   Variations of X9.17

There are numerous ways to establish secret keys without using public key techniques or being ANSI X9.17 compliant. Public key techniques for key exchange are discussed later in Chapter 9. Secret key techniques generally reduce to a protocol working roughly the same as X9.17. A comparison of the relative merits of public and secret key techniques for rekeying appears in Section 9.3.2.

Some vendors sell devices that claim to generate keys automatically between pairs of devices without ever transmitting the keys. This seems to violate the concepts of information theory the same way that perpetual motion machines violate the laws of physics. If we look closely we will usually find that the keys are, in fact, transmitted between devices in some coded form.

One vendor uses a PRNG to produce random bits that the devices exchange through point-to-point messages. Once the devices have collected enough random bits from themselves and from their partner, the two devices use the bits to construct a shared random number. This is fed as a seed value into another PRNG that yields a crypto key. Since both devices use the same generator and the same seed, they get the same key value as a result.

While this may sound very different from X9.17, it is in fact very similar. Two particular types of data figure prominently in both protocols—secret key value that is shared between the two devices and randomly generated bits that are transmitted between the two devices across the untrusted data link. In both cases the session key is formed by a mathematical function that uses the transmitted data and the shared secret.

It is hard to tell how much security this provides, since the protocols and the PRNG are proprietary to the manufacturer and protected as trade secrets. Given the difficulty of constructing a good PRNG, there is a real risk that a sophisticated, well-funded adversary could reverse engineer such a system. If the proprietary techniques turn out to be weak, a capable adversary could crack the system by analyzing the key exchange messages. On the other hand, the implementation could be a simple and secure variant of X9.17 hiding behind proprietary marketing jargon.

This example illustrates why it can be hard to determine the strength of commercial crypto devices. If important functions like random number generation are trade secrets, there is no simple way to compare it with other devices with security that has been analyzed. Perhaps the vendor simply wrapped the device with idiosyncratic terminology. This might help the vendor differentiate the device from others in the marketplace and, in some cases, make the device patentable. However, it does not help us understand the security properties of the device. When faced with such a situation a buyer must either choose a different product or decide to trust the vendor's statements.

NO MAGIC BULLETS

Although it is wise to minimize the amount of data protected by a single key, it might be possible to overdo it. There is one key exchange system that claims to rekey itself automatically every few minutes or after carrying a given number of kilobytes. In a busy system this may yield enough key exchanges to make the exchange messages themselves a reasonable target for cryptanalytic attack.

A former cryptography expert with the Soviet KGB once described how they exploited a series of interruptions of the communications lines going into the U.S. Embassy in Moscow. Each time a line was interrupted, the cryptographic equipment in the embassy had to rekey itself and resynchronize with the device on the other end. The KGB carefully collected this information to try to crack the American crypto devices.

In practice, rekeying becomes an interesting trade-off. If the crypto is relatively weak, perhaps from using too short of a key, then steps must be taken to minimize the loss when a single key is cracked. Frequent rekeying would provide some protection against this, especially if a simple, secure rekeying protocol is used.

However, there is some evidence that the newest protocols deserve to be approached with some caution. Security expert Gustavus Simmons identified a number of problems that have appeared in modern protocols based on various number theoretic techniques. The essential problem tends to be that, like traditional communications protocols, these sophisticated new protocols work well when everyone follows the rules. But, like traditional protocols, they fail when some assumption is unexpectedly violated. For example, some protocols required that a particular value be a random number, and it could be manipulated if the number was not. Simmons recommended that all protocols be rigorously analyzed in a process he characterized as "formalized paranoia."

In practice, most of the problems to which Simmons alluded are the province of systems based on public key algorithms. The simpler procedures based on X9.17 are less susceptible to such attacks. However, public key systems yield several benefits that make the extra analysis and potential risks worthwhile. This choice is examined further in Section 9.3.2.

4.5.3 Technical Security Requirements

Here is an ordered list of security requirements for devices with point-to-point automatic rekeying. Keep in mind that while a protocol may include particular features, not all product implementations will include all features:

1. **Generate good random keys.** This is essential or the rekeying facility is worthless. It is better to use a key continually that is practically impossible

to guess and hard to change than a key that is both easy to change and easy to guess.

2. **Use a separate KEK to protect rekey messages.** The KEK must be a key produced and used exclusively to protect data keys when they are being exchanged with an authorized recipient. The KEK must never be used to encrypt other data. The goal is to give the KEK a relatively long life by encrypting as little data with it as possible.

3. **Provide a mechanism to update the KEK.** Since the KEK will probably have to be updated via some manual distribution process, we may not want to update it very often. However, we must provide a method of updating it, if only in support of a key compromise procedure in which the KEK may have been stolen.

4. **Use a published protocol for automatic rekeying.** The principal benefit here is that published protocols have been reviewed and discussed in the open literature, especially the more mature protocols. A product's strengths and weaknesses are far less likely to take everyone by surprise if the essentials of its behavior are public knowledge. Proprietary implementations present too many opportunities for hidden flaws.

5. **Protect against replay attacks.** This has to be a property of the key exchange protocol being used and should be explicitly included in the product implementation. This is a standard feature in X9.17.

4.6   Key Distribution Centers (KDCs)

A *key distribution center* is a device that simplifies the secret key distribution nightmare posed by a large community of hosts that must communicate directly with one another. Instead of having pairwise keys for every pair of hosts, each host has a secret key for communicating with the key distribution center. Hosts establish keys for talking directly with other hosts by contacting the center and requesting keys for the particular hosts that need to communicate. The center provides randomly generated keys that only those two hosts can read.

For Alice and Bob to communicate, they each need an individual secret key they share with the key distribution center ("Alice's key" and "Bob's key"). Once they have been issued these keys, they can contact the center to establish a key whenever they need to communicate. Note that the key they set up between themselves is supposed to be used as a session key. It should be discarded when they are finished with their current message exchange and they should get a fresh key from the center the next time they need to talk.

So, when Alice needs to send a message to Bob she contacts the key distribution center to request a session key for them to use. Alice's request identifies herself as the originator of the request and Bob as the other recipient of a key. The center generates a fresh, acceptably random session key and sends two copies of it back to Alice—one encrypted with her key and the other encrypted with Bob's key (Figure 4-9).

Alice takes the copy of the session key encrypted with Bob's key and sends it to Bob, notifying him that she needs to send him a message (Figure 4-10). She decrypts her own copy of the random session key and uses it to encrypt the actual message being sent to Bob.

Bob receives a sequence of two messages from Alice. The first message contains the session key encrypted with Bob's key. Note that Alice couldn't read this version of the key, but Bob can. He decrypts the session key and then uses it to decrypt Alice's second message. Since they have established a session key, Bob can immediately send a response if he has one.

KEY DISTRIBUTION CENTERS IN PRACTICE

The banking industry incorporated key distribution centers into ANSI X9.17, and also described a variant called a *key translation center* that allowed other hosts to generate keys. As with point-to-point rekeying, the protocol was designed for use with manually exchanged text messages. Some vendors have produced automated versions integrated into commercial encryption products. There is also the Ker-

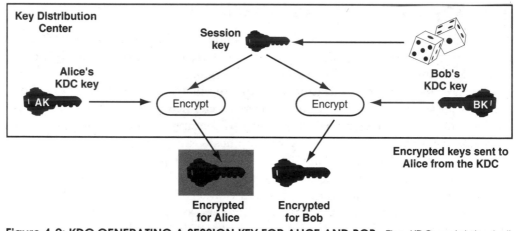

Figure 4-9: KDC GENERATING A SESSION KEY FOR ALICE AND BOB. The KDC maintains individual secret keys for each of its users. When Alice needs a session key for communicating with Bob, the KDC sends two copies of the session key to Alice—one encrypted with Alice's secret key and the other encrypted with Bob's secret key. It is up to Alice to forward Bob's copy of the key to him.

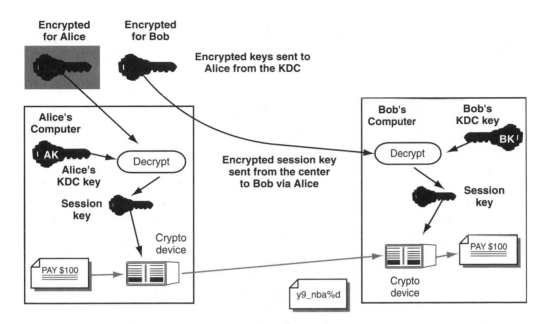

Figure 4-10: ALICE RECEIVING SESSION KEYS FROM THE KDC. Alice decrypts the session key that was encrypted with her secret KDC key. She forwards the other one to Bob and he decrypts it with his secret KDC key. Now they have both decrypted the same session key, so they each install it into their crypto device.

beros system, a very well-known package built around the concept of a key distribution center. Kerberos uses secret keys and a key distribution center to provide reliable access control in a network of computers. Authorized users each have a memorized secret password that is used as their personal key for communicating with the Kerberos key distribution center (also called the *Authentication Server*).

The protocol described here for a KDC is relatively simple and in fact it is inadequate for most security-conscious applications. As given here, it does not provide any authentication between users. If Henry the Forger also uses the same center, he can forward an appropriately encrypted session key to Bob and simply claim the key and message are coming from Alice. Practical systems require more sophisticated protocols. ANSI X9.17 includes additional features for authentication and message integrity protection, and Kerberos incorporates even more sophisticated mechanisms.

Selecting a key distribution center for production use is a difficult problem. Standards like X9.17 do not reflect the latest analytical studies of such protocols. A naive implementation could leave users open to attack. The fact that Kerberos has gone through several major versions reflects how knowledge of the problem has evolved. The latest Kerberos version is version 5, although version 4 is still very widely used. Kerberos is more of a tool kit than a turnkey product, so it generally requires appropriately trained technical experts to ensure it is properly deployed.

4.7   Maintaining Keys and System Security

Key distribution isn't a one-time operation. It's part of the ongoing activity of maintaining the crypto system's security. The following is a summary of activities that should take place in order to maintain security as time goes on.

- **Key aging**
  The period a key is in service is generally referred to as its *cryptoperiod*. Keep a record of when individual keys were issued and ensure that a key does not remain in service too long. KEKs can safely stay in service for years in a medium-risk environment. In some applications you might plan to do rekeying as part of periodic software upgrade activities.
  If the crypto system being used does not support automatic rekeying, arrange to rekey all devices as often as possible. The inevitable inefficiencies and delays of manual procedures will prevent you from rekeying "too often" under such circumstances.

- **Key revocation**
  Rekey at once if there is any risk of a key having been stolen or improperly disclosed. If the equipment can't be rekeyed at once, you must make a judgment call and balance the threat of someone improperly exploiting the key against the loss of service resulting from the revoked key. This is typically a business decision that balances the potential loss of business against the risk of fraud.

- **Operation review**
  Periodically review the operation of crypto systems and keying mechanisms with users to ensure that such systems are running smoothly and correctly. Many users will not hesitate to disable or bypass security mechanisms that interfere with their professional duties. Security measures may be obtrusive but they must not seriously interfere.

- **Security assessment**
  The lists of requirements given in this book provide a guide for assessing the security of crypto applications. Periodically reassess how well the deployed system complies with these requirements. While it is unlikely that a practical, working system will comply with every requirement, it is important to identify a set of requirements you intend to meet and ensure that you are

meeting them. This requires a periodic reassessment, since equipment and behavior will change over time.

4.8   For Further Information

- **ANSI Standard X9.17,** *Financial Institution Key Management (Wholesale)*
  The standard for automated DES key management, both point to point and through centralized keying centers. Also includes interesting appendices of requirements for crypto hardware and for key handling in general.

- **Greenlee, "Requirements for Key Management Protocols in the Wholesale Financial Industry"**
  This thorough and entertaining article provides requirements and the historical background behind the ANSI X9.17 standard specification.

- **Kaufman, Perlman, and Speciner,** *Network Security: PRIVATE Communication in a PUBLIC World*
  An informally written but fairly sophisticated textbook covering network security mechanisms. It provides good, basic coverage of protocols for key distribution centers, including introductions to Kerberos 4 and Kerberos 5.

- **Knuth,** *The Art of Computer Programming, Vol. 2: Seminumerical Algorithms*
  This is the classic computer science reference on random number generation, but be warned that this is about *statistical* random numbers not *cryptographic* random numbers. Still, it contains valuable insights.

- **Sheymov,** *Tower of Secrets*
  The author was a crypto security expert at the KGB, then he defected and wrote his memoirs. Sheymov demonstrates a knack for thinking about security problems that can be quite educational.

- **Simmons, "Cryptanalysis and Protocol Failures"**
  A cautionary tale about putting too much faith in sophisticated crypto protocols.

- **Schneier,** *Applied Cryptography: Protocol, Algorithms, and Source Code in C*
  This is the place to go for source code or algorithms to generate keys.

<u>5</u>

Security at the IP Layer

What is the use of running when we are not on the right road?

—Old saying

IN THIS CHAPTER

This chapter introduces the IP Security Protocols (IPSEC) that provide crypto protection to TCP/IP communications at the network layer. These protocols allow sites to protect their traffic while they intercommunicate over a public Internet connection. The following topics are discussed:

- Security objectives and issues associated with IPSEC

- Overview of network-layer IP security

- Cryptographic checksums for message integrity protection

- IPSEC encryption and authentication headers, and how they interact

This chapter has no deployment examples. They appear in the following chapters.

5.1   Security Objectives

IPSEC is a set of general-purpose protocols for protecting TCP/IP communications. In practice they work best for protecting traffic between hosts and not between users on a given host.

- **Protect traffic between trusted hosts from forgery or eavesdropping.**
  Network traffic to and from trustworthy hosts needs to be protected. The traffic between pairs of hosts might pass through hostile hosts or be accessible by adversaries. Attackers could do damage either by forging messages or by eavesdropping on them.

- **Protect the whole range of Internet software currently in use.**
  Several different network applications are currently in use: e-mail, World Wide Web, file transfer, remote terminal access, and so on. TCP/IP has become the lingua franca of networking. Every notable proprietary protocol has made accommodations to interoperate with Internet protocols. This traffic must be protected as it travels between sites, but it is often too expensive to modify or replace all the TCP/IP software currently in place.

- **An untrusted network is in place and cost is very important.**
  An existing, less trustworthy network can carry the traffic between the trusted hosts. In many cases the untrusted network is the public Internet. It is often too costly to implement an independent network between the trusted hosts.

- **Protection is automatic between hosts configured to need protection.**
  Many organizations prefer not to make individual users decide whether traffic should be protected or not. Instead, the system applies protection automatically between hosts needing the security. This is important if users do not have sufficient training or understanding to apply crypto protections correctly. This can also be inefficient since both sensitive and nonsensitive traffic will be automatically protected.

5.2   Basic Issues with Using IPSEC

Network-layer crypto and IPSEC have certain properties that distinguish them from other techniques, including link-layer crypto. Here are some issues raised by those properties:

- **Security must be independent of and transparent to existing Internet service providers (ISPs).**
  A major motivation of IPSEC is that people want to connect safely with other trusted sites and use the existing ISPs to carry the packets. Unfortunately, the architecture of the Internet makes it impossible to enforce any service or integrity requirements on ISPs. Therefore, IPSEC is designed to provide protection against threats that ISPs usually can't block.

Link encryption is not transparent to ISPs. It can only be applied to dedicated connections between pairs of cooperating sites.

- **Crypto applied at the network level leaves more plaintext in the packets.**
  As shown in Figure 5-1, network-level crypto will leave even more address information in plaintext. All data that isn't required to route the packet is encrypted. The internet header is in plaintext so that ISPs can route the packet to its destination even though its data contents are encrypted.

- **Site-level security yields per-site authentication.**
  Network-level security measures can distinguish between traffic from approved sites and other sites, but it can't reliably distinguish between traffic from individual users at an approved site. This is acceptable for many sites. Individual authentication is then handled by other mechanisms, like passwords, as long as the activity clearly originates from an approved network.

  This yields *virtual private networks* (VPNs) that link geographically distributed sites. In a VPN, traffic from one site destined for another must traverse an untrusted public network like the Internet. The site-to-site traffic is protected from outsiders. Separation of traffic between insiders is not generally a problem addressed by VPN facilities.

- **Numerous factors have bred uncertainty in key management.**
  Developers, vendors, politics, and rapidly evolving public key technologies have bred competing alternatives for IPSEC key management. Internet standards promote one protocol while product availability promotes alternative protocols. The only consistently supported technique is for basic manual keying.

5.3   Technology: Cryptographic Checksums

Crypto techniques have long been used to lend authenticity to messages. Sixteenth century correspondents of Mary, Queen of Scots, assumed messages from her were authentic if they were in fact written in her personal code. Twentieth century

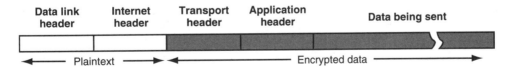

Figure 5-1: BASIC PACKET FORMAT WITH IPSEC PROTECTIONS. IPSEC encrypts and seals the transport and application data during transmission. Integrity protection is also provided for the Internet header. Since the Internet header is in plaintext, IP routers can deliver encrypted IPSEC messages to the destination host.

armies have relied on encrypted radio communications to ensure their orders came from a legitimate source as well as to ensure the orders' secrecy. Naturally this could work to an army's disadvantage if the codes were cracked. Major units of the Yugoslav Army during World War II were induced to halt their offensive and even retreat by radio broadcasts that were forged by the Italians after they broke the Yugoslav radio code. However, as we illustrated earlier in Section 3.2.3, encryption alone does not protect the integrity of messages, even if the keys have not been cracked. We must use techniques that are specially developed to protect message integrity with strong crypto.

The essential technique is the *cryptographic checksum,* which detects changes in a protected message (Figure 5-2). Unlike encryption, this crypto technique does not hide a message's contents; instead, it uses the crypto computations to "seal" the message against changes. An effective crypto checksum will not allow an attacker to produce or modify a protected message.

A checksum is a computational procedure with an answer that depends on the contents of some arbitrarily large block of data. Ideally, any change in the data contents will yield a different checksum. If the data and checksum are sent across the network in the same message, the recipient can verify that the data arrived intact by repeating the checksum computation and comparing the result against the checksum in the message.

Checksums by themselves are intended to detect random errors in data as it is handled by automatic equipment. The problem with network security is that some

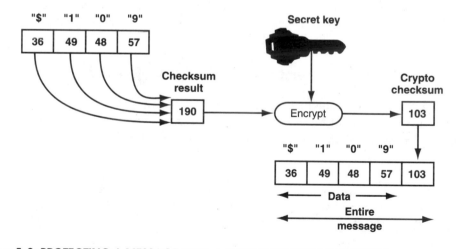

Figure 5-2: PROTECTING A MESSAGE WITH A CRYPTOGRAPHIC CHECKSUM. The sender computes the checksum of the data being sent and encrypts it using a secret key. The recipient can verify that the message is authentic by recomputing the checksum. The encrypted checksum must match the value sent with the message. Forgers cannot compute valid checksums without the key.

people are motivated to modify messages systematically in order to somehow bene-fit themselves. For example, Bailey the Switcher could modify the message, recom-pute the checksum, and replace the checksum in the original message with the new, forged one. The recipient will not be able to detect the difference, since the forged checksum validates the forged contents.

The cryptographic checksum defeats this type of forgery by using a crypto key when forming the checksum value. For example, we could use the DES algorithm with a secret key to encrypt a message's 64-bit checksum. The receiving host would then take the result of the checksum of the received data, encrypt it using the same secret key, and compare the result with the encrypted checksum in the message.

To prevent attackers from forging or modifying messages, the crypto checksum should resist two general attacks. First, the attacker should not be able to construct a legal crypto checksum for a forged message. The computation should be based on secret information of some sort that the attacker can't have, and then should be used to produce the checksum in a way the attacker can't duplicate. Second, the attacker should not be able to take an existing message with a legal crypto check-sum and be able to construct a different message that would have the same crypto checksum.

Figure 5-3 illustrates this second case. Bailey the Switcher doesn't need to know the secret key to substitute the message's legitimate contents with bogus information. Since the plaintext is readable, she only needs to know how the check-sum is computed and she can compute the plaintext checksum value. If she finds a different and profitable message that yields the same plaintext checksum, she can substitute it for the original message. In this case, the weak checksum on the mes-sage yields the same value for "$109" as it does for "$910." Since the plaintext checksum values match, the crypto checksum values would match. The recipient won't be able to tell that the contents were changed. This type of attack has driven the evolution of crypto checksum techniques.

5.3.1 One-way Hash Functions

One-way hash functions are checksumlike functions, but they are explicitly designed so that an attacker can't construct a forged message that yields the same result as a legitimate one. Like checksums, one-way hash functions take an arbi-trarily long data sequence and compute a check value of a fixed size, called the *hash value*. Unlike checksums, one-way hash functions try to generate a "fingerprint" of the data. The functions are designed to make it as difficult as possible to construct another data sequence that yields the exact same result.

Hash functions are more sensitive to minor changes in the input text, so they provide the best protection for larger data items. For example, Internet-savvy soft-ware vendors often publish patch software on the Internet so that customers may

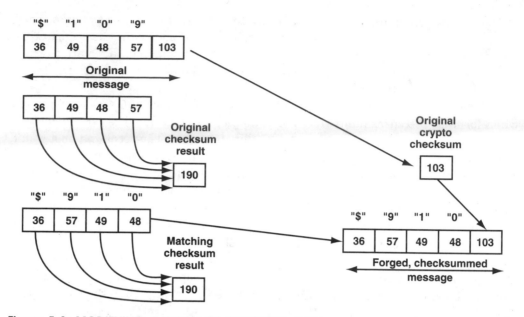

Figure 5-3: MODIFYING A MESSAGE PROTECTED WITH A CRYPTOGRAPHIC CHECKSUM.
Bailey the Switcher notes that the more profitable message "$910" has the same plaintext checksum as the legitimate message "$109." Bailey can substitute the higher amount and use the same crypto checksum value. The message looks legitimate because the crypto checksum value is still correct.

conveniently download the latest fixes to their software. The vendors always publish hash values, usually computed with the MD5 algorithm, so recipients can verify the software's integrity after downloading. Changing even a single bit will change the MD5 hash. If the hash on the downloaded file matches the published value the recipient can be sure that the file wasn't modified since the vendor created it.

The published hash value protects against both accidental and intentional changes. Accidental changes occasionally happen, particularly as important data items are "mirrored;" that is, copied from one Internet distribution site to another. Intentional changes also occur, particularly when a modified patch could render several Internet sites vulnerable to attack. Bogus patches and subverted software have been encountered in the Internet community several times. The published checksums help protect customers by giving them a positive check that the software they received is authentic and intact. Particularly enterprising crackers have even backed up bogus patches with forged announcements from vendors or from CERT, but such antics typically raise a hue and cry in Internet security circles.

KEYED HASH COMPUTATIONS

Published hash values give effective protection to data that is being broadly distributed, especially if the hash value itself is likely to reach the right people via many paths. If, on the other hand, we must protect data that makes a single trip between two sites, then the published hash value really isn't feasible. The published hashes are trustworthy because they travel many paths, but efficient communications between two sites must find security through something other than redundancy. If we simply include the hash with the message, Henry the Forger can modify messages or produce new ones that look just as authentic by including the hash computed from the forged contents. However, Henry's forgery is blocked if the hash operation incorporates a secret key. This is the basis of the keyed hash.

Figure 5-4 illustrates the generation of a keyed hash. The data being sent is combined with the secret key value and the hash is computed over both. The hash result is sent with the message as in the earlier crypto checksum examples. Unlike the earlier, trivial checksum, the keyed hash effectively blocks both types of attacks against crypto checksums. First, attackers can't generate the right checksum value for a given message unless they have a copy of the secret key being used. The correct hash value depends on constructing the same input data, which includes both the data sent and the secret key. Second, attackers can't construct a similar, beneficial message that yields the same hash value. Even if, by some remote coincidence,

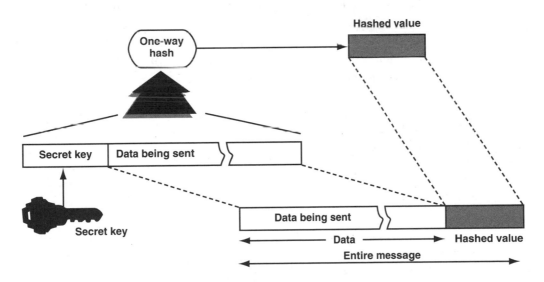

Figure 5-4: PROTECTING MESSAGE DATA WITH A KEYED HASH. We append a secret key to the message contents and compute a one-way hash. We then send the message data plus the hash. The recipient uses the same secret key to recompute and validate the hashed value.

they happened to construct a message that would yield the same hash value, they have no way of verifying that fact before sending it. Given how difficult it is to construct a message that matches a given hash value, the chances are remote that any particular attempt would succeed.

5.3.2 Technical Security Requirements

Here are the security requirements for a cryptographic checksum operation:

1. **One way function.** An attacker should not be able take the checksum result and "backsolve" to determine the original data that produced the checksum. If the attacker has the original hashed text minus the secret key, there should be no way (short of brute force) to recover the key value.

2. **Single bit changes should change the checksum value.** The attacker should not be able to change $100 to $900 without invalidating the checksum value.

3. **Bit transpositions should change the checksum value.** If the attacker changes $109 to $901, the checksum value should change.

4. **Changes in message length should change the checksum value.** This is particularly important for keyed hash computations since the secret key is generally appended to the data being hashed. Keying provides no protection if we get the same hash value after keys are cut from the computation.

5. **It should resist collisions.** To some extent this is implied in the previous requirements. The essential requirement, however, is that an attacker should not be able to construct a message systematically with the same hash value as an existing message, except through brute force.

Reasonable choices for keyed hash functions include MD5 (developed by Ron Rivest of RSA) and the Secure Hash Algorithm (SHA-1; developed by the NSA). Effective keyed hashes can also be constructed using a good block cipher like DES in an appropriate chaining mode like CBC or CFB. Table 5-1 summarizes these choices.

Table 5-1: Recommended algorithms for keyed hash computations

Hash Algorithm	Key Size (bits)	Hash Size (bits)
SHA-1	128 (variable)	160
MD5	128 (variable)	128
ANSI X9.9 with DES CBC	56	64

Keep in mind that while keyed hash functions provide a certain degree of authentication, they are not the same as digital signatures, which we examine in Section 11.5. Keyed hash functions generally use a secret key that is shared between the sender and the recipient. This means that the sender and recipient can both generate authentic messages. Digital signatures are generally based on public key encryption technology, which provides unique "private" keys to individuals. Recipients can validate a message without being able to generate an authentic message containing different data. Keyed hash functions associate the protected data with the group that shares the key, while digital signatures can associate the protected data with a particular individual or device.

5.4   IPSEC: IP Security Protocol

IPSEC is an extension to the existing IP networking protocol to protect IP packets from snooping or modification. IPSEC evolved as part of the development of the new IP version 6 and has been adapted to work with existing IP version 4 protocol implementations. By operating at the network level, IPSEC protections do not interfere with existing application software or protocols, and packets protected by IPSEC can be handled by existing routers and routing hosts (Figure 5-5).

IPSEC is designed to provide privacy, forgery detection, or both for IP packets. IPSEC defines two optional packet headers, one for each type of protection. The headers both contain a numerical value called the *security parameter index* (SPI). Whenever a host processes an IPSEC header it uses the SPI to identify the crypto keys and proce-

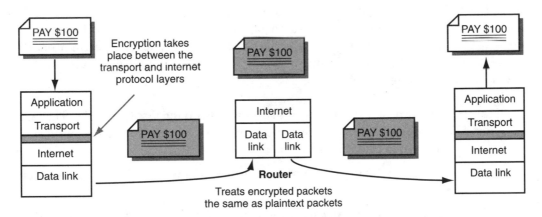

Figure 5-5: IPSEC CRYPTO IS TRANSPARENT TO INTERNET APPLICATIONS AND ROUTERS. IPSEC protections are applied "above" the IP routing information and "below" the application data. Routers ignore the extra IPSEC headers, and applications never see the IPSEC crypto services.

dures to use with it. A packet may contain one or both headers, depending on which security services are needed. In practice, most packets use both.

- **Authentication Header (AH)**
  This AH provides integrity-checking information, so we can detect if the packet's contents were forged or modified while traveling across untrusted networks.
  The AH contains a cryptographic checksum to vouch for the fact that the packet's contents were not changed. If the contents of the packet were in fact changed, the checksum computation would fail. The cryptographic checksum incorporates secret keying information so that an attacker cannot compute an alternate checksum that checks correctly.

- **Encapsulating Security Payload (ESP)**
  The ESP encrypts the data contents of the remainder of the packet so that the contents cannot be extracted while traveling across untrusted networks. The format of the ESP varies according to the type and mode of the encryption being used. In all cases the key associated with the encryption is selected using the SPI.

The following section describes how IPSEC associates different keys and crypto procedures with different hosts, and coordinates their use with the IPSEC headers.

SECURITY ASSOCIATIONS IN IPSEC

In order to communicate, each pair of hosts using IPSEC must establish a *security association* with one another. The security association establishes the what and how of IPSEC protection: what types of protection to apply, how to do encryption or authentication, and which keys need to be used. The security association that applies to a given IPSEC header is determined by the packet's destination IP address and the SPI in the packet header. IPSEC software must maintain the following information for each SPI:

1. **Specification of the crypto methods to be used by that SPI.** The AH and ESP formats are very general and must be tailored to specific encryption and crypto checksum methods.

2. **Keys to be used by the crypto methods when processing traffic for that SPI.**

3. **The hosts or other entities associated with this traffic.** This information helps disambiguate security associations if two or more hosts happen to assign an identical SPI.

When a host applies IPSEC protection to an outgoing packet, it uses a security association belonging to the destination. The host applies the association's crypto method and key to the data to protect it, and inserts the association's SPI in the IPSEC header. This process is then repeated if a second IPSEC header is applied in front of the other one.

When a host processes the first IPSEC header in an incoming packet, the SPI is used to identify the appropriate security association. Then the host applies the indicated crypto method to the header using the indicated key. Since there is probably a separate AH and ESP, the process is repeated on the next IPSEC header, using its SPI to locate the appropriate crypto material. If the header's SPI doesn't exist or the packet is invalid after processing, it is silently discarded; that is, no indication is given to the sending host that the packet was rejected.

REPLAY ATTACKS

TCP/IP protocols are designed to operate correctly even if data packets are retransmitted. The IPSEC protocols being used in today's products reflect this philosophy. There is no replay protection built in to any of the essential protocols. However, this does not mean that replay is not a risk. Like all other aspects of the internet protocols, its toleration of duplicate packets is tailored to handle communications errors. Duplicate packets are a natural result of retransmissions that occur to ensure that data is sent reliably. The protocols are not explicitly designed to identify and reject packets that are cleverly collected and maliciously replayed at a different time.

The practical threat to Internet traffic depends on the protocols being used. Connection-oriented applications that use TCP are unlikely to be fooled by maliciously replayed packets. When two hosts establish a connection, they exchange randomly selected sequence numbers and must use those numbers cooperatively for the connection to work correctly. While it is not impossible for Play-It-Again Sam to encounter an opportunity where TCP packets could be replayed, the process would not be clean, simple, or reliable. Malicious replay of packet-oriented traffic using the User Datagram Protocol (UDP) is much more likely to cause trouble. Some protocols, like Network File Service (NFS), do not need to contain any indicator that could detect a packet that is replayed several minutes or hours later. Newer versions of the Simple Network Management Protocol (SNMP), on the other hand, contain time stamps that were specifically designed to detect and block replay attempts.

The practical threat of replay attacks is still a matter of uncertainty. It is clear that an attacker could retransmit packets that would on occasion be accepted as genuine. The actual result of this behavior would depend on the particular packet that is retransmitted. If performed randomly, this retransmission could disrupt computer operations in unpredictable ways, causing minor and unexpected changes in data or possibly even major and devastating changes. This style of attack may appeal to some attackers despite the uncertainty of dramatic results. A successful fraud based on this type of replay attack would probably require a large amount of insider information about the traffic being attacked.

Antireplay protocols are being designed into future improvements of IPSEC. Products that provide such features today have had to develop them independently of the currently listed IPSEC standards.

5.4.1   IPSEC Authentication

The IPSEC AH is a header in an IP packet that contains a cryptographic checksum for the packet's contents. The AH is simply inserted into the packet between the IP header and any subsequent packet contents. No changes need to be made to the packet data contents. Security resides entirely in the contents of the AH.

Figure 5-6 shows the AH format and the data it protects. The AH format is very simple. The first word identifies the type and location of the next protocol header, and an implementation could even skip the AH without authenticating it. The SPI tells the destination host which security association applies to this header. The rest of the header is a multiple of 32-bit words that contains the cryptographic checksum. The exact format and contents of the checksum depends on the authentication method being used for this security association.

The crypto checksum is computed over the packet's IP header combined with the headers following the AH. By including the IP header in its computation, the AH can detect any changes in the packet's addressing information or attempts to bypass the AH itself. Since the IP header contains fields that are changed during transit, the computation is performed on a standardized version of the header. First, each field is set to the value the recipient should see in it on receipt. Next, any fields that might otherwise change during transit are set to zero. Then this ide-

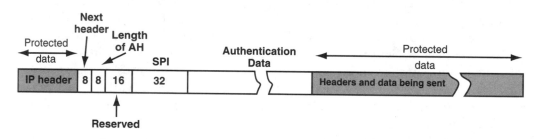

Figure 5-6: FORMAT AND CONTENTS OF THE IPSEC AH. The AH begins with a 64-bit header that identifies the header following it, specifies the AH's length in 32-bit words, and identifies the security association for authenticating the packet. The authentication data field contains a variable number of 32-bit words. Typically it contains a keyed hash value computed over the protected data.

alized IP header is combined with the headers following the AH to compute the cryptographic checksum.

The receiving host repeats this process to verify the cryptographic checksum. Any fields with values that are unpredictable on receipt are set to zero. The key associated with the SPI is used to compute the crypto checksum. If the results do not match the checksum value received in the AH, the packet is silently discarded.

The AH format itself does not define the size or nature of the cryptographic checksum. The actual checksum is formatted as a variable number of 32-bit words. The security association must be used to specify the type of checksum, how large it is, and how it is computed. The SPI also indicates what secret key, if any, should be used in the checksum computation.

DEFAULT METHOD: KEYED MD5 HASH

All IPSEC implementations are required to handle an AH that uses the MD5 hash algorithm with a secret key, yielding a 128-bit hash value. Interoperability testing has typically used 128-bit keys. The protocol leaves the size of the secret key unspecified. Two hosts can interoperate as long as they agree on the key's size, contents, and the ordering of its bits.

Figure 5-7 illustrates the authentication process. The crypto key associated with the SPI is appended to the protected data twice—once at the beginning of the data and once at the end. Analysis has shown that this format is more resistant to attack than a single use of the key. The MD5 hash is then computed over the combined data. The resulting 128-bit hash value is inserted in the packet's AH. The recipient validates the hash by reconstructing the hashed value, with the same secret key appended at the beginning and end of the message data. If the message arrived intact, the resulting MD5 hash value should match the one delivered in the AH.

5.4.2   IPSEC Encryption

The IPSEC ESP also defines a new header inserted in the IP packet. ESP processing also includes transforming the protected data into an unreadable, encrypted form. The ESP header simply contains the SPI for the destination host's security association (Figure 5.8). The format of the encapsulated data depends entirely on the crypto processing being used with that security association.

Under normal circumstances the ESP will be "inside" the AH. The host generating a packet will encrypt the data using the procedure and key chosen in the security association, and place the SPI in the ESP header. The authentication is then computed over the packet's encrypted contents.

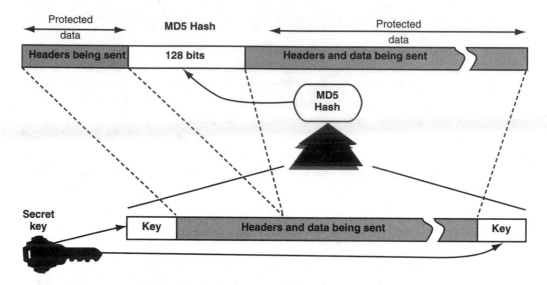

Figure 5-7: IPSEC AH WITH THE KEYED MD5 HASH. We append a secret key to the beginning and the end of the message's protected data and compute the MD5 hash. The SPI in the AH tells the recipient which key to use when verifying the hash.

On receipt, the AH will be processed first, if it is present. If the encrypted data has been tampered with in transit, AH processing will detect this tampering and the packet will be silently discarded. Then the host will extract the key and the crypto procedure associated with the ESP and decrypt the data.

DEFAULT METHOD: DES WITH CBC

All IPSEC implementations are required to support ESP encryption using the DES in CBC mode. (CBC is described in Chapter 2.) A security association using this method must have a 56-bit DES secret key associated with it.

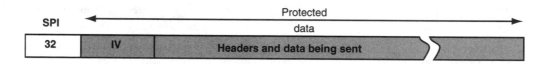

Figure 5-8: FORMAT AND CONTENTS OF THE IPSEC ESP. The ESP consists of a 32-bit SPI field, followed by data with a format that depends on the encryption procedure being used. The ESP incorporates all remaining data in the packet. If there are embedded headers or other fields, they will not be processed until after they have been decrypted at the receiving end.

For its cipher block chaining to operate correctly, DES requires the usual 56-bit key plus a 64-bit Initialization Vector (IV) and stream of 64-bit data blocks. The procedure cannot process partial blocks, so the data must be padded out to a 64-bit boundary. Figure 5-9 shows how the ESP and its encapsulated data are formatted to handle this. Following the SPI value in the header is the IV value that "seeds" the cipher block chaining. DES requires a 64-bit value for the IV. Some IPSEC implementations use a 32-bit value that is concatenated to its complement to produce the necessary data block. Padding and a payload type indicator are added to the end of the data before encryption.

The receiving host uses the SPI in the ESP header to determine how to decrypt the encapsulated data, and to identify which key to use. If the ESP was not protected by an AH during transit, there are only two relatively unreliable methods to indicate if the encrypted contents used a bogus key or were modified in transit. First, the DES CBC process can verify that the encapsulated data is on a 64-bit boundary and reject it if it is not. Second, the DES CBC process can verify that the Payload Type contains a legal value. Effective integrity checking must be handled by the AH, though there are a few cases in which higher level protocols could handle it instead.

ALTERNATIVE ENCRYPTION TRANSFORMS

A variety of other transforms are either available in products or under development. Here are some examples of other encryption transforms that are in products or on the drawing boards:

- **RC4 with Anti-Replay (product).**
  This nonstandard encryption transform provides some degree of replay detection along with the exportable RC4 crypto algorithm. The transform is used in Secure Computing's Border Firewall Server.

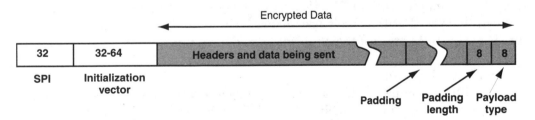

Figure 5-9: ESP FORMAT WHEN USING DES IN CBC MODE. When using DES in CBC mode, the ESP contains the IV for the chain and the encrypted data. The payload type for the encrypted data is appended to the end before encryption. Padding is also added before encryption to ensure that the encrypted data falls on a 64-bit boundary.

- **3DES (standard).**
  This encryption transform provides DES encryption with a longer key by using the 3DES construct. It is currently an Internet-proposed standard, like the other IPSEC protocols. However, it is not currently a required part of IPSEC, like the DES transform just described.

- **Combined Encryption, Authentication, and Antireplay (proposal).**
  This transform has been published as part of planned improvements to IPSEC. This transform would allow hosts to use the ESP by itself to provide both encryption and authentication. It would also provide strong antireplay measures. There is a long term plan to require antireplay features in all IPSEC implementations.

5.5   IPSEC Key Management

An essential requirement for IPSEC or any other security protocol is that there be a way to define the relationship between particular authorized entities, their crypto keys, and identification codes within its messages. This corresponds to the establishment of security associations in IPSEC. We have just looked at how the SPI is used to select the correct security association for a particular IPSEC header. What is needed is a method for establishing security associations and assigning SPIs to them.

As noted earlier, IPSEC key management is an area of conflict among competing objectives and solutions. Several protocols have been proposed and a few have been used in practice. The most practical approach today is to look at what is really available and what compatibility objectives are sought by various vendors. The principal venue for IPSEC interoperability testing is the S/WAN Initiative sponsored by RSA Data Security, which verifies interoperability with static keys, and with emerging key management protocols.

Today there are four standard approaches to IPSEC key exchange. This includes techniques that are in actual use today as well as techniques that hold enough promise that they have been extensively documented and reviewed. They are listed below in order of their current operational status:

- **Manual keying**
  All IPSEC implementations must provide a way to configure security associations manually. This includes specifying SPIs, crypto methods, and keys, as well as identifying with which communicating hosts these items are used. The crypto material is distributed manually whenever keys are to be changed. The S/WAN Initiative has published a recommended file format for

specifying security association data. The S/WAN Initiative has completed interoperability testing with a variety of IPSEC vendors using manual keying.

- **Simple Key Interchange Protocol (SKIP)**

  SKIP negotiates and exchanges session keys between IPSEC hosts by inserting a special header into each IP packet, preceding the IPSEC headers. Key exchange can be based on a shared secret, similar to ANSI X9.17, or it can perform an authenticated Diffie-Hellman key exchange. Diffie-Hellman is a public key algorithm that can establish a shared secret between two entities without them having to exchange secret information ahead of time (Section 9.1.2).

  The design of SKIP makes it easy to integrate with the IPSEC software, which makes it easier to insert in existing network protocol stacks. The SKIP header adds 20 to 30 bytes of overhead to each packet. This extra overhead makes SKIP less attractive in some applications, especially those using slow data links.

  Sun Microsystems developed SKIP and uses it in their SunScreen product to negotiate keys for VPN support. Sun is encouraging other vendors to use SKIP and has sponsored interoperability testing with participating vendors.

- **Internet Security Association and Key Management Protocol (ISAKMP)**

  ISAKMP is a broad, general-purpose protocol intended both to manage security associations and to handle key exchange. It is currently the key management protocol of choice according to the IPSEC Committee of the Internet Engineering Task Force (IETF). However, there are very few implementations of it available in products or in source code.

  A full ISAKMP implementation promises to be quite complex. The S/WAN Initiative has proposed a basic implementation profile that uses shared secret keys to establish per-session keys. The ISAKMP specification also provides guidance for using a more sophisticated key exchange protocol called *Oakley*, which is based on an authenticated Diffie-Hellman key exchange. Unlike SKIP, ISAKMP is intended to operate as an application-level protocol. This integrates poorly into some implementations as discussed in Section 7.3. However, ISAKMP uses the communications bandwidth more efficiently, since key management data isn't passed in every data packet.

- **Photuris**

  Photuris is a competing alternative to ISAKMP that also establishes security associations and exchanges keys, again using the Diffie-Hellman algorithm. The protocol is neither as flexible nor as complex as ISAKMP. Photuris is not designed to include a subset that simply and directly implements secret key-based session key exchanges. Although reference implementations of Photuris exist, many doubt it will progress much further toward standardization or adoption by vendors.

The distinctions between these alternatives have more to do with product availability and operating convenience than they do with security. Manual key management is available in any compliant IPSEC implementation. However, the manual management of secret keys becomes unwieldy as the number of communicating hosts grows large. Key exchange protocols based on public key techniques can handle communications between larger populations of encrypting hosts, but the product implementations are still maturing. Section 9.3.2 contains a discussion of the trade-offs between secret key and public key exchange techniques.

In addition to these standardized techniques, some vendors implement nonstandard key exchange protocols. Until recently this was the only reasonable approach for a vendor to take, since the specification documents and sample implementations for the key exchange protocols were not very mature. As discussed in Section 4.5.2, it can be difficult to assess the security of a product that uses a proprietary protocol.

S/WAN MANUAL KEYING: LEVEL 1 INTEROPERABILITY

Interoperability testing by the S/WAN Initiative has enjoyed the largest participation of any IPSEC testing. This is perhaps because "Level 1 interoperability" places the fewest requirements on an IPSEC implementation. This yields the greatest likelihood that systems will interoperate.

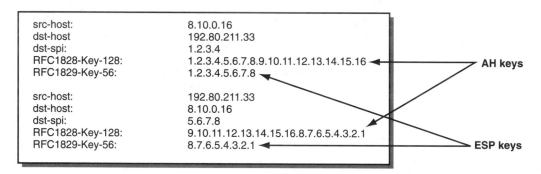

Figure 5-10: S/WAN FORMAT FOR SPECIFYING AN IPSEC SECURITY ASSOCIATION. This example contains two entries—one for data traveling in each direction. The two hosts sharing this association could both use this file to process the security association.

The Level 1 interoperability profile gives a more detailed description of an acceptable implementation than is spelled out in the published standards. Details are provided as to which options must be available and which capabilities might be omitted. Such profiles illustrate what you are likely to find in a compatible product and which features are less likely to work.

Level 1 key management is fully manual. A host's security associations are defined in a text file with a uniform format (Figure 5-10). All numbers are represented as decimal bytes. Numbers containing multiple bytes have decimal points separating the bytes. The file also shows that the same SPI value is used in both the AH and the ESP for a given security association.

5.6   Other TCP/IP Network Security Protocols

Here is a summary of other security protocols developed for TCP/IP to be integrated into the network protocol stack. These techniques were generally applied somewhere above the device driver interface and at or below the socket interface. Some did not even involve cryptography.

Like link encryption, network-layer crypto provides security without affecting the behavior of applications software. Existing software and operating procedures remain largely unaffected, except that interactions with untrusted hosts can be blocked

IPSO: IP SECURITY OPTION

The IP security option (IPSO) is an evolving series of protocols that insert "sensitivity labels" into IP packets. These labels work in conjunction with specially built, highly trusted routers and other network components that prevent sensitive information from reaching untrustworthy destinations. These protocols do not protect the information itself while in transit, since IPSO doesn't incorporate any form of crypto protection. IPSO simply puts markings in packets to prevent sensitive information from reaching an untrustworthy or risky location. It provides no protection if sensitive data does in fact encounter less trustworthy networks or hosts. IPSO-related protocols include Commercial IPSO (CIPSO), revised IPSO (RIPSO), and DNSIX (used in military applications).

SDNS: SECURE DATA NETWORK SYSTEM

The Secure Data Network System (SDNS) is a family of protocols developed to provide crypto protection to network traffic at a variety of protocol layers. Work in application-level protocols yielded the Message Security Protocol (MSP), which evolved into PEM, which is discussed further in Chapters 11 and 12. SDNS also developed lower level network and transport layer protocols: the SDNS security protocol for layer 3 (SP3) and the SDNS security protocol for layer 4 (SP4). The protocols were intended to work with internet protocols, but the principal objective during development was to provide strong security for the International Standards Organization (ISO) network protocol suite.

The SDNS protocol development process was largely funded by the NSA with the objective of protecting sensitive U.S. government and military communications. A handful of special-purpose security products were developed that used the protocols. Additional host-based implementations were developed during a series of technology demonstration projects in the late 1980s. Today, the HannaH protocol suite from SecureWare is one of the few remaining products based on the lower level SDNS protocols.

The SP3 protocol was designed to provide similar protections to the IPSEC protocols. Certain features of the ESP format are very similar to SP3. However, SP3 does not provide a separate authentication header.

The SP4 protocol was designed to provide security at the "transport" layer. In effect, it applied crypto services to socket connections instead of packets. This makes it similar in design and application to the SSL protocol described later.

Perhaps from today's perspective the SDNS protocols should have appealed to vendors and been incorporated into products long before IPSEC appeared. Two factors probably contributed to its commercial failure. First, there was relatively little potential for commercial Internet use at the time the SDNS protocols evolved. Some networks comprising the Internet backbone explicitly prohibited commercial use. Noncommercial Internet users had little to protect, so vendors had little market for security products. Second, the protocols' legacy with the NSA of the 1980s made commercial deployment difficult. Although the protocols were in fact published by the National Institute of Standards and Technology (NIST) as U.S. government standards, much of the supporting technical work was closely held by the NSA.

NETWORK LAYER SECURITY PROTOCOL (NLSP)

The ISO merged this variant of the SP3 protocol into their OSI protocol suite. Unfortunately, this protocol suffered from what unsympathetic observers might call the "OSI disease" of giving developers too many options. Without a focused, well-defined set of necessary services it was too daunting for vendors to design and build compatible products.

POINT-TO-POINT TUNNELING PROTOCOL (PPTP)

This protocol is an extension of the Point-to-Point Protocol (PPP), which is the protocol of choice when connecting dial-up serial modems to ISPs. PPTP tries to behave like a single, coherent link-level protocol while being carried on a mixture of link-level or higher level protocols. This allows it to carry a variety of Internet and non-Internet networking protocols between the devices that support it.

PPTP and PPP do not themselves provide crypto services. Such protections are defined by extension protocols. Sites can use the combination of a tunneling protocol and crypto services to protect traffic between sites. This provides the essential building blocks for a VPN. Several vendors, including Microsoft, have formed a group called the PPTP Forum that is developing a standard protocol profile that includes crypto protection. At present, Microsoft is recommending PPTP as a general solution for constructing VPNs and has announced plans to integrate it into future products.

SECURE SOCKETS LAYER (SSL)

Like the SP4 protocol developed for SDNS, the SSL protocol provides transport-layer encryption. SSL applies protection through a variant of the TCP socket interface. SSL is usually bundled with an application so that the underlying protocol stack simply needs to provide a socket interface with conventional TCP/IP networking services.

SSL was originally developed by Netscape Communications as part of their security package for the World Wide Web. The Netscape Commerce Server uses SSL to provide secure Web service and the Netscape Navigator provides the corresponding client. SSL is covered in detail in Chapter 9.

5.7   For Further Information

- **Atkinson, IPSEC specifications: RFCs 1825 ("Security Architecture for the Internet Protocol"), 1826 ("IP Authentication Header"), and 1827 ("IP Encapsulating Security Payload [ESP]")**
  ftp://ftp.internic.net/rfc/rfc1825.txt
  ftp://ftp.internic.net/rfc/rfc1826.txt
  ftp://ftp.internic.net/rfc/rfc1827.txt
  These are the authoritative descriptions of the IPSEC protocols. They are published as "requests for comments," or RFCs, by the IETF.

- **Metzger, Simpson, "IP Authentication using Keyed MD5"**
  ftp://ftp.internic.net/rfc/rfc1828.txt
  All AH implementations are required to support keyed MD5 as a possible choice for producing the cryptographic checksum. This describes how to format the AH when MD5 is used.

- **Metzger, Karn, Simpson, "The ESP DES-CBC Transform"**
  ftp://ftp.internic.net/rfc/rfc1829.txt
  All ESP implementations are required to support encryption using the DES in CBC mode as one of the available options. This describes how to format the ESP when DES CBC is used.

- **RSA Data Security, *S/WAN Interoperability Testing***
  http://www.rsadsi.com/swan
  A summary of interoperability testing performed on IPSEC implementations through the S/WAN Consortium. This identifies the interoperability participants and describes the technical profiles with which the systems are tested to comply.

Chapter

6

Virtual Private Networks

Only those defenses are good, certain and durable, which depend on yourself alone and your ability.

—Nicolo Machiavelli, *The Prince*

IN THIS CHAPTER

This chapter presents the modern, low-cost alternative to link encryption—the *virtual private network*, or VPN. This technique uses relatively low-cost, widely available access to public networks like the Internet to connect remote sites together safely. Like link encryption, a VPN can provide transparent access between sites for a broad range of protocols. Much of what is said will apply to both IPSEC and non-IPSEC solutions. The following topics are discussed:

- Security objectives and special issues for VPNs
- The concept of proxy encryption
- IPSEC encrypting router products for constructing VPNs
- Example VPN deployment with IPSEC

This chapter does not discuss controlled access to the Internet. That difficult topic is discussed in Chapter 7. This chapter concentrates on protecting your private network, and assumes that you are not interconnecting it with potentially hostile outside networks.

6.1 Security Objectives

The objectives pursued here for a VPN are similar to those provided by link encryption, though the issues of cost and simplicity are more important here.

- **Isolate a distributed network from outsiders.**
  The principal objectives are to prevent outsiders from interfering with messages sent among insiders and to block forged traffic from entering any of the network's sites. Insiders are trusted not to mount sophisticated attacks on internal computing resources. There is no immediate need for controlled access by outsiders or access to external, untrusted Internet sites.

- **Protect the privacy and integrity of messages traversing untrusted networks.**
  Traffic between sites is vulnerable to attacks like forgery and eavesdropping. Users may be transmitting passwords or valuable transactions between sites, so the traffic needs protection from outsiders.

- **Handle the whole range of internet protocols currently in use.**
  The sites that require protection are already making extensive use of networking software and protocols. It is necessary to support those capabilities. New security measures must not require extensive software replacement. Practically every widely used protocol today is either internet based or has a defined mechanism for using TCP/IP as its transport protocol.

- **Public Internet access is available, and cost is very important.**
  A high bandwidth, dedicated Internet connection is often available for a lower cost than a point-to-point leased line.

6.2 Basic Issues with VPNs

The essential differences between link-level crypto and network-level crypto show up as we use IPSEC as an alternative. For now we will treat them the same in the way they handle "outsiders;" that is, we will use IPSEC crypto to block outsider traffic from mingling with the shared, internal network.

- **Lower cost protection for traffic on untrustworthy network links.**
  An IPSEC encrypting router or similar device can use a connection to the public Internet to replace one or more leased lines connecting to other sites. Existing Internet protocol software does not have to be modified. The existing Internet backbone can route IPSEC-protected traffic since the packets conform to the IP protocol.

- **Security associations are between pairs of hosts.**
  In link encryption, the security association is between pairs of devices that talk across a connection of some sort, usually a telephone call or a leased line. In IPSEC, the security association is between pairs of IP hosts. Regardless of the path a packet follows between those two hosts, it will use the same keys and crypto procedures.

- **Outsiders will see more of your traffic than with link encryption.**
  Snooping incidents are rare on private leased lines, or at least they are very rarely publicized. Snooping incidents on the public Internet are common, so your encrypted traffic might be examined by unfriendly eyes. Depending on how your IPSEC is set up, outsiders might be able to see which hosts in one of your sites talks to which host in other sites. They will at least know how much traffic passes between your sites.

- **There is a cost trade-off against private leased lines.**
  A recent study commissioned by Sun Microsystems analyzed the financial implications of using IPSEC-based VPNs instead of dedicated private networks in two scenarios: a corporate frame relay backbone and a branch office leased line network. In the frame relay scenario the VPN approach yielded a 50% cost savings. In the private leased line scenario the VPN approach yielded a 23% cost savings.

6.3 Technology: IPSEC Proxy Cryptography

In *proxy cryptography,* a crypto service is shared among multiple entities, like users or hosts, that might otherwise have their own crypto services. IPSEC is designed so it can be installed on any host that uses the IP protocols. However, there often will be reasons not to run IPSEC on individual hosts. In particular, crypto processing requires a lot of resources and many hosts will reap significant performance benefits if IPSEC processing is performed elsewhere. Some older hosts might not have enough extra storage to hold the additional protocol software or to run it efficiently. Or perhaps it is too difficult to key all the hosts securely. Larger sites may have dozens or hundreds of hosts but not have the necessary resources to install IPSEC on every host.

Using IPSEC in a proxy mode means that message traffic of several hosts is all funneled through a single encrypting host (the *proxy*) before it traverses a potentially hostile network like the public Internet. The destination host itself might have IPSEC support or the messages may again travel through a proxy to have the IPSEC headers validated and removed.

Figure 6-1: DATA SENT BY CONVENTIONAL SOFTWARE IS PROTECTED WITH PROXY ENCRYPTION. Traffic between Alice, Bob, and Carl is protected with IPSEC headers applied by the proxy devices P1 and P2. Protections are added to packets leaving each site. On arrival, the IPSEC headers are validated and removed.

A typical proxy arrangement is shown in Figure 6-1. When Alice sends Bob a message, it is in plaintext while it traverses their respective local networks. When the message reaches the boundary between the local network and the Internet, it encounters the proxy device. Outbound from Alice, a message encounters device P1, which applies the IPSEC headers (Figure 6-2). The proxy device may be a router or a firewall; the latter is examined in more detail in Chapter 8. When the message

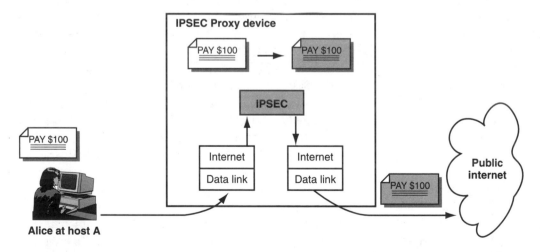

Figure 6-2: THE IPSEC PROXY IS SIMILAR TO AN IP ROUTER. Incoming plaintext packets enter the proxy on their way to an untrusted network and are routed through an IPSEC package where protections are added to them. Then packets are routed to the untrusted network.

arrives at Bob's site, it encounters proxy device P2, which validates and decrypts the IPSEC headers. The message is then forwarded, unprotected, to Bob's computer. No equipment at either site needed to deal with cryptography or keys except the proxy device itself. Since IPSEC crypto does not affect the routing information in an IP header, the untrusted Internet can route IPSEC traffic just as effectively as any unprotected traffic.

Typically the proxy devices establish and maintain individual security associations with one another. In other words, the proxy hosts in Figure 6-1 will use the same security association and related crypto keys regardless of whether Alice is communicating with Bob or with Carl. If the three colleagues all had IPSEC installed on their own workstations, Alice would have established separate security associations to talk to each. In theory, proxies could use separate end-to-end associations for each host, but this is complicated and less likely in practice. The simpler approach dramatically reduces the complexity of key management, since keys only need to be assigned to proxy hosts. However, the shared security association could open traffic to a *header cut-and-paste attack*, which is discussed in Section 6.5.1.

There are essentially two approaches to IPSEC proxies: *transport mode* and *tunnel mode*. In transport mode each IP packet carries the address of the ultimate source and destination hosts, as described in Chapter 5. To do this, the proxy device must apply the right security association to messages in a "wild card" mode, since a variety of end point hosts will share a single security association. In tunnel mode the ultimate host addresses are carried inside the ESP header, and the security association is clearly established between the proxy hosts alone.

6.3.1 ESP Tunnel Mode

In tunnel mode we establish an encrypted "tunnel" between two hosts. While this can be used between two hosts, its most obvious application is to proxy crypto. The encrypted tunnel is established between two proxy hosts, and all traffic between hosts served by those two proxy hosts will travel through that tunnel. When Alice tries to send a message to Bob, the packets travel to the proxy device P1, the entrance to the tunnel to Bob's site. Each IP packet traveling through the tunnel is encapsulated, IP headers and all, inside the encrypted portion of the ESP. This encapsulated packet is then sent to the host at the other end of the tunnel, proxy device P2. On receipt, P2 strips off the encryption and forwards the original IP packet to its real destination. Figure 6-3 illustrates the packet header encapsulation that takes place.

The handling of security associations is relatively straightforward with tunnel mode, particularly with inbound packets—those from an untrustworthy network like the Internet. The proxy device maintains a small number of security associations that identify all other proxy devices to which it can talk. It can quickly find

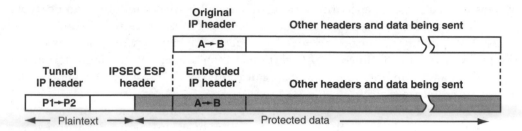

Figure 6-3: TUNNEL MODE ESP FOR HIDING IP PACKET ADDRESSES. In ESP tunnel mode the entire IP packet is encrypted and embedded in another IP packet sent between two "tunnel end point" hosts, P1 and P2. On receipt, P2 strips off the ESP encapsulation and delivers the packet.

the right security association for an inbound packet. The IP host address identifies the originating proxy device, and the SPI in the header selects the correct keying material. The decrypted and validated packet can then be passed to the IP routing software for delivery to its destination.

Tunneling appeals to many because it takes the extra step of hiding a packet's real source and destination addresses. ESP already hides what is being said; tunneling retains and encrypts the packet's original header, hiding who is talking as well. All an outsider can tell is that some amount of traffic is moving between the two sites. This subtle addition to site security is probably unnecessary for most applications, but it gives extra peace of mind to some sites. Another security benefit of the encapsulated header is that it foils header cut-and-paste attacks (see Section 6.5.1).

Extra security is never free. The cost of tunneling is that the packet must carry two IP headers instead of just one, as shown in Figure 6-3. This reduces communications efficiency somewhat, since more bits must be transmitted and cryptographically processed.

People familiar with TCP/IP routing might feel uneasy about how tunneling mode hides the IP header and ships the packet between sites. This is beneficial if the two sites are using unregistered IP host addresses, an increasingly common occurrence as the existing Internet address space fills up. The approach also provides a straightforward approach to proxy crypto. However, it also negates the benefits of IP routing. Packets that enter one end of an IPSEC tunnel must always be routed to the proxy host at the other end. There is no mechanism to redirect a tunnel mode packet if the tunnel's destination gets overloaded or crashes. On the other hand, if proxy devices at the destination can share security associations among one another (along with the corresponding crypto keys), then standard IP routing will deliver the packets to the other proxy device.

6.3.2 ESP Transport Mode

In transport mode we retain the original IP header when we apply the IPSEC crypto services at the proxy device. This reduces the communications overhead but increases the complexity of handling security associations. Transport mode discloses the actual source and destination of each packet. While this disclosure may be a problem in some situations, it can also allow packets to be routed among alternate, cooperating proxy devices.

Proxy behavior is similar to that with tunnel mode except that the end point IP addresses are not hidden. Correct packet delivery in transport mode depends on IP routing instead of explicit proxy addressing. This should work correctly since the only route should always travel through a proxy device. In other words, sites using proxies must use nothing but encrypting proxy devices for connecting to external networks, otherwise they may end up with a route that bypasses the proxies. Such a route will render the proxy encryption unreliable or make it fail completely. Also, it probably indicates that the site has unintended "backdoor connections" to the Internet (see Section 3.4.2).

With transport mode crypto it is relatively straightforward to establish separate proxy security associations between separate communicating host pairs. Packets traveling between Alice and Bob can be given different encryption than packets travelling between Alice and Carl. This helps block the header cut-and-paste attack, but it also increases the complexity of keying. Each communicating pair of workstations in different sites would need their own set of keying material on the proxy hosts. This brings back much of the keying complexity that proxy encryption should eliminate. The increased complexity is not justified however, since the cut-and-paste attack is also foiled by always using the AH

We can perform keying per proxy if there is a way to "wild card" the IP addresses that use a particular security association and its keying material. For example, proxy device P1 in Figure 6-1 would have a wild card security association that is used for all traffic to hosts behind proxy P2. When Alice sends her message to Bob, proxy P1 would look at its host address ("B") and match it with a security association. After applying the IPSEC headers, P1 sends the packet to the Internet, and it is eventually routed to P2. Unlike the case with tunneling, the IPSEC-protected packet does not contain the P2 address; the packet goes to P2 because the Internet itself routes traffic for host B through P2.

When the packet arrives at proxy device P2, the same wild card security association is identified, based on the packet's SPI and its destination address. This yields the same keying material that was used at P1 to construct the IPSEC headers. After P2 validates and removes the headers, it again forwards the plaintext packet, just like it does in tunnel mode.

6.4 Product Example: IPSEC Encrypting Router

An *encrypting router* is a device that encrypts enough of an IP packet to protect its data contents but leaves enough of it readable so that the packet can traverse the Internet. A variety of devices have been developed over the years to do network encryption and protect classified military traffic, including the ARPANET Private Line Interface, BLACKER, and Motorola's Network Encryption System. A small number of commercial products have also evolved as the Internet has evolved. Today, several vendors in the router and firewall markets provide products that can implement VPNs (Figure 6-4). But until the development of IPSEC, no security protocol gained broad enough vendor support to promise interoperability between different vendors' products.

IPSEC encrypting routers provide proxy encryption in transport mode, tunnel mode, or both. The routers allow the site to establish security associations with

Figure 6-4: AN ENCRYPTING ROUTER PRODUCT. This device connects a frame relay system and provides network encryption. Photo courtesy of Cylink Corporation.

other Internet sites and to protect all traffic with those sites by applying IPSEC authentication and encryption. All traffic to and from internal hosts is in plaintext form without IPSEC headers. All external traffic with the Internet must carry IPSEC headers or somehow be processed via an IPSEC security association. This yields a device with something very similar to the traditional "red/black separation" associated with link encryption (Section 3.2.1).

An IPSEC encrypting router needs a way to specify security associations with remote hosts along with the crypto material needed to support those associations. Routers should always support fully manual keying, since this is required by the standards and it provides the greatest promise for interoperability. Section 5.5 describes the basic requirements for IPSEC manual keying. Models that support automatic keying will need additional parameters depending on the keying protocol supported.

The router should allow for the distribution of manual keying material either on magnetic media (diskettes) or on paper. Magnetic media is probably best. Administrators never actually have to look at keys and there is less of a risk of mistyping the security association data. However, magnetic media are harder to produce and deliver. The file format for magnetic media should be similar in content to that suggested by the S/WAN Initiative (see Section 5.5). Paper copies of keying data can be generated and distributed efficiently and securely (see Section 4.4.3), and can be delivered via secure fax or even recited over the telephone in an emergency. Both diskettes and paper keys can be distributed via postal or parcel delivery services with similar levels of security.

6.4.1 Blocking Classic Internet Attacks

For many organizations, the only reason to connect to the Internet is to acquire a lower cost communications channel between trustworthy sites. This benefit is not worth the cost savings over other techniques (like link encryption) if it opens up the site to external attacks. Fortunately, an IPSEC encrypting router will block attacks from the Internet, either by hiding sensitive information under encryption or by blocking forged external traffic with packet authentication. The following is a summary of how a variety of well-known Internet attacks are blocked by an IPSEC encrypting router.

PASSWORD SNIFFING

Cautious Internet users have been aware of the risk of password sniffing for a very long time. It became an issue of broad concern in late 1993 when a large Internet service provider discovered that someone had secretly penetrated their system and installed *password sniffers*. A typical password sniffer is a program that collects the first hundred or so bytes transmitted on each connection passing through the host. This program often manages to intercept the login names and passwords used to connect to various hosts. Ever since, CERT's quarterly Internet security reports note that more sniffers have been found at various Internet sites.

ESP encryption protects all traffic from disclosure to outsiders, including reusable, secret passwords. If you have taken reasonable measures to secure your internal hosts against such attacks, this completes the task by protecting them from outsiders.

IP SPOOFING

The IP spoofing attack was made famous during the Christmas season of 1994 when Kevin Mitnick, holder of an impressive criminal record involving abuse of telephones and computers, allegedly penetrated a personal Internet site in southern California. The sophisticated attack caught the attention of Internet security experts, who dubbed it *IP spoofing*. Essentially, the attackers' host "spoofed" a vulnerable host into believing the attackers' messages came from a different, trusted host. The attackers exploited the misplaced trust and coerced the vulnerable host into letting the attackers in.

Such forgeries are detected during AH processing and are discarded. The attacking host does not have access to the crypto key needed to generate an acceptable AH for the forged packet.

IP HIJACKING

IP hijacking raised notice at roughly the same time as IP spoofing, and in fact it is similar to the attacks Kevin Mitnick performed many years earlier using vulnerable telephone switches. In this attack, an active, authenticated connection between two hosts is disrupted and the attacker takes the place of one of the hosts. One host is cut off and sees the connection drop. The other host cannot necessarily tell that anything changed. The attacker can then masquerade as the host that was cut off. For example, an attacker might cut off a legitimate user during an authenticated remote terminal session. The attacker takes the user's place and the server host does not know that commands are now coming from an attacker.

Connections with packets that are protected with an AH can not be hijacked successfully. Attackers could not continue using the session because they cannot generate the valid AH for a packet they produce. Valid packets for the connection can only come from a host that has the key required to generate an AH.

SYN FLOODING

SYN flooding first became significant in the fall of 1996, when simple programs to perform it appeared in hacker circles. A large Internet provider in New York City was attacked and essentially shut down for several days. The site was taken "off the air" by using up its available incoming connections without actually establishing any. The attackers sent the TCP "SYN" message to request a connection, but they never responded with the final message required to establish the connection fully. TCP software typically leaves such "half-open connections" around for a few minutes in the hope that the connection will be completed soon. Meanwhile attackers send additional SYN messages with varying, forged source addresses, each appearing to request its own connection. This uses up the available connections faster than the host can recover them. With all incoming connections used up, the host automatically refused connections to legitimate users.

This attack is blocked because the TCP SYN messages must have a legitimate AH with a valid cryptographic checksum. The attackers cannot generate numerous requests from random hosts because they cannot produce a legitimate AH for every such host. Attackers could, in theory, mount an SYN attack by replaying authentic SYNs that were sniffed during normal host operation. However, this would be very difficult to do, and would not work at all if the site periodically rekeys its associations and assigns new SPIs.

6.4.2 Product Security Requirements

Here are security requirements that can apply to encrypting routers, with the most important listed first:

1. **Separate network connections for plaintext and ciphertext.** Explicit red/black separation is always the safest approach. The most secure devices will reject everything without an IPSEC header that arrives on the encrypted side, except perhaps key exchange protocols.

2. **Crypto key length.** The device must provide a key size consistent with the sensitivity of the information you send across the data link. Review the questions in Section 2.3.4 for guidance on establishing your key size requirement.

3. **Crypto algorithms.** The default DES CBC encryption algorithm and MD5 hash algorithm are adequate for medium-risk uses of IPSEC. Higher risk uses may also be adequately protected by DES CBC if combined with automatic rekeying. Products will undoubtedly support other algorithms in the future, like the encryption algorithms noted in Section 2.3.2 and the hash algorithms discussed in Section 5.3.2.

4. **Application of the AH to the ESP.** The device must be able to apply both the AH and the ESP to every packet. Both need to be applied in order to block the classic attacks noted in the previous section.

5. **Security association configuration.** The router should support manual input of security associations, preferably from a file similar to the S/WAN format shown in Figure 5-10. There should also be a method of specifying "wild card" security associations to simplify proxy configuration.

6. **Protection against key leakage.** The router should provide mechanisms and recommendations to protect secret and private keys from being unnecessarily disclosed to operations personnel or others with incidental access to the device.

7. **Interoperability testing.** The router should have passed interoperability testing with one or more of the active interoperability groups. At present there is the S/WAN Initiative sponsored by RSA Data Security and the SKIP Forum sponsored by Sun Microsystems.

8. **Automatic rekeying.** The best devices will provide mechanisms to change the crypto key automatically and periodically or whenever a connection is established. Ideally such devices should use one of the proposed IPSEC keying protocols so that it will interoperate with a variety of vendors' products. Automatic rekeying is particularly important for high-risk and critical applications.

9. **Replay protection.** This is not currently a standard feature in IPSEC products that comply with the protocol standards, though it is probably going to be added to future revisions of the IPSEC protocols. Some vendors currently offer nonstandard IPSEC variants that provide some protection against replay.

10. **Event logging and incident detection.** The IPSEC protocols establish requirements for logging failures encountered when processing a header. Be sure that the router in fact logs these packets and can report on such events. Ideally the router should be able to generate some sort of alarm if some persistent activity takes place that may indicate a systematic attempt to breach site security.

11. **IP tunneling support.** The device should support the IP tunneling mode of IPSEC. This disguises all addressing information except what is absolutely necessary to deliver the packet between sites. This mechanism is particularly beneficial when the two sites aren't using registered Internet host addresses.

6.5 Deployment Example: Site-to-Site Encryption

This example uses IPSEC technology to protect traffic moving between pairs of sites in a single, cooperating corporate network. Users of the network should see no difference in behavior between this configuration and the deployment based on link encryption that is described in Section 3.4. Traffic inside the network is generally plaintext and protection is handled with techniques other than IPSEC. When traffic must move between sites it is protected with IPSEC headers. Inbound traffic either contains valid IPSEC headers or it is discarded. A two-site VPN is shown in Figure 6-5.

Physical security for this environment is similar to that for link encryption. As shown in Figure 6-6, the hosts inside the sites reside inside the site's physical perimeter. All links to outside systems must go through encrypting routers. The connection between the site's internal networks and the external networks should be in locked machine rooms with restricted access. Individuals authorized to use computers within the site do not need access to the encrypting routers. Such access should be strictly restricted to individuals who are required to administer and maintain the routers. This reduces the risk of accidentally or intentionally disclosing the crypto keys being used, as well as the risk of encryption being disabled or bypassed.

There must be *no* links to outside systems except those that go through encrypting routers. Any "backdoor" connections open the site to attacks like those described in Section 6.4.1. Back doors also make it possible that site traffic will traverse the Internet without IPSEC protection. If transport mode proxies are

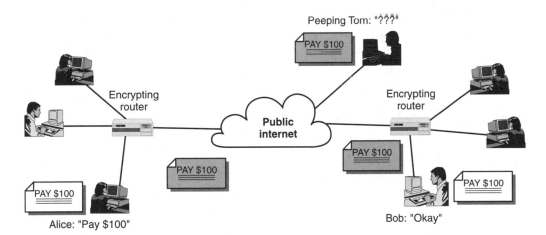

Figure 6-5: A VPN USES THE UNTRUSTED PUBLIC INTERNET TO CARRY MESSAGES SAFELY.
Only messages validated by the encrypting router will enter or leave the sites. Encryption and authentication prevent outsiders like Peeping Tom from reading or forging messages.

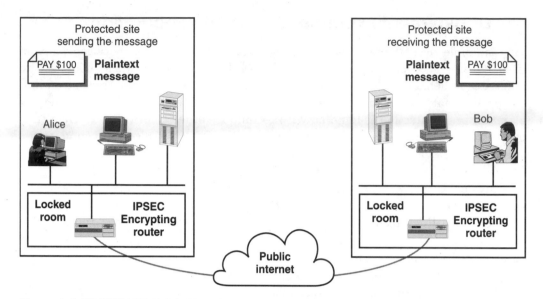

Figure 6-6: HARDWARE ARRANGEMENT FOR IPSEC ENCRYPTING ROUTER. The site's perimeter protects the hosts from unauthorized access. Like a link encryptor, the encrypting router must be further protected since it contains secret keying material and must not be bypassed.

used, there is also a risk of bypassing the proxy at only one site—a situation that will probably prevent traffic flow. If the proxy is bypassed by an outbound packet, the destination proxy will reject it since it lacks the required IPSEC headers. If the proxy is bypassed by inbound traffic, the packets will arrive at the destination host with the IPSEC headers still in place. Older IP implementations will almost certainly discard such packets since the IPSEC protocols won't be recognized. If the packet is encrypted, the destination host will still discard it in most cases since the host won't have the right crypto keys for the security association.

VPN TOPOLOGY AND KEY ASSIGNMENT

Key assignment is the same as for link encryption: You establish a set of keys for each link. With IPSEC, all sites are probably connected to the Internet and could conceivably communicate directly with any other site. If secret keys are being used, key assignment and management can get complicated. Many enterprises naturally expect that every site on the VPN should be able to send traffic directly to every other site. As the number of sites grow, the number of keys grows very rapidly. The total number of keys will be roughly the square of the number of sites.

However, enterprises that use secret keys can use simpler approaches. If the IPSEC VPN is replacing a previously existing, leased line network, then a reasonable first step is to establish security associations between the same sites that had direct leased lines. This yields some inefficiency, since some traffic will need to make an IPSEC-protected hop more than once. Additional security associations can be established when traffic patterns warrant direct links.

Many organizations already implement a "star" or "hub-and-spoke" topology in their network traffic patterns. The enterprise network in Figure 6-7 began with a star topology and then evolved. There is a central site, perhaps the home office, and all other geographically remote sites tend to send their network traffic to the central site. Security associations and their corresponding keys are assigned according to the permitted traffic flow. Keys K1 through K5 allow traffic to flow from remote offices and business associates (the bank) to the main office. After a review of network usage showed that Plant #1 and Plant #2 exchanged a lot of messages, they established K6, an additional security association that allows the plants to communicate directly.

Some large organizations even establish network flow restrictions along those lines when typical organizational operations are centralized. This is sometimes seen as a security measure, particularly if users at one branch office really don't have a particular need to access another branch office directly. Such restrictions are probably reasonable if all shared resources really reside in the central office. This arrangement provides a measure of "least privilege," increasing internal security.

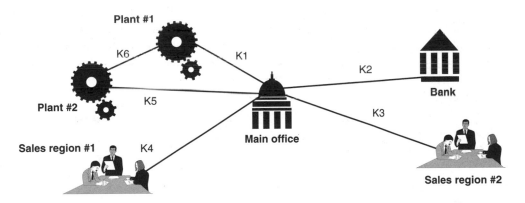

Figure 6-7: STAR OR "HUB-AND-SPOKE" SECURITY ASSOCIATION TOPOLOGY. In this example, the assignment of IPSEC security associations causes all IPSEC-protected traffic to be routed from distant sites and outside organizations directly to the main office. Without a security association, a given site cannot directly route IPSEC traffic to another site. IP-level routing can then pass traffic between distant sites. If two specific distant sites exchange a lot of traffic, it may be worthwhile to establish an additional security association between the two sites (K6).

Secret key techniques work reasonably well for star topologies and for other network topologies with a relatively small number of interconnecting links. Unfortunately, secret keys are very hard to manage as the number of communicating host pairs gets large. In such situations you must look at public key techniques for key exchange (Chapter 9). Public key systems require a minimal amount of shared information in order to exchange keys securely with any other device in a community. The trade-offs between these different techniques are examined in Section 9.3.2.

6.5.1 Header Usage and Security

The IPSEC headers were explicitly designed to allow them to be used individually. There are important trade-offs to be considered when omitting one or the other. In some places the IPSEC standards recommend using the AH to protect the ESP, although it is occasionally suggested that the opposite order could be useful. In practice, it is best to use both headers, and to use them in the recommended order.

In theory, sites could achieve some security benefits by using just one of the two headers. In practice, however, the benefits seem unlikely to justify the risks. Separately, the AH and ESP provide some protections, but the protections are most effective when both headers are used.

OMITTING THE ESP

The message integrity provided by the AH may be the principal security requirement in many business environments, but such organizations also need some measure of confidentiality. Without the ESP, it is possible to eavesdrop on the authenticated data. This will pose a threat in computing environments for as long as reusable, secret passwords are used. Most commercial software systems still rely on them heavily. Today most database servers use reusable passwords to enforce access control. The same is true for off-the-shelf server software of all kinds. The integrity of internal processing depends on correctly authenticating users, which in turn depends on the secrecy of passwords. In practice, then, the ESP is necessary for most installations.

OMITTING THE AH

The ESP protects against disclosure, but it does not generally protect against modification. As illustrated with link encryptors in Section 3.2.3, there are several techniques for modifying or otherwise exploiting encrypted data without extracting the key. The ESP is particularly vulnerable to a disturbing header cut-and-paste attack. Data encrypted with the CBC mode used in the default ESP is vulnerable to having data cut out or truncated, though this will usually produce some garbage at the deletion point. In practice, the AH provides the only reliable protection against modification.

HEADER CUT-AND-PASTE ATTACKS ON PROXY CRYPTO

The *header cut-and-paste attack* plays a trick on the IPSEC proxy by making it encrypt or decrypt someone else's data. The result allows the trickster either to forge a message or to eavesdrop on an encrypted one. Both situations require an accomplice inside one of the secure sites. Most organizations grudgingly admit they must tolerate some level of insider threat; however, the potential risks of some of these attacks deserve a defense.

Both forms of the attack, forgery and eavesdropping, are described in a paper by Steven Bellovin. The eavesdropping is the most automatic and requires the least amount of collusion by the insider. This makes it a relatively likely scenario, so we will examine it here.

We set the stage with an IPSEC VPN that connects two remote sites, shown in Figure 6-8. The encrypting routers are configured to only use an encrypting ESP; the AH is not used at all. Alice sends confidential messages to Carl, and certain

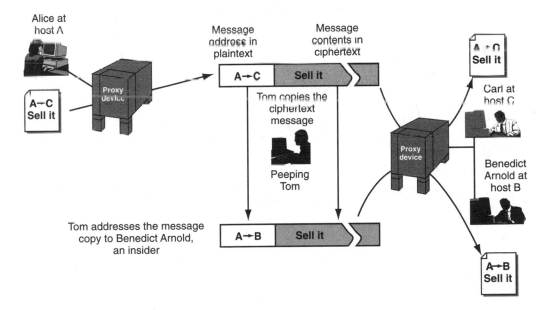

Figure 6-8: HEADER CUT-AND-PASTE ATTACK ON PROXY VPN TRAFFIC. Peeping Tom makes copies of all encrypted packets sent from Alice to Carl and forwards the copies to Benedict Arnold by changing the messages' destination IP address to Arnold's workstation. Each copy is decrypted when it passes through the proxy, so Arnold receives copies of all messages from Alice to Carl.

third parties seek to benefit by eavesdropping on Alice's messages to Carl. They do so with an automated attack that operates on ciphertext intercepted on the Internet and retransmitted to Carl's site.

The attack causes a plaintext copy of every message Alice sends to Carl to also be sent to Benedict Arnold, a subverted insider at Carl's site, courtesy of Peeping Tom. Without this attack, Arnold might have to do something risky in order to collect this data, like break into Carl's office and fiddle with his computer or install a sniffer somewhere. This is more than Arnold is capable of doing reliably without detection. However, Arnold can reliably collect packets at his computer. So Peeping Tom, an outsider, arranges to send copies of all of Alice's messages to Arnold's computer.

Tom implements this particular attack by installing a "cut-and-paste repeater" program on a routing host that carries the traffic between proxy A and proxy B. The repeater copies the ESP out of packets destined for Carl's machine and inserts them into new packets destined for Arnold. When these copied packets arrive at proxy B they are decrypted like any other packet and are delivered as addressed— to Arnold's machine.

The cut-and-paste attack is made possible by two general problems with the VPN's configuration—one fixable and one chronic. The fixable problem is that there is no mechanism to ensure the integrity of packet addresses as the data traverses the untrusted Internet. The chronic problem is that crypto transforms are being shared by a population of users that don't necessarily want to share data with one another. However, the chronic problem is rarely addressed in commercial environments.

At first glance it might appear that we could use ESP tunneling to hide the destination address under encryption. There are shortcomings to this since some encryption transforms are vulnerable to rewrite attacks. We might expect this to confound most attackers and be particularly effective when the default DES CBC transform is used. If Peeping Tom can intercept a tunneled packet traveling between Alice and Benedict Arnold, he can stitch that together with a packet from Alice to Carl to construct a tunneled packet. The technique isn't reliable but will recover data even when used with DES CBC.

There are two security measures to take against header cut-and-paste attacks:

1. Use the AH since it validates both the IP addresses and the message contents. When the destination address of a signed and encrypted packet is changed to point to a different host, the hash value in the AH will no longer match the data contents. This will cause the modified packet to be discarded during AH processing.

2. Assign unique security associations to different pairs of communicating hosts. This solution is consistent with the security architecture of IPSEC, but it also places the heaviest burden on administrators. Good security technology that is hard to use rarely yields good security in practice.

6.5.2 Deployment Security Requirements

Here are the requirements for constructing a VPN using IPSEC encrypting routers:

1. **Effective IPSEC router.** Select an encrypting router after reviewing them against the requirements in Section 6.4.2.

2. **Effective physical site protection.** The requirements here are the same as those for IP-routed link encryptors. Review the deployment security requirements listed in Section 3.4.3. The principal difference is that an encrypting router combines the encryptor and the router into a single device.

3. **Both AH and ESP protect all traffic.** The ESP protects reusable passwords and other sensitive information that is exchanged between protected sites. The AH protects any transactions involving valuables and prevents changes that might cause other types of damage. Neither can substitute for the other.

4. **Incident detection and handling.** Establish mechanisms and procedures to monitor IPSEC processing and to respond promptly to attacks on it. A good IPSEC encrypting device will log any unusual behavior. Use that information to ensure that you are not under attack.

5. **Automatic rekeying.** The VPN should periodically rekey all IPSEC security associations and assign new SPIs for use in the protocol headers. This increases the security provided by the crypto services and also protects against an SYN flood replay attack. Rekeying is particularly important if data security would benefit from a longer key length than your equipment can support. Rekeying can at least limit the amount of data disclosed if a key is recovered and it prevents a real-time attack based on a previously recovered key.

6.6 For Further Information

- **Atkinson, "IP Encapsulating Security Payload (ESP)"**
  ftp://ftp.internic.net/rfc/rfc1827.txt
  Describes the ESP format in general and tunneling behavior in particular.

- **Bellovin, *Problem Areas for the IP Security Protocols***
  ftp://ftp.research.att.com/dist/smb/badesp.ps
  A compendium of situations in which IPSEC protocols don't provide the security the designers expected. Although the paper doesn't explicitly discuss the implications of proxies, some of the problems are especially serious there.

Remote Access with IPSEC

He is most free from danger, who, even when safe, is on his guard.

—Publilius Syrus

IN THIS CHAPTER

This chapter explores how to use IPSEC to protect TCP/IP traffic with remote, possibly mobile hosts like home computers and laptops. A software package we will call the *IPSEC client* provides IPSEC protection to traffic between the client and a secure remote site using IPSEC. The following topics are discussed:

- Security objectives and basic issues faced by remote hosts
- Overview of IPSEC client software
- Example deployment of mobile IPSEC hosts

7.1 Security Objectives

For the most part, the objective is to support numerous potentially mobile hosts in a VPN. Thus, the objectives are very similar to those in Chapter 6.

- **Give traveling Internet clients access to the enterprise's internal network.**
  Associates of your organization need to access computers remotely without exposing the site or their transmissions to serious Internet attacks. You need to prevent outsiders from reading or interfering with messages sent among insiders, and to block forged traffic from entering any of the network's sites.

- **Handle the whole range of Internet protocols currently in use.**
  The central site makes extensive use of a broad range of TCP/IP protocols, and remote hosts need to access these services. You do not want to do extensive software replacement in order to provide security.

- **Public Internet access is available, and cost is very important.**
  A fundamental shortcoming of link encryption is that it requires sites to install expensive, dedicated links between sites or else it must rely on low-speed dial-up connections. Most organizations can acquire a high bandwidth, dedicated Internet connection for a lower cost than a point-to-point leased line.

7.2 Basic Issues with IPSEC Clients

Remote and mobile clients present several issues beyond those of VPNs and proxy crypto.

- **Client security**
  The security of the underlying crypto and the confidentiality of the keys can, in theory, be subverted by a variety of techniques ranging from specialized viruses to simple, physical theft. This becomes a particularly serious risk when dealing with host computers outside the physical protection of the organization. Computers at home and on the road are broadly vulnerable to physical theft or other forms of surreptitious access.

- **Floating security associations**
  The VPNs discussed in the previous chapter usually connect sites together that have fixed IP host addresses. Mobile and home-based hosts do not necessarily have fixed IP addresses. Some dial-in service providers assign IP addresses only for the duration of a dial-in phone connection. Some traveling laptops may need to connect via different service providers and each will need to assign to the laptop a different address. The security association must be with the mobile host itself and not with the host's IP address.

- **IPSEC client software packaging**
  IPSEC client software may be bundled with a full TCP/IP network stack implementation or be provided by itself as a "shim" implementation. Some host operating systems will be more supportive of one form than the other.

7.3 Product Example: IPSEC Client

An IPSEC client is a software package that provides IPSEC protections for TCP/IP network traffic on a workstation or laptop. The client may include full TCP/IP as well as IPSEC, or it may be packaged as a shim that fits between an existing TCP/IP stack and the host computer's device drivers. The client provides IPSEC protection without affecting the behavior of existing applications or device drivers. Protection is applied according to the security associations established by the workstation's operator. Example IPSEC client products include Secure Computing's NetCourier and FTP Software's VIP Secure Client.

Figure 7-1 illustrates the basic operation. Alice produces a message for Bob using a TCP/IP application. The application passes the message to the TCP/IP stack. As individual packets pass through IPSEC processing, they are protected if so required by the established security associations. The data link layer receives protected packets for transmission to the message recipient, Bob. The data link layer on Bob's machine passes the packets upward through the protocol layers until they reach IPSEC processing, where the IPSEC headers are processed, validated, and removed. The application software on Bob's machine receives the plaintext data from Alice.

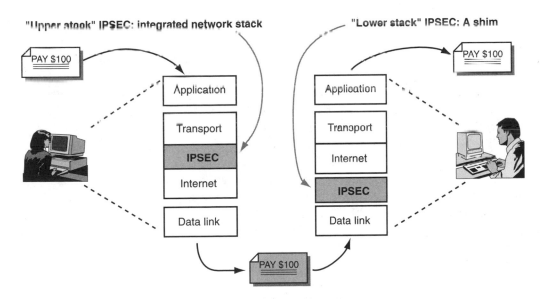

Figure 7-1: IPSEC CLIENT SOFTWARE FOR END USER WORKSTATIONS AND LAPTOPS. IPSEC client software is transparent to applications and to the data link interface. IPSEC can be integrated into the TCP/IP stack at a higher point ("upper stack") to provide more flexibility with security associations. However, "lower stack" implementations are easier to integrate into hosts using existing TCP/IP products.

Figure 7-1 also illustrates different approaches for building and integrating IPSEC into the workstation software. In the "upper stack" approach, IPSEC is integrated directly into the TCP/IP stack, while in the "lower stack" approach it is a separate package residing between an existing TCP/IP stack and the network device drivers. While any IPSEC package should be able to interoperate with any other regardless of the design, these different approaches have different strengths.

The upper stack approach is best for sophisticated systems like Unix or Windows NT, since it can allow software with differing security attributes to use separate security associations. For example, a workstation operator might want to run without IPSEC protection in most cases, but require IPSEC encryption when operating in an administrative role like "root." The association between network data and the user that created it is better preserved at higher levels of the protocol stack. However, an upper stack implementation must be integrated into the TCP/IP protocol software itself. This yields a more complex product and forces users to replace the TCP/IP stack they currently use. This is not always a realistic alternative.

In the "lower stack" approach, IPSEC appears at a lower point in the protocol stack, typically between the data link device drivers and an existing TCP/IP network stack. This approach is often referred to as a *shim*. David Wagner and Steve Bellovin used the phrase "bump in the stack" to describe a pilot implementation they developed using this approach. The shim uses the device driver interface between the existing TCP/IP stack and the device drivers. This is generally a very well-defined interface. Unlike upper stack implementations, the shim does not replace the existing TCP/IP stack. This saves the user from the dilemma of choosing between IPSEC security and the operational benefits of other TCP/IP implementations. Also, the shim is generally a much simpler software component to construct and maintain than a package including full TCP/IP support.

Balanced against these benefits, the shim forces a much more rigid handling of security associations. The shim can only enforce security associations at the host IP address level, since that is the only information it has for making its decisions. User identities cannot be associated with network data since such information is generally lost at these lower levels of the TCP/IP stack.

The packaging of an IPSEC client does not reliably indicate whether the implementation is an upper stack or lower stack one. While a shim will always be a lower stack implementation, IPSEC integrated into a TCP/IP network stack will not always provide an upper stack implementation. Some vendors have used a lower stack reference implementation to add IPSEC to an existing TCP/IP stack. The resulting product is packaged like an upper stack implementation but behaves like a lower stack implementation. Given this state of affairs, it is safest to assume that typical IPSEC products provide lower stack capabilities and, at best, support host-based security associations.

7.3.1 Client Security Associations

Security association handling for IPSEC clients is closer to the original intent of IPSEC than that for proxy implementations. However, there are some special considerations. Client security associations need to be generated centrally and often in large numbers. Also, client IP addresses are likely to vary, particularly when associated with a traveling laptop.

SITE-BASED ASSIGNMENTS

A typical IPSEC client application is to protect mobile users when connecting to a central site (Figure 7-2). The most practical way to do this is to allow the central site to generate all IPSEC security association parameters needed and to provide a mechanism to import them into the client. For example, the central site could generate security association data in S/WAN format (see Figure 5-10) and send the appropriate information to each client user. The IPSEC architecture is designed on the assumption that hosts assign the SPI for inbound IPSEC headers, but the essential requirement is simply that inbound SPIs be unique. Operationally it will probably work best if the central site generates keying material and assigns the SPIs to use them.

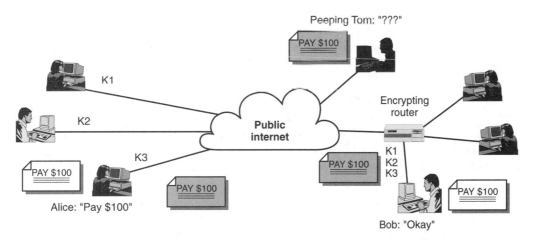

Figure 7-2: IPSEC CLIENTS SAFELY EXCHANGE MESSAGES WITH AN IPSEC CENTRAL SITE.
The clients generate and accept IPSEC-protected traffic only when communicating with the central site. Encryption and authentication prevent outsiders like Peeping Tom from reading or forging messages.

CLIENT MOBILITY

Unlike VPN hosts, IPSEC clients occasionally will have variable IP host addresses. Most mobile clients will access their ISP via a dial-in phone line. In some cases these clients will use a unique, permanently assigned IP address. However, ISPs that use the Dynamic Host Configuration Protocol (DHCP) will assign the client an address that is good only for the duration of the dial-in phone call. In other cases, a traveling client might use a variety of ISPs according to location. Each ISP will have to assign a different IP address to the mobile host. Thus, the client's security association with the central site has to be able to work with a variety of IP addresses, and the addresses might not be known ahead of time.

One approach for dealing with this is for the client not to make assumptions regarding its local IP address. This requires an extension to the S/WAN security association format to identify when the source or destination addresses refer to the client's host. There may also be a need to use a wild card specification of the central site addresses, particularly if an IPSEC proxy is being used. This is discussed in the previous chapter.

7.3.2 Client Self-Defense on the Internet

When a client connects to the Internet it becomes "just another host" and thus can become a target of attack. Fortunately, clients are less of a target than servers for two reasons. First, clients belonging to typical users are not perceived to be worthwhile targets, since people rarely keep items of real value on their home computers or laptops. Second, clients lack the continuous accessibility of servers. They aren't always on-line either, because they are turned off or because they connect via a dial-up telephone line that is not in constant use. In many cases a client's IP address may change from one session to the next, so that even if attackers wanted to target a particular individual, they might not be able to identify the client when it does come on-line.

Despite all this, some client systems are at risk and need to protect themselves. The simple fact that a client contains IPSEC keying material that gives it access to a site may make it an interesting target to attackers. The presence of keying material is clearly broadcast the moment your client starts talking with the central site—why use IPSEC headers if you don't have the keying material to make them work?

There are two general approaches to protecting your client system from Internet attacks: either you block all communications that don't use IPSEC or you configure the rest of your system to resist Internet attacks. The former approach is the most secure, but it blocks you from being able to access public Internet resources. The latter approach is more complicated and thus less reliable. However, the benefits of Internet access will probably lead many users to take the risk.

The safest approach is to program the client to accept only valid, IPSEC-protected messages. Different client packages may require different procedures to set this up. Ideally, the client should have a specific configuration option that tells it to reject all non-IPSEC packets. In the worst case it may be necessary to set up a wild card security association to capture all hosts not specified in other security associations. This will cause all traffic from those hosts to be rejected. In most cases the traffic won't contain IPSEC headers and will be rejected simply on that basis. If packets do contain IPSEC headers, they still will be rejected since there is no way for the hosts to know the key you assigned to the wild card security association.

If for some reason the client system cannot block all access by public Internet hosts, then other protective measures should be taken. In particular, you should take a close look at every TCP/IP software component residing on the client and ensure that it is configured in a safe manner. This difficult problem is discussed further in Section 7.4.1.

7.3.3 Client Theft and Key Protection

The security of a computer system depends heavily on its physical security. No defenses are effective unless we keep the hardware away from potentially hostile individuals. In most environments we depend heavily on physical security to protect the computer's software from subversion and to protect any private or secret keys from disclosure. This makes sense in offices where walls, doors, locks, alarms, and even guards keep outsiders away.

Portable systems, however, are a different matter. Laptop theft is a big business, and some have estimated that as many as 10% of all laptops are stolen. Rumors claim that laptops stolen in particularly interesting locations, like Washington National Airport, command as much as $10,000 from buyers hoping to recover valuable information from them, even though such recovery may also be illegal under trade secret laws. Another report claims that there is a standing bounty of $80,000 for any laptop belonging to a Fortune 100 executive. Laptops are extremely attractive targets of theft, and client software security must take that into account.

The principal risk from a crypto standpoint is that the thief will recover and use the keying material that enables the client's IPSEC connection. In the worst case this could allow the thief to masquerade as the laptop owner. Some organizations that rely heavily on laptops for traveling agents often will set up a fully automated connection so that the owner doesn't need to provide any passwords or other error-prone interactions. While this is a boon for ease of use, it also lets anyone possessing the laptop, whether legitimately or through theft, to look like a legitimate user. In some applications this may be a necessary security trade-off, but a reasonable client package must also support stronger protection.

There are essentially three techniques for protecting keys from theft (Figure 7-3):

1. Store the keys on a removable device like a diskette and carry it separately from the client. If the client gets stolen, the thief won't have the keys.

2. Encrypt the keys with a secret password or phrase and require the client to verify the password before IPSEC can be used.

3. Encrypt the keys with a secret password or phrase and let IPSEC processing fail if the wrong password is used. This is the most secure approach.

The removable key device approach is risky. Client software that uses this approach should contain a mechanism to remind users automatically to remove the key device and store it in a safe place. However, the "safe place" is too likely to be the case that carries the laptop, either through accident or carelessness. Furthermore, the key device itself is an attractive target and must be carefully protected.

The password gives more reliable protection than the removable keys as long as it actually *encrypts* the keys. It is not enough for the software simply to collect and validate the password before using the keys. If the keys are "hidden" but not encrypted, then a reasonably motivated attacker will simply pick apart the client software files and extract the key directly. The keys should be stored in a state that makes them completely unusable unless the correct password is provided. Ideally

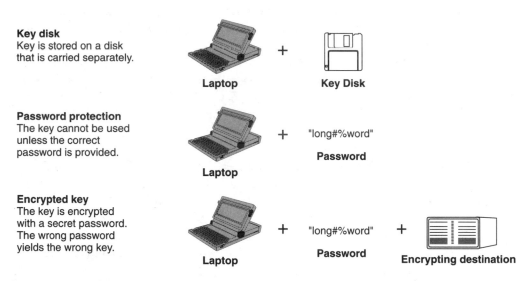

Key disk
Key is stored on a disk
that is carried separately.

Laptop   +   **Key Disk**

Password protection
The key cannot be used
unless the correct
password is provided.

Laptop   +   "long#%word"
                   Password

Encrypted key
The key is encrypted
with a secret password.
The wrong password
yields the wrong key.

Laptop   +   "long#%word"   +   **Encrypting destination**
                   Password

Figure 7-3: ALTERNATIVES TO PROTECT A LAPTOP'S CRYPTO KEYS FROM THEFT. The goal is to keep a thief from recovering and using the client's crypto keys. We increase security by putting only part of the information on the laptop itself and requiring more interaction to verify the correct key.

they should be encrypted with a strong crypto algorithm. The password is used as the algorithm's key.

If the client's keys are encrypted, the attacker can only recover them by exhaustively testing plausible password values. The attacker could write a program that takes the encrypted form of your keys and runs the decryption algorithm to guess the password through brute force. The safety of the keys then relies on the unpredictability of the password. A smart attacker will start by checking shorter, plausible passwords first. Refer to Table 2-2 to see how quickly an attacker can exhaustively search the possible choices for a four-letter password, and how much harder it is to search all possible eight-character passwords. Longer phrases may be easier to remember and pose a more daunting computational challenge. The client should give you as much latitude as possible for choosing a memorable and long password or phrase.

The client software can make matters even more difficult if there is no quick and unobtrusive way to tell if the decrypted result is in fact the correct password. This yields the third and most secure approach. The client software collects the password from the user, applies it to the encrypted keying material, and then uses the decrypted result as its operating keys. If the password was correct, communications proceed normally. If the password is wrong, all packets will be discarded by the central site. Attempts to find the password through brute force are discouraged because the central site must validate the guessed password. The brute force search would generate enormous numbers of invalid IPSEC packets that would reveal the penetration attempt to the central site.

Unfortunately, this approach makes innocent password errors very user hostile. The incorrect password will cause the packets to be discarded on receipt, and this will appear the same as a host or network communication problem. The user will not get a clear indication that the password was wrong.

An important point of the last approach is in "who decides" if the password is correct or not. If the client is solely responsible for deciding, then users must either use long, hard-to-guess passwords or run the risk of losing stolen keys to a brute force search. However, this is far more usable since errors by legitimate users are easier to identify. If the client must send IPSEC messages to the server, the server can detect brute force penetration attempts. On the other hand, if a legitimate user enters the wrong password and thereby generates the wrong key, the resulting error condition will be hard to distinguish from other types of communications failures.

7.3.4 Product Security Requirements

Here is a list of security requirements for IPSEC clients, listed with the most important requirements first.

1. **Compatible IPSEC configuration parameters.** Since an IPSEC client is generally used to communicate with specific IPSEC-capable sites, it is important to match the client's capabilities to the site's encrypting server. Crucial parameters include

   • Headers used (in other words AH, ESP, or preferably both)

   • Order in which the headers are applied (preferably the AH applied to the ESP)

   • AH cryptographic checksum algorithm and key length

   • ESP crypto algorithm and key length

   • Choice of ESP tunnel mode or transport mode

   • Use of key exchange protocol, if any

2. **Clear indication when IPSEC is working.** The client software system must provide a clear indication that encryption and authentication are active and being used. This is the old problem of "crypto bypass." You don't want the system to transmit your data unless you know it is being properly protected.

3. **Download security associations.** A busy central site will probably need to generate security associations in batches and distribute the associated crypto material on paper or diskettes. The client needs to be able to install the complete specification of a security association as generated by the site.

4. **Mobile security associations.** The client must be flexible enough to handle dynamically assigned IP addresses. Users at home or on the road cannot depend on having a single, preassigned IP address. The client must be able to apply its security associations correctly, even though its own IP address may change when it uses a particular association.

5. **Theft protection.** The client must provide mechanisms to protect the keying material from theft. The most effective and least convenient method is to encrypt the keys with a password so that the central site rejects the client's messages if the password is incorrect. Protection should be optional since it may be unnecessary and interfere with operations in some cases.

6. **Automatic rekeying.** The best devices will provide mechanisms to change the crypto key automatically and periodically or whenever a connection is established. If your client can do this, compare its capabilities against the automatic rekey requirements listed in Section 4.5.3. Also review its capabilities against the following:

   • Passed the compatibility tests using one of the proposed, standard IPSEC keying protocols

- Can dynamically assign new SPI numbers during rekeying

- Uses a cryptographically strong random key generation procedure to generate its keys

7. **Explicit blocking of non-IPSEC traffic.** Client users that are especially cautious or especially at risk will want to block communications with all hosts except those that have an explicit security association with them. This is done most reliably if the client has a specific configuration option for it.

7.4 Deployment Example: Client-to-Server Site Access

In this example, we use IPSEC clients to protect traffic between a central site and remote hosts. The central site has an IPSEC encrypting router or a similar IPSEC device, used as described for site-to-site encryption in Section 6.5. As shown in Figure 7-2, the principal difference is that the communicating hosts are arranged in a "star," with the central site in the middle. The central site assigns security associations and keys to the individual clients. Incoming traffic that uses assigned associations is then admitted to the site. All other traffic is blocked.

The IPSEC protections described in Section 6.4.1. are thus provided to remote clients as they communicate with the central site. Password sniffing is no problem since ESP encryption will protect secret passwords from disclosure. IP spoofing, either to fool a client or to fool the central server, is blocked by authentication of packet IP addresses. An attacker cannot forge an acceptable IP packet without knowing the key being used in the AH. IP hijacking is also foiled by authentication. Even if the attacker is able to take over the client's IP address completely, the attacker can't generate an AH that the central site will accept or even one that the client will accept. SYN flooding also fails since the SYN won't be processed unless the packet's AH is authentic. Client-level IPSEC thus provides a broad and effective level of protection to remote hosts and traveling users.

However, security always comes with a price. Since crypto protections apply complex mathematical operations to every bit of protected data, message processing is always slower when you use IPSEC. For some applications, like X Windows, the slowdown might render the service unusable. However, the actual effect depends on how powerful the particular host might be and the speed of the communications link being used. Faster hosts used with slower links might not see any performance degradation since IPSEC processing might be faster than the data link.

Another shortcoming is that IPSEC protection occasionally will be applied even when not really needed. The deployment described here applies IPSEC protection automatically whenever there is a security association in place between the client and the central site. Thus, traffic is protected between the client and server regardless of whether the messages really need protection or not. For example, a user might be viewing public reference material that has been provided as Web pages on the corporate intranet. If the information is truly "public," then the expense of protecting it during transmission is largely wasted. In practice, however, there is no way to tell the IPSEC proxy at the central site that a particular data item or even a particular connection does not need to be encrypted. IPSEC works at the packet level and protects everything traveling between a given pair of hosts. There is no safe way to enable it sometimes, disable it other times, and not open the hosts to attack.

REMOTE ACCESS KEY ASSIGNMENT

Generating security associations for remote access is simpler in some ways than it is for networks of encrypting routers. While a VPN may evolve into an arbitrary web of site interconnections, remote access is almost always between each client and the central site, yielding a star topology. Thus, each client only needs one security association—the one between itself and the central site. In Figure 7-2 this is shown by the key assignments K1, K2, and K3. Note that each client has its own key (Alice's is K3) and the central site (the encrypting router) contains a copy of all three keys.

The star topology simplifies the key generation process described in Section 4.4. by eliminating almost half of the key deliveries. The database described in Table 4-1 supports key distribution to pairs of recipients. In the star topology, one of the recipients is always the central site. In short, we can initialize the database fields SERIAL2, CUSTODIAN2, and LOCATION2 to point to the central site or we can simply eliminate these database fields and modify the procedures accordingly. It is probably best to modify the procedures, since then we can produce a single file containing all of the clients' security associations. The modified procedure will work more smoothly and reduce the risk of mishandling the keying data.

7.4.1 Remote Access Security Issues

There are two parts to remote access security: risks to the central site and risks associated with clients. The central site risks are essentially the same as those described in Chapter 6 that apply to VPNs. While risks to the IPSEC client software were discussed in the previous section, there are other risks to the mobile clients that must be considered. The following risks are discussed:

- Client attacks from the Internet
- Virus-based attacks on clients
- Client theft

CLIENT ATTACKS FROM THE INTERNET

Clients are at risk of attack simply because they are hosts on the Internet. Section 7.3.2 explored this problem and focused on the simple approach of blocking all messages that don't carry valid IPSEC headers. However, this approach prevents the client from being able to visit public, unprotected Internet sites, whether for business or recreation. The lure of the Internet is strong and the risk to clients is as yet small, so few users will restrict their traffic only to IPSEC. The alternative is to configure the software on the client to resist Internet attacks as much as possible.

To protect the client system best, take a close look at every TCP/IP software component residing on the client and ensure they are all configured in a safe manner. Unfortunately, this subject demands a book of its own and the specifics will vary from one type of system to another. A reasonable rule of thumb is to look for any mechanism that allows an outside system to modify data on your machine, and then block that mechanism or service. In some cases the outside access is allowed by some unnecessarily permissive software. Other cases are caused by *executable content*, that is, data that is read into your computer and then automatically executed. This increasingly common phenomenon on the Internet is discussed in Section 10.5.3.

Here are a few well-known examples of mechanisms to block:

- Will your Web browser automatically read a Microsoft document into the appropriate application like Word or Excel? The proliferation of Word macro viruses makes this a risky proposition. Although Excel viruses have not spread in the same way as Word viruses, similar viruses have been demonstrated.

- Does your Web browser support Java or ActiveX? If you don't want to use these new languages and the potential risks they carry, be sure to disable them. If you want to use Java but wish to limit the risks, be sure to switch on the Java security controls contained in your browser. It is not clear that security controls are available that will prevent a malicious ActiveX control from damaging your client.

- Do you use NCSA Telnet from the National Center for Supercomputer Applications? Its file transfer mechanism is built around an FTP *server* that could open your workstation's files to everyone on the Internet. Assign a hard-to-guess password to the FTP service and then disable it. If you must use the FTP service, enable it only for the time that you really need it and disable it when you are finished. This limits your window of vulnerability. NCSA Telnet is often configured with no password and with FTP enabled. This means the files on the client's workstation are fully accessible whenever Telnet is being used.

It is hard to make clients secure. Much of the problem is that most client users do not have the specialized knowledge required to configure all the different software packages securely. Another problem is that client software is usually built for user convenience, and security is added as an afterthought. Fortunately, most clients present a hard-to-hit target with an unpredictable payoff. This reduces the risk somewhat.

VIRUS BASED ATTACKS ON CLIENTS

There are two parts to this issue: Does IPSEC provide any protection against viruses, and what special threats might viruses pose to IPSEC clients? The only virus protection IPSEC might provide is indirect at best. It limits the way in which information can enter the client, and this might prevent a virus from entering the system. For example, if the client only accepts IPSEC-protected messages from the central site, then it can't download a virus-infested file from an unprotected public Internet site. On the other hand, if the virus has infested the central site, IPSEC provides no protection against it. IPSEC will treat the virus-infested message the same as any other data it carries and protects.

If a typical virus does infect the client, the client will suffer the usual problems, such as changes in software behavior and potential damage depending on how the virus operates. In theory the virus could be tailored to attack IPSEC clients. This could pose an even nastier risk since the virus could extract and disclose the IPSEC keys being used. If a sufficiently clever virus infected the IPSEC software itself, it could simply steal the keys while they are being used to protect traffic. This would bypass any theft protection mechanisms that might be in place. Fortunately, such viruses are only theoretical at this point.

CLIENT THEFT

The basic issue is, of course, physical security. The client's keying material should not be usable except when the client is in the physical possession of the authorized user, safe from tampering, and actually being used. If the user has shut down the system, the keys should not be in a usable state. For example, password protection can protect the keys from theft. Physical protection must then extend to the password. The user must not type it in or store it in a place where someone else will see it. Ideally the user only types the password when in a safe place where others won't observe it and where there is no serious risk of someone taking control of the machine after the password has been entered.

Section 7.3.3 discussed the protection of IPSEC keying material. If the client does not provide password protection for keys, or if the password protection is poorly implemented, file or disk encryption might provide a reasonable security alternative. If the keys are stored on the hard drive, and all data on the hard drive is encrypted, then a thief should not be able to recover the keys. The effectiveness of such protection depends, of course, on the effectiveness of the encryption. Such products need to be approached with caution. The U.S. National Computer Security Center (NCSC) evaluated several products providing such facilities. In most cases the products earned a "D" rating (the lowest), because the protections were judged ineffective. If you intend to rely on hard drive encryption, be sure to select effective software to do it.

A final issue is that of detecting attempts to use stolen keying material. If properly keyed, it should be virtually impossible for an attacker to forge IPSEC traffic. However, the risk of client theft raises the risk of outsiders having access to valid keying material. To reduce the risk, users must promptly report all instances of actual or potential key theft.

7.4.2 Deployment Security Requirements

Here is a list of security requirements for remote site access, listed roughly in order of decreasing priority.

1. **Deploy IPSEC effectively at the central site.** The deployment should follow the VPN requirements listed in Section 6.5.2.

2. **Use a good IPSEC client.** The client should comply with the requirements listed in Section 7.3.4.

3. **Have a good key generation procedure to support the clients.** Follow the recommendations in this chapter and in Chapter 4.

4. **Train client users on physical security expectations.** Establish realistic and effective expectations based on theft protections in the IPSEC client and the remote computers themselves. Then be sure that all client users are trained on how to protect their keying material.

5. **Detect and respond to security incidents.** This requires mechanisms and procedures for clients and for the central site. Client users should know how to report suspected leaks of keying material or other security-relevant incidents. Theft of a client is an important incident regardless of how the keying material is protected. The central site itself should also have mechanisms to monitor invalid IPSEC traffic and to look for attempts to crack password-protected keys.

6. **Block executable contents from operating on your host.** Most programs that support executable content also provide mechanisms for disabling them. Microsoft Word has a mechanism that prevents "macros" inside of word processing documents from automatically executing. Disabling this feature will prevent the spread of the Word macro virus. The latest Web browsers support several forms of executable content including Java, JavaScript, and ActiveX. These can be disabled in full function browsers.

7.5 For Further Information

- **Cohen, *A Short Course on Computer Viruses***
  This book provides broad, no-nonsense coverage of the general problem of viruses.

- **Wagner and Bellovin, *Bump in the Stack Encryptor for MS.DOS Systems***
  This paper describes a pioneering IPSEC client implementation for MS-DOS. The architecture is a prototype for the shim approach to IPSEC.

Chapter
8

IPSEC and Firewalls

Sed quis custodiet ipsos custodes?
(Who guards the guardsmen?)

—Juvenal, *Satires VI*

IN THIS CHAPTER

This chapter introduces *firewalls*, devices that allow users at a protected site to use Internet services in a relatively safe manner by restricting incoming access by potential attackers. Previous chapters used crypto techniques to prevent outsiders from communicating with your site, either for good or bad. However, most organizations with Internet connections wish to access the vast array of public information it has to offer. Such access opens your site to attack. Firewalls are a way of managing that risk. The following topics are discussed:

- Security objectives that call for firewall systems
- Overview of firewall technology
- IPSEC-encrypting firewall products
- Example VPN deployment with a firewall

8.1 Security Objectives

The objective is to support both VPN connections and unprotected connections to public Internet sites. This allows protected communications to colleagues at other sites, as well as connections with potentially hostile sites and users.

- **Ensure controlled access to Internet services.**
  Authorized people inside the site need to access public Internet services. This capability must not open the site to attack by outsiders.

- **Protect a distributed enterprise network from outsiders.**
  The enterprise network spans geographically distributed sites that all have Internet access. The sites comprising this network need to exchange traffic safely between each other without having outsiders on the Internet interfere with that traffic. All messages traveling between sites should be protected from eavesdropping or forgery. Outsiders should not be able to play the part of insiders.

- **Protect the whole range of Internet protocols currently in use.**
  The sites are already making extensive use of networking software and protocols; it is necessary to support these capabilities. Extensive replacement of existing software is not an option for providing security.

- **Public Internet access is available and cost is very important.**
  Any service like an Internet connection is easier to justify from a business standpoint when it can be used for a variety of purposes. Many organizations can justify Internet access as an information resource. Others justify it as a low-cost data link to other company sites, especially when the traffic between sites is protected.

8.2 Basic Issues with IPSEC and Firewalls

The decision to connect to the public Internet must balance the business benefits against potential risks.

- **Weigh permissive versus restrictive Internet access.**
  There are two general approaches to controlling a site's Internet access: either permit everything except risky traffic (*permissive access*), or permit nothing except necessary traffic (*restrictive access*). Early firewall techniques supported permissive access, since the security problem was perceived as a small number of flaws in particular software components. Also, the permissive approach is consistent with the Internet's architectural traditions. Restrictive firewalls emerged as it was realized that security was not some simple property that could be easily imposed on a large, complex environment like the Internet. Cautious sites now use restrictive firewalls and only take the risks they require for business purposes.

- **Perimeter protection will not stop everything.**
  Firewalls stop a variety of recognized attacks at the site's perimeter because firewalls detect and block messages that do obviously improper things. They cannot block attacks hidden inside innocent-looking traffic. While some fire-

walls can support virus checking, they cannot block viruses for which they
don't know how to look.

- **Crypto bypass is a bountiful source of security flaws.**
An IPSEC firewall must process both plaintext and ciphertext through the same
connection to the Internet. This means the firewall occasionally must reject
plaintext data and occasionally pass it through, bypassing the crypto protection.
The problem is, if you can bypass the protections on purpose you can also bypass
them by accident. It is hard to build such systems to work correctly.

8.3 Internet Firewalls

An *Internet firewall* tries to protect the site from attacks originating at other Internet sites. Typically the protection consists of restricting the types of network traffic
that can flow between the Internet and the site's internal network. The site decides
the types of Internet traffic it needs to have and which types it can handle safely.
Those types of traffic are permitted and all other traffic is blocked.

In the early days of the Internet, most sites ran as much Internet service software as they could. They'd give outsiders the ability to look at many files, transfer
public ones, even log in as a "guest." Then the modern cracker culture developed
and people started to exploit the fragility of rapidly changing software.

Firewalls allow users at a protected site to use Internet services in a relatively
safe manner by blocking incoming access by potential attackers (Figure 8-1). Some
products also provide some protection for services that accept incoming connec-

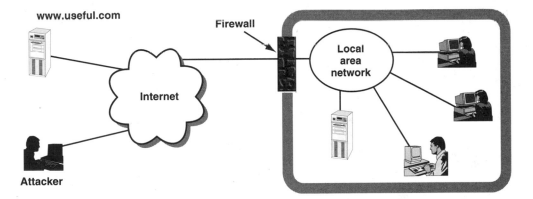

**Figure 8-1: AN INTERNET FIREWALL PROTECTS A SITE WHILE PROVIDING OUTBOUND
ACCESS.** Users inside the protected site can access useful Internet hosts while blocking attackers
from their site.

tions, like Internet e-mail servers. In all cases a firewall essentially enforces a site-specific set of access control rules intended to allow acceptable Internet access and block all others.

8.3.1 What Firewalls Control

Firewalls control the flow of traffic between internal, relatively safe networks and external, potentially hostile networks (Figure 8-2). Those intending to provide good protection generally block all traffic, except what is explicitly allowed by the site. Typically the access controls can be categorized according to the direction of access, since this also reflects the population making the accesses.

OUTBOUND ACCESS

The firewall can provide internal users with outbound access to the Internet. Users can use TCP/IP client software like a Web browser or remote terminal program to open connections to server hosts on the Internet. When a firewall permits outbound traffic, the permission can be subject to the following:

- The type of service: Web, file transfer, remote terminal, and so on
- The client hosts and/or server hosts being accessed
- Authenticated user name of the client's user

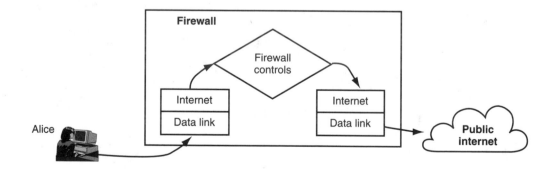

Figure 8-2: FIREWALL CONTROLS ARE APPLIED TO MESSAGES AT THE IP LEVEL AND ABOVE.
The firewall processes the flow of messages and controls access according to the site rules on what is allowed. Traffic is blocked if the user uses unauthorized services or requests them from the wrong side of the firewall.

INBOUND ACCESS

Inbound access is a far more serious issue. A firewall can allow users outside the site to connect to services inside and inbound access can be subject to the same controls as outbound traffic. However, the user population for outbound traffic is limited to users that are physically located at the site. If they are allowed into the site they probably can be trusted to some degree. Inbound connections, on the other hand, could come from anywhere on the Internet, and could certainly come from people with malicious intent. If a site allows inbound connections of some type, they must consider the risk of an attacker penetrating the server that accepts those connections.

A cautious site will not allow outside connections into the internal network unless they can be certain that the incoming user can be trusted. They must be able to authenticate that user and be sure that nobody has hijacked the connection. Inbound sessions from an IPSEC client can be adequately authenticated and protected from forgery or hijacking.

INBOUND SERVICES

It is dangerous to allow inbound service messages to flow right through the firewall and into the site. If the server software for the permitted service contains a security flaw (and this happens too often for many sites' comfort), then the attacker can piggyback an attack on the supposedly legitimate service traffic. Some sites deal with this by placing servers outside their protected site or on a separate network (a "demilitarized zone" or DMZ) that limits access from the outside and to the inside. Other sites run their externally visible services on special, high-security firewalls. Several high-end firewalls are expressly designed to provide services such as e-mail and the Web without placing the site at risk.

8.3.2 How Firewalls Control Access

Firewalls use four general techniques to control access and enforce the site's Internet usage objectives: service control, direction control, user control, and behavior control. Originally firewalls focused primarily on service control, but have since evolved to provide all four.

SERVICE CONTROL

Service control determines the types of Internet services that can be accessed—inbound or outbound. In many cases this consists of allowing or blocking packet flow according to the packets' TCP/IP port number, which generally indicates the service being accessed. The specifics of which packet flow is allowed is usually captured in a set of *permit/deny rules* that are tailored to each device. In some cases the firewall may provide *proxy* software that receives and interprets each service request and forwards it, if appropriate, to the destination server on the other side. In other cases the firewall may instead provide the service by hosting the server software on the firewall itself, like with e-mail or the Web.

DIRECTION CONTROL

Direction control determines the direction in which particular service requests may be initiated and allowed to flow through the firewall. Some sites want to allow clients inside the site to access Internet servers while blocking Internet clients from connecting to the site's internal servers. Direction control is also implemented with permit/deny rules or with proxies.

USER CONTROL

User control controls access to a service according to which user is attempting to access it. In some cases this is as simple as associating a unique workstation IP address with the workstation's usual operator. The site then controls that user's access with rules that allow or block data flow based on the workstation IP address. A more reliable but complex technique uses specially constructed proxies to authenticate the user when access is to be controlled by identity.

External access adds an interesting wrinkle to user-based access control. Most sites would like to allow authorized individuals to use internal computing resources from outside locations. Unfortunately, it is difficult to ensure that the connections really come from the authorized individuals. The site must prevent attackers from masquerading as authorized users and prevent hijacking of authenticated connections from authorized users. IPSEC is often used to prevent connection hijacking.

BEHAVIOR CONTROL

Behavior control controls how particular services are used, often on the basis of other control information collected. For example, the firewall might block e-mail messages containing profanity or the names of sensitive company projects. Some firewalls support Web page classification procedures that can be used to block access to Web pages containing "inappropriate" subject matter. Sites that are concerned about risks from executable contents or about viruses in general might block downloading of Java scripts or Microsoft Word files.

8.3.3 Firewall Control Mechanisms

Firewalls have evolved using three general mechanisms to control TCP/IP traffic. Figure 8-3 illustrates how each mechanism makes its access control decisions. The different mechanisms each have their own benefits and are all widely used in one form or another:

1. **Packet filtering.** This is the simplest mechanism, based entirely on the contents of individual packets. Most modern IP routers provide some packet filtering.

2. **Circuit filtering.** This mechanism controls access by reconstructing the flow of data associated with the traffic and blocking the flow if it is not permitted.

3. **Application gateway.** This mechanism controls access by processing the messages specific to particular TCP/IP application protocols.

All three mechanisms evolved around the notion of passing data through the firewall on the behalf of a pair of entities that are authorized to communicate. The term *proxy* is often applied to the software that passes the data through a firewall, especially in the more sophisticated implementations.

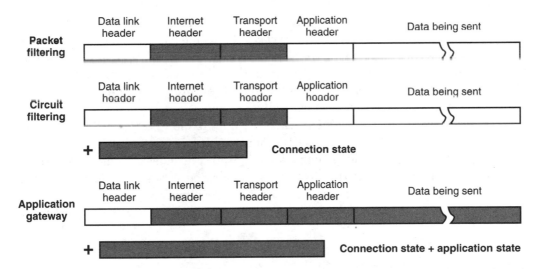

Figure 8-3: GRAY AREAS SHOW THE DATA USED BY THE DIFFERENT FIREWALL CONTROL MECHANISMS. Packet filtering relies entirely on individual packet headers. Circuit filters collect connection state data and use it in addition to packet header data. Application gateways use circuit filter information as well as application-specific information to apply access controls.

Firewalls provide access controls according to the amount of data they use to make their decisions. More elaborate decision making is less efficient but allows more specific control of site access.

PACKET FILTERS

Packet filters were originally developed as a "filtering" feature on IP routing hosts and routers. As firewalls evolved, packet filters were promoted as a fast, efficient tool for site access control. Indeed, the principal strength of a packet filter is its speed and not its security capabilities. Packet filters remain the most widely used type of firewall.

Filtering is based on a set of rules that identify the properties of individual packets that are to be blocked or passed through. All access control decisions are based on the information available in individual IP packets: the IP addresses, service port numbers, and flags indicating connection status. Each packet filter at a given site usually has its own distinctive set of filtering rules.

Service control is provided by examining TCP and UDP port numbers, and filtering packets accordingly. Direction control can only be applied to TCP connections, blocking packets with flags that indicate an attempt to open a new connection in the wrong direction. User control can be provided only by filtering the host IP address, which may be adequate in sites with users who are assigned to individual, dedicated workstations.

However, packet filters' sheer simplicity have opened them up for a variety of attacks. Individual packets don't always carry the whole story, so sometimes the filters can be tricked. For example, there was one style of attack that sent connection requests through a packet filter by breaking them into multiple, separate packets. The individual packets looked acceptable to the filter, but the reconstructed sequence actually bypassed the access control rules.

The low level of packet filtering makes it impossible to apply certain types of access control rules simply because the decision-making information isn't organized into packets. For example, many sites want to control access based on authenticated user identities, but the authentication procedures rarely operate at the packet level. Most application-level protocols are designed to ignore packet boundaries, so there is no way to control application-specific behavior with a packet filter.

CIRCUIT FILTERS

A circuit filter is a device that passes a connection from a client on one side of the firewall to a server on the other. Unlike a packet filter, a circuit filter gets actively involved in the connection and allows it to operate as long as it complies with the firewall's access control rules. For example, a site might need to allow outbound Telnet connections, so the circuit filter will accept outbound connection requests to port 23, the Telnet connection port. The circuit filter accepts the connection on the inside and echoes it on the outside, addressing the server selected by the inside client. Traffic flowing in either direction is handled inside the firewall on behalf of the circuit set up for that particular connection. The internal connection is often referred to as a *proxy* for the external connection.

An important difference between circuit and packet filters is that circuit filters are essentially *restrictive* devices while packet filters are essentially *permissive* devices. A circuit filter won't pass a packet from one side to the other unless it is part of an established connection. Thus, a circuit filter automatically filters out all low-level TCP/IP traffic that is not associated with active connections. A packet filter, on the other hand, might accidentally pass low level-control and status packets that are not associated with authorized traffic.

Circuit filters do not pay attention to the information carried on the connections, so they fall victim to the same higher level shortcomings of packet filters. Circuit filters cannot do user authentication and they cannot detect misuses of the service protocols that they carry. Thus, a circuit filter can carry an attack constructed with an authorized protocol just as efficiently as it carries genuine traffic.

An interesting technical variation is the *stateful packet filter*. Unlike a generic packet filter, a stateful filter will maintain information about connections and, in some cases, about application-level activities. In practice such devices can provide similar features to circuit filters and some of the features of application gateways. Stateful filters can be as permissive as generic packet filters, while circuit and application gateways are rarely that flexible. However, it can be a technically challenging and error-prone task to graft additional application protocol filtering onto a stateful filter.

APPLICATION GATEWAYS

Application gateways are restrictive devices like circuit filters, except that they are tailored to handle specific TCP/IP application protocols. This allows such gateways to apply true user-based access control and behavior control. Since these are tailored to specific protocols, they cannot be generalized easily to protect traffic using newer protocols. This decreases flexibility and increases costs in exchange for more precise security controls.

Software packages that handle specific protocols are often called *application proxies*. Commercial application gateways generally provide an extensive suite of proxies. Different versions of the proxies provide different controls, so it is important to examine specifically what a particular vendor or package provides. Commercial application gateways usually include the following proxies:

- **World Wide Web**
  Some versions support user authentication with passwords. Many allow filtering on particular uniform resource locator (URL) contents. Sites use this to block access to particular sites or to filter out specific content types, like Java applets. Some even classify URLs by content type and block access to contents deemed inappropriate by the site administration, like sports or other entertainment-oriented sites.

- **Internet e-mail**
  The first objective of e-mail proxies was to ensure that only legitimate e-mail would flow through an e-mail service connection. For many years the most common e-mail package on the Internet has suffered from a legion of security bugs. Firewalls use a variety of proxying techniques to prevent exploitation of those bugs. More recently, proxies include varieties of message filtering to check for data leaks and even viruses.

- **Telnet remote terminal protocol**
  Telnet proxies often support user authentication, either with passwords or with more sophisticated challenge/response systems. Unfortunately, it is impractical to implement behavior constraints in a Telnet proxy because the underlying protocol is so free form and its semantic content varies dramatically from one server host to the next. If a Telnet proxy is permitted, then there is no practical way to restrict what is done through that proxy after the connection has been authenticated.

- **File Transfer Protocol**
  The FTP proxy was an early entrant because the protocol does not use predefined TCP port numbers in the simple manner of other protocols. The proxy had to intercept FTP messages that identified the ports being used and ensure that port was available through the proxy. Typical proxies also provide some measure of behavioral control by specifying which FTP commands may be used. Some proxies also support authentication, usually with passwords.

- **Internet service protocols**
  This covers a variety of application proxies, including the lookup of host names via Domain Name Service and time of day via the Network Time Protocol.

- **New multimedia protocols**
  This is an area of great Internet activity with new protocols being developed and distributed constantly. Occasionally the developers also prototype an application proxy for use by firewall vendors.

SUMMARY OF FIREWALL MECHANISMS

Packet filters and circuit filters operate entirely on the basis of generic TCP/IP protocol information, so they can be tailored to control almost any TCP/IP service. However, these filters can only apply a limited amount of control, as shown in Table 8-1. Their ability to restrict access to particular users is limited and they cannot restrict behavior within an authorized protocol. Application gateways must be constructed to control specific application protocols, but they provide the broadest range of control.

8.4 Product Example: IPSEC Firewall

An Internet firewall with IPSEC permits a site to use a single device to mediate all of its Internet access (Figure 8-4). Encrypted messages between different sites are processed at the firewall, and plaintext messages to browse the public World Wide Web are passed through as permitted by the site's rules. The site must configure the firewall to identify the services that may be accessed from the public Internet and the traffic that must be protected with IPSEC. IPSEC firewalls may provide their controls with packet filtering, circuit filtering, or application proxies, depending on the design and construction.

Table 8-1: Controls provided by different firewall mechanisms

Type of Control	Type of Firewall Mechanism		
	Packet Filters	Circuit Filters	Application Gateways
Service control	√√	√√	√√
Direction control	√	√√	√√
User control	√	√	√√
Behavior control			√√
√√ = a technique strongly supports a given goal; √ = partial support.			

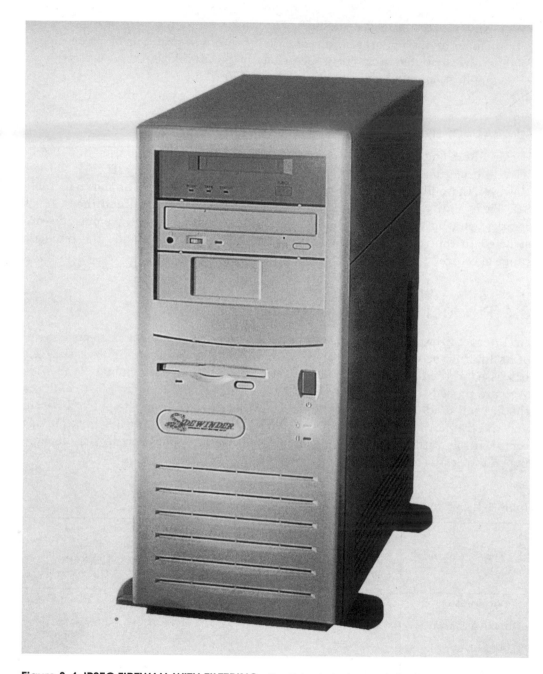

Figure 8-4: IPSEC FIREWALL WITH FILTERING. The Sidewinder is an application gateway that provides proxy IPSEC crypto and also passes all external traffic through the standard application filtering controls. Photo courtesy of Secure Computing Corporation.

There are two general approaches to implementing IPSEC in a firewall: the *unfiltered* and *filtered* approach (Figure 8-5). In the unfiltered approach the IPSEC traffic is handled the same as it is in an encrypting router, as discussed in Chapter 6. The IPSEC-protected data is dropped directly into the internal network without any filtering or controls on its contents. In the filtered approach, the firewall's filter and proxy controls are applied to the IPSEC traffic before it is allowed into the internal network. Such control can be used if IPSEC access is granted to business partners or others that should not have unconditional access to the site's internal network.

8.4.1 Administering Multiple Sites

The essential challenge in operating multiple sites is to maintain consistent firewall access control across all sites. Consistent access control gives consistent service to internal users as well as consistent protection against attack. If access control is inconsistent, both user traffic and potential attacks can change direction

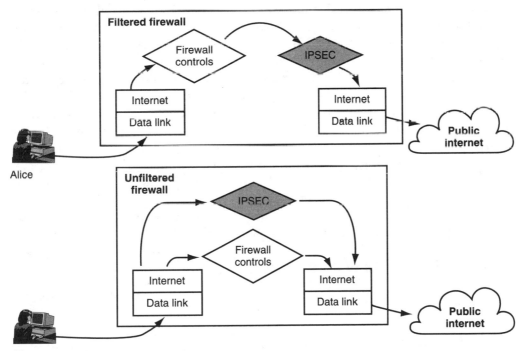

Figure 8-5: FILTERED AND UNFILTERED IPSEC FIREWALLS. An IPSEC firewall may or may not be able to apply its filtering and proxy controls to IPSEC traffic. Filtered firewalls apply such controls while unfiltered firewalls do not.

to exploit weaker controls. Users may reroute their Internet service requests to use the most permissive firewall. Incoming attacks that bypass a weaker firewall can use VPN connections to attack other sites from the inside. Consistent access control requires careful administration and benefits from appropriate support in the IPSEC firewalls being used.

Configuration and access rules should be the same for every firewall in the entire enterprise. The firewall at Site A should enforce the same access control restrictions as the firewall at Site B, and so on. Many firewalls require that such consistency be achieved by hand, with administrators at each site carefully updating their own copy of the global rules. Alternatively, some firewalls maintain their security rules and configuration in a set of files that can be copied from one firewall to another. If this is implemented correctly, then the access control rules will be interpreted consistently in each firewall. This does require careful design on the part of the firewall manufacturer, since some configuration data will always be "local" even though much of it will be global. If local information is included with the global data, it will have to be manually tailored at each site. However, such manual tailoring is likely to be an error-prone activity.

If the firewall's configuration files can be transported and installed in the other firewalls, then the next problem is to deliver these files safely. This is similar to the key distribution problem. These configuration files are crucial to the security of the system and must arrive without change. If the files include secret keys for security associations, then they require even more stringent care in delivery. One approach would be to use a secure e-mail package to encrypt and sign the files as described in Chapter 11. This would provide appropriate protection to the files and would ensure that they could only be extracted by a specifically identified individual at the receiving end. However, this does in a sense simply rearrange the problem, since we still would be left with the problem of exchanging the keys or certificates needed by the secure e-mail package. Updates could be easily handled, though, once the secure delivery mechanism was in place.

Key assignments for IPSEC firewalls will be similar to that for IPSEC router networks. Consult Section 6.5 for a discussion of this topic.

8.4.2 Product Security Requirements

The security requirements for an IPSEC-capable firewall, in order of decreasing priority, are as follows:

1. **IPSEC encrypting router capabilities.** A capable IPSEC firewall must meet the same requirements as an IPSEC encrypting router, as described in Section 6.4.2.

2. **Appropriate controls for Internet access.** At a minimum, this includes the ability to forbid all inbound connections and allow outbound connections only. All state-of-the-art firewalls allow selection of which services to permit and can restrict access by host IP address. Application gateways can further control access based on user identities and types of operations performed.

3. **Real-time alarms for serious incidents.** A state-of-the-art firewall should be able to detect various types of serious attacks. A serious attack may include systematic attempts to do any of the following:

   - Crack a crypto key or password through a series of failed access attempts

   - Probe for accepted inbound services

   - Repeatedly attempt to violate access rules over a limited time period

   - Cause unauthorized behavior by server processes, indicating a server overrun

   - Cause resource exhaustion within the firewall

4. **Synchronized administration of multiple sites.** The firewall should provide the tools necessary to apply uniform access controls easily at every enterprise site.

5. **Detect/block nonlocal forwarding.** As described later in Section 8.5.2, it is possible to perform a minor attack on the IPSEC firewall's crypto system if packets received by a site from outside hosts will be delivered to another site via the enterprise VPN.

The National Computer Security Association (NCSA) has established a basic evaluation program for Internet firewalls. The program "certifies" all firewalls that meet its requirements and pass its basic tests after being submitted by the manufacturer. NCSA certification does not currently address crypto capabilities, although it does verify basic functions and capabilities. The certification process also tests the firewalls against well-known Internet attacks.

8.5 Deployment Example: A VPN with a Firewall

This example combines access to the public Internet with the enterprise network protection of a VPN. The site can grant access to individual users to access public Internet resources, and specify the types of services they may use. Access is also provided to enterprise resources at other sites, and all traffic between sites is protected with IPSEC crypto services.

8.5.1 Establishing a Site Security Policy

The first step for any organization when connecting to the Internet is to ask a fundamental question: What is the business purpose of this Internet connection? Given that the Internet connection can open your internal business operations to outsiders, you must have a good reason for taking this risk. Perhaps you need it to better reach your customers and provide service for your products. Perhaps your research department needs Internet access for creative input. Perhaps you need it as a "perk" for your sophisticated team. Whatever the reason, it is important to identify it so you can tailor your Internet access rules to your needs.

The second question that must be asked is about your organization's internal network: What do you need to protect? Large sites in financial industries probably have a good deal to protect. Insurance companies, for example, track the status of their policy portfolios as well as individual decisions on benefit payments for thousands or even millions of dollars. Even internal equipment-ordering systems can be vulnerable to manipulation. A classic story of computer crime involved a college student who sold equipment from Pacific Telephone to a variety of customers and then instructed Pacific Telephone's computers to ship the equipment as an internal company transfer. Other companies have genuine corporate secrets to protect.

Once you have identified the services you need and the assets you must protect, you can organize your Internet access accordingly. If your Internet access requirements are modest, you may be able to provide general desktop Internet access with little risk. For example, there is at least one large corporation with a firewall that blocks all direct Internet access except World Wide Web browsing, which it only allows to specifically authorized individuals. The corporation also has a special, dedicated LAN for its advanced development group and they are connected to the Internet via a relatively permissive packet filter. This special LAN itself has a firewall between it and the corporate LAN as well. The advanced development group gets complete access to the Internet while limiting the risk of an Internet-based attack on other corporate networks.

Each organization is different. The arrangement of its Internet access and how it is integrated with its other computing resources will depend on what it needs and what it must protect.

Once the enterprisewide policy is established, be sure to enforce it consistently at all VPN sites. Inconsistent filtering across multiple firewalls will tend to concentrate traffic flow on the most permissive firewall. VPN firewalls will end up processing traffic that simply allows users in one site to exploit the permissiveness of a different site. This is inefficient and it renders the more restrictive rules irrelevant. It is better to have weaker rules consistently applied and enforced than to have stronger rules bypassed by clever users.

8.5.2 Chosen Plaintext Attack on a Firewall

Earlier discussions of attacks against crypto systems have noted that the attackers' job can be simplified if they can produce *chosen plaintext;* that is, select what information is to be encrypted, send it through the encryptor, and collect it for exploitation. The task of extracting a particular key through brute force cryptanalysis is easier and more efficient to do if they have the plaintext that goes with the ciphertext. And Bailey the Switcher has several tricks she can try if she can produce correctly encrypted pieces of ciphertext from carefully crafted pieces of plaintext. Cut-and-paste attacks are especially easy if she can construct the exact pieces she wants to paste into a forged message. Since VPNs with firewalls accept plaintext from the Internet and transmit ciphertext between associated sites, attackers might be able to run chosen plaintext attacks against them.

Occasional, unpredictable forwarding of Internet data across encrypted VPN links should not pose a threat. However, Figure 8-6 illustrates how Peeping Tom can generate all the chosen plaintext he wants completely under his control. If shortcuts were taken in implementing IPSEC protections, then Tom and his associates might be able to use the chosen plaintext as an entering wedge to attack the site's message traffic.

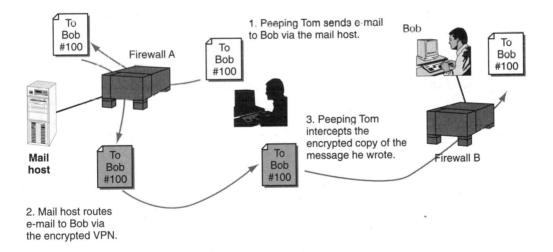

Figure 8-6: CHOSEN PLAINTEXT ATTACK ON A VPN WITH A FIREWALL. Peeping Tom sends plaintext messages into the site, and the messages are forwarded to the recipient via encrypted VPN connections. Tom can then collect encrypted copies of his messages. This allows him to select information to be encrypted and collect the encrypted result, which he might use in forgeries or key cracking.

The attack shown in Figure 8-6 proceeds in three steps that are repeated as needed. Bob is part of an enterprise that has a VPN running between Firewalls A and B. The attacker, Peeping Tom, resides on an Internet routing host that can intercept all traffic between Firewalls A and B.

Tom proceeds as follows. First, Tom composes a plaintext e-mail message to Bob and sends it to him at Site A, which is behind Firewall A. The e-mail is accepted by the mail host at Site A, which realizes that Bob is really at Site B. The mail host dutifully forwards the e-mail to Site B. However, since the enterprise has implemented an encrypted VPN between its sites, all data going between Sites A and B will be encrypted. So Tom's plaintext e-mail messages gets encrypted for its journey to Site B.

As the encrypted message passes Peeping Tom's site, he intercepts a copy of it, possibly recognizing it by its size or perhaps because the packets are addressed to Bob's computer. Tom can even use this technique to run a more sophisticated attack—an *adaptive chosen plaintext* attack—by varying the chosen plaintext according to how the cipher permutes his earlier chosen plaintext.

This technique is powerful enough to cause real concern. It can obviously aid the attacks noted earlier—brute force cracking and message modification. We can anticipate how these attacks might proceed, examine our IPSEC operations, and assure ourselves that Tom and friends can't profitably exploit this chosen plaintext through any obvious attacks. Therefore, this style of attack should not be a concern for low- or medium-threat applications as long as the IPSEC implementation is strong enough. Specifically, (1) use longer crypto keys to make brute force attacks infeasible and (2) use the AH to detect cut-and-paste attacks.

Unfortunately, this chosen plaintext could aid a broad range of unanticipated attacks in addition to the ones we've already noted. Therefore, it should be taken very seriously in higher risk applications. This is a very powerful technique for an attacker to use to go after a crypto system and can provide an entering wedge to exploit all kinds of weaknesses in crypto systems. Here are three countermeasures to use to block or prevent this behavior:

1. Configure the firewall and internal systems so that they will not accept plaintext messages from outside the firewall and forward them to other sites across encrypted connections. This will block Peeping Tom's ability to run the entire attack at his leisure.

2. Some enterprises have corporatewide e-mail addresses that do not change as employees move from one location to another. Inbound Internet e-mail then has to be forwarded to the correct corporate site. This can be handled by an e-mail server that resides outside the VPN and forwards plaintext, external e-mail across the Internet in plaintext.

3. It is acceptable from a security standpoint for someone inside the site to forward plaintext e-mail manually from Tom to Bob across the encrypted VPN. This is because the forwarding operation is not under Tom's control—he cannot control whether or how much of the message is in fact forwarded and encrypted.

8.5.3 Deployment Security Requirements

Here are the requirements for a VPN configuration with a firewall. The most important requirements are listed first:

1. **Use an appropriate encrypting firewall.** The device should comply with the requirements listed in Section 8.4.2.

2. **Apply consistent security filtering at each site.** Inconsistent filtering across multiple firewalls is ineffective and inefficient.

3. **Accept local input at each site.** If outsiders need to send messages to your sites, make it most efficient for them to send the data directly to the destination site. Do not force the VPN to transmit an encrypted version of the same data across the Internet. It is inefficient and risky.

4. **Don't encrypt and forward between sites.** This is the other side of the previous requirement. Wherever possible, block automatic delivery across the VPN of plaintext messages received from outsiders. Again, this raises the spectre of a chosen plaintext attack.

8.6 For Further Information

- **Cheswick and Bellovin, *Firewalls and Internet Security: Repelling the Wily Hacker***
  The classic reference on firewalls. It provides a wealth of low-level technical details as well as practical high-level recommendations.

- **Chapman and Zwicky, *Building Internet Firewalls***
  This is the bible of packet filtering, and a valuable reference when using routers to set up an Internet connection.

- **Holbrook and Reynolds, "Site Security Handbook"**
  ftp://ftp.internic.net/rfc/rfc1244.txt
  This report provides sensible basic suggestions on Internet security policy and on how to manage an Internet site securely.

- **National Computer Security Association,** *NCSA Firewall Certification Program*
  http://www.ncsa.com/fpfs/fwindex.html
  This introduces the NCSA's certification program, lists all certified products, and describes the certification requirements.

Chapter
9
Public Key Crypto and SSL

It's a poor atom blaster that doesn't point both ways.

—Isaac Asimov, *Foundation*

IN THIS CHAPTER

This chapter introduces *public key cryptography* and its most familiar application, the Secure Sockets Layer (SSL) protocol that is widely used in conjunction with the World Wide Web. The following topics are discussed:

- **Public key encryption**
- RSA public key encryption
- Use of RSA encryption for key exchange
- The SSL protocol and how it is used to protect Web transactions

The crypto deployments we examined earlier would generally protect a predefined population of communicating hosts, and protect all traffic automatically, whether sensitive or not. SSL, on the other hand, does not require a prior arrangement like a key exchange between the two communicating hosts in order to establish crypto keying safely. SSL is a transport level protocol, so traffic is only protected when SSL is specifically used. This leaves the choice of crypto protection largely up to the client user.

9.1 Public Key Cryptography

Public key cryptography is a set of techniques that allows people to share secret information by exchanging information entirely in public. The secret key techniques described in the previous chapters can do this only after we have taken the separate step of exchanging crypto keys in complete secrecy. Public key techniques replace the secret exchange with one that does not require secrecy.

This capability is so important that some observers have called it the first major breakthrough in cryptography in hundreds if not thousands of years. Public key techniques have yielded new and better techniques for exchanging keys and also for associating crypto keys with individuals. However, the mathematics behind public key crypto make it vulnerable to a variety of peculiar attacks that limit how it can be used.

Effective public key techniques have been developed for key management and for *digital signatures*, an improved and personalized form of crypto checksum. These applications are used in conjunction with established secret key cryptography and with one-way hash functions. Public key does not replace existing crypto techniques; instead, it makes them easier to use for some applications.

While the actual and theoretical benefits of public key techniques are significant, so are the limitations. It is important to recognize what public key crypto is *not*. It is not a new set of encryption algorithms that replace the existing secret key algorithms. Not all public key algorithms really do encryption in the usual sense. Encrypting data with a public key may guarantee privacy when sending data to the key's owner, but it does not implicitly provide privacy for return data. While public key techniques may reduce the need for secrecy when distributing keys, it does not eliminate security risks during key distribution. Manual techniques still play an important role when using public key techniques to distribute keys.

Even with these limitations, public key crypto is the most promising technique available for key management. The principal shortcoming of secret key crypto is that a cautious enterprise will assign separate crypto keys to every pair of communicating entities. While this provides the best security, it also produces a huge key management burden. This burden grows rapidly out of control as the communicating population grows. In a population of a thousand hosts there are a million pairs of hosts that can communicate. There is no practical way to produce and distribute the million pairwise keys needed to allow all hosts to communicate with each other.

With public key techniques, hosts can simply keep lists of public keys (or get them from a common directory) and use public key techniques to establish individual pairwise keys as they are needed. The NSA is said to have used public key techniques in the STU III encrypting telephone to allow any pair of telephones to establish their own encrypting key without having to distribute all the keys ahead of time. There are more that 320,000 STU III telephones and any one of them can establish a secure conversation with any other. Clearly, there is no place in a STU III to store and update billions of pairwise keys (Figure 9-1).

Figure 9-1: THE STU-III ENCRYPTING TELEPHONE USES PUBLIC KEY TECHNOLOGY. Any one of the 320,000 STU III telephones supported by the NSA may establish an encrypted connection with any other without prior arrangements. The telephones use their public keys to establish a shared secret key that is used to encrypt that particular conversation. Without public key techniques, each phone would need to store billions of keys in order to allow any phone to connect directly to any other.

9.1.1 Evolution of Public Key Crypto

Public key techniques are based on numerical tricks used in a carefully crafted series of arithmetic computations. We start with randomly selected secret numerical values and combine them in a peculiar way that is hard to reverse. These initial values comprise a *private key* that the crypto user keeps secret and the combined result is the *public key*. If Alice wants to communicate with Bob, she applies the public key algorithm to her own private key or to Bob's public key, or both, depending on the particular technique being used. Alice never has to share her private key with Bob, or vice versa.

The basic concepts of public key crypto were first publicized in the mid 1970s, around the time DES was developed. Following the pattern of many modern inventions, public key techniques were developed almost simultaneously by at least three different teams: Ralph Merkle at Berkeley; Whitfield Diffie and Martin Hellman at Stanford; and Ron Rivest, Adi Shamir, and Len Adelman of the Massachusetts Institute of Technology. According to rumor, cryptographers at the NSA developed their own variation of public key techniques as much as ten years earlier.

While the details of the NSA's approach aren't known publicly, the other three teams developed algorithms that exploited difficult but different mathematical problems. In all three cases, the problem involved strings of computations that are easy to compute in one direction and extremely difficult to compute in the other. Merkle's algorithm was based on the knapsack problem, which encrypts a message by computing the vector product of the plaintext and the key bits, relying on the difficulty of reversing that computation for security. However, attempts to build a practical system from the algorithm failed. The failure was dramatically illustrated at the Crypto '82 technical conference when Len Adelman presented a paper on cracking the knapsack algorithm and simultaneously demonstrated the cracking procedure on an Apple II personal computer. Subsequent attempts to strengthen the knapsack approach have failed.

The other two approaches have more successfully stood the test of time and clever mathematics. The Diffie-Hellman approach is based on the difficulty of computing discrete logarithms as opposed to doing exponentiation. The resulting algorithm can establish a shared secret key that can then be used with a conventional secret key algorithm. The third approach (developed by Rivest, Shamir, and Adelman) is known as the RSA algorithm. This approach is based on the fact that it is easy to find and multiply large primes together but extremely difficult to factor their product. Diffie-Hellman has been a popular choice among developers of IPSEC key management protocols. However, RSA is the algorithm most people associate with the notion of public key cryptography (Figure 9-2).

9.1.2 Diffie-Hellman Public Key Technique

The Diffie-Hellman technique was the first practical public key crypto algorithm and it is still widely used. Two entities can use it to produce a shared secret value that can then be used as a common crypto key for a secret key encryption algorithm. As shown in Figure 9-3, Bob and Alice each generate a random number and this becomes their private key. If they need to communicate, then they exchange some public data that comprises their public key. Alice applies her private key to Bob's public key to compute the shared secret value. Bob applies his private key to Alice's public key and computes the identical value.

If someone intercepts the Diffie-Hellman public values, they can't easily compute the random, secret values from them. However, Alice and Bob can each combine their own secret value with the other's public value to yield the secret key value. The crucial point of the Diffie-Hellman algorithm is that Alice and Bob will

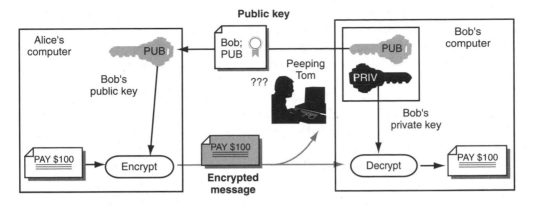

Figure 9-2: USING RSA FOR PUBLIC KEY ENCRYPTION. Anyone with Bob's public key can send him a message that only he can read. Bob keeps his private key secret and creates his public key from it. Alice uses Bob's public key to encrypt her message to him. The public key alone cannot decrypt the message. Only Bob's private key can decrypt it.

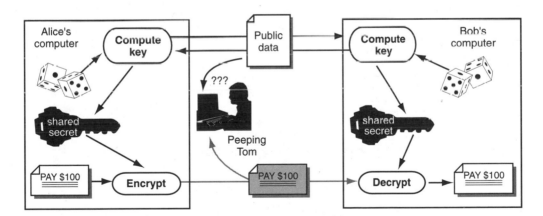

Figure 9-3: PRODUCING A DIFFIE-HELLMAN SHARED SECRET KEY. Alice and Bob exchange some information in public and then use that information to generate a private crypto key that nobody else can guess. Each generates a local secret (the *private key*), combines it with public data, and distributes the resulting *public key*. Alice combines Bob's public key with her private key to yield the shared secret; Bob produces the same number when applying his private key to Alice's public key. Peeping Tom can neither derive the key from the public data nor can he read a message encrypted with the key.

both end up with the same numerical result and nobody else can easily compute the same result from publicly available information. The resulting shared secret key can then be used with any secret key algorithm.

In practice, Diffie-Hellman is primarily used in key management procedures. For example, Alice and Bob exchange their Diffie-Hellman public keys and use them to compute their shared secret value. They each then use that shared value to compute a secret key that is used with a conventional secret key crypto algorithm like DES or IDEA. Since they both apply the same procedure to the same shared secret value, they will end up with the same shared secret key. This can then be used as a key encrypting key (KEK) to negotiate a session key, like with ANSI X9.17 (see Figure 4-8). The basic convenience and security is far superior to ANSI X9.17 however, since Alice and Bob never have to send the KEK itself between them. They only have to exchange their public keys, which do not have to be kept secret. All three of the automatic key exchange protocols proposed for IPSEC use Diffie-Hellman to implement the key exchange (see Section 5.5).

A variant of Diffie-Hellman, called *ElGamal*, provides functions similar to RSA: the encryption and digital signature computations. The encryption, however, has the peculiar feature of generating twice as much ciphertext as it is given plaintext. The Digital Signature Standard (DSS) established by NIST uses a variant of the ElGamal digital signature algorithm. DSS is described in Section 11.5.2.

Basically, Diffie-Hellman works because you can apply exponentiation in different orders and still get the same numerical result. This is shown in Figure 9-4. Note the math fact showing that we get the same answer even if we apply the exponents in different orders. The exponents are our private keys. We pick a huge prime number n and a small Base value that is shared publicly between Alice and Bob.

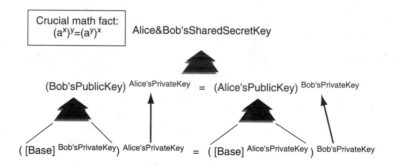

Crucial math fact:
$$(a^x)^y = (a^y)^x$$

Alice&Bob'sSharedSecretKey

$(Bob'sPublicKey)^{Alice'sPrivateKey} = (Alice'sPublicKey)^{Bob'sPrivateKey}$

$([Base]^{Bob'sPrivateKey})^{Alice'sPrivateKey} = ([Base]^{Alice'sPrivateKey})^{Bob'sPrivateKey}$

Figure 9-4: THE BASIC MATH CONCEPT BEHIND THE DIFFIE-HELLMAN ALGORITHM. This is a simplified portrait of how the Diffie-Hellman algorithm produces its shared secret. Alice and Bob choose huge random numbers (hundreds of bits) to use as private keys. Their public keys are produced by raising an agreed Base value to the power of their private key. Alice and Bob will compute a secret value that is unique to their two private keys when they exponentiate each others' public key.

Then they each choose a large integer to use as their private key. Alice computes her public key by exponentiating the base value by her private key and taking the remainder divided by n. Bob does the same. Alice computes the shared secret by exponentiating Bob's public key with her private key in the same manner. Bob does the same, and computes the same shared secret key value. Although Figure 9-4 doesn't show the remainder calculations, the essence of the calculation is the same: Bob and Alice exponentiate their keys and end up with the same shared secret value. Attackers like Peeping Tom can't derive the shared secret value or the private keys from the publicly disclosed information.

The principal reason why attackers can't generally crack Diffie-Hellman is because there are no general shortcuts to find the secret exponents Bob and Alice used in that computation. This is the same as the general problem of computing discrete logarithms in a finite field, a problem for which mathematicians know no shortcuts. Mathematicians have centuries of experience with logarithms and have not found ways to compute them in these cases. Some have suggested that, given enough time and memory, an attacker could generate an enormous table of values for a particular Base value and use it compute discrete logarithms on that Base.

Diffie-Hellman has produced a lot of interest in IPSEC circles largely because it can be used to achieve *perfect forward secrecy*. This is a crypto protocol that eliminates the need for using long-lived KEKs to distribute session keys. One of the perceived shortcomings with key exchange systems like ANSI X9.17 is that a KEK may be used to distribute numerous session keys. If the KEK is leaked somehow (perhaps by theft of a crypto device), then the thief can use the KEK to decrypt traffic that may have been recorded earlier. A perfect forward secrecy protocol generates temporary Diffie-Hellman secret keys in order to establish a session key. If any of these keys are recovered, they will only provide access to that session's information. The keys used to encrypt other sessions aren't compromised. So far, this capability has achieved very little use in commercial products.

9.2 Technology: RSA Public Key Cryptography

The public key technique developed by Rivest, Shamir, and Adelman is known as the RSA algorithm. The security of this approach is based on the fact that it can be relatively easy to multiply large primes together but almost impossible to factor the resulting product. RSA has become the algorithm that most people associate with the notion of public key cryptography. The technique literally produces public keys that are tied to specific private keys. If Alice has a copy of Bob's public key she can encrypt a message to him, and he uses his private key to decrypt it (Figure 9-2). RSA also allows the holder of a private key to encrypt data with it so that anyone with a copy of the public key can then decrypt it. While public decryption obviously doesn't provide secrecy, the technique does provide *digital signatures*, which attest that a particular crypto transform was performed by the owner of a particular private key. This is discussed further in Chapter 11.

RSA keys consist of three special numeric values that are used in pairs to perform encryption or decryption (Figure 9-5). Figure 9-6 illustrates how RSA keys are generated. The public key value is generally a selected constant that is recommended to be either 3 or 65,537. After choosing the public key we generate two large prime numbers, P and Q. The private key value is derived from P, Q, and the public key value. The distributed public keying material includes the constant public key value and the modulus N, which is the product of P and Q. The modulus is used in both the encryption and decryption procedures when either the public or private key is used. The original primes P and Q are discarded.

RSA is arguably the most widely used public key crypto technique. This is primarily because it is used in SSL to negotiate session keys between Web clients and secure servers. Since Netscape Navigator has been freely distributed to interested Web users, RSA has found itself on countless desktops worldwide. However, this is not RSA's only use. It is also used in secure e-mail packages like Privacy Enhanced Mail (PEM) and Pretty Good Privacy (PGP), which are discussed in Chapter 11. RSA digital signatures are also widely used to protect public key certificates as discussed in Chapter 12.

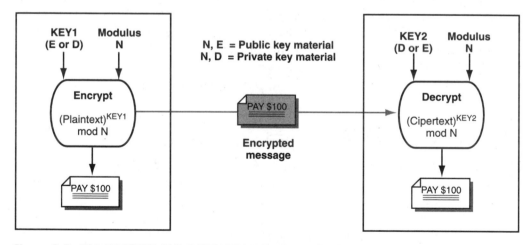

Figure 9-5: RSA ENCRYPT AND DECRYPT MAY USE EITHER THE PUBLIC OR PRIVATE KEY. The crypto functions take a key and the modulus value as arguments. The public key value and modulus are distributed together as the public keying material. If data is encrypted with the public key value, then only the holder of the private key can decrypt the message. If data is encrypted with the private key value, then anyone with the public key value can decrypt it.

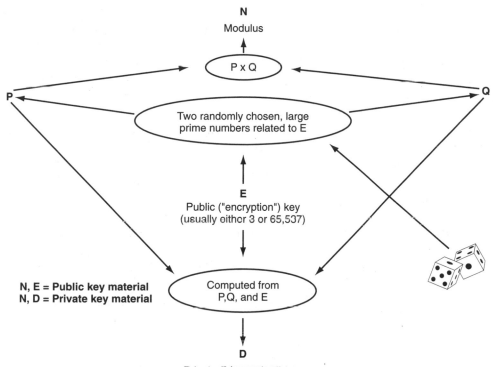

N
Modulus

P x Q

P

Two randomly chosen, large
prime numbers related to E

Q

E
Public ("encryption") key
(usually either 3 or 65,537)

N, E = Public key material
N, D = Private key material

Computed from
P,Q, and E

D
Private ("decryption") key

Figure 9-6: GENERATING KEYS FOR RSA CRYPTO ALGORITHMS. The RSA public key consists of the public key E and the modulus N. The public key is usually either 3 or 65,537. The modulus N is the product of two large prime numbers, P and Q, that are mathematically related to the chosen public key. The private key is computed from P, Q, and the public key value. The private key cannot be derived in practice because there is no practical way to compute the values P and Q by factoring N.

9.2.1 Brute Force Attacks on RSA

In general, analysts recognize that the first step in cracking the private key is to find the two prime numbers, P and Q, that were multiplied together to produce the modulus N. Mathematicians have analyzed variants of RSA and have proved conclusively that cracking one of these variants is equivalent in difficulty to factoring the modulus N. While this doesn't confirm that RSA itself is as difficult as factoring, it is a promising result. With practical crypto systems this is often the best assurance we can find. Since we can brute force crack a private key by factoring N, the security of RSA depends on how difficult it is to factor large numbers.

In 1977, Rivest, Shamir, and Adelman described their algorithm to Martin Gardner of *Scientific American* magazine, and this led to its first description in public. The inventors were fully aware that factoring the modulus was a critical vulnerability and they firmly believed that factoring would remain a difficult problem. They predicted that a number with as many as 129 decimal digits would confound the available computing resources for the foreseeable future. They even suggested that Martin Gardner publish a little challenge: They encrypted a brief message using a public key with a 129-digit modulus and offered a $100 reward to anyone who could crack the message.

In 1993, an international team of volunteers combined the idle computing time of more than 1,600 computers to crack the code. It took eight months to find the factors. A number with 129 decimal digits is the same length as one with 429 bits, so a 429-bit key represents today's upper limit on factoring technology. We know that it is possible to factor that large of a number, though it can take more than a thousand workstations and most of a year to do so.

Bit for bit, factoring N turns out to be a much easier problem than brute force cracking a secret key of a similar size. This is clearly shown in Figure 9-7. The cryptanalytic effort required to crack a secret key rapidly escalates beyond anything practical as it approaches 200 bits, while public keys of similar length are easily within reach of today's cracking technology. This is because public keys are

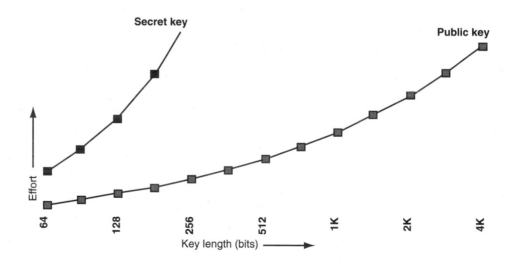

Figure 9-7: RELATIVE WORK FACTOR FOR CRACKING SECRET AND PUBLIC KEYS. The upper curve shows how quickly the brute force cracking effort increases with the number of bits in the secret key. The lower curve shows that cracking the same size public key requires much less effort. Secret key cracking exceeds physical cracking limits before reaching 200 bits, while a public key needs thousands of bits.

attacked differently from secret keys. If we have a secret key with 128 bits, for example, then we probably have to try every possible value that can be represented with a 128-bit number. When cracking an RSA key, the procedure of factoring N does not need to test every possible value of P and Q. If N is 128 bits long, then the cracking effort is dramatically less than it would be if we were cracking a secret key of similar length.

KEY SIZE RECOMMENDATIONS

If we are using public key and secret key crypto together, it is important to pick key sizes that are comparably strong. The public key should be at least as hard to crack as the secret key, and for many applications the public key should probably be even stronger. Table 9-1 lists secret key sizes along with public key sizes that would present a cryptanalyst with as tough a challenge. The sizes are based on models to estimate amounts of cryptanalytic effort published by the National Research Council. When trying to decide between longer or shorter key sizes, consult the criteria in Section 2.3.4.

In practice, many experts recommend choosing a public key length that is much harder to crack than the secret key length. This is because the public key is both easier to attack and a more valuable target. To find the secret key, attackers need to collect adequate amounts of ciphertext along with some notion of what the corresponding plaintext could look like. They will have a hard time judging if the ciphertext has been decrypted correctly unless they can anticipate whether it is

Table 9-1: Secret keys and public keys of comparable strength

Secret Key Sizes		Comparable Public Key Sizes	
No. of Bits	Algorithms	No. of Bits	Example Applications
56	DES	256	
70		384	Old PGP, minimum size
80	SKIPJACK	512	Short DSS, PGP "low grade"
96		768	PGP "high grade"
112	3DES with 2 keys	1,024	Long DSS, PGP "military grade"
128	RC4	1,440	
150		2,047	PGP "alien grade"
168	3DES with 3 keys	2,880	
192	Annual solar output	3,000	Annual solar output

ASCII text or binary text of some known format. To crack the public key they simply have to check potential values of P and Q against the number N. The public key is a more valuable target because it is generally used as a key encryption key for establishing secret keys. If the attackers crack the public key, they can then crack any other traffic if they manage to collect the key exchange messages that preceded them. If the attackers crack a secret key under these circumstances, they only retrieve the contents of the messages encrypted with that key. In many cases the key won't be in use any more, so attackers can't use the key they recovered to forge encrypted traffic. While the public key might not encrypt as much data, its effectiveness is crucial.

Although the resistance to brute force cracking is a reasonable starting point, it isn't clear that this tells the whole story. So little public key software has been deployed that there isn't much operational experience on which to base decisions. We don't really know if it is necessary to rely on a particular private key value for such a long time that it could lead to disaster. If we assume that public keys are replaced when equipment is replaced or software is updated, then in most cases we only need a private key that will resist attack for a few years.

9.2.2 Other RSA Vulnerabilities

The security of public key techniques like RSA rely on the fact that combining numbers in particular ways like multiplication or exponentiation can be very hard to reverse. Transformations like encryption can be easily reversed only if the original factors or exponents are already known. The factors or exponents become the private keys, and their combined forms become the public keys. This mathematical element is different from earlier crypto design techniques, when codes were constructed piecemeal from the lessons of previous, failed codes. However, this mathematical factor also leads to some novel vulnerabilities. An attacker can use the mathematical relationships to construct attacks. Such threats force us to use public key techniques in fairly limited ways.

While RSA naturally suffers from predictable vulnerabilities to brute force attempts at key recovery, its peculiar mathematical nature also makes it vulnerable to other attacks. These include attacks against message confidentiality and attacks against public key generation techniques. Mathematical attacks have been identified against encrypted data and against digital signatures; the digital signature attacks are discussed in Chapter 11.

Fortunately, we can generally defend against mathematical attacks by using RSA carefully. The practical result is that RSA must be used sparingly. When encrypting for confidentiality, it is best to limit the plaintext to random, unpredictable data. When signing, it is best to do so with a very rigid and carefully structured format. RSA Data Security Inc. (RSADSI) has developed a set of standards for applying public key crypto. These standards are called the Public Key Cryptography Standards (PKCS) and are available from RSADSI.

ATTACKS AGAINST MESSAGE CONFIDENTIALITY

It is now possible to make strong, mathematical arguments about why various codes are hard to crack, and how hard they are to crack in comparison with other provably hard mathematical problems, like extracting the prime factors comprising a large number. Some of these arguments are based on mathematical conjectures that no one has yet been able to prove. Even in such cases, however, the conjectures themselves have generally stood the test of time and mathematical progress has tended to support them.

However, the same mathematics can be used to identify attacks against RSA encryption. These attacks all exploit mathematical properties of messages and the keys that encrypt them. All of the attacks can be prevented by careful use of RSA in the application software. In some cases there are specific PKCS that include features to block specific attacks.

- **Timing attack**

  It has been observed that the RSA algorithm takes different amounts of time to perform its crypto operations according to the key's value. Some researchers have refined this to the point of being able to make estimates of a private key's value based on the time required to apply the private key to some information. The significance of this risk increases according to how close an attacker can get to the process performing the crypto operation. The attack is not feasible unless the attacker can closely monitor the processing time. Rivest has suggested a countermeasure that normalizes the amount of computation time so that different keys take similar execution times.

- **Small private key attack**

  There is a mathematical shortcut for recovering a private key if it is relatively small and the corresponding public key is relatively large. Since the public key is small in typical applications (either 3 or 65,537), there is never a corresponding private key that is vulnerable to this attack.

- **Small plaintext attack**

  If the public key value is 3 and the message length is less than a third the length of the modulus N, then there are shortcuts for trying to recover the message. If the message is smaller than the cube root of N, then the message can be recovered simply by taking the cube root of N. PKCS data formatting defeats this by forcing the message always to be larger than N.

- **Low-encryption exponent attack**

  If a particular message or series of mathematically similar messages are all encrypted with the same, low value for the public key E, like the value 3, then there is an attack that will recover the plaintext. However, this attack is thwarted if all messages contain random padding so that no two messages are similar. The PKCS defeat this by putting random padding in all RSA-encrypted messages.

- **Chosen ciphertext**

  This allows an attacker to decrypt a selected message if he can get the private key holder to encrypt or decrypt a mathematically related message. Peeping Tom intercepts a message from Bob to Alice that he wishes to read, but the message is encrypted with Alice's public key. Alice can decrypt it with her private key, but Peeping Tom doesn't have access to her private key. However, Tom can get Alice to apply her private key to another message that she knows isn't one of hers and give him the result.

  So Tom constructs a message that is mathematically related to the message from Bob. Alice decrypts this message for him and perhaps notices that it looks like gibberish before she releases it to Tom. But then Tom takes this apparent gibberish and mathematically combines it with Bob's original message to Alice. This produces a copy of Bob's original message in plaintext.

The essential lesson is that RSA isn't simply a "plug-in" crypto algorithm that consistently provides security. It must be used very carefully so that none of these vulnerabilities can be exploited by attackers. An implementation needs to follow the published recommendations in the PKCS and apply the crypto operations to data in a carefully controlled manner. If the system is too flexible about encrypting and decrypting, an attacker can exploit this to attack the private key or decrypt messages.

KEY GENERATION VULNERABILITIES

As with secret key systems, the key generation process itself can be a source of vulnerability. In RSA the key is constructed from two very large prime numbers, P and Q. If P and Q are not really primes, an attacker will have a dramatically easier time trying to factor N and derive the private key. So key generation must generate both an unpredictable number and ensure that P and Q are truly prime numbers.

Generating an unpredictable number is similar to the problem described for secret keys in Chapter 4. Recommendations in Section 4.3.3 also apply to the problem here. We are generating two large numbers, so we will probably use a random seed value and a PRNG to generate P and Q. As with secret key generation, the random "seed" must be truly random. If a PRNG must be used to generate additional random values, the PRNG must be cryptographically random and not simply a statistical PRNG.

Typically, P and Q are generated by starting with two completely random values that are each applied to a random prime-generating procedure. The procedure takes a random binary value and computes a prime number from it. This typically involves generating a candidate prime number and then applying statistical tests to ensure that the number is truly prime. RSA key-generating software usually makes a trade-off between key generation efficiency and security. Software that generates larger keys to protect more sensitive information will apply numerous lengthy tests to ensure that each number is a prime. As more tests are applied, the likelihood increases that the number is in fact prime. If the application has lower security requirements, fewer tests can be applied.

Another concern that is occasionally voiced is whether there are "enough" primes to serve as keys. It is true that within any given numeric range there are far fewer primes than there are nonprimes. Some people occasionally wonder if it is possible to make a huge table of primes and simply use a dictionary lookup to attack private keys. This is not a realistic risk. It is estimated that there are 10^{151} primes available simply in the range of 512-bit key values, and that far exceeds the physical capabilities of an exhaustive search.

9.2.3 Technical Security Requirements

The following requirements for secure use of RSA are roughly in priority order with the most important requirements first:

1. **Adequate key size.** Review the recommendations in Section 2.3.1 on how to select a secret key size. Choose a public key size that requires as much or more cracking effort by consulting Figure 9-7 or Table 9-1.

2. **Effective key generation.** Keys must be generated from a truly random seed and the prime generation process should apply multiple tests to ensure they are prime.

3. **Limitation on access to crypto functions.** Access to the encryption and decryption operations should be limited to carefully crafted application functions that don't pass arbitrary data through them. This prevents attackers from mounting chosen plaintext or chosen ciphertext attacks.

4. **Adherence to PKCS.** These standards block a variety of mathematical attacks on public key crypto and they define standard formats for interoperability between different public key system implementations.

5. **Timing attack countermeasures.** If the public key crypto software must operate in an environment where attackers can monitor the time needed to apply the private key to a crypto function, then the function should include wait loops to ensure that the computation time does not disclose information about the private key.

9.3 Technology: Secret Key Exchange with RSA Crypto

RSA is particularly well suited for key distribution. It requires a minimal amount of information sharing among users, and it allows an arbitrary user to send a key to another, specifically identified user. All of this can happen safely without the users having to exchange secret keys manually. All the sender needs is the recipient's public key and the sender can safely transmit a secret key that only the recipient can read.

For example, assume that Bob has generated a private key and has made his public key available to people who may want to communicate with him. When Alice wants to talk to Bob, Alice retrieves his public key and uses it to pass a secret key to him safely. Nobody except Bob will be able to decrypt the secret key after it is encrypted with Bob's public key. This is illustrated in Figure 9-8.

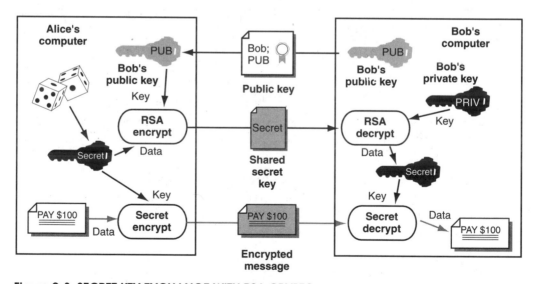

Figure 9-8: SECRET KEY EXCHANGE WITH RSA CRYPTO. Alice needs to send Bob a message using secret key encryption. She has generated a random secret key to use and she must send it to him. Alice retrieves Bob's RSA public key and uses it to encrypt the secret key. Bob uses his private key to decrypt the secret key. He uses the secret key to decrypt Alice's message.

This technique makes use of the best features of both public key and secret key crypto. Public key crypto lets anyone send an encrypted message to a specific recipient, but it is vulnerable to attacks if used in a general manner to encrypt a lot of data. Keys are relatively small compared to sensitive documents or transactions and their contents are completely unpredictable to an outsider. Secret key crypto is very fast and very secure, but is only as secure as the secret keys themselves. By using public key crypto we can greatly simplify the problem of exchanging secret keys. The procedure can even take place automatically and as often as needed.

This technique eliminates the need to establish and distribute individual pairwise keys for every pair of hosts that must communicate. In a secret key arrangement, a careful enterprise must generate individual keys for every pair of hosts that must communicate. This yields huge numbers of keys and rapidly becomes unworkable as the host population grows large. An organization with thousands of hosts could require millions of keys—an impossible administrative task. When we use public key crypto to exchange secret keys, we never generate the pairwise secret key until it is needed. At worst, each host might keep a list of public keys for all other hosts. This is more workable, even in larger networks.

Figure 9-8 also illustrates an alternative to storing public keys on every host. Instead of Alice keeping a copy of Bob's key, she sends an automated request to Bob's host to retrieve the key. This allows Bob to change the key if he needs to and ensures that Alice still gets the proper key value. This has led to elaborate architectures involving public key *certificates* and directory servers to hold them. Certificates will be discussed in detail in Chapter 12, but the reason for using certificates will be covered in the next section.

LEGAL RESTRICTIONS

Under the current U.S. export rules, RSA public key systems used for key exchange must restrict the size of the modulus (N) to no more than 512 bits in order to receive the most favorable export treatment. Systems with longer key lengths can not be exported unless they qualify under some other condition, like restricting encryption to purely financial data or providing an approved key escrow mechanism.

9.3.1 Attacking Public Key Distribution

There is a "gotcha" in the key exchange in Figure 9-8. Remember that whenever an important message is sent across a network, you need some way to authenticate it. In this case, Alice has no way of knowing if the public key she receives is in fact Bob's. This is a problem. The problem leaves us open to the *man-in-the-middle*

(MIM) attack, which sometimes carries the more gender-neutral title of *bucket brigade* attack.

In Figure 9-9, Bailey the Switcher has set up shop in a node sitting between Bob and Alice. Bailey plays the part of the "man in the middle" since she sees all traffic that passes between Bob and Alice. Since Bailey stands to benefit by interfering with messages between Bob and Alice, she decides to insert herself into their conversations. When Alice tries to retrieve a copy of Bob's public key, Bailey interferes and passes Alice a copy of her own public key instead. Note what happens when Alice now tries to send Bob a shared secret key.

Alice encrypts the secret key with Bailey's secret key, thinking it is Bob's key. Bailey intercepts the encrypted key, decrypts it, and saves it. Then she encrypts the key with Bob's public key and sends it on to Bob, who successfully decrypts it. Now Bob and Alice both have the secret key and they can exchange encrypted messages.

The problem is that neither Bob nor Alice will be aware that Bailey is part of the conversation. Alice doesn't use the public key any more, so she discards it and never figures out that it was really Bailey's key. Both Bob and Alice have the same secret key since Bailey repackaged and forwarded Bob's message to Alice. As is typical with good eavesdropping, there is no technical test you can perform to know whether it is happening or not in a case like this. Bailey can monitor the conversation until it's almost finished, and when one of them signs off, she can jump in and masquerade. All she has to do is discard the sign-off message and continue with, "By the way, be sure to pay $1,000 to Bailey the Switcher this week."

The solution to the problem is to provide a reliable way of associating public keys with individuals. There are essentially two approaches: manual distribution

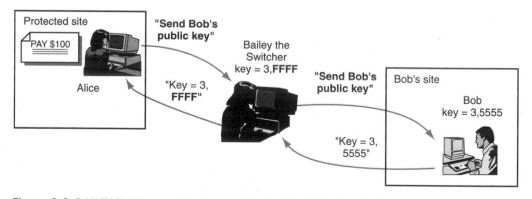

Figure 9-9: BAILEY THE SWITCHER IN A MAN-IN-THE-MIDDLE ATTACK. Bailey intercepts messages between Alice and Bob. She forwards Alice's request for Bob's public key but substitutes her own public key for Bob's. This tricks Alice into encrypting messages for Bob with Bailey's key. Bailey intercepts the messages and forwards them to Bob after encrypting them with Bob's real public key. Alice and Bob can't tell that Bailey is part of their conversation.

or public key certificates. In manual distribution, the keys can be sent out individually using some protected form of delivery, like what was described for secret keys in Chapter 4. The distribution process would certainly be easier for public keys since elaborate confidentiality procedures wouldn't be necessary. However, many experts are promoting the certificate-based approach.

A public key certificate is a specially formatted block of data that contains a public key, something to identify to whom the public key belongs, and a digital signature to verify the data's integrity. Certificates are issued by some trusted third party that vouches for the certificate's authenticity. Individual hosts use the third party's public key material to validate the certificate. In a sense, certificates simply defer the problem of checking the public key, since the checking procedure depends on the presence of at least one authoritative and correct public key. Certificate systems allow a single, authoritative public key to be used to authenticate the owners of numerous public keys. Certificates are discussed further in Chapter 12.

9.3.2 Public Key versus Secret Key Exchange

While public key procedures for key exchange hold great promise, they represent a relatively new technology that does not suit every purpose. The discussion of key exchange protocols in Section 4.5.2 noted the uncertain risks of rekeying protocols in general and of public key protocols in particular. Practical protocols have seen little widespread use and only a limited amount of in-depth analysis. Their very newness should raise a red flag for the extremely cautious. On the other hand, secret key techniques suffer from a variety of shortcomings, some of which were noted in the previous section. The practical result is that there are still situations when secret key exchange protocols should be used. There is no product or system based on either approach that solves all key exchange problems, so individual applications need to decide which approach best suits their situation. The following is a summary of the issues involved in choosing among these alternatives.

CHOOSING SECRET KEY

Secret key techniques for key management are best used under the following situations:

- **Communication between a small number of host computers**
  Unique secret keys should always be assigned to every pair of communicating entities in the system. If Bob, Alice, and Carl should all be able to communicate securely with one another, then each pair (Bob/Alice, Alice/Carl,

Bob/Carl) must have their own, unique key. This only works if the number of pairs is kept small.

- **Communication with a central host or KDC**
  We can efficiently assign individual keys to a large user population if users only need a few keys each for accessing central systems. For example, we can assign an individual key to each user that needs to access a central modem bank via an IPSEC client.

- **All communicating hosts are efficiently identified beforehand**
  Secret keys must be distributed carefully, and key distribution is a security-critical operation. This can only take place effectively if we know ahead of time who needs the keys and we can distribute them reliably before they will be needed.

- **Central hosts are adequately protected against key leakage**
  If we are using secret keys to access central hosts, then those hosts must have a database of all the keys of their authorized users. This database is a very attractive target to an attacker like Henry the Forger, since the keys would allow him to masquerade as any other user on the system. This approach is risky if we can't protect the central host's key lists from disclosure.

- **Access revocation must be timely and reliable**
  If it is absolutely necessary to revoke access quickly, reliably, and efficiently, then secret keys are currently the best approach. If one side of a secret key association has become compromised, the other side can simply revoke the appropriate secret key. Public key techniques typically rely on a separate "revocation list" to disable an invalid key, but these lists have not been fully implemented in the available public key systems.

- **Off-the-shelf availability**
  Secret key systems are widely available and extensively deployed, particularly in the banking industry. They are relatively simple to construct and test.

Secret key-based systems become impossible to manage as the number of communicating hosts increases. If every host needs to talk to every other host, the number of keys needed rapidly escalates. The only way to make such a system work is to force all traffic through central hosts and then distribute keys that allow individual hosts to connect to the central hosts. These techniques and trade-offs were discussed in Chapter 4.

CHOOSING PUBLIC KEY

Public key techniques for key management are best used under the following situations:

- **Point-to-point communication between a large number of host computers**

  If individual hosts must be able to communicate directly with one another without some intermediary like a KDC or central host, then public key exchange is the only reasonable approach. Secret key techniques become intractable very quickly as the number of hosts increases.

- **Central hosts that cannot safely store a large database of secret keys**

  Public key exchange protocols do not require the central host to store secret keys. The central host can use individuals' public keys to authenticate authorized users. The public keys are not vulnerable to abuse simply because someone makes a copy of them.

- **Inefficient revocation is an acceptable risk**

  The strength of public key protocols is that the public keys can be easily and widely distributed. The system works better when as many users as possible have easy access to copies of other users' public keys. Unfortunately, this is also a weakness. If Bob's keying material is stolen, he has no way to reach out to every copy of his public key and invalidate them all. Even if the key is carried within a public key certificate, there is no easy way to revoke the certificate reliably and immediately.

  The suggested solution to this problem is the "revocation list," a list of every public key certificate that has been canceled. Sophisticated systems will automatically consult these revocation lists when validating a certificate. Unfortunately, such capabilities are not widely available in commercial systems.

- **Custom engineering costs are acceptable**

  Although many vendors are promising to ship products soon that provide comprehensive public key crypto support, it is unlikely that the first generation of such products will be easy to use. Highly visible public key systems in use today were developed by specialized organizations that have a lot of expertise in public key systems and in security. Except for proprietary, integrated systems like Lotus Notes, it is rare to find a "homegrown" public key system being used for even a medium-risk application.

9.3.3 Technical Security Requirements

Here are the security requirements for the use of public key crypto to distribute secret keys, given roughly in priority order with the most important requirements first:

1. **Generate good random secret keys.** This is essential or the rekeying facility is worthless. It is better to use a key continually that is practically impossible to guess and hard to change than a key that is both easy to change and easy to guess. Secret key generation should comply with the requirements in Section 4.3.3.

2. **Use a good RSA implementation to encrypt the keys being exchanged.** RSA relies on subtle mathematical features in order to provide its security, so it must be applied with caution. The implementation should comply with the requirements listed in Section 9.2.3.

3. **Provide a mechanism to authenticate public keys.** While public keys don't need protection against disclosure, they do need protection against modification. This protects the keys against a MIM attack. The keys may be authenticated through a trustworthy manual distribution procedure (Chapter 4) or through public key certificates (Chapter 12).

4. **Provide a mechanism to update the public keying material.** Keys are always at risk of being compromised, and the compromise of your private key will render your public key worthless for protection. You must have a way to update your public key and private key in order to handle such a risk.

5. **Use an accepted, published protocol for automatic rekeying.** Many public key techniques are relatively new and untested, but they have sparked intense interest in the research community. These protocols have been scrutinized for vulnerability to classic attacks like spoofing, forgery, and replay. A protocol's strengths and weaknesses are far less likely to take customers by surprise if the essentials of its behavior are public knowledge. Proprietary implementations present too many opportunities for hidden flaws.

9.4 Secure Sockets Layer

The SSL protocol combines the capabilities of three separate IPSEC protocols and applies them to transport-layer protection (Figure 9-11). In practice, SSL implementations are usually bundled with specific applications that use SSL to protect the application's data while in transit (Figure 9-10). By far the most common use of

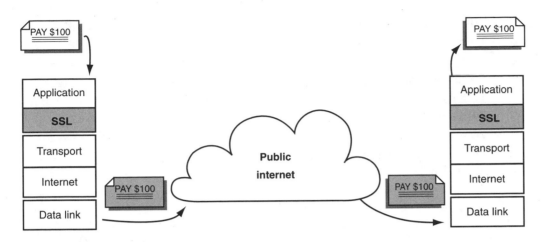

Figure 9-10: TYPICAL SOFTWARE ARRANGEMENT FOR THE SSL PROTOCOL. SSL is typically bundled with an application like a Web browser. Cryptographic protection is applied before the data is given to the TCP/IP stack, so it is treated like generic TCP/IP data. SSL-capable applications can work with any TCP/IP stack.

SSL is on the World Wide Web. Netscape Communications estimates that there are more than 40 million users of its SSL-capable Navigator software.

The three protocol capabilities bundled into SSL include authentication, encryption, and key exchange. In IPSEC these are provided by separate protocols: the AH, the ESP, and the key exchange protocols like SKIP and ISAKMP. SSL data is always transmitted in a special format that incorporates a cryptographic checksum like the AH and a security association identifier like the ESP. When two hosts first start communicating with SSL, the initial messages use a special handshake protocol to establish the crypto algorithms and keys to be used.

SSL is designed to always work between a host behaving as a client and one behaving as a server. The SSL protocol consists of the following major elements:

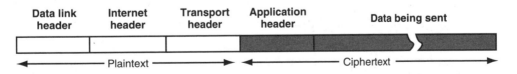

Figure 9-11: BASIC PACKET FORMAT USED FOR TRANSPORT LAYER CRYPTO LIKE SSL. Most of the communications protocol data is passed in plaintext; only the application header and actual data being sent to the application is cryptographically protected.

- **The record protocol**

  This functions as a layer beneath all SSL messages and indicates the encryption and integrity protection being applied to the data.

- **The handshake protocol**

  This negotiates the use of new crypto algorithms and keys between the communicating client and server.

- **The alert protocol**

  This indicates when errors have occurred or when a session between two hosts is being ended.

Instead of the security association used by IPSEC, SSL maintains its security state according to *sessions* associated with a particular set of TCP/IP host addresses and corresponding server port numbers. Thus, both Alice and Carl might have SSL sessions established with Bob, and each will have their own crypto parameters. Alice and Bob might agree to use RC4 for encrypting Web traffic while Carl and Bob might be using DES. Whenever Alice sends an SSL-protected Web request, Bob will automatically use their established RC4 keys to protect the traffic. As long as they have a session established, Alice and Bob will continue to use the same crypto parameters.

With Version 3.0, SSL has become a fairly sophisticated protocol, but its typical use follows a model established with SSL Version 2.0. This earlier version was widely distributed in early releases of the Netscape Navigator, and it gave Web users a way to access Web servers securely to perform simple commercial transactions. SSL provided its security services without requiring users to manipulate cryptographic keys or other such things personally. If a hypertext link in a page specified "https," then the browser would automatically try to use SSL without requiring extra work by the user. SSL 3.0 preserves this transparency while providing additional crypto capabilities and protection against ever more subtle attacks.

Figure 9-12 illustrates the basic handshake protocol. Alice, taking the place of the client, exchanges "Hello" messages with Bob, who takes the place of the server. These Hello messages contain random data. Then Bob sends Alice his public key embedded in a signed certificate. Alice generates some random data to use as a shared secret, uses Bob's public key to encrypt the secret, and sends the encrypted secret to Bob in a "Client Key Exchange" message. Alice also sends a "Change Cipher Spec" to switch to the selected cipher services and key, followed by a "Finished" message. Bob replies by sending both a Change Cipher Spec and a Finished message himself. The Finished messages are both protected with the new crypto parameters, so both Bob and Alice can verify that the other is ready to communicate.

Now that the crypto parameters are established, Alice and Bob will exchange application data using SSL's record protocol. Each record is individually encrypted

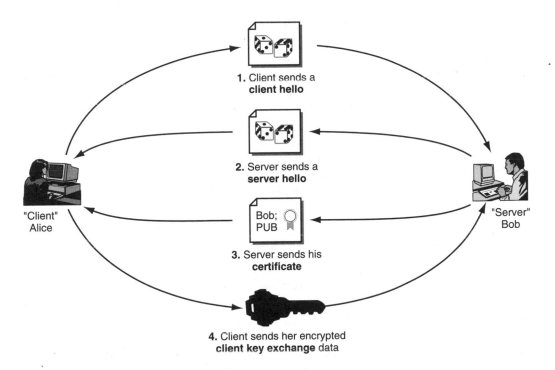

1. Client sends a
client hello

2. Server sends a
server hello

3. Server sends his
certificate

4. Client sends her encrypted
client key exchange data

"Client"
Alice

"Server"
Bob

Figure 9-12: ESSENTIALS OF THE SSL HANDSHAKE PROTOCOL. The client (Alice) and server (Bob) exchange "Hello" messages containing random data. Then Bob sends his public key embedded in a signed certificate. Alice generates some secret random data and sends it to Bob in a "Client Key Exchange" message encrypted with his public key. Then Bob and Alice use a combination of their publicly exchanged random data and Alice's secret random data to generate the keys they will use. Finally they exchange "Change Cipher Spec" and "Finished" messages (not shown here) to verify that they have generated the same keys. The mixture of public and private random data is exportable and it defeats replay attacks.

and hashed, and the recipient will treat it as a fatal error if a message arrives with an invalid hash. This is because the underlying TCP service should automatically correct unintentional transmission errors. When Alice or Bob are ready to close the connection, they send a "Close Notify" message to each other.

If Alice needs to establish another Web connection to Bob, she can resume the previously established session by providing its session identifier in the Client Hello message. This invokes an abbreviated version of the handshake protocol that reuses the previously established crypto parameters, including the shared secret value. This efficiency step is particularly useful for Web traffic since it typically consists of numerous, separate connections by the client to the same server.

While the preceding discussion describes how SSL is typically used to handle Web traffic security, this is not the only way SSL works, nor is it necessarily the only way a Web-based application might use it. SSL in general and Version 3.0 in particular support a broad range of cryptographic algorithms and even provide a mechanism to use public keys for authentication in both directions. The typical Web-based key exchange just described is built around the authentication of the server's RSA public key, and SSL performs no cryptographic authentication of the client. However, SSL 3.0 also supports key exchanges between a client and a server using the following:

- RSA using anonymous public key values
- Diffie-Hellman using anonymous or signed public key values
- Fortezza key exchange to use the SKIPJACK crypto algorithm

SSL VERSIONS AND OTHER TRANSPORT SECURITY PROTOCOLS

While Netscape is encouraging all SSL users to convert to servers and browsers that support SSL Version 3.0, support for Version 2.0 will probably need to persist for a long time. Furthermore, the Transport-Level Security Working Group of the IETF has been drafting a "standardized" transport security protocol, probably under a name other than SSL. Microsoft Corporation has also produced the Private Communication Technology (PCT) protocol that is compatible with SSL Version 2.0.

While it is true that these protocols are different, the essential behaviors described in the previous section are the same. Some features do not appear in SSL 2.0, like the Close Notify message and support of additional crypto suites like anonymous RSA, Diffie-Hellman, and Fortezza.

9.4.1 Other SSL Properties

There are two SSL features that aren't called out in the operating concept we have just outlined, but are clearly of interest. The first is *key recovery,* a mechanism that leaks keying material in order to comply with export laws on cryptographic systems. The second is *client certificates,* which is the ability of clients to have their own private keying material and the public key certificates to go with them.

KEY RECOVERY

A variety of laws in the United States and other countries restrict the export and import of crypto systems. Netscape Communications negotiated with the U.S. government to permit the export of a basic encryption facility with Netscape's SSL products. These negotiations limit the encryption to use the RC4 algorithm with no more than 40 bits of secret key, and the RSA algorithm for key exchange using a modulus of 512 bits.

To comply with this, SSL defines a special version of RC4 that uses a 128-bit encryption key constructed of no more than 40 secret bits. The secret bits are taken from the shared secret passed between client and server in the Client Key Exchange message. The 128-bit key is constructed by hashing the 40 secret bits with random bits sent in plaintext in the Hello messages exchanged by the client and server. Thus, an outsider can reconstruct all possible 40-bit keys by hashing these Hello bits with different instances of the random 40 bits.

This approach allows an enterprise with adequate computing power (such as a government) to crack an SSL-encrypted message if necessary, but protects the messages from casual prying. However, 40 bits is no deterrent to large-scale attacks, as was demonstrated by three separate teams in 1995. In early 1997, another challenger cracked a 40-bit crypto key in only three and one-half hours.

CLIENT CERTIFICATES

SSL provides several optional protocol messages that allow a server to ask for a public key certificate from a client. The server can then authenticate the client by sending it a "challenge" encrypted with its public key. This allows SSL to provide reasonably strong authentication based on private keying material instead of reusable passwords or access codes.

There are a variety of issues associated with certificate-based authentication, particularly where naive users and mobile clients are concerned. These are examined in more detail in Chapters 10 and 12.

9.4.2 Basic Attacks Against SSL

This is a summary of the "classic" security problems against which SSL was designed to protect. These include brute force, known plaintext, replay, and the MIM attack. There are also some specialized attacks that SSL Version 3.0 contains specific measures to prevent. These are all examined here, followed by a review of how SSL handles the classic Internet attacks.

BRUTE FORCE CRYPTANALYTIC ATTACK

SSL implementations support a variety of public and secret key crypto algorithms. The secret key algorithms use key lengths ranging from 40 bits to 168 bits. The most common SSL software is limited to 40-bit secret keys and 512-bit RSA keys because of export restrictions. While there has been no public demonstration of cracking a 512-bit public key, there have been several public demonstrations of cracking 40-bit secret keys. This follows the intent of crypto design: The difficulty of the attack is tied to key length.

KNOWN PLAINTEXT "DICTIONARY" ATTACK

The known plaintext attack could be a particular risk in Web applications since many messages will contain predictable data, like the HTTP **GET** command. The most efficient form of known plaintext attack is a dictionary attack, and it is particularly effective when only a small number of secret crypto keys are used. The attackers construct a dictionary containing every possible encryption of the known plaintext message (the **GET** command for example). When they receive an encrypted message, they take the portion containing the encrypted **GET** command and look up the ciphertext in the dictionary. The ciphertext should match against a dictionary entry that was encrypted with the same secret key. If they get a "hit," they immediately know the secret key. If they get several hits, they can simply apply each of them to determine which is the right one.

SSL protects against dictionary attacks by not really using a 40-bit key. The key is really 128 bits long with only 40 bits of the key kept secret. The rest of the key is constructed from data that is disclosed in the Hello messages. However, this arrangement means that the dictionary cannot be simply 40 bits long. Since the 40-bit secret key is combined with 88-bit "disclosed" key, the resulting encryption does in fact use all 128 key bits. Thus, the dictionary must also have separate entries for all of the 128-bit keys. This makes the attack impractical. Thus, the only practical attack is the brute force attack noted previously, and it is significantly more difficult than a 40-bit dictionary attack.

REPLAY ATTACK

In this attack, Play-It-Again Sam collects messages sent earlier and replays them so that an interesting transaction gets repeated. For example, this could be a transaction that sends Sam some money. SSL defeats replay attacks during the handshake protocol by using a 128-bit nonce value that is unique to that connection. Sam cannot predict the nonce in advance, since it is based on events he likewise cannot predict. Therefore, a replayed nonce value won't look right to the client or the server if Sam tries to replay a previous set of SSL handshake messages.

MAN-IN-THE-MIDDLE ATTACK

The MIM attack is the same attack described earlier in Section 9.3.1. In the SSL case, Bailey the Switcher tries to masquerade as an SSL server to outside users like Alice, perhaps to forge extra payments to herself. SSL blocks this attack by using signed certificates to authenticate the server's public key. The certificate contains the name of the server host, its public key, and the digital signature of a trusted entity called the certificate authority. The certificate authority's public key is distributed with the SSL client software, which allows the client software to verify that the certificate's contents are genuine and unmodified. This lets the SSL client verify both the server's name and its public key value.

CLASSIC INTERNET ATTACKS

Here is how SSL by itself responds to the general Internet protocol attacks described in Section 6.4.1. While SSL is effective against most of these attacks, it provides no protection against SYN flooding.

- **Password sniffing**
  It is safe to carry reusable passwords under SSL encryption as long as the secret crypto key is long enough to defeat exhaustive key searches. This is because SSL normally encrypts all data traffic it carries. Therefore, forms can carry secret passwords and other such data as long as the server or client requires a sufficiently long crypto key. If an attacker can tangibly benefit from extracting a password from one of your transactions, then shorter keys (such as 40 bits) might not provide adequate security.

- **IP spoofing**
  IP spoofing uses forged IP addresses to fool a host into accepting bogus data. SSL does not rely on IP addresses alone to process messages securely. The messages must also have been correctly processed with a shared secret key. Attackers would not possess this key, so they cannot spoof the server or the client.

- **IP hijacking**
  The crypto protections applied to SSL traffic have always protected it against basic hijacking attacks. SSL 3.0 also blocks more sophisticated hijacking attacks in which attackers try to replay encrypted data collected earlier from the same session.

- **SYN flooding**
  SSL provides no protection against SYN flooding. This is because the SYN flood attack is made against the TCP layer and SSL's protections are applied

above that layer. The SSL software must wait for a TCP connection to be fully established before it can begin to determine whether the connection is legitimate or not. The SYN flood attack involves partially open TCP connections and does its damage long before SSL receives any messages.

SYN flooding in SSL servers must be prevented using the same general mechanisms used in any other service that must accept unprotected public connections.

9.4.3 SSL Security Evolution

SSL is one of those rare commercial crypto systems that has evolved in the public eye. The Netscape Navigator, its server counterparts, and the SSL protocol specification have all been subjects of intense interest and extensive public discussion on the Internet. Earlier chapters have noted random number problems in early Navigator software releases and the weakness of 40-bit encryption. However, it is worthwhile to note that every reported problem, whether theoretical or practical, has been answered with an additional security measure. These fixes don't always solve the problems completely, but they generally improve the system's security in some sensible way.

This process is particularly fascinating because these threats never manifested themselves in terms of lost assets of Internet vendors or customers. The problems were all identified by the professional computer security community and associated experts. In some cases the threats were demonstrated, like the teams that cracked 40-bit encryption keys. However, there have been no public reports of individuals or enterprises suffering a loss due to an attack on SSL-protected traffic. Unlike those with cellular telephones and credit cards, SSL security problems were identified and fixed before they could be exploited for fraudulent purposes.

The following is a summary of security problems found and fixed in early versions of SSL and of Netscape client software. As noted, these problems were generally found by members of the computer security community and were reported in open discussions. There are no recorded instances of costly attacks using any of these techniques. All of these attacks have been effectively blocked in later protocol and software revisions.

- **Generating predictable keys**

   This was an implementation problem in the key generation software for the Netscape Navigator. Early versions generated keys based on a small amount of internal information that proved too easy to predict in some cases. A team of students at the University of California, Berkeley, demonstrated that they could dramatically reduce the time it took to crack SSL encryption by predicting likely values for the secret key being used. Subsequent versions of the Navigator use a more elaborate technique to generate keys that is argu-ably harder to predict.

- **MIM attack with incorrect certificate**
  In theory, SSL stops a MIM attack by validating the public key certificate before using its public key. However, this does not prevent a MIM attack when the client receives a valid certificate with the wrong name on it. Early versions of the Navigator left it up to the user to verify that the public key certificate did in fact belong to the entity that owned the Web server. This meant that a MIM attack would certainly succeed against a naive user, and that is just the user for whom the Netscape Navigator was designed. This problem was in part due to the implied architectural barrier between the transport-layer security protocol and the application-layer activities that identified a particular server in a URL. Subsequent releases of the Navigator extract the host name from the server's certificate and verify it against the host name in the URL.

- **Integrity attacks on data with short crypto checksum keys**
  SSL Version 2.0 used the same crypto keys for encryption and for computing a keyed hash on the data. This meant that a successful brute force attack on the encryption key would also let the attacker forge data sent with that key. The 40-bit encryption key is required by various export laws, but there is no similar restriction on keys for integrity checks. Therefore, this integrity weakness was unnecessary. IPSEC uses separate keys for encryption and integrity, and SSL 3.0 uses separate keys as well.

- **Hijacking a connection for replay**
  While the handshake protocol does a reasonable job of preventing a replay, the SSL Version 2.0 protocol had limited protection against clever replay attacks. An attacker could, in theory, collect a dictionary of ciphertext from the session, and all that ciphertext would have been generated with the correct key. If the attacker can guess which ciphertext is worthwhile to replay, he could replay it on the hijacked connection that the authorized server and client established. If the hijacker jumps in when the client tries to close the connection, the client never knows that an attack took place, and the server simply thinks the client is continuing the original connection.
  SSL 3.0 incorporated security measures that block this type of attack. Every message sent by SSL now includes a sequence number within the message's protected contents. The sequence number is incremented for each message sent, so a replayed message would almost certainly show up out of sequence.

9.5 For Further Information

- **Kaufman, Perlman, and Speciner,** *Network Security: PRIVATE Communication in a PUBLIC World*
  Contains a good, practical overview of the mathematics of public key cryptography.

- **RSA Laboratories,** *The Public Key Cryptography Standards (PKCS)*
  The published standards for how to implement secure, interoperable public key crypto facilities.

- **Rivest, "On the Difficulty of Factoring"**
  A set of estimates on how hard it is to brute force crack an RSA key.

- **Netscape Communications,** *SSL 3.0 Specification*
  http://www.netscape.com/libr/ssl/ssl3/index.html
  The official definition of SSL. The appendix on attacks is especially interesting.

Chapter

10

World Wide Web Transaction Security

It is common sense to take a method and try it. If it fails, admit it frankly and try another. But above all, try something.

—Franklin Delano Roosevelt, Speech at Oglethorpe University

IN THIS CHAPTER

This chapter talks about using the World Wide Web to perform simple commercial transactions. The most common approach for securing such transactions is to use SSL or a similar transport-level protocol. The following topics are discussed:

- Security objectives and basic issues in protecting Web transactions
- The basic mechanisms of the World Wide Web and Web forms
- The essentials of SSL-capable Web browsers and servers
- An example deployment showing a Web catalog vendor

While the specific examples, in most cases, involve SSL, the general concepts apply to all Web browsers that implement transport-level protection, including Microsoft's PCT protocol.

10.1 Security Objectives

These objectives are tied to the handling of commercial transactions between a large community of vendors and customers using compatible software.

- **Protect transactions against attack on the Internet.**
  Transactions should be safe to perform but difficult for others to replay, modify, or otherwise interfere with. Both the client and server need to identify reliably who is on the other end of the connection, and the messages must not be modified in transit. If the transaction involves confidential information (such as credit card numbers), then the information must be adequately protected from eavesdropping.

- **Ensure security without prior arrangements between customers and vendors.**
  Customers who are browsing the Internet will not necessarily have established any relationship with a company before they decide to perform a commercial transaction. The customer and vendor must be able to protect their transaction even if they have never communicated with each other before.

- **Apply crypto protections selectively as needed.**
  Most traffic on the World Wide Web consists of visits to unprotected public sites. Crypto always causes a performance penalty, so users are not going to want to use it except when really needed. Protection should only be applied when it is really needed to protect transaction data, and it should not be applied to static Web pages.

- **The receiving host must be protected from attack by incoming messages.**
  Both servers and clients on the Web are vulnerable to attack. Those indulging in commercial transactions are even more vulnerable since there may be tangible benefits to attacking commercial traffic. The vendors' computing systems are targets of Internet attack simply because they are on the Internet and reside at a fixed address. Client software packages are attractive targets if they store crypto keys, pass codes, or account numbers that validate Internet transactions.

Security systems in earlier chapters were designed to protect a large community of users without making them explicitly invoke security measures when needed. On the World Wide Web, typical data transfers are completely unprotected. SSL allows individual users to decide when to protect their own data.

10.2 Basic Issues in Internet Transaction Security

Internet transaction security poses special problems because it attempts to reach a vast community of users that span the full range—from novice to expert computer user. This, combined with the essential technical differences between transport security and lower level techniques, yields a different set of benefits and problems.

- **Widely available, user-friendly transaction protocol**
  The economic viability of Internet commercial transactions requires that a large number of customers have the right software to reach a large number of vendors. This makes it possible to generate enough revenue from Internet transactions to justify the costs of the Internet connections, vendor software, and associated facilities. The "forms" facility in the Hypertext Transfer Protocol (HTTP) used in the World Wide Web has proven sufficient for handling transactions and has been adopted by a broad range of Internet users.

- **Authenticating the customer and vendor**
  Nobody wants to take part in a transaction where it isn't possible to identify the entity on the other end. While we may be willing to purchase a garment from Lands' End over the Internet, we want some assurance that it is Lands' End with whom we are speaking and not someone masquerading as Lands' End. By the same token, Lands' End wants to be certain that the person paying for the merchandise is the person who ordered it.

- **Key management with naive users**
  To make Internet transactions work we need a way of establishing keys so that customers can safely communicate with vendors. Customary techniques of software packaging and selling make it far too expensive to use secret keys for this. The Web's ease of use and the extensive distribution of browser software have put millions of people on the Internet with very little training. These people expect security measures to work correctly with as little muss and fuss as possible. While reasonably sophisticated users should be able to handle simple key management tasks, most users will either avoid such tasks or do them incorrectly.

- **Liability for bogus transactions**
  This is the problem of ascribing costs when a bogus transaction occurs and cannot be reversed. For example, someone may masquerade as an existing customer and extract goods or services from the vendor. Does the customer lose out, does the vendor make up the difference, or does some designated third party (such as a credit card issuer) pick up the cost? It all depends on how various agreements are written. Typical credit cards in the United States tend to place the liability for bogus transactions on the vendor.

10.3 Transactions on the World Wide Web

The World Wide Web is the one application that has brought the Internet within everyone's reach. While some point out that Internet e-mail and file transfers have for years carried the most Internet traffic, there is little doubt that more people have used Web browsers than any other Internet service. This is primarily because they are so easy to use: It's the ubiquitous point-and-click interface and it takes you all over the globe in moments. Documents retrieved from the web typically contain *hypertext links* which in turn refer to other documents on the Web. If you click on a hypertext link the associated document is immediately retrieved and displayed for you. Practically every important specification document regarding the Internet is available via the Web, and most computer system vendors provide their latest product descriptions through the Web, too. The "forms" extensions to the Web provide the essentials needed to perform transactions between users and Web based-vendors.

There are four essential elements to the Web: browsers, servers, URLs, and pages. A *Web browser* is the client software that people use to access the Web. The browsers send requests to Web servers which contain *Web pages* containing the information for which the users can ask. Each Web page is identified by a unique *Uniform Resource Locator* or URL (Figure 10-1). The browser requests a page by sending that page's URL to the server. Pages are generally written in a document markup language called Hypertext Markup Language (HTML).

Traffic between browser and server follows a protocol called Hypertext Transport Protocol (HTTP) which uses the TCP transport protocol. Retrieving a page always starts with the browser being given a URL. An experienced user might actually type in a URL: They appear everywhere, from billboards to television commercials. More typically the URL comes from a hypertext link on a previously retrieved Web page. Each URL contains three major fields: the protocol field, the server

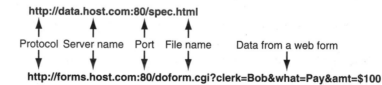

Figure 10-1: FORMAT OF A UNIFORM RESOURCE LOCATOR (URL). The URL tells what protocol to use (usually HTTP), the server host name, the port number (optional), and the Web page's file name. The host name may take any conventional form. The port number is left blank when using a protocol's standard port number. Typical Web pages have the ".html" suffix. Responses to forms will have the ".cgi" suffix to indicate that data is being returned for processing by the given file. In those cases the URL includes the data being returned, presented in a "name=value" format.

name, and the page's file name on the server (Figure 10-1). The protocol field could indicate one of several TCP/IP application protocols, but it will say "http" if we are retrieving a Web page.

The process for retrieving a Web page is illustrated in Figure 10-2. The browser uses the server name to open a TCP connection to that server, usually through TCP port 80. Once the connection is open, the browser sends an HTTP **GET** command that includes the URL and a list of data formats the browser will accept. If the server can fulfill the browser's request, it sends the Web page back to the browser via the same TCP connection. The server closes the connection as soon as the entire page has been sent. Many pages include references to graphical files to be displayed on the page. The browser retrieves these files by repeating the connection process for each file.

10.3.1 Transactions with Web Forms

A typical Web access consists of a single TCP connection that requests a page from the server and fetches it back to the client. A *transaction* requires that the client send information to the server. This requires special Web features to collect the data and process that data on the server. A Web transaction consists of a pair of connections—one to fetch the Web *form* that collects the transaction data and another connection to transmit the collected data to the server. This is shown in Figure 10-3.

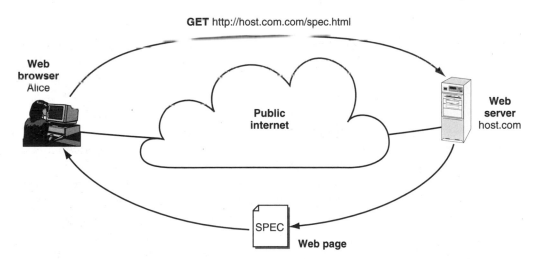

Figure 10-2: RETRIEVING A PAGE FROM THE WORLD WIDE WEB. When the user with the browser selects a URL (possibly via a hypertext link), the URL is passed to the Web server for retrieval. The server sends the page back. Each file is retrieved via a separate connection.

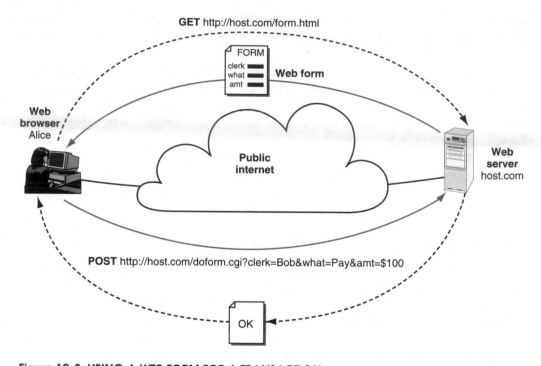

Figure 10-3: USING A WEB FORM FOR A TRANSACTION. The Web form is retrieved the same as any other Web page. The recipient fills in the form and then chooses a hypertext link that transmits ("posts") the information filled in by the recipient. The server runs a special program (a "cgi script") that processes the form's contents and then returns a page indicating the result ("OK").

Web transactions rely on three key elements of the Web protocols: forms, the **POST** command, and common gateway interface (CGI) scripts. Forms are Web pages containing special HTML functions that instruct the browser to collect particular types of data from the user. The HTML **POST** command transmits the data values collected by the form to the server. The command also indicates a CGI script that has been programmed to collect the form's data, process it, and return a Web page in response. CGI scripts can be tailored to run custom programs capable of implementing typical automated transactions.

In Figure 10-3, Alice's organization has set up a Web server to receive transactions from her while she is on the road. Instead of sending her "Pay $100" messages directly to Bob, she reads a form on the company's Web site, fills it in with what she needs, and submits it to the Web server. Her Web browser software performs the transaction as a two-step process. First, Alice locates the form at the Web site, possibly by following a hypertext link to it. When the form is read into her computer, the browser displays it in a typical form style: There are boxes that must be filled in with text or numbers, there are multiple-choice lists of items, and there are various push-button controls. This particular form contains three fields: clerk, what, and amt. Alice naturally needs "Bob" to "Pay" the amount of "$100" so she fills in the form accordingly. After Alice has filled in the necessary information she will click on a button to send the entered data to the server. This generates the **POST** command that delivers Alice's data to a CGI script titled "doform.cgi."

10.3.2 Web Form Security Services

Web forms are naturally vulnerable to the usual Internet security threats. Attackers on the Internet can eavesdrop on Web traffic, modify forms while in transit, or fabricate their own forms and try to masquerade as a different user. Transactions based on Web forms generally need the following security services in priority order:

1. Transaction integrity
2. Customer authentication
3. Vendor authentication
4. Transaction secrecy

TRANSACTION INTEGRITY

Transaction security refers to whether outsiders can modify a form's contents while in transit. There is no point in performing a transaction unless both the customer and vendor are sure that their intentions are accurately communicated. The items ordered, the agreed price, and delivery plans must be seen as the same by both parties. This can only happen if both are assured that their messages are received intact.

CUSTOMER AUTHENTICATION

Vendors want to know for certain who you are so they can reliably determine who should pay the bill. Vendors will not perform a transaction without some assurance that they can reliably identify the recipient of goods and services so that the recipient can be billed.

In computer security we typically distinguish between *identification* of a person and *authentication*. Identification simply provides the name; authentication gives us the assurance that the correct name was provided. Better authentication systems are those in which it is harder for someone to masquerade as another.

VENDOR AUTHENTICATION

Vendor authentication refers to how reliably a customer can identify the server site. If you connect to a particular vendor, you want to be certain that you did indeed connect to that particular vendor and not to some other site masquerading as the vendor. Customers will not initiate transactions without some assurance that the recipient of their messages can in fact perform the transaction. It is important both to try to communicate with a specific vendor and to have some assurance that you are in fact communicating with that vendor.

TRANSACTION SECRECY

Commercial transactions are rarely matters of public record. In fact, most people find it better to limit the amount of information generally available about their commercial transactions. In some cases, transactions must be kept secret for business reasons. Also, many computing systems use secret passwords, access codes, and account numbers to authenticate the participants in a transaction.

It is important to keep these needs in perspective. To some extent, any commercial transaction document carries similar information and could face the same general threats. A postcard requesting a magazine subscription contains the same general information as a commercial Web transaction. Keep in mind the relative security of such methods when assessing security measures and costs for Internet transactions.

In many cases security measures can be reduced if there are obvious techniques to detect bogus transactions eventually and limit any financial loss they might carry. Keep in mind that despite hundreds of millions of dollars in fraud losses, the cellular phone industry continues to be incredibly profitable with a product that has little effective security. Such trade-offs are difficult to judge, however, and many potential participants in Internet commerce have already voiced significant concerns about transaction integrity, privacy, and fraud risks.

10.4 Security Alternatives for Web Forms

The following is a review of candidate techniques for providing the security services noted in the previous section:

- Protection with passwords
- Network security (IPSEC)
- Connection security (SSL)

- Application security (secure HTTP [SHTTP])
- Review of authentication alternatives

All of these address some requirements, but not all yield successful solutions today.

10.4.1 Password Protection

This approach collects a secret password or other personal identifier from the customer. Passwords by themselves provide no crypto protection. There's nothing to prevent an attacker from eavesdropping on a transaction or, if they're nimble, from modifying it while in transit. The transactions are vulnerable to password sniffing, so the password could be stolen and used by someone else to masquerade as a legitimate user. On the other hand, this approach is available and reasonably easy to implement. It is best restricted to low-risk applications.

Of the four security services noted earlier, passwords only provide customer authentication, and only a relatively weak form of that. Web servers typically collect passwords using either of two mechanisms. Some use the simple password mechanism integrated into more sophisticated Web browsers like the Netscape Navigator. Typically, the browser collects this information with a dialog box and only asks for a password if the browser encounters an "authentication failure" when requesting a page. Once the browser has collected the user's name and password, that information will be embedded in subsequent HTTP requests sent to that server. An alternative to using the browsers' built-in password function (some browsers don't support it) is to collect a password or other personal identifier on a Web form.

Transaction secrecy and integrity with this approach rely on the standard and vulnerable Internet protocols. Customers authenticate vendors solely by network address. When they request a connection to a particular vendor by using the vendor's domain name or numeric IP address, they assume that only that vendor is likely to respond in a consistent manner. Vendors authenticate customers with a preassigned password or other access code. The value may simply be the customer's account number.

Note, however, that the password mechanism *can* be used securely. If the server establishes some type of protected connection with SSL or perhaps IPSEC, then the password will be protected from sniffing by outsiders. This is discussed in Section 10.4.3.

10.4.2 Network-level Security (IPSEC)

The network level IP Security protocol (IPSEC) was introduced in Chapter 5. Network level-security, like IPSEC, is often seen as a general antidote to the security shortcomings of passwords. As summarized in Section 6.4.1, IPSEC can block a variety of important threats to Internet traffic like sniffing, spoofing, hijacking, and flooding. However, its tendency to provide all-or-nothing security yields a number of practical shortcomings when using IPSEC to protect Web transactions. So, while it will in fact provide all four of the protections noted earlier, it also blocks access to hosts that don't support it or don't have a security association with your own host.

As described in Chapter 5, IPSEC can provide confidentiality and integrity protection to any type of Internet traffic. It can be installed below the Web software so that protection does not require changes to the Web server or client software packages. However, IPSEC's network-layer protection is generally applied to all traffic between the client and server, and not only to transactions. This has two problems. First, it is inefficient to apply crypto to all Web traffic between the client and server. Web traffic tends to carry lots of data that does not require protection. Crypto processing tends to slow things down, and the Web's effectiveness generally depends on fast response times. The second problem is that we increase the risk of bogus transactions if we encrypt everything. If all traffic is treated the same as a transaction, then it's easier to confuse a mistaken or bogus transaction for a legitimate one.

Another IPSEC shortcoming is in key management. The common denominator for most IPSEC implementations is still pairwise secret keys. This is not a practical technique for protecting transactions between arbitrary Internet customers and vendors. Even the more sophisticated key management protocols still expect that both client and server will have their own public keying material and that it has been validated by a third party. This exceeds the sophistication of most Internet users.

10.4.3 Transport-level Security (SSL)

Security applied at the transport level provides better control over when security measures are used. An application like a Web browser can choose whether a particular connection is going to use transport-level security or not. This is the approach behind SSL, developed by Netscape Communications to protect Web traffic. Variants of this approach have been suggested by the Transport Level Security Working Group of the IETF, and a compatible alternative protocol was developed by Microsoft in its PCT protocol. SSL was described in detail in Section 9.4.

SSL can automatically apply encryption and integrity protection to the data it carries. The client and server negotiate to establish a satisfactory set of crypto parameters including an acceptably strong encryption cipher and a shared secret key. Clever use of public key cryptography allows SSL to negotiate shared secret keys based on a small amount of public keying data embedded in the browser software. The use of public keys allows the browsers to be commercially marketed on a broad scale and still provide good communications security.

The SSL-enabled Web software uses separate protocol identifiers and port numbers to distinguish between normal Web traffic and SSL-protected traffic. A hypertext link on a Web page will use SSL if the protocol identifier says "https" instead of the usual "http." SSL-protected Web traffic generally travels through a connection to server TCP port 443. If the server receives a connection to port 443, it applies SSL to the connection and then passes the Web data to the Web server. This arrangement gives both the client and server some control over what traffic is protected and what traffic moves fast.

Putting the crypto services in the transport layer can pose an architectural problem in some applications, since the crypto activities will be hidden from the application by a protocol interface. Typical SSL applications deal with this by integrating the SSL software into the application. This allows the application to monitor crypto activities when appropriate. For example, an SSL-enabled browser can fetch a crypto certificate retrieved by SSL from a server and verify that the host name in the certificate matches the host name in the requested URL. This prevents a host with a legitimate certificate from masquerading as another, and the test can only be performed inside the client application.

SSL suffers from other shortcomings due to its location in the protocol stack. As noted earlier, everything that passes through an SSL-protected connection is cryptographically protected whether it needs it or not. Fortunately, SSL-enabled Web clients and servers can interactively choose whether or not individual connections need to be protected. Typical IPSEC products do not implement this degree of control. However, SSL's transport nature also means that crypto security measures are only applied to the data in transit and are lost once a connection is closed. There are a variety of Web and transaction-oriented applications that would benefit from the ability to apply encryption and/or digital signatures directly to Web data for later processing.

10.4.4 Application-level Security (SHTTP)

The Secure Hypertext Transfer Protocol (SHTTP) is a set of security functions defined for protecting Web traffic, including forms and transactions. It carries many of the same benefits as transport-level security like SSL. From the standpoint of a network protocol architecture, many argue that an application protocol like SHTTP will always yield the best security results. In practice, however, SHTTP has enjoyed very limited success.

SHTTP supports both authentication and encryption of HTTP traffic between a Web client and server. Both client and server must implement SHTTP in order to apply the protections, though a server does have the option of allowing a transaction even when the client doesn't have the appropriate crypto capabilities. The crypto services use encryption and digital signature formats that were originally developed for Privacy Enhanced Mail (PEM, see Chapter 11).

The principal benefit of an application-specific protocol like SHTTP is that the protocol can define security very specifically in terms of the application's activities. For example, the application could handle a message containing digital signatures by several different agents and make decisions based on who signed what, or optimize the application of crypto services to different parts of a large message. When crypto processing is pushed into the transport layer, it must treat all application messages essentially the same. In practice, however, transport crypto seems sufficient for most transaction applications.

Embedding crypto services in HTTP does offer other possibilities. For example, SHTTP could define crypto security measures to apply to individual Web pages. Each page could carry its own crypto checksum or digital signature, allowing much safer distribution. Individually encrypted pages could be published on any Web server and still only be read by those with authorized keys. Signed pages could be reliably authenticated regardless of how they are replicated and distributed. SHTTP has been defined in a way that permits such mechanisms to be integrated with it.

In practice, SHTTP has achieved limited use. In the United States SHTTP is principally supported by the CommerceNet consortium and marketed by Terisa Systems. SHTTP-enabled browsers have not become as widely and easily available as the SSL-enabled browsers from Netscape.

10.4.5 Client Authentication Alternatives

Some of the security alternatives noted earlier, particularly SSL, do not necessarily provide client authentication. The following is a review of client authentication alternatives that focus on choices that work with SSL. The authentication method is a pivotal choice we must make when providing security for a Web service. The following alternatives are examined:

- Reusable passwords
- One-time passwords
- SSL client certificates

REUSABLE PASSWORDS

The authentication method with the longest history in computers is the reusable password—usually a memorable word kept secret by a given individual. For example, Alice might have the password "potatoe" which she uses when logging in to a particular computer: the computer requires her to type her name ("Alice") and her password ("potatoe"). The computer recognizes her as Alice simply because she knew the secret password that went with her name. Neither Bob nor Henry the Forger can masquerade as Alice because they don't know her secret password. However, Peeping Tom can masquerade as Alice because he happened to see her password one day. This illustrates the strengths and weaknesses of passwords. They are easy to handle and they are easy to steal.

Modern Web browsers typically support two general techniques to authenticate the browser's user to Web servers: passwords or SSL authentication with the user's public key. The password technique was described earlier in Section 10.4.1. Given that we can hide passwords from eavesdropping by using SSL, they actually represent a reasonable approach. They are easy to distribute to a large community and they can be easy to change. We can distribute them on paper or fax. In a special case we can even recite them over the telephone. The only shortcoming is that they must be kept secret or they are useless for authentication. If an attacker intercepts the password, we may suffer some losses before we detect and correct the problem. Passwords are easy to intercept since they are easy to reproduce and distribute. It is best to treat them like secret crypto keys and use some variant of the key distribution technique described in Section 4.4.

ONE-TIME PASSWORDS

If you need very reliable, hard-to-crack authentication and you are limited to 40-bit encryption due to export restrictions, one-time password systems provide a strong alternative. These are systems that use *authenticating tokens*, small calculatorlike devices, to authenticate their users. For example, Alice might have a token for authenticating herself to the home office. When she connects to the Web server it asks for her one-time password. She activates her token and it responds by displaying an access code. She types in the access code and the server verifies that it is the right code for Alice to use that time. If Peeping Tom intercepts the access code and tries to reuse it, the server will reject it. The code only works once. The next time Alice logs in, the token will display a different code for her to use.

There are several authenticating tokens that provide distinctive operational and security features. The SecurID card by Security Dynamics is fairly common. It displays a time-dependent access code that changes every thirty or sixty seconds. Other devices, like Secure Computing's SafeWord, use a *challenge response* approach: The server generates a random code and the token must convert it into the correct pass code. Many of these systems are available both in hardware and software versions. Security-critical applications can use tokens that require a PIN in order to work correctly.

However, keep in mind that these authentication systems have their own equipment and administrative costs. These systems may in practice be as complex to manage as a comparable system of encryption keys. In fact, authentication systems are generally built on crypto algorithms like DES and the tokens essentially contain user-specific secret keys. Authentication is performed by verifying that the user is in possession of the appropriate secret key.

SSL CLIENT CERTIFICATES

The most recent SSL-capable Web browsers and servers can authenticate the Web browser's user by validating a public key certificate issued to that user. This is described in Section 10.5.2. If an organization needs strong authentication and has no other particular use for the authenticating tokens described earlier, then SSL client authentication may some day be a reasonable choice. Keep in mind, however, that authentication tokens are a well-developed, mature product available from a variety of reputable sources. The SSL client certificate mechanism is new and suffers from a lack of supporting products.

The basic question with client certificates is the issuing of certificates. Some organizations may be willing to purchase that service from an existing certification authority while others may prefer to perform such a sensitive activity in-house. At present there are very few real products that handle client keying and issue client certificates.

However, the problem is not solved once certificates are created. They must also be installed in the corresponding Web browsers and perhaps in directory systems. Some first steps have been made to solve these problems, but the solutions are limited and not yet very robust. SSL client authentication is probably an appropriate solution in organizations with sophisticated technical talent that can deal with the rough edges of this new technology.

10.5 Product Example: Web Browser with SSL

The SSL-based Web browser is the essential tool for any customer that shops on the Internet. The Navigator by Netscape Communications was the first such product, and Netscape has freely distributed millions of copies of it. Their latest estimate is that they have distributed more than 40 million copies worldwide. Microsoft's Internet Explorer also supports SSL, as do various other browsers. When communicating with an SSL-enabled Web server (see Section 10.6), the browser can exchange transaction data that is protected from access by others. The newest browsers incorporate mechanisms to try to detect bogus commercial Web servers and to provide cryptographically strong authentication of the browser's user.

Typical Web browsers can access information using a variety of Internet application protocols. Aside from the Web's HTTP, the most commonly supported protocols are FTP, Gopher, Network News Transfer Protocol (NNTP), the Telnet remote terminal protocol, and the Internet e-mail protocols. In practice, however, servers only use SSL with HTTP traffic. This is not a shortcoming of the SSL protocol itself, rather it is because the HTTP traffic is seen as needing protection the most, particularly when performing transactions.

An important feature of SSL browsers is that they do not apply SSL to every Web access. Most Web accesses are to pages made available to the general public, and there is rarely a worthwhile security benefit to encrypting them. Since encryption is expensive, we don't want to apply it to data that doesn't need protection. Instead, the browser only applies SSL protection when it is specifically called for in the protocol field of the URL (Figure 10-4).

Just as there are specific identifiers for conventional protocols accessed by URLs there is a special identifier when SSL is applied to a protocol. When SSL is

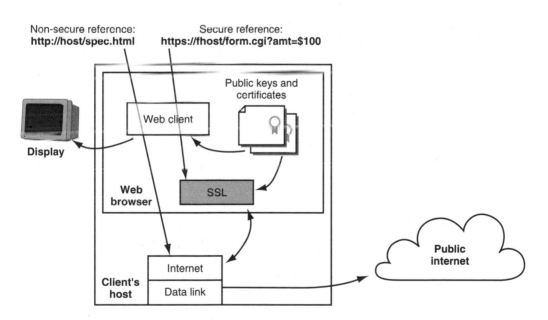

Figure 10-4: WEB BROWSER WITH SSL SUPPORT. The Web browser applies SSL protection when specified in the URL. The https: protocol identifier is used to apply SSL to a Web request. The browser's certificates and public keys are generally used to authenticate the server during the SSL handshake operation. The latest browsers can also handle public and private keys for the browser's owner. These keys can be used to authenticate the user to participating SSL server sites.

being applied to HTTP traffic, the URL contains the https: protocol identifier instead of the conventional http: identifier. As a result, users will automatically invoke SSL when they follow the appropriate links in a Web page. The page's author simply has to use the correct protocol identifier in the URL and the page access will automatically use SSL.

10.5.1 Browser Cryptographic Services

While the SSL specification lists a large variety of protocols for both key exchange and for traffic encryption (called *bulk ciphers* in the SSL specifications), actual products generally provide a smaller choice. The available services depend in part on whether you have the "U.S." version or the "export" version of the browser, because of the legal restrictions on crypto exports as noted in Section 1.6. Here are some typical services provided in Web browsers:

- **Key exchange protocol**
  SSL Version 3.0 defines a variety of key exchange techniques including RSA, "anonymous" RSA, and Diffie-Hellman. In practice, most browsers and servers only use RSA.

  The U.S. government places the fewest restrictions on the export of products that limit the modulus to 512 bits when using RSA for key exchange, so this is what generally appears in browsers that are exported from the United States. This is what is provided in exportable versions of the Netscape Navigator.

- **Authentication options**
  All SSL browsers will authenticate the server using an RSA digital signature. This is always an "out-of-the-box" capability. More advanced browsers can authenticate the browser's user to the server with the user's personal RSA public key certificate. However, this capability is not yet widely deployed in servers.

- **Exportable bulk cipher**
  The U.S. government places the fewest export restrictions on products using the RC4 encryption algorithm as long as the key only contains 40 bits of secret information. This is implemented in exportable versions of the Netscape Navigator and in other exportable products.

- **Stronger bulk ciphers**
  Browsers that are not for export from the United States generally support RC4 with a full, 128-bit secret key along with single- or multiple-key implementations of DES.

The presence of these options brings up two important considerations: How much choice in crypto algorithms should a browser have and how many bits of secrecy are necessary for Web transactions?

Regarding algorithm flexibility, it is generally better to have a small number of good choices than a large number. If a server and browser can choose between something stronger and something weaker, they should always choose the stronger alternative. If weaker alternatives are available, there is always a risk they might be used by accident. Worse, the server and browser might be unintentionally coerced into using a bad alternative by attacks on the SSL handshake protocol. While it is true that the handshake protocol is specially designed to thwart such attacks, caution is still recommended.

Key length is a very controversial topic. Some experts argue that the only safe course is to identify the most critical, vulnerable data you will ever transport with this system and choose a key to keep that data fully protected. Others point out that highly sensitive data might rarely traverse an SSL-protected link. In practice, 40 bits of secrecy might give as much protection as we give to similar commercial paperwork traveling through mail rooms and unsecured mailboxes. The most sensitive information that is probably carried by typical SSL connections will be pass codes or other confidential account identifiers. The degree of protection needed by such data is determined by the cost and amount of inconvenience caused when such access codes are misused. Some organizations might find 40 bits of protection sufficient while others might not. Refer to the key length discussion in Section 2.3.4 for further information.

10.5.2 Authentication Capabilities

The latest SSL browsers provide ways for the server and client to authenticate one another. Netscape extended HTML to include a user ID and password. The Naviga tor will prompt the user for this information if certain types of authentication failures are detected. The latest browsers also include SSL-based authentication methods to validate the identities of both the server and the client. Server authentication is widely deployed among SSL servers. Client authentication is a fairly recent development.

SERVER AUTHENTICATION

An important feature of SSL Web browsers is the ability to authenticate the Web server being accessed. This is particularly important when using SSL, since users will rely on SSL to protect confidential account numbers and pass codes. Users do not want to connect to a host masquerading as a particular server and disclose confidential identity information. Multiuser systems like Unix have fought similar problems where a prankster would run a program that looked and acted like the standard "login" procedure, but would simply collect the victim's user ID and password. SSL provides server authentication in order to avoid similar problems with bogus servers. This is illustrated in Figure 10-5.

Server authentication in the Web browser validates both the Internet identity of the server and the integrity of the public key certificate. For example, when Bob's browser accesses a secure URL pointing to host.com, the SSL protocol delivers the public key certificate from host.com to Bob's browser. First, the browser verifies the digital signature on the certificate, essentially verifying that its crypto checksum is intact. Then the browser compares the host name in the certificate against the host name in the URL. If the two match, then Bob is definitely establishing an SSL session with host.com. If the two do not match, then Bob may be connected to a bogus server masquerading as host.com.

The first step, verifying the certificate, is a standard function performed on public key certificates. The process uses the public key of a certificate authority to verify the digital signature on the certificate. If the signature checks correctly, then the certificate is intact. If not, then the name in the certificate does not necessarily go with the public key provided. This may indicate that someone is attempting a MIM attack against the public key. Certificate validation is described in Chapter 12.

An important aspect of server authentication, however, is the collection of public keys available to the Web browser. Early versions of Netscape Navigator provided a single public key that would verify certificates issued by a special authority at Verisign, Inc., and not recognize any other certificates. More recent versions

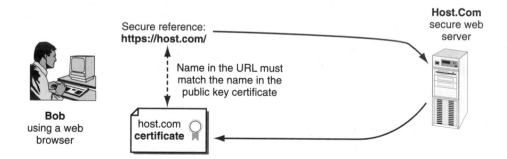

Figure 10-5: THE WEB BROWSER AUTHENTICATES THE SERVER DURING THE SSL HANDSHAKE.
During the SSL handshake the server must send its public key certificate to the browser. The browser verifies that the host name in the URL is the same as the host name in the certificate. The browser also verifies the certificate's digital signature using the public key of the certificate's issuing authority.

allow users to add public keys for other authorities and are in fact distributed with several such keys already installed.

SSL CLIENT AUTHENTICATION

The SSL handshake protocol also provides a mechanism to authenticate the browser's user. This mechanism uses RSA public keys and a personal certificate issued to each participating user. In a sense, it behaves like the challenge response tokens described earlier, except that the process is embedded in the SSL handshake. In fact, the process is essentially the same as that used by the browser to authenticate an SSL server.

Client authentication requires that the user do two things: First, generate a personal set of RSA keying material and second, have the public key placed in a signed certificate by a *certification authority*. The user can then install this certificate inside the browser, and the browser can use it when a server tries to do SSL client authentication. Additional information about public key certificates and certificate authorities can be found in Chapter 12.

This technique holds a lot of promise since it is reasonably secure, invisible, and automatic. Once the appropriate keys and certificates are installed, the user's authentication takes place automatically as part of the SSL handshake. However, the process only works once the user has generated the keys and received a signed certificate, and this is the source of the problem. Key generation and certificate management are time-consuming, complex processes. Netscape has attempted to automate the process in the latest versions of the Navigator, but the activity can take hours to complete if anything goes wrong. Sophisticated computer users can be stumped by the process as well as novices.

In practice, SSL client authentication is primarily used for special applications and not for general-purpose authentication of Internet users. Organizations that need to publish information on the Internet use it to strictly control access to authorized people. The organization generates and distributes the appropriate keys and certificates to the authorized users, and the users install them into their browsers. The organization's Web server can verify that the certificate was one that they issued and that the identified user is still permitted access. Additional passwords or token-based authentication is unnecessary.

10.5.3 Client Security and Executable Contents

A Web browser shares many of the security problems faced by the IPSEC client examined in Chapter 7. Theft remains a risk, particularly when the browser resides on a laptop. A security conscious browser should provide password protection if it carries any private or secret keying material.

Today, Web browsers face additional risks because of *executable contents*, little programs that reside on Web pages. Unlike plain text or HTML data, executable contents are capable of modifying files on the client's host computer or even transmitting files to other computers. The best known examples are Java and JavaScript (developed by Sun Microsystems), and ActiveX (developed by Microsoft). These are programming languages, not unlike the more traditional ones like C, Fortran, or Basic. The principal difference is that these languages are being embedded in the most recent Web browsers, which allows programs written in these languages to run on the computer that is running the Web browser.

While some visionaries predict that someday this will somehow make the Web better for everyone, the near-term problem is that it takes control out of the hands of the Web browser's operator. There is no way for a casual Web user to predict reliably what will happen when they click on a hypertext link. If the link carries an executable content, all sorts of unpredictable and unwanted things could happen to their workstation.

Executable contents represent a very interesting experiment with technology, but the uncertainty they breed does not mix well with commercial activities. They should only be used in low-risk applications, especially if the associated browser software carries cryptographic keys. The technology is very sophisticated and has proven to be vulnerable to obvious, if sophisticated, attacks. Researchers have demonstrated a number of ways to make executable contents attack the browser running them.

The problem with executable contents is that they might carry a "Trojan horse" that, while performing its expected behavior, also takes steps to subvert the Web browser's integrity. While promoters of these languages have made some attempts to provide reasonable security, especially with Java, the attempts have not been consistently successful. Experiments with early versions of Java uncovered several ways for a Java program to break out of its operating area and touch parts of the client system that should have been blocked from it. ActiveX, on the other hand, lacks even the generic restrictions available in Java browsers and can perform serious damage.

A particularly dramatic example of an attack by Web-based executable contents was a malicious ActiveX control written by the Chaos Computer Club. This control would search a user's computer to look for the Quicken personal financial program. If found, the control would create an additional, fraudulent payment. Since this malicious program looks just like any other hypertext link on a Web page, a malicious page author could place this control where innocent browsers won't realize the threat it poses. When users click on the control, they don't know that it is modifying their Quicken files. A naive or careless Quicken user may not detect the bogus transaction until after it has been sent to the bank and paid.

Fortunately, the only reports of malicious Java or ActiveX programs have been demonstrations, like the example from the Chaos Computer Club. Just as that example threatened users' financial transactions, the same mechanism could threaten browser keys and other crypto activities. Cautious sites and users tend to disable such capabilities until time and usage further clarify the security situation. Unfortunately, it is difficult or impossible to block ActiveX effectively in current products.

One way to minimize the risk of key theft by executable contents, Trojan horses, and viruses is to use a hardware module to store the encryption facilities. U.S. government applications of SSL are using the Fortezza crypto card (Figure 10-6), which carries its own crypto algorithms and keying material in a PC card device. Fortezza cards provide strong protection for crypto keys and for the integrity of the crypto algorithms. Attackers cannot extract keys from them even if they are in their normal operating mode. At worst an attacker might coerce an active card to apply crypto to some available data, and the potential damage is thus limited to the time available to perform separate crypto operations. Commercial versions that implement standard crypto algorithms like DES, RC4, or IDEA are also being produced by Nortel, Spyrus, Hewlett-Packard, and others.

There have been other techniques suggested for reducing the risk of executable contents. Sun originally applied classic computer security analysis to the basic architecture of the Java language in the hope that the analysis would provide assurance against misbehavior by Java applets. Unfortunately, the security model did not take into account the higher level activities of browsers—those activities that most directly concern a workstation's owner. In any case, there have been a series of reports by researchers of flaws that have allowed various types of executable contents to exceed their intended range of behavior, potentially damaging a browser's workstation.

Another proposal that has received a good deal of attention is crypto integrity checking on all executable contents. Vendors suggest that they would apply digital signatures to all Java applets and ActiveX controls that are produced by approved developers, and cautious users could reject all incoming contents that aren't properly signed. The signature would be validated against a public key certificate installed in the browser. This would work the same way as server certificate authentication. This might be an acceptable approach in a commercial setting if the digital signature could provide the basis for legal action against the purveyor of contents that cause damage, or against the enterprise that certified its safety. However, this technology is not yet widely deployed, and the practical aspects of enforcing legal liability are untested and unclear.

Figure 10-6: FORTEZZA CRYPTO MODULE PACKAGED IN A PC CARD. This is a Fortezza crypto module, developed by the U.S. government to provide crypto services for Web browsing and e-mail applications. It is installed in standard PCs and laptops. Photo by Marcus Ranum.

10.5.4 Product Security Requirements

Here are the product security requirements for an SSL-enabled Web browser, with the most important requirements given first. These should also apply to software like Microsoft's Internet Explorer, which is SSL compatible.

1. **Implement the latest version of the SSL protocol.** SSL continues to evolve as security and operational problems are identified and corrected. Profit from the collective efforts of a large community of users and analysts who have studied, used, and proposed improvements to SSL.

2. **Implement a good RSA key exchange.** The SSL handshake protocol implementation should comply with the key exchange protocol requirements listed in Section 9.3.3. The SSL protocol specification provides ways of using key exchange algorithms other than RSA. These should be avoided for compatibility reasons.

3. **Support a few effective secret key ciphers.** The SSL specification lists a large number of ciphers, but only RC4 and DES are really needed in most cases. These should provide compatibility with most SSL-capable servers. Other algorithms are defined, but are probably unnecessary for most applications. Do not provide a large variety since it opens a risk of using a weak cipher when a stronger one is more appropriate. However, be sure to provide whatever ciphers are required for interoperability.

4. **Disable any inadequate crypto.** If you are using SSL in sensitive applications, be sure the browser allows you to disable any bulk ciphers that don't give the protection you need. Left to itself, a browser might negotiate only 40 bits of secrecy even if your application really needs more protection than that. If you are bearing the liability for a key compromise, be sure you are satisfied with the key lengths you have available for SSL-protected transactions.

5. **Ensure interoperability with SSL servers.** The browser must interoperate with the community of SSL servers you intend to access with it. This may be the community of Internet vendors or it may be a special-purpose set of servers you have established for your own purposes. The browser must be able to support whatever ciphers the targeted servers require.

6. **Provide a clear indication when SSL is working.** The browser must provide a way to tell you for certain that encryption and authentication are active and being used. This is the old problem of "crypto bypass." You don't want the system to transmit your data unless you know it is being properly protected.

7. **Protect against theft.** The client must provide mechanisms to protect the keying material from theft. The most effective and least convenient method is to encrypt the keys with a password. Protection should be optional since it may be unnecessary and may interfere with operations in some cases.

8. **Support hardware crypto modules as well as software.** Hardware crypto modules provide incomparable protection against software subversion.

9. **Block or restrict downloaded executable contents.** This is to prevent attackers from manipulating the user's crypto credentials—either the server public key certificates or any client private keys.

10. **Use preinstalled public keys to validate server certificates.** This yields the simplest deployment scenario. The preinstalled keys allow "shrink-wrapped" distribution of keying material.

11. **SSL client authentication.** If you want to automatically authenticate the browser's user, this is the most secure and automatic approach. However, your site will need additional software and facilities to do public key certification in order to make it work.

12. **Support additional server authority keys.** If your enterprise establishes its own public key certification authority, this allows you to use that authority to generate SSL server certificates. However, the authority's public key must be installed in each Web browser that talks to these servers.

10.6 Product Example: Web Server with SSL

The SSL-capable Web server is the other side of the equation for Web-based commerce. Netscape has sold a series of SSL-based Web server products including the Netscape Commerce Server and the Enterprise Server. Other vendors have also implemented SSL-capable Web servers, including Microsoft's Internet Information Server. There is also the Apache server, which is available in source code form.

Figure 10-7 illustrates the essential components of an SSL-capable Web server. The data link software and the network protocol stack are usually components of the underlying host system. The Web server consists of the server itself, the SSL protocol, and CGI software. The host also carries the Web pages and SSL keying material, including the server's private key. The network protocol stack passes TCP traffic to the Web server if it arrives on one of that server's ports. While the default port number is 80, many servers also accept Web requests to other ports. If the TCP traffic arrives for port 443, then it is passed to SSL. After the SSL protocol has extracted the data from the incoming message, it passes the data to the Web server. Regardless of the source, the Web server processes the request as described in Section 10.3. Responses pass back through the same path they arrived. SSL requests

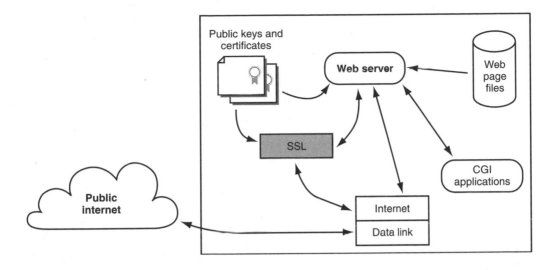

Figure 10-7: WEB SERVER HOST WITH SSL SUPPORT. An SSL-capable Web server is a collection of software modules that processes Web requests and optionally applies SSL crypto protection to them. Normal Web requests will serve up Web pages or execute CGI applications. SSL requests will act the same except that they have SSL protection applied to them.

go back through the SSL software first, while unprotected requests go directly back to the network stack.

10.6.1 Web Server Vulnerabilities

Reports from CERT and even the press show that Web servers are very popular targets of attack. In the fall of 1996 alone the Web sites of both the U.S. Justice Department and the Central Intelligence Agency were successfully attacked. Vandals essentially rewrote the sites' home pages to reflect their own peculiar concerns. Sites belonging to the major presidential candidates also suffered attacks with varying degrees of success. A year earlier, participants in a hacker's convention attacked a Web site advertising a movie called *Hackers*, though some observers suspected that the vandalism was more effective advertising than the undamaged site. However, most Web site owners want their site to present a specific message they choose and not one by someone else.

The risks to a Web site are more profound when the site is participating in commercial transactions. Computer-based transactions like that have a long history of abuse. A college student in the early 1970s ordered several hundred thousand dollars worth of telephone equipment just by calling up the phone company's equipment ordering system. The system generated the appropriate paperwork, the equipment was delivered to a spot he named, and the fellow simply picked it up and resold it. A catalog vendor does not want all of this week's orders shipped to a single mail drop in Brooklyn simply because someone broke into their site.

This section reviews the following Web site vulnerabilities:

- Host setup
- CGI attacks
- Buffer overrun

Attacks on Web sites are made possible through a range of problems, from egregious carelessness on the part of administrators to unsafe software defaults to bugs in the software. CERT has reported on many widespread problems, though basic flaws in the host system setup often account for a site's problems. Once the Web site's host is in an essentially secure condition, there are still the problems of bad defaults and bugs.

HOST SETUP

Typical commercial systems are not designed to be plugged into the global Internet, they are designed to be plugged into the departmental LAN. Every TCP/IP service provided by the vendor is turned on and available by default so that people on the network can use them. This is very convenient for everyone in the office and isn't necessarily a security problem. There are rarely vandals or other attackers on your internal network, especially if it's a small one. But once you connect that network to the Internet you make your computers accessible to a huge population, and they are not all well behaved.

Section 1.3.4 summarized the evolution of Internet security problems. This evolution has produced a very rich set of literature on security for Internet hosts. Most of this is written for Unix systems since they have had the largest Internet presence for the longest time. Regardless of the system you use, it is vital that you review whatever security configuration information you can find about it and be sure to plug those holes. They are there, regardless of the operating system or vendor.

Always be sure to apply the standard Internet server security measures. Here is a summary of several basic steps that are generally followed to increase a host's resistance to Internet attack:

- **Place no unnecessary Internet services on the Web server.**
  Every piece of software that accepts Internet traffic is also a potential security hole. No internet software is perfect, regardless of its maturity or the claims of its vendor. A new security hole could appear in any network service. The more services you run, the more likely you'll be running a service that's affected by the next bug.

- **Prohibit conventional login access to the server.**
  The experience in the computer security community has been that a knowledgeable attacker can generally penetrate a system given only a conventional login connection. Experts have demonstrated this over and over with each new operating system that has come along. This is a very good reason not to allow Internet users to log in remotely to your server.

- **Restrict access to a small list of authorized administrators.**
  Only specifically authorized individuals should be allowed to manipulate your Internet Web site. Some enterprises would see this as obvious. The Web site is part of the corporate image and should only be changed by those responsible for such things. More casual organizations should also control access, if only for security reasons. Individuals could unintentionally install software that makes the server more vulnerable to attack.

- **Keep track of Internet software and security problems.**
  There is an active Internet community that tracks software and security problems. Administrators can easily arrange to receive CERT advisories, although problem announcements are more timely through the less formal newsgroups and mailing lists dedicated to particular products. Seek out your colleagues on the Internet and be sure you are on the same distribution lists for reports, comments, and other useful information.
  Most importantly, once you are plugged in to the information stream, be sure to pay attention to it. This takes some practice since there is a lot of rubbish on the Internet along with the nuggets of priceless information.

- **Apply patches promptly.**
  Knowing that you have a problem can make you more vigilant, but it's also important to block its effects. If a fix is available for a problem, be sure to apply it before someone tries to use it against you. However, you must also take care about patches. Bogus patches have occasionally been distributed on the Internet, though they generally produce a lot of comment on administrators' mailing lists.

The preceding list is not complete. Find a good book on security for your host system and lock down your system.

CGI ATTACKS

Programmable components are always a rich source of security problems. CGI scripts fill this purpose in Web servers. CERT has reported problems with sample CGI scripts that are provided with various Web server products. Typically there is some flaw in the script that allows a browser to fetch or even modify arbitrary files on the server host. For example, an attacker might be able to trick the CGI script into sending a copy of the system's password file to the browser, or perhaps to add another user (the attacker) to the password file. This problem can be solved in a number of ways. The easiest approach is to remove all CGI scripts that aren't absolutely necessary to provide the Web service you offer. If you are fortunate, none of the scripts you keep will have security bugs in them. You can reduce the risk of such bugs by reviewing the CERT advisories associated with CGI scripts and by applying any other published recommendations you can find. Another approach is to use mandatory protection on your server to limit the potential effects of a misbehaving CGI script. Mandatory protection is discussed further in Section 10.6.2.

BUFFER OVERRUN

Buffer overrun is a situation in which an attacker exploits a bug in the software and confuses the software into running a program the attacker provides. The attacker literally loads a new program into your computer and your computer runs it. If the buffer overrun bug is in the Web server, then the attacker's program can manipulate any computer resource that the Web server software can touch, probably including your server's private crypto key. The Internet Worm exploited a buffer overrun bug in the "finger" server, and the first CERT report against a Web server was for a buffer overrun bug. In a perfect world we could simply insist on bug-free software and this would not be a problem. However, it has been proved to be impractical to expect software to be bug free. It is safer and more realistic to plan for the problems caused by bugs.

The best way to deal with buffer overrun attacks is to minimize the amount of damage they do. This requires that the Web server operate with as few privileges as possible. In no case should it ever run with some high-powered administrative identity like "root" on Unix systems. If a server has extensive privileges and it is successfully attacked, you have given the attacker essentially free run of your host. It is best to run the server with as few privileges as possible. In fact, the Web pages themselves should be made read-only relative to the server. The benefit of giving the server more access to the pages is usually offset by the risks of an attack. Again, mandatory protection techniques can greatly increase the server's security condition.

10.6.2 Mandatory Protection

Mandatory protection is the notion that there should be security boundaries inside a computer that can't be modified or disabled by system users. The idea first appeared in the late 1950s with the earliest multiprogrammed machine, the Ferranti Atlas in England. This system incorporated separate modes for "kernel" and "user" programs. A kernel program could do anything, including access memory and device control registers, while user programs were restricted to basic computational functions and various services provided by the kernel.

A quarter century later the concept was applied to computer systems intended to protect military secrets. These systems were designed so that users couldn't even be tricked into giving secret data to users not allowed to see it. The specifications for these systems appeared in the document *Trusted Computing System Evaluation Criteria*, also known as the Orange Book by virtue of its cover. In order to provide the desired secrecy, these systems implemented a mechanism called *multilevel security* (MLS), which controlled what data various programs could see and what data they could modify. Such systems are often evaluated by the National Computer Security Center (NCSC), earning a B or A rating if they provide the right features and strongly resist attack. Although MLS systems were originally constructed to protect data secrecy, they are also being used to protect server software from sophisticated attacks. Several vendors, including SecureWare, AT&T, and Hewlett-Packard, have applied MLS to the protection of commercial servers on the Internet.

MLS is not the only mandatory protection mechanism used to protect Internet servers. Another mechanism, called *type enforcement*, provides a way to establish specific rules about how different programs could access different types of data. It is used in Secure Computing's Sidewinder to run e-mail and Web servers in a protected manner. Type enforcement prevents the server from being able to corrupt Web page contents or to modify configuration data since access is unconditionally blocked. This also provides a method to reliably detect attacks on the Web server by identifying violations of the server's normal behavior patterns, as captured in the type enforcement rule specifications.

A third mandatory protection technique, available in most modern Unix systems, is the chroot() system call, though it is the least capable of the three.

These mechanisms are mandatory mechanisms because their rules cannot be disabled or bypassed by any system user. They are applied whenever a program tries to touch some data. Typical commercial systems only provide discretionary controls, and these can be turned off accidentally or intentionally by privileged system users. A mandatory rule will limit the conditions under which a program can read or modify various kinds of data regardless of who is running the program. For example, mandatory rules can be established that prevent the Web server from modifying Web pages. Even if an attacker overcomes the Web server and manages to acquire a privileged user ID, the mandatory rules applied to the Web server will prevent the attacker from modifying the Web pages. Mandatory protection can also be used to restrict access to keying material, keeping it out of an attacker's hands even if the server is subverted.

An alternative to mandatory protection for protecting keying material is the use of hardware crypto devices that contain the keys. The Fortezza PC card is an example of the technology, although it does not support commercial crypto algorithms. Several other vendors offer PC cards that provide various commercial algorithms as an alternative to the Fortezza card.

10.6.3 Product Security Requirements

Here are the product security requirements for an SSL-enabled Web server, with the most important requirements given first. These should apply to any Web server that intends to be SSL compatible.

1. **Security on the Web server host must be as tight as possible.** If your server is vulnerable to Internet attacks then no crypto mechanism will protect you from damage. Select a host for which there is a lot of security information available. If you can't find two or three books on "How to Secure Your Host" for that product, don't assume you can secure it. No conventional commercial system is really secure enough for the Internet, especially right out of the box.

2. **Implement the latest version of the SSL protocol.** SSL continues to evolve as security and operational problems are identified and corrected. Profit from the collective efforts of a large community of users and analysts who have studied, used, and proposed improvements to SSL.

3. **Implement a good RSA key exchange.** The SSL handshake protocol implementation should comply with the requirements listed in Section 9.3.3. The SSL protocol specification provides ways of using key exchange algorithms other than RSA; these should be avoided for compatibility reasons.

4. **Support a few effective secret key ciphers.** The SSL specification lists a large number of ciphers but only RC4 and DES are widely supported by browsers. Other algorithms are defined, but are unnecessary for most applications. Do not provide a large variety since it opens a risk of using a weak cipher when a stronger one is more appropriate. However, be sure to provide whatever ciphers are required for interoperability.

5. **Configure the secret key length to the application.** Different applications will carry different types of data that require different degrees of protection. The server should provide the mechanisms necessary to indicate which key lengths are acceptable. If 40 bits of secrecy is adequate, the server should support it; if not, the server should not allow a 40-bit session to be established.

6. **Ensure interoperability with SSL browsers.** The server must interoperate with the community of SSL browsers intending to access it. This includes support of bulk ciphers and key lengths as well as the underlying protocol.

7. **Provide server event logging.** The server should be able to log all URL references including CGI script invocations. CGI scripts should perform their own logging, and there should be a method to validate the contents of one log against the other.

8. **Protect against host subversion.** There should be mechanisms that prevent or at least limit the damage that can be caused by an attacker overrunning the server host. Ideally, this should be a mandatory protection mechanism. Alternatively, a hardware crypto module can protect the server's keys from compromise even if an attacker completely takes over the server host.

9. **SSL client authentication.** If you want to automatically authenticate a browser's user, this is the most secure and automatic approach. However, your site will need additional software and facilities to do public key certification in order to make it work. If you need this function, be sure it is supported by your server.

10.7 Deployment Example: Vending with Exportable Encryption

The World Wide Web has become a natural medium for publishing merchandise catalogs. Unlike paper catalogs, there is no printing or mailing cost. Updates can take place very quickly and tomorrow's customers see the catalog material just posted, not the material sent to the printer several weeks ago. Web vending can be convenient for customers, too. The catalog isn't lost in a pile somewhere; it's on the Web in the same location every time. There's lots of software out there that lets customers visit a Web site, and most of it can display at least some types of pictures.

One of the remaining problems for many potential customers and vendors is security. Vendors don't want to be defrauded out of merchandise and customers don't want the aggravation of improper charges against their accounts. However, many customers and vendors have come to accept telephone catalog ordering. It seems likely that an acceptable implementation of Web vending would be one that works, as much as possible, like telephone catalog ordering.

Telephone Sales	*World Wide Web*
• Almost everyone has a telephone.	• Millions of people have Web browsers.
• Phone tapping takes minutes or hours.	• Cracking a 40-bit SSL key takes hours or days.
• We can limit liability by restricting orders.	• We can limit liability by restricting orders.
• We can use private accounts or bank cards.	• We can use private accounts or bank cards.

However, there remain several differences between the two:

Telephone Sales	*World Wide Web*
• All telephones work the same.	• Different Web browsers behave differently.
• Phone tapping leaves physical clues.	• Internet cracking leaves few traces.
• Criminal phone tapping is very rare.	• Internet crackers will do it just for fun.

Web-based sales definitely present different risks, benefits, and opportunities. Ultimately it becomes a highly individual decision. However, this deployment example will proceed on the assumption that we will provide the following services:

- Sell merchandise described on Web pages
- Accept bank credit cards or a company-issued credit account in payment
- Make order processing and shipping as efficient as possible for the customer
- Validate as many order details as possible to look for potential fraud
- Manually review orders for obvious irregularities

The last item on this list may sound peculiar to readers with more of an auto-mation background, but it reflects an important security issue: People are very good at spotting oddities while computers are not. Even if the manual order review becomes a "spot check," it really needs to take place. If irregularities or fraud is detected, it is smart to build checks into the automated portions of the system to flag any peculiar-looking orders for manual review. The system should not reject odd-looking orders automatically any more than a retail store can bar the door to people "dressed like thieves."

Keep in mind that the objective of this Web site is to serve customers that might not be served otherwise. It is important to make the process as efficient as possible, but automation must be applied appropriately. Automated fraud preven-tion is probably an unrealistic expectation.

10.7.1 Export Restrictions and Transaction Security

In order to provide as much security as possible to the largest population possible, the potential risks associated with the weaker, export-authorized crypto mecha-nisms must be taken into account. These mechanisms reside in millions of copies of the Netscape Navigator that have been distributed worldwide through the Inter-net. While many of these programs support the latest and most secure protocols, many support earlier and less secure versions. It is important to examine the prop-erties of these weaker protocols and consider the potential risks. The following is a summary of the security issues.

RISKS OF 40-BIT ENCRYPTION

This is the topic that gets the most publicity. Several teams have demonstrated that it is possible to crack 40-bit encryption in a matter of days or even hours if the right processing power is applied to it. So it is within available technology to attack indi-vidual SSL messages that use exportable crypto. However, this capability has mostly been demonstrated as a parlor trick among technical experts with lots of computing power at their disposal. How can it injure either the vending site or a customer?

Risk to the customer is generally perceived as the risk of compromising the cus-tomer's bank credit card number or other payment authorization data. SSL trans-actions used in typical cracking examples always contain simulated credit card numbers, presumably to illustrate how these numbers could be acquired by the attacker. In practice, however, cracking a 40-bit SSL transaction requires signifi-cantly more effort than numerous other techniques for acquiring credit card num-bers (for example, dumpster diving, shoulder surfing, and other such activities in places where cards are used). This may not be true in a few years if processor performance continues to improve, but today the cost of the attack is far out of proportion to its benefit.

Risks to the vendor are restricted to losses from masquerades based on stolen account numbers. For example, if the vendor assigns its own account numbers for use in Web transactions and an attacker intercepts and abuses one of these numbers, then the vendor must take the loss. There is a similar risk of a transaction using a bank card number stolen through some other means. However, this is the same risk encountered in telephone catalog sales.

RISKS OF 40-BIT INTEGRITY PROTECTION

A problem with older versions of the SSL protocol is that it used the same secret key for integrity protection that it used for encryption. Thus, the integrity protection provided in older systems is as vulnerable to cracking as the encryption protection. Systems that were limited to exportable encryption were likewise limited to 40 bits of secrecy protecting the integrity of messages. In fact, the legal limitations on encryption keys do not apply to secret keys that protect message integrity. This shortcoming was eliminated in newer versions of the SSL protocol, which applies integrity protection with a 128-bit secret key. However, numerous Web browsers are still in use that support the older protocol, so we must consider how it might affect transaction security.

In practice, this weakness should not affect the security of SSL transactions. The transactions are performed interactively based on secret keys established for that particular session. If a secret key is successfully cracked, it can only be exploited while that particular session is still in progress. Given that the fastest recorded attacks on 40-bit keys still take several hours to complete, it seems unlikely that a cost-effective attack can take place.

10.7.2 Site Configuration

Figure 10-8 shows a typical arrangement for running a catalog sales site on the Internet. Users on the Internet contact the vendor's Web server. The server is accessible by both legitimate customers and by attackers. The customer browses the vendor's Web site, selects merchandise, and then pays for it. Payment may involve a credit card or perhaps a personal account number provided by the vendor. The actual order entry operation may reside on the server, but many sophisticated organizations use their corporate database management system (DBMS) instead. In that case the Web server simply provides a graphical front end to the corporate

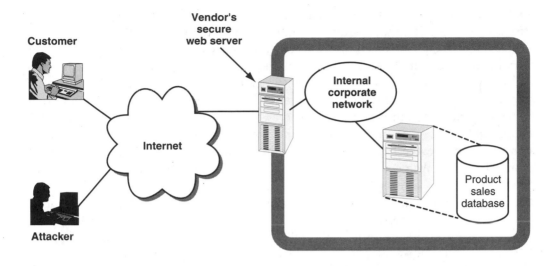

Figure 10-8: BASIC CATALOG SALES OPERATION ON THE INTERNET. The vendor's Web server is accessible to both legitimate customers and to attackers. Customer orders are collected by the Web server and sent to the corporate database for processing.

system. The customer's Web forms are transformed into database transactions, transmitted to the DBMS, and then processed.

Figure 10-9 illustrates a typical transaction in such a system. Bob is buying a hat from the company "Tops." He connects to their Web server, locates the hat he wants, and submits the order. Note that the order involves a CGI script. This script converts the order into a DBMS function, posting Bob's "buy" order to the database. The DBMS returns a status result to the CGI script, which in turn sends an acknowledgment back to Bob's browser.

This particular arrangement for Internet catalog sales is the result of several things. First of all, corporate DBMS interfaces tend to be arcane and idiosyncratic,

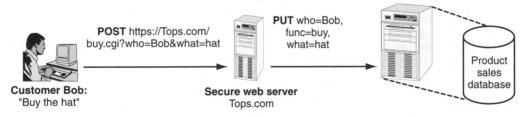

Figure 10-9: WEB-BASED CATALOG TRANSACTION SCENARIO. Bob fills in a form and his request is sent to a CGI script, which converts it to a DBMS transaction. After processing it, the DBMS returns an acknowledgment that the CGI script inserts into a page sent back to Bob.

so that it's unlikely that many customers could or would want to submit orders directly to the DBMS in its query language. Second, few commercially popular DBMSs have been subjected to the security scrutiny or even the attacks that Web servers have suffered. As with server hosts, there are a handful of expensive DBMSs that have earned B-level security ratings from the NCSC, but they aren't widely used commercially. The industry has developed a fairly good notion of how much security one can get in a Web server, but few DBMSs have passed through comparable struggles. In short, we cannot expect a commercial DBMS to hold up against sophisticated Internet attacks, so it is better to place a stronger system in front of it. The Web server provides a uniform and user-friendly interface to the DBMS, as well as protects it against attack.

Another important aspect of this arrangement is the protective perimeter around the internal network that holds the DBMS. Attackers should not be able to access the internal network directly. All access to the DBMS should be through the Web server. All other inbound access should be rigidly controlled through a firewall system as described in Section 8.3. If attackers can reach the DBMS directly through the internal network, then the Web server cannot block attacks against it.

In part we achieve this protective perimeter by implementing a sort of red/black separation, in which the suspicious network is connected to one network interface and the more trustworthy internal network is connected to a completely different network interface. We can separate traffic more reliably if we use physically different devices and networks. The cost for the extra hardware is balanced by the greater likelihood that our security will work correctly. We achieve even more certainty of correct operation if we use a system that provides completely different protocol stacks for the two different networks (Figure 10-10). This is provided in some systems that support mandatory protection, like Sidewinder, and in some "security-modified" versions of Unix that form the basis for commercial firewalls like the V-One SmartWall or the TIS Gauntlet.

10.7.3 Deployment Security Requirements

The requirements for deploying a Web application that uses exportable crypto are given here, with the highest priority requirements appearing first:

1. **Use a capable SSL Web server.** The Web server should comply with the appropriate requirements given in Section 10.6.3.

2. **Use a dual-home host for the SSL Web server.** The server host must have two separate network interfaces: Connect the Internet to one and the internal enterprise network to the other. Configure the host so that no traffic can flow directly from one network to the other (in other words, no IP forwarding).

3. **Identify the browsers you expect customers to use.** Decide if you intend to support plaintext transactions as well as SSL-protected transactions, and configure the server accordingly.

4. **Determine the types of payment you will accept.** This will affect other choices you must make regarding fraud prevention.

5. **Apply Internet server security measures.** Consult a recent reference on Internet site security. Establish an effective firewall system. Place no unnecessary Internet services on the Web server. Prohibit conventional login access to the server except by a small list of authorized administrators. Keep track of software and security problems reported against your software and apply patches promptly.

6. **Apply Web server security measures.** Consult a recent reference on Web site security. Eliminate all CGI scripts that are not explicitly required to operate your site. Place read-only protection on Web pages that should not be changing; the Web server should not have write access to these pages.

7. **Select a widely supported certification authority.** Customers will only be able to establish SSL sessions with the server if the server's certification

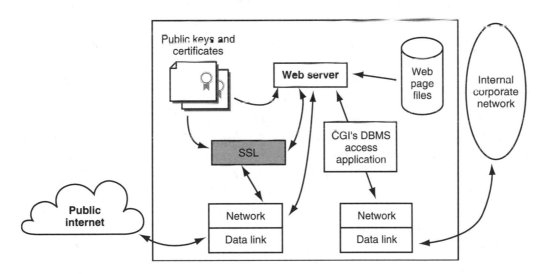

Figure 10-10: HIGH-SECURITY WEB SERVER SOFTWARE ARCHITECTURE FOR CATALOG SALES. Internet traffic enters through one interface, passing through a dedicated protocol stack. The Web server passes customer orders to the DBMS access scripts, which generate DBMS transactions. The DBMS traffic is sent to the internal corporate net through a separate protocol stack and independent network interface.

authority is identified within the customers' Web browser. Verisign administers the authority that issued the earliest SSL server certificates, so it is probably recognized by the largest number of Web browsers currently in use. However, the latest browsers contain a veritable library of keys for validating server certificates issued by the major public key issuing organizations.

The National Computer Security Association (NCSA) has established a service for assessing the security of commercial Web sites. They issue an endorsement to sites that are verified to meet their published requirements.

10.8 For Further Information

- **Stein, *How to Set Up and Maintain a Web Site***
  A thorough explanation of the practical details in operating a Web site.

- **Garfinkel and Spafford, *Practical Unix and Internet Security***
  Sensible and comprehensive coverage of Internet security, with recommendations for improving host security through proper configuration.

- **Stein, *World Wide Web Security FAQ***
  http://www.genome.mit.edu/WWW/faqs/www-security-faq.html
  On-line, up-to-date information on Web security.

- **Kalakota and Whinston, *Frontiers of Electronic Commerce***
  A thorough survey of electronic commerce topics, from Web systems to electronic payment protocols to wireless systems. Covers existing commercial systems as well as emerging concepts and protocols.

- **Netscape Communications, *SSL 3.0 Specification***
  http://www.netscape.com/libr/ssl/ssl3/index.html
  The official definition of SSL. Describes everything a modern SSL server and client should support. Keep in mind that practical servers and browsers only support a subset of the protocol options.

- **National Computer Security Association, *Certified Secure Web Site Certification Program***
  http://www.ncsa.com/webcom/webcert.html
  A description of the NCSA's program for testing and certifying the security of commercial Web sites.

11

Secured Electronic Mail

Secrecy is as indispensable to human beings as fire, and as greatly feared.

—Sissela Bok, *Secrets*

IN THIS CHAPTER

This chapter examines the application of modern crypto techniques to e-mail security. E-mail is arguably the most pervasive Internet service available, and a special collection of crypto techniques have evolved for it. The following topics are discussed:

- Security objectives, basic issues, and an introduction to Internet e-mail
- Introduction to crypto keying for e-mail messages
- Introduction to digital signatures
- Properties and features of secure e-mail packages
- Deployment of secure e-mail

Crypto techniques for Internet e-mail have undergone a significant amount of evolution, dating back to the 1980s. Only rarely have these techniques found their way into widely used commercial e-mail packages. In practice, the cost and behavior of secure e-mail is heavily influenced by the certificate management system being used; these are discussed in Chapter 12.

11.1 Security Objectives

These objectives seek to provide similar features to paper mail messages between a large community of senders and recipients.

- **Protect message contents from modification or disclosure.**
  E-mail should be easy to produce but difficult for others to replay, modify, or otherwise interfere with. Both the sender and recipient need to identify reliably who is on the other end of each message, and messages must not be modified in transit. If a message involves confidential information, then the information must be protected from eavesdropping.

- **Reliably identify who wrote a message.**
  An e-mail message should not prompt any costly activities unless we can be reasonably certain that the message is genuine. In practice we need to know who really wrote the message. If it contains Alice's name, for example, we need some assurance that she wrote her name there and that the message was exactly the one she wrote.

- **Apply crypto protections selectively as needed.**
  Crypto always causes a performance penalty, so users are not going to want to use it except when really needed. Protection should only be applied when it is really needed to protect e-mail. Furthermore, users will also need to communicate with others whose e-mail clients don't support the same e-mail crypto protocols, or any crypto at all.

- **Protect the receiving host from attack by incoming messages.**
  E-mail servers and clients are both vulnerable to attack. Servers are the most at risk because they have fixed network locations and generally run software with behavior that is far too complex to predict. E-mail clients are generally immune to attack if they only handle traditional text-oriented e-mail. Unfortunately, many e-mail clients will accept executable files embedded in e-mail messages, and these files can themselves contain viruses or other subverted programs.

11.2 Basic Issues with E-Mail Security

E-mail security measures and capabilities are quite different from those examined in earlier chapters.

- **Application-level security**
  Techniques developed to provide security to e-mail are applied to data at the application level. In other words, the data is protected before the e-mail software hands it off to another layer of protocol software. This means that much of the protocol information involved in delivering the e-mail is itself unprotected. The only part of the e-mail that is protected is the message text itself (Figure 11-1).

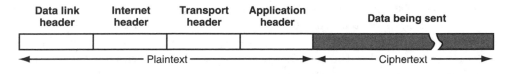

Figure 11-1: BASIC PACKET FORMAT USED FOR APPLICATION-LAYER CRYPTO. Everything   is transmitted in plaintext except for data that the application itself has explicitly encrypted.

- **Nonrepudiation versus deniability**
  Nonrepudiation is a security property indicating that the author of a message cannot deny authorship of that message. Paper contracts strive for this property by using witnesses and notaries to attest to the fact that people signing the contract did in fact sign it. A message is *deniable* if there are plausible reasons to explain why, despite evidence to the contrary, the apparent author or signer of a message may not have actually signed it. High-quality e-mail security systems strive to achieve nonrepudiation so that digitally signed e-mail may have a legal standing comparable to paper documents.

- **Public key distribution**
  Modern Internet e-mail security systems all rely on public key techniques to protect messages and to identify authors reliably. However, these techniques depend in turn on reliable distribution of public keys. The security can be subverted if a public key is associated with the wrong individual. This problem is examined in detail in Chapter 12 which describes public key certificates.

- **Mailing list handling**
  Conventional e-mail can be sent to a long list of recipients in a relatively simple manner. However, it is much harder to encrypt messages sent to mailing lists. The crypto protection must be tailored so that each recipient is able to decrypt the message.

11.3 Basics of Internet Electronic Mail

For many years, electronic mail has been the most widely available Internet service. Today this dominance has been strongly, even decisively, challenged by the World Wide Web, but e-mail continues to hold a vital role. E-mail reaches more users than the Web, and in many offices e-mail has replaced countless paper notices, paper reports, and paper reminders.

Modern Internet e-mail originally evolved on the ARPANET—an experimental wide area network produced by the U.S. government. In the 1970s the ARPANET

connected almost all of the major organizations doing advanced computer development in the United States. This was the test bed for several other well-known
Internet protocols, principally the Telnet remote terminal protocol and FTP. Any
host directly connected to the ARPANET could send e-mail, transfer files, or run a
remote login session on any other ARPANET host.

The original specifications for today's Internet e-mail were developed for the
ARPANET, along with the notion of a simple protocol for stuffing e-mail into designated user files. The techniques were very simple and very effective. ARPANET e-
mail produced several important features of today's Internet e-mail:

- **Address included in the message's body**
  E-mail did not rely exclusively on lower level protocols to say where a
  message must go.

- **Text only**
  E-mail messages must contain readable text, not raw binary data.

- **Accept from anywhere**
  Any delivery service or individual is allowed to submit messages that go into
  users' e-mail boxes.

- **No acknowledgment**
  Like the postal service, a sender rarely gets any acknowledgment that a
  message was received, unless the recipient explicitly sends one.

E-mail delivers complete messages between named entities. Unlike other protocols, e-mail can deliver its message even if the recipient isn't immediately available. Most internet protocols won't work unless both the sender and recipient,
server and client, are on-line and available simultaneously. E-mail systems will
save messages and try again at several points in the delivery process. If the recipient, the recipient's e-mail server, or some other e-mail relay point is off-line, the
sending e-mail server will hold the message and try again later. In short, e-mail
transfers its messages through a *staged delivery* process instead of relying entirely
on real-time connections.

E-mail evolved as the first true "internet" protocol because of its staged delivery
approach. Originally, ARPANET e-mail users could only read their mail by logging in
to a multiuser host that was directly connected to the ARPANET. However, this soon
proved inconvenient and sites developed "mail relay" mechanisms. This carried
ARPANET e-mail across internal networks within different organizations. Eventually relays were also established to carry e-mail between the ARPANET and other
wide area networks, including the BITNET system connecting IBM systems worldwide, and the CSNET system connecting universities that weren't already on the
ARPANET. Thus, a single e-mail message could easily traverse a variety of networks.

The advent of the Internet did not eliminate mail relays. The Internet permits e-mail to flow directly between any pair of Internet hosts using the Simple Mail Transfer Protocol (SMTP). However, Internet e-mail can still reach numerous other hosts through mail relays. Numerous proprietary systems have been developed that do not support Internet protocols like SMTP but do provide e-mail relaying between themselves and Internet e-mail servers. E-mail remains the most globally available Internet capability since it is often available even when lower level Internet protocols are not (Figure 11-2).

11.3.1 Internet E-Mail Software Architecture

Unlike the Web, e-mail is sent from one client to another, and not simply between a client and a server. The clients compose messages to send and display messages received; servers transmit messages to intermediate and final destinations or hold them while in transit (Figure 11-3). All Internet e-mail systems require an SMTP server to receive and forward messages between sites. When a message arrives at the host to which it is addressed, the SMTP server places the message in a mailbox file for the message's addressee. Multiuser systems like Unix provide client software that accesses e-mail directly from these mailbox files.

Organizations with a more distributed environment will deliver e-mail directly to individual desktops. Desktop delivery sometimes involves proprietary e-mail systems like CE Software's QuickMail, CCMail, or Microsoft Mail. These systems use a

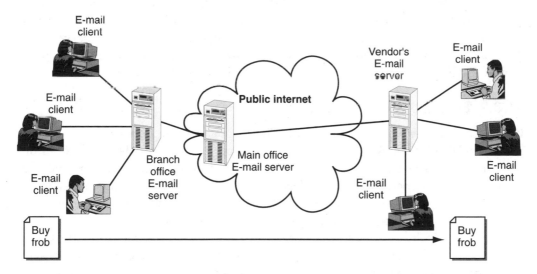

Figure 11-2: INTERNET E-MAIL MAY BE RELAYED THROUGH SEVERAL SERVERS. An e-mail message originating at a branch office may be routed through a main office e-mail relay before it enters the Internet. It is then relayed to the destination server, where it is held for the recipient.

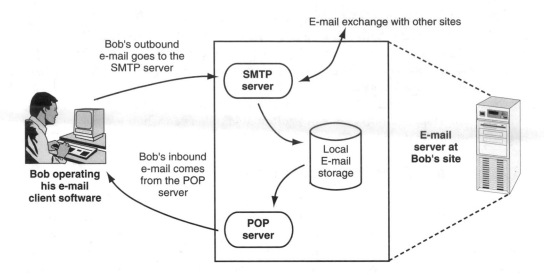

Figure 11-3: INTERNET E-MAIL USES THE SMTP AND POST OFFICE PROTOCOL (POP) PROTOCOLS. The SMTP server accepts incoming e-mail messages and forwards them in the direction of the host, whose address appears in the message. SMTP places e-mail in local storage when it arrives at the destination SMTP server. The POP server delivers stored messages to individual recipients when they call for them.

mail gateway program that converts Internet e-mail addresses and message formats into something compatible with the particular proprietary system. Many desktop systems also use the Post Office Protocol (POP), which is an Internet standard protocol for retrieving personal e-mail messages from an Internet server host. There are a number of commercial e-mail clients that support POP, notably Qualcomm's Eudora as well as the mail support in Netscape's Navigator.

11.3.2 E-Mail Security Problems

E-mail became the most widely available Internet service in part because a system had to fulfill relatively few requirements to support it. The simplest of text editors can produce Internet e-mail and the simplest of text-oriented protocols is needed to deliver e-mail to another server. In fact, some experienced users may occasionally compose and deliver e-mail using nothing more than a Telnet remote terminal program. They simply establish a connection to the server's e-mail port, type the appropriate SMTP commands, and then type the e-mail message directly to the server. SMTP is simple enough that the server can't tell the difference between e-mail from another server program or from a typing user.

This is the source of Internet e-mail's legendary insecurity. If Bob gets standard Internet e-mail from Alice, he can't be certain that the message wasn't a complete fabrication by Henry the Forger. Henry may have constructed the entire message and fed it directly to Bob's e-mail server. Since e-mail travels over the same transport service as other Internet traffic, it is generally vulnerable to snooping, just like the reusable passwords "sniffed" in Section 6.4.1. So Peeping Tom has an opportunity to discover any information placed in an e-mail message.

E-mail also faces security problems from attacks on e-mail servers and clients. These risks are examined in the following sections.

ATTACKS ON E-MAIL SERVERS

> *Better the devil you know.*
>
> —Anonymous proverb

Internet e-mail servers have been attacked with a variety of evolving techniques and varying degrees of success over the years. The classic Unix e-mail server, *sendmail*, has developed a reputation as being an insecure piece of software because of continuing reports of actual and potential security flaws. Although sendmail has long suffered from security problems, they were largely tolerated until 1988, when the Internet Worm used a well-known vulnerability in sendmail's SMTP implementation to penetrate unprotected hosts. Additional security flaws are detected and fixed in sendmail every year, though they tend to be increasingly subtle and harder for attackers to exploit.

The problem isn't simply sendmail. The problem is software reliability in general. Sendmail's problems are well publicized because the software is maintained by a vocal, public community instead of a single proprietary vendor. Anyone with the appropriate software development experience is familiar with the long lists of software problems that develop with any widely used software product. The only advantage other products might have is that vendors don't publicize the entire contents of their problem lists. Many vendors only report problems after a fix has been distributed to sites it is likely to affect.

The only general solution to server vulnerabilities is to implement a layered software defense against attacks. Simple firewall systems (proxies) do not provide this type of protection. Instead, there must be a software component that intercepts the e-mail and is either too simple to allow attacks to work or is well-enough armored to ride out the attack. The simple approach is reflected by Marcus Ranum's *smap* program, developed as part of the Firewall Toolkit distributed by Trusted Information Systems. Smap is a grossly simplified SMTP server that collects e-mail as a front end for sendmail and then simply forwards the individual e-mail messages to sendmail for actual processing. This blocks most attacks on e-mail servers.

The armoring alternative is used by firewalls hosted on high-security platforms like Secure Computing's Sidewinder or systems hosted on B-level trusted computing systems like the Cyberguard and the BMD Cybershield products. On these systems, the e-mail server runs in a highly restricted environment. The restricted environment is enforced using the mandatory protection techniques discussed in Section 10.6.2. This protects the site from damage even if the e-mail server software falls to a sophisticated new attack.

ATTACKS ON E-MAIL CLIENTS

Typical text-oriented e-mail poses no risks for clients or servers. The vast majority of e-mail virus scares are hoaxes. As long as e-mail users exchange normal text messages there is no danger of attack. Approximately twice a year there is a wave of e-mail messages traversing the Internet that warn of the "Good Times" e-mail virus. It is a hoax. The warnings tell of a dangerous e-mail message with the subject Good Times and how it will damage the computer of anyone who reads the message. Text e-mail messages can not harm a computer. But this will not prevent the warnings from spreading on a regular basis. Some argue that the "virus" is really just the warning messages themselves and the damage is the amount of time wasted explaining the hoax to the uninitiated.

However, the proliferation of "macro languages" embedded within word processing systems and other forms of executable contents has made e-mail less safe than it used to be. The problem is increased by mail client "features" that allow the user to easily (or even accidentally) execute a program attached to an incoming message. Occasionally, malicious executables are distributed through e-mail. In 1995 someone distributed a package of DOS programs claiming to "optimize America On-line access." In fact, the programs would delete files from the user's hard drive. The e-mail client included in more sophisticated versions of Netscape Navigator will automatically execute Java or JavaScript programs embedded in e-mail messages. This opens e-mail users to the Java risks discussed in Section 10.5.3. Fortunately, the Navigator provides controls to disable the execution of Java and JavaScript.

Many vendors and software developers see the uncontrolled distribution of executable software as a positive benefit instead of a risk. Therefore, it is up to individual computer users to be wary of potential Trojan horses in software they receive. There is no technology in theory or practice that will reliably identify hostile software, any more than there is technology to automatically detect all software bugs.

Virus scanners may help prevent some problems, but newer viruses can always defeat such methods.

11.4 Technology: Off-line Message Keying

The key interchange protocols discussed in earlier chapters will negotiate a key between two hosts by interactively exchanging a series of messages. This does not work with e-mail. Typical e-mail messages are stored for some period of time before the recipient reads them, and the recipient's workstation might not even be running when a message is produced. So the sender needs a way to generate a key for the message without involving the recipient. The general approach used is similar to the other protocols except that the encrypted key is delivered as part of the e-mail message.

The process takes place as shown in Figure 11-4. Again, Alice is sending her message to Bob. First, as with any key exchange, Alice must generate a random secret key value. Next, she produces a *token*, which contains the secret key encrypted with Bob's public key. If the message needs to go to additional people (Carl, for example) then she generates additional tokens that encrypt the secret key with other recipients' public keys. Finally, she encrypts the e-mail message with

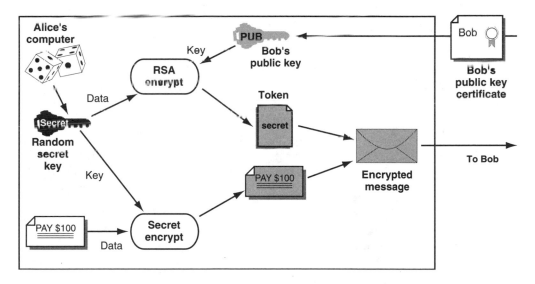

Figure 11-4: OFF-LINE MESSAGE KEYING FOR ELECTRONIC MAIL. Alice needs to send Bob a message. She generates a random secret key to use and encrypts the message text with it. Then she produces a key token for Bob by encrypting the secret key with Bob's public key. Alice combines the token and the encrypted text in an e-mail message and transmits it to Bob.

this secret key using a secret key crypto algorithm. The e-mail message actually sent through the standard e-mail system will contain all of the tokens as well as the encrypted message.

On receipt, Bob locates his token in the message's header and decrypts it using his private key. This yields the message's secret key. Bob then uses the secret key with the chosen secret key algorithm to decrypt the message (Figure 11-5). Bob can simply ignore or discard any other tokens Alice provided, since he can't decrypt them and doesn't need them.

This technique allows an e-mail sender to protect an e-mail message so that nobody except the authorized recipients can decrypt it. The message can be delivered through any number of e-mail gateways. Copies can be misdelivered to potentially or actually hostile people that could do damage if they could read the message. But the encryption is keyed so that only the recipient can decrypt it.

11.4.1 Encryption Tokens

Encryption tokens take on a variety of forms in different implementations, but all of them include the following:

1. **Recipient identifier.** This tells whose public key was used to encrypt this token.

2. **Encrypted secret key.** This is the secret key encrypted with the identified public key.

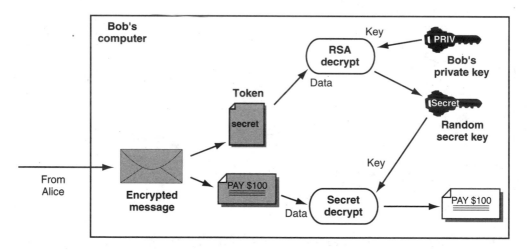

Figure 11-5: DECRYPTING A MESSAGE KEYED OFF-LINE. Bob receives a message from Alice. He extracts the token and decrypts it with his private key. This yields the secret key. Bob uses the secret key to decrypt the message text.

The recipient identifier may take on whatever form is convenient. Systems that use public key certificates often use the certificate's serial number or a similar numerical identifier for the public key. However, any unique identifier will do, as long as it tells the recipient which token they can decrypt with their own private key.

The encrypted secret key must comply with format rules for the public key algorithm being used. When using RSA, the encrypted key should comply with PKCS #1 or at least fulfill the standard's intent. This ensures the encrypted key value is within size constraints of the public key being used and that it contains random data.

It is important that the secret key be combined with random data so that every token is different. The secret key could be vulnerable to attack when the same secret key value is encrypted by a variety of public keys. A message with multiple recipients will contain the same secret key in each token, encrypted by different public keys. If random data is appended to each secret key before encryption, we avoid the risk of encrypting identical data items. When the key is decrypted, the random data is easily removed.

PKCS #7 defines a format for carrying encrypted messages and their tokens. This is essentially the format used by PEM and MSP. This standard calls tokens *recipient info* and includes two additional fields. The first field specifies the version of the token's format to allow for future changes in the format. The other field identifies the algorithm used to encrypt the key. This field can include parameters for the algorithm if necessary. The recipient identifier contains the certificate serial number and the name of the certificate's issuer. PGP tokens contain roughly the same data, although the binary format is different.

11.4.2 Technical Security Requirements

Here are the technical security requirements for generating off-line secret keys to be exchanged using public key cryptography. The highest priority requirements appear first:

1. **Generate good random secret keys.** This is essential or attackers will be able to crack the encrypted e-mail messages. Secret key generation should comply with the requirements in Section 4.3.3.

2. **Use good-quality secret key crypto.** Review the mail system's features against the algorithms and key size recommendations in Section 2.3.

3. **Use a good public key implementation to encrypt the tokens.** RSA-based implementations should comply with the requirements listed in Sec-

tion 9.2.3. Tokens need to be formatted so that their size and padding data are consistent with RSA's security requirements.

4. **Provide a mechanism to authenticate public keys.** While public keys don't need protection against disclosure, they do need protection against modification. This protects the keys against a MIM attack. Keys may be authenticated through a trustworthy manual distribution procedure (Chapter 4) or through public key certificates (Chapter 12). The latter is more common in e-mail systems.

5. **Provide a mechanism to update the public keying material.** Keys are always at risk of being compromised, and the compromise of your private key will render your public key worthless for protection. You must have a way to update your public key and private key in order to handle such a risk.

11.5 Technology: Digital Signatures

The *digital signature* is the most novel mechanism provided by modern crypto technology. It's a mechanism that does not involve secrets but it protects data from undetected change. Moreover, the digital signature associates the data with the owner of a specific private key. If we can verify the signature with Alice's public key, we can be certain that the data was signed with Alice's private key. Experts widely believe this technique will form the bedrock of electronic commerce by providing digital credentials that are extremely hard to forge.

In Chapter 9 we noted that public key encryption can associate the encrypted data with the specific entity that holds the private key. If you can decrypt a message successfully with a particular public key, say Public Key X, then it can only have been encrypted with the corresponding private key, Private Key X. If that private key is under the control of a single identified user or other entity, then we can be sure that the original message was signed by that entity.

Digital signatures use a private key to produce a crypto checksum. Unlike the secret key crypto checksums discussed in Section 5.3, anyone with the signer's public key can verify the digital signature and only the signer can actually create it. Crypto checksums based on conventional secret key techniques can only be verified by people who are trusted with the secret key, and the technique can't tell which key holder actually produced the crypto checksum. Digital signatures are tied to a particular private key, so we can safely assume that only the private key's holder could have produced the corresponding digital signature. Anyone with the corresponding public key can validate the hash or checksum themselves, tying the message's contents to the holder of the corresponding private key.

Figure 11-6 illustrates how it works. Alice writes a message to Bob and "signs" it. In the simplest case she simply encrypts the message with her private key. She transmits the message to Bob. Somehow Bob has also retrieved a copy of Alice's public key, but since it is "public knowledge" it is also known by potential attackers. Bob can verify that a message is from Alice by decrypting it with her public key. He should get back a recognizable plaintext if it was in fact encrypted by her.

Henry the Forger cannot directly construct a believable forgery and send it to Bob. If he sends a plaintext message saying "Pay $100" it will be reduced to gibberish when Bob decrypts it. If Henry encrypts a forged message with Alice's public key, Bob will still get gibberish when he decrypts it. Remember that a message encrypted by Alice's public key can only be recovered by decrypting it with her private key, and Bob only has Alice's public key.

But, as we have seen before, there are often ways that a clever attacker can undermine the crypto mechanism. It's not an issue of keeping a secret, since everyone including Henry the Forger has a copy of the public key. Instead, we have to worry about Henry constructing a new message that decrypts into a sensible message when Alice's public key is applied to it. We need to prevent Henry from being able to present a message to Bob that is signed by Alice but says something she didn't intend to say. Unfortunately, there are a variety of techniques that Henry could use, particularly since the data being encrypted is the actual plaintext that Henry is trying to construct.

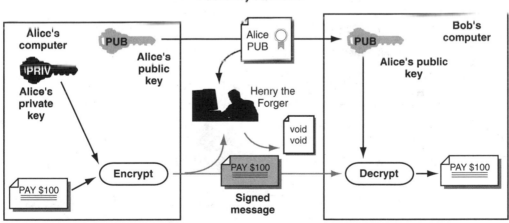

Figure 11-6: USING RSA TO PRODUCE A DIGITAL SIGNATURE. Alice can uniquely "sign" any message she sends by encrypting it with her private key. Anyone, even Henry the Forger, can decrypt and read it with her public key. But Henry cannot produce an acceptable forgery without Alice's private key. Alice's public key will decrypt the message only if her private key encrypted it.

We make Henry's forgery job all but impossible if we add an extra step to make the digital signature more like a conventional crypto checksum. To do this we compute a hash of the message to be signed and then encrypt the hash, as shown in Figures 11-7 and 11-8. This technique also removes various mathematical vulnerabilities associated with digital signature computations. These vulnerabilities are described in the next section.

11.5.1 Attacks on Digital Signatures

Section 9.2.2 summarized a variety of mathematical attacks on RSA encryption. This section summarizes similar attacks against digital signatures and the keys that encrypt them. All of the attacks can be prevented by careful use of digital signatures in the application software. In some cases there are specific PKCS standards that include features to block specific attacks. The following attacks are described:

- Smooth number attack
- Cube root attack
- Varying the ciphertext
- "Birthday attack" on hash functions

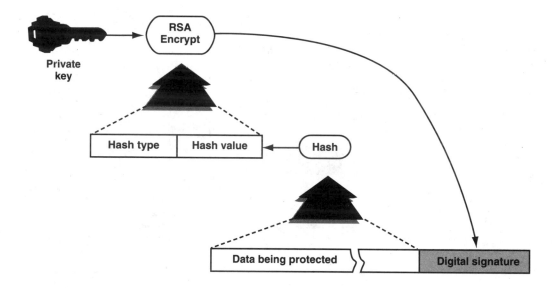

Figure 11-7: PROTECTING DATA WITH A DIGITAL SIGNATURE. We produce an RSA digital signature for a data message by hashing the message contents and then encrypting the hash with the author's private key. We include the hash type in the digital signature for both cryptographic security and compatibility reasons.

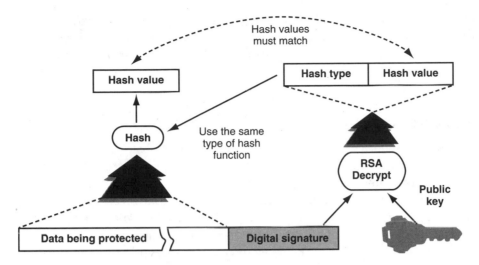

Figure 11-8: VALIDATING A MESSAGE'S DIGITAL SIGNATURE. The recipient validates the data by checking the encrypted hash value. The recipient decrypts the digital signature with the author's public key, yielding the hash type and value. Then the indicated hash function is applied to the data received. This hash result is compared to the one protected by the digital signature.

SMOOTH NUMBER ATTACK

A *smooth number* is the product of reasonably small primes. If Henry the Forger has a collection of Alice's signed messages, and the message texts are composed of small primes or products of small primes, he can use these messages to construct an "alphabet" of Alice's signature values. He can then construct any "signed" message that uses an existing value or a product or power of the values in his "alphabet."

This is easily defeated by padding the signed value with random, nonzero data. Such padding is required by the PKCS standard format for digital signatures.

CUBE ROOT ATTACK

If the public key value is 3, as suggested in Section 9.2, then a valid digital signature is generally a cube root. If you pad on the right with zeros and then sign, an attacker can generate different text to sign (zero padded), take its cube root, and add "random" digits to the right to fill it up to the next integer cube root value. This effectively forges the signature.

This is countered by always signing the result of a one-way hash that has been embedded in an ASN.1 encoding along with an indicator of what hash function was used. Nonzero padding is added to the left in a controlled manner. After being properly formatted, the entire field is signed. This is the technique recommended in the PKCS specifications for digital signatures, and is illustrated in Figures 11-7 and 11-8.

VARYING THE CIPHERTEXT

Alice needs to send a message to Henry the Forger. Nobody but Henry should be able to read the message. She also wants to sign the message to ensure that Henry doesn't modify it and pass around a forgery. So, she encrypts the message with Henry's public key and then applies her private key to the message to sign it. Since the message is encrypted with his public key and the encrypted version is signed, Henry can modify the signed message by modifying how his encryption is performed. One way to do this, in theory, is to vary the encryption exponent being used in the public key algorithm. He can compose a new message and compute a different public key value that yields that message.

Since Alice signed the encrypted text, her signature does not detect the fact that the transformation from plaintext to ciphertext was modified. Thus the signature still matches, but Henry can claim that the message really says something different from what Alice really said.

Alice protects herself by making it nearly impossible for Henry to construct alternate messages that produce the same digital signature. The usual approach is to use a hash function like MD5 to construct the digital signature. This reduces the problem to one of finding a second message with the same hash as the first one. Another step Alice can take is to sign the message in plaintext before encrypting it, instead of signing the ciphertext version. However, there are occasions where it is worthwhile to be able to validate a signature without decrypting the underlying data, so signing plaintext is not always the best solution.

"BIRTHDAY ATTACK" ON HASH FUNCTIONS

Just as encryption must be designed to resist brute force key searches, a hash function must resist attempts to build different versions of a message that yield the same hash. Computing a matching hash value for two different messages is called a *collision*, and puts us at risk of the same problem we saw with trivial crypto checksums in Section 5.3. Hash functions are carefully designed to make it as hard as possible to cause collisions. A hash function that generates 64-bit hash values will require 2^{64} random messages before a collision is sure to occur. If it takes 50 μsec to generate hash values, then it will take more than 12 million years on average to match a 64-bit hash value. However, we can dramatically reduce the search for messages with matching hash values: the *birthday attack*.

There is a famous statistical parlor trick in which the magician bets a group of a couple dozen people that at least two of them were born on the same day of the year. While it may be true that the odds are small that you and I have the same birthday, the odds increase dramatically as people are added to the group. This is because we must consider every possible pairing of people, and that produces a lot of possibilities as the group grows in size. Once a group contains at least 23 people, the odds are even that at least two of them have the same birthday.

We use this trick to attack hash functions by generating a large number of random messages simply to locate two messages with the same hash value. It turns out that statistically such a search should require only half the number of bits. For example, it should only take $2^{64/2}$ or rather 2^{32} on average to find two texts that produce the same 64-bit hash value. If it takes 50 μsec to generate hash values, then the birthday approach will take less than a half a day on average to attack a 64-bit hash function.

This attack is largely theoretical since digitally signed agreements are in their infancy today. However, we can guess how such an attack might occur. Henry the Forger has agreed to buy a rare postage stamp from Bob for $1,000 after failing to bargain him down to $750. But Henry knows Bob will honor his agreement if presented with a digitally signed sales agreement, and that Bob might forget what price was really negotiated. To set up the attack, Henry constructs two long, flowery messages full of purple prose: one agreeing that the price is $1,000 and another agreeing that the price is $750. Then Henry varies the wording in each, changing between "Henry" and "Henry the Forger," between "Bob" and "The Seller," and between synonyms for thirty other words in the agreement. This quickly yields several billion variations (at least 2^{32}) of each message. Henry computes the hash for each, searching for any pair of messages with the same hash value.

Once Henry finds two texts with a matching hash value, one saying "$1,000" and the other saying "$750," he sends the "$1,000" version to Bob for his digital signature. When Henry receives the signed agreement back from Bob, he cuts the original, signed message out and inserts the "$750" message. When it comes time to close the transaction, Henry produces the "$750" message and asks Bob to verify that he signed it. The signature will be valid because the hash values matched.

As a practical matter, this attack probably cost Henry far more than $250 in time, equipment, and effort. However, some transactions may in fact be large enough to make this attack worth protecting against. The basic countermeasure is to always use a hash size that's at least twice as large as a practical brute force attack. MD5 generates a 128-bit hash value while SHA produces 160-bits, and there are no reported instances of successful attacks against actual users.

Another technique for the cautious is to never sign a message if the sender can predict the message's hash. If you suspect the sender can predict the hash, then make a minor change (any change will do) to the message before you sign it. Simply adding a blank line with a random number of spaces will make an unpredictable change that affects the hash. If the sender computed a matching "birthday" message, its hash will no longer match the one for the message you signed.

11.5.2 The Digital Signature Standard (DSS)

The digital signature discussion has focused on RSA signatures because the RSA algorithm is the one found most often in commercial systems. However, there is also a Digital Signature Algorithm (DSA) that signs data hashed by the Secure Hash Algorithm (SHA). Both the DSA and the SHA were developed by the NSA. The NIST has issued the DSS as a Federal Information Processing Standard (FIPS). In short, the U.S. government established a national standard for a digital signature (the DSS) based on other algorithms (the SHA and the DSA).

The DSA used for producing DSS signatures is a variant of the ElGamal digital signature algorithm, which in turn is a variant of the Diffie-Hellman algorithm described in Section 9.1.2. The DSS process is shown in Figure 11-9. First, the message is hashed using the SHA, which generates a 160-bit result. Then the signer must generate a random number that must be kept secret. The signed hash value is generated by applying the DSA to the hash with the random number and the signer's private key. The random number is erased and the computed signature value is appended to the message.

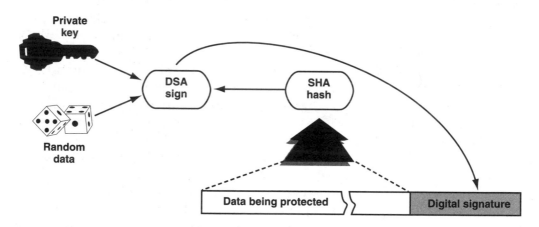

Figure 11-9: SIGNING DATA WITH THE DSS. A DSS signature is produced by hashing data with SHA-1 and signing it with the DSA. The signature computation requires a random number, and random numbers must never be reused. Misuse of the random number value can lead to disclosure of the private key.

The DSS has been implemented in the Fortezza crypto card that is being used in the DMS, the U.S. military's evolving system for digital messages. There are systems deployed and in use that judge the authenticity of messages based on DSS signatures. The NSA cites its endorsement of DSS for these military applications as evidence that it believes in the security of the underlying algorithm.

A practical weakness in DSS is in the random, secret value required for each signature. The DSS private key that signs a message is vulnerable to mathematical attacks if this random value is used incorrectly. Section 4.3 described how hard it is to generate truly random, hard-to-guess numbers in a deterministic machine like a computer. If attackers can guess the random number used when computing a digital signature, they can use it to extract the private key used to compute the signature. Another problem with the random, secret value is that every signature must be computed with a different random value. If two or more messages are signed with the same random value, attackers can use that fact to extract the private key again. Once the private key has been extracted, the attackers can forge messages under that signature.

The risks associated with the random number are caused by mathematical properties of the DSS computations. Some analysts suspect some other potential weaknesses, depending on certain implementation choices. For example, the DSS public key contains numbers that could be made constant as an implementation convenience (the modulus numbers P and Q) but there is a theoretical concern that this could simplify cryptanalysis of DSS signatures.

Another area of concern is key generation. Like RSA, DSS must generate large, high-quality primes for strong private keys. Furthermore, it turns out that certain primes are much easier to crack than others. However, the published definition of DSS describes a procedure for generating high-quality primes that explicitly checks for and rejects any of these weak primes if they are generated as candidate keys.

The preceding observations yield the following list of requirements to follow when implementing the DSS. As usual, they are given in priority order with the most important first:

- **Use a capable random number generator.**
  These numbers must be essentially impossible to predict, so follow recommendations given in Section 4.3.

- **Generate strong DSS keys.**
  Use the procedure recommended in the standard so that weak keys are identified and discarded.

- **Use varying modulus values.**
  The public key P and Q values should not be set constant within the implementation. Make them a varying part of the public keying material.

- **Use a trustworthy implementation.**
  Be sure you can trust the DSS software on which you intend to rely.

While it is always important to deal with reputable, trustworthy vendors, the DSS makes this particularly important. A quirk in its behavior allows a DSS developer to embed small amounts of information in each DSS digital signature. This mechanism is called a *subliminal channel* because it can leak information while still functioning normally. An unscrupulous developer could use this channel to transmit data about the DSS software's user. In the worst case the channel could secretly broadcast bits from the user's private keys. There has never been a report of this type of subversion actually occurring in a genuine product, but it is a risk of which to be aware.

11.5.3 Technical Security Requirements

Here are the technical security requirements for digital signatures. The highest priority requirements appear first:

1. **Follow the security rules for the algorithm.** For RSA, the implementation should comply with the PKCS requirements for digital signatures. For DSS, the implementation should comply with the requirements specified in FIPS and with those noted at the end of Section 11.5.2.

2. **Sign the result of a good hash function.** Do not simply sign the data itself. Sign a hash of the data. Reasonable choices for the hash functions include MD5 and the SHA. The hash function should comply with the requirements described in Section 5.3.2.

3. **Use a sufficiently large public key.** As discussed in Section 9.2.1, public keys must be significantly larger than private keys to pose a comparable challenge to a brute force attacker. Table 9-1 and Figure 9-7 compare the relative effort needed to crack public and secret keys of comparable sizes.

4. **Use a separate public key for digital signatures.** In theory you can use the same public key for both encryption and for digital signatures, especially if RSA is being used. However, it should also be possible to use separate keys for each. Legal restrictions might limit the size of the key used for encryption, but no similar restriction applies to digital signature keys. If you can have separate keys then you can make your signature hard to forge even if the encryption is vulnerable to brute force cracking.

5. **Avoid signing others' unchanged messages.** You want your message to yield a different hash value from any value the sender might predict. Any

trivial change will do this. Add a greeting or other content-free comment, or make some purely cosmetic change. This prevents a "birthday" attack. While a practical birthday attack is probably unlikely, this is probably a worthwhile practice in which to indulge.

11.6 Product Example: Secure E-Mail Client

The essential e-mail security software is a client that applies crypto security to e-mail messages (Figure 11-10). Since e-mail is designed to pass data between end users, the e-mail client software can provide all the services all by itself. The sending client can apply encryption and digital signatures; the receiving client can decode and verify them. The crypto services can be embedded within a standard e-mail message. Existing e-mail servers and storage systems require no special changes to handle encrypted or signed messages.

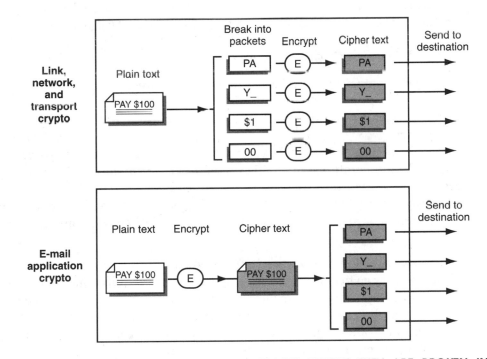

Figure 11-10: E-MAIL CLIENTS ENCRYPT MESSAGES BEFORE THEY ARE BROKEN INTO PACKETS. Crypto services applied at other protocol levels will apply crypto processing to the data piecemeal. E-mail applies the crypto services to a complete, logical message and then hands the encrypted message to the underlying delivery process to packetize the data and deliver it.

There are three principal Internet e-mail crypto protocols, and clients have been developed for them that provide crypto security services:

- Pretty Good Privacy

- Privacy Enhanced Mail

- Fortezza Message Security Protocol

There are a variety of other systems, more or less proprietary, that provide similar services. These have the most stature in the Internet community. These systems are currently in use on the Internet and are recognized as standards for one reason or another.

Another technique for e-mail crypto protection is called *S/MIME*, where *S* stands for "secure" and *MIME* stands for multipart internet mail extensions. MIME is a package of Internet standards for embedding data other than text in e-mail messages. In theory, S/MIME can provide the "hooks" necessary in the standard e-mail formats for integrating all three e-mail security protocols. There is some hope that S/MIME capabilities will find their way into a variety of mail clients, eventually superseding the alternatives. However, this has not happened yet.

11.6.1 Basic Secure Client Features

Secure e-mail clients typically provide the following features:

- **Sending and receiving e-mail, with or without crypto protection**
  Many packages are e-mail clients first and crypto service software second. A few applications like PGP and the ArmorMail product developed for MSP are add-ons that operate in conjunction with other e-mail clients. PGP applies crypto to message text that goes into the body of an e-mail message. An incoming message is decrypted by extracting the embedded PGP data from it. ArmorMail is an add-on for the Microsoft Mail package and interacts with it to provide crypto services.

- **Establishing a list of recipients for an outgoing message**
  Messages may go to one or more recipients, and this requires special processing. Public keys must be available for all recipients of crypto-protected e-mail. Note that it can be risky to send a message to some recipients in plaintext and others encrypted, since there is the risk of failing to apply crypto protections in every case that requires them.

- **Fetching public keys for potential message recipients**

  The client must have a mechanism for fetching and/or maintaining a list of public keys. This generally means the client needs to locate public key certificates for potential e-mail recipients. PGP's public key certificates are formatted so that they may be sent in e-mail messages, posted on Web pages, or retrieved by sending a "finger" request to the certificate's owner. These certificates are then stored in the user's personal "key ring" for later use.

- **Authenticating public keys**

  The client must be able to authenticate public keys for potential recipients, usually by validating a public key certificate. There are several ways to approach this problem and PGP, PEM, and MSP have each taken a somewhat different approach. This is discussed in Chapter 12.

- **Message encryption and decryption**

  Encryption follows the process outlined in Section 11.4, encrypting the message and constructing key tokens for each recipient. Likewise, decryption involves locating the client's key token, decrypting it with the private key, and then decrypting the message text with the encrypted secret key.

- **Applying or checking digital signatures**

  Digital signatures follow the process outlined in Section 11.5, signing with the client's private key or verifying with the sender's public key.

- **Creating or updating your own public key**

  This capability appears in some, but not all, secure e-mail clients. PGP provides functions to create a private key and a public key certificate. PEM requires that public keys be signed by a separate certification authority and implementations may have that authority generate all keys as well. Fortezza keys are all produced by the certificate authority.

- **Handling mailing lists**

  This is not necessarily a feature of an e-mail client, but it is a feature that needs some degree of support in a practical e-mail security system. A client should provide mechanisms for establishing and processing e-mail to reasonably sized lists of recipients. However, the problem of sending a protected message to hundreds or thousands of recipients is beyond the scope of typical e-mail clients. It must be provided by an external device that is part of the e-mail security system.

11.6.2 E-Mail Client Security Issues

This section reviews the following e-mail client security issues:

- Client theft or subversion
- Piggybacked authentication
- Classic Internet attacks
- MIM attacks

CLIENT THEFT OR SUBVERSION

As with other client software, theft and software subversion are important concerns. Keying material should be protected by a pass phrase so that a thief can't simply extract the keying material and use it to masquerade as the theft's victim. This is a standard feature in e-mail software like PGP. The host computer running the client software should be protected against virus attacks and Trojan horse software. While there is no way to unconditionally protect against viruses or other software subversion, we significantly reduce risks simply through basic caution: Avoid installing and running software from uncertain sources.

The Fortezza MSP implementation, like any hardware-based crypto solution, has some distinct benefits when faced with client theft or subversion. The Fortezza card stores all of its keying material inside and it will not disclose its keys even to its authorized user. At worst a Trojan horse attack might manage to trick the Fortezza card into encrypting, decrypting, or signing something the user didn't intend. The Fortezza card also requires a memorized PIN phrase before it will operate at all, so a thief is unlikely to get much use out of it.

PIGGYBACKED AUTHENTICATION

This is a peculiar problem with "multipart" e-mail. Developers of e-mail standards have realized that many e-mail users like to send many types of data in e-mail messages, and if possible send several different items, possibly of different types, in a single message. This led to the MIME standard. This allows Internet e-mail messages to carry a variety of different types of data and to carry many different items in a single message. Variations of this approach were defined for embedding MSP messages in Internet e-mail, and the S/MIME effort promises to provide similar encapsulation for other types of secure e-mail. The result is that an e-mail message may contain one or more components that have had crypto protection applied to them and one or more components without any protection.

The problem here is that the crypto protection on some components tend to suggest that all components were created by the same author. Unfortunately, this is not necessarily true. If a component is unprotected then we have no way of knowing if it was tampered with in transit or not. An attacker could have rewritten the unprotected part of the message or fabricated it completely. The crypto protections on other parts of the message won't necessarily be disturbed by changes to the unprotected parts of the message. Therefore, we can't assume anything about the unprotected components.

CLASSIC INTERNET ATTACKS

E-mail security services provide (or lack) similar protections against classic Internet attacks to those described for SSL in Section 9.4.2. The classic attacks mostly involve attacks on active connections. Since e-mail security is in the messages themselves, attacks on the connection won't affect the security. At worst an attack can prevent a message from being sent. None of the attacks can successfully forge or modify messages. Like SSL, e-mail security measures do not provide any protection against SYN flooding attacks.

MIM ATTACKS

The MIM attack was described in Section 9.3.1. In the discussion, Bailey the Switcher intercepts a public key being sent between Bob and Alice, substituting her own public key for it. This allows Bailey to play an invisible part in their communication, impersonating Bob to Alice and Alice to Bob. Public key certificates are intended to block such attacks by authenticating the owner of each public key. However, this assumes that the client handles the certificates correctly. Two problems could crop up here.

The first problem is that the client might skip the step of validating the certificate signature. In some applications this might be considered a useful feature, since the client might not be able to validate the signature for a variety of reasons. However, the client should be able to validate the certificate under normal conditions if the e-mail system is set up properly. If the client can't validate the certificate signatures, then a MIM attack could occur.

The second problem is that the client might ignore the identification data in the certificate, regardless of whether the certificate's signature has been checked or not. An early version of the Netscape Navigator checked the signature on a certificate, but never verified that the name in the certificate was what it should have been. This could have allowed a MIM attack by a site with a valid certificate.

A "low-tech" way of sidestepping the mechanical requirements for checking certificates while preserving some measure of security is to rely exclusively on manual distribution of public keys. The MIM attack can't happen if the public keys don't travel along the route that the attacker has staked out.

In practice, nobody has ever reported a successful MIM attack for any purposes other than demonstration. The attack has never been reported against valuable e-mail traffic, but then very little valuable e-mail traffic has traveled the Internet so far. E-mail vulnerable to fraud is a relatively new phenomenon on the Internet.

11.6.3 Product Security Requirements

Here are the product security requirements for a secure e-mail client. They are given in priority order with the most important requirements appearing first:

1. **Use a recognized protocol like PEM, PGP, MSP, or S/MIME.** The e-mail client should implement one or more of these protocols. There should be some statement of the compatibility of the client with other implementations, and of how the compatibility was validated.

2. **Provide appropriate secret key crypto.** The client should provide a recognized secret key algorithm with a sufficient key length for the intended application. Appropriate algorithms and key lengths are discussed in Section 2.3. The choices may be constrained by the e-mail security protocol or the implementations available.

3. **Off-line key exchange should be effective.** The client's off-line key exchange operation should comply with the requirements stated in Section 11.4.2.

4. **Digital signature implementation should be effective.** The client's digital signature software should comply with the requirements given in Section 11.5.3.

5. **Provide pass phrase protection for private keying material.** This is necessary to protect against theft and is discussed in Section 7.3.3.

6. **Protect against MIM attacks.** One approach is to deploy a certificate system with appropriate signature-checking software in the client (see Chapter 12). The major e-mail crypto protocols support certificate systems that provide varying degrees of security and convenience. Another approach is to distribute public keys manually.

11.7 E-Mail Deployment

This section examines two important issues in deploying a number of crypto e-mail clients to support secure communications:

- Client key generation and certification
- Message content filtering

CLIENT KEY GENERATION AND CERTIFICATION

There are two general alternatives regarding where a client's public keying material is generated—at the client or at the certification authority. Ideally a client's private keying material should be moved, copied, and distributed as little as possible. Every time the keying material moves around, it runs a bigger risk of being stolen or accidentally disclosed. This would suggest that it is safest to generate the keying material on the client. Then the client can send just the public key to the certification authority, which simply inserts the key into a certificate and signs it. The certification authority never needs the client's private key at all. PGP, Netscape, and a few other public key software clients generate private keys on the client workstation and never export them.

There are, however, a few advantages to key generation by the certification authority. In some cases the authority might be able to generate better keys (for example, if the authority's workstation contains high-quality random number generation hardware). Some enterprises also like the opportunity to make backups of private keying material, and this provides a simple and reasonably secure situation for doing so. These alternatives are examined further in Section 12.3.1.

MESSAGE CONTENT FILTERING

Modern enterprises use e-mail so extensively that it is sometimes hard to keep track of who is really receiving various messages. It is not unusual for a technical discussion to be prompted by an outside expert and continued among company insiders. Such discussions often lead to sensitive and proprietary discussions. Careful e-mail authors must be constantly aware of who is on the recipient list. Note that crypto services do not prevent such a problem. Outside recipients might even have crypto certificates available so that they get encrypted messages just like the insiders.

One technique used in high-security sites is to scan outgoing messages for messages that contain words uniquely associated with sensitive or proprietary activities. This is not done as a punitive measure, but rather to prevent accidental spillage. Some organizations block all outgoing messages unless they include a special word or phrase like "Unclassified" or "For Public Release." This approach usually requires the message's author to take the overt act of typing the right words in order to make a message fit to leave the proprietary boundaries of their site.

Unfortunately, such measures cannot be applied easily to encrypted messages. If such scanning is important enough, the outbound e-mail filter can also be programmed to decrypt outgoing messages. Message keys must be provided to the filtering software in such cases.

11.8 For Further Information

- **Garfinkel, *PGP: Pretty Good Privacy***
  Broad coverage of the PGP, including history, politics, math, and detailed examples of PGP operation.

- **Schneier, *E-Mail Security: How to Keep Your Electronic Messages Private***
  A survey on PGP and PEM that includes reprints of PGP's user guide and PEM's Internet RFCs. A useful source book.

- **Kaufman, Perlman, and Speciner, *Network Security: PRIVATE Communication in a PUBLIC World***
  Solid explanations of the technical underpinnings of the major electronic mail systems.

- **Linn, Kent, Balenson, and Kaliski, "Privacy Enhancement for Internet Electronic Mail: Parts I–IV"**
  The Internet RFCs (1421–1424) defining PEM. The certificate management discussion is still the industry's primary blueprint on the subject.

- **RSA Laboratories, *The Public Key Cryptography Standards (PKCS)***
  The published standards for how to implement secure, interoperable public key crypto facilities. Several standards focus on e-mail formats and operation.

- **Smith, "Securing Client/Server TCP/IP"**
  A proposed approach to using e-mail for secure transaction and order processing.

12

Public Key Certificates

The major difference between a thing that might go wrong and a thing that cannot go wrong is that when a thing that cannot possibly go wrong goes wrong it usually turns out to be impossible to get at or repair.

—Douglas Adams, *Mostly Harmless*

IN THIS CHAPTER

This chapter describes the creation and use of *public key certificates*—digital data structures that reliably associate a public key with the identity of its owner. Certificates are actually used in different ways, so we will examine three specific approaches. The following topics are discussed:

- Security objectives for public key certificates
- Basic technology behind certificates
- Simple, centralized certificate deployment used initially by Netscape
- Hierarchical certificate structure used in other large-scale systems
- Web-of-trust certificate system used by Pretty Good Privacy

Study and analysis of certificate systems has far outpaced their actual use in broadly based, sophisticated applications. This is important to keep in mind when considering practical applications of them.

12.1 Security Objectives

These objectives reflect the need to protect information being used in commercial activities. The principal risks are forgery or modification.

- **Reliably associate an identity with a public key**
  Public keys provide effective security only if they are distributed correctly and are associated with the right owner.

- **Off-line procedures to judge whether a given certificate is valid**
  Software must be able to recognize valid certificates without having to contact a separate authority to authenticate it. Reliable procedures must identify and reject both completely forged certificates and legitimate certificates that are not supposed to be used with the system.

- **Minimal amount of user interaction required**
  The system is less likely to work securely or even correctly if users are burdened with numerous obscure tasks like downloading keys, doing bookkeeping on them, analyzing them, and so on. The system is more likely to work well if such activities are either eliminated or performed automatically.

- **Administration by a changing population of employees**
  The integrity of the system must be maintained when employees come and go. It is not acceptable to require a major overhaul of the system when an administrator leaves.

12.2 Distributing Public Keys

Unlike secret keys, public keys can protect information even if they become public knowledge. While this makes them somewhat easier to distribute than secret keys, delivery problems persist. Section 9.3.1 discussed the MIM attack where Bailey the Switcher tricked a pair of public key users into sharing their private conversation. We can't rely on a public key's crypto capabilities if we can't be sure who really owns the corresponding private key. The essential and tricky objective is to deliver both the public key and the correct name of its owner. In practice, systems use a combination of two mechanisms to safely distribute public keys:

1. **Certificates.** We try to distribute the majority of keys in special data blocks called *certificates*. A certificate always contains three pieces of information: a name, a public key, and a digital signature computed over those other two (Figure 12-1). The certificate's purpose is to show us that a particular name goes with a particular public key.

2. **Trusted manual distribution.** We distribute the remaining keys through trustworthy manual delivery techniques like those described in Section 4.4 for secret keys. The process is much easier for public keys since the primary goal is to deliver the keys accurately and secrecy is not important. Typically,

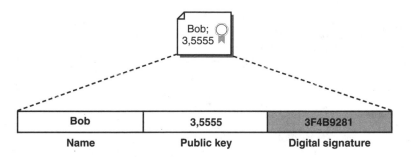

Figure 12-1: CONTENTS OF A PUBLIC KEY CERTIFICATE. The certificate tells us a public key value and the name of whoever controls the corresponding private key. We validate the certificate's contents by checking the digital signature.

the only public keys we distribute manually are those we use to verify signatures on certificates.

Certificates are signed by a trusted third party called a *certification authority* (or CA). If you have a copy of the authority's public key, then you can use it to check the certificates it signed. For example, Bob needs to send Alice a copy of his public key. To do this he turns to Honest Abe, a CA that Bob and Alice both trust. Honest Abe signs his certificate, and Bob can now safely send it to Alice. On receipt, Alice validates Bob's certificate by checking its digital signature with a copy of Honest Abe's public key. Figure 12-2 illustrates this process.

Now certificate validation gets complicated. Where does the authority's key come from? How does Alice get a copy of Honest Abe's key? In a sense, we have simply rearranged the problem. We can safely fetch Bob's key only if we can safely fetch Abe's key. In fact, the public keys for CAs are the ones we usually distribute manually. A certification system is only practical if a very small number of manually distributed keys let you validate certificates containing any other keys you might need. So we manually distribute the public keys we use when validating certificates—the keys of CAs.

The relationship between keys, certificates, authorities, and trust are all based on how the particular certification system is set up. At present there are three general types of certificate systems:

1. **Central authority.** All certificates are signed by a single authority and we can check them with that authority's public key. The central authority's key is manually distributed to each host that must validate certificates, often by being embedded in the certificate-checking software. This is the classic approach used in early versions of the Netscape Navigator.

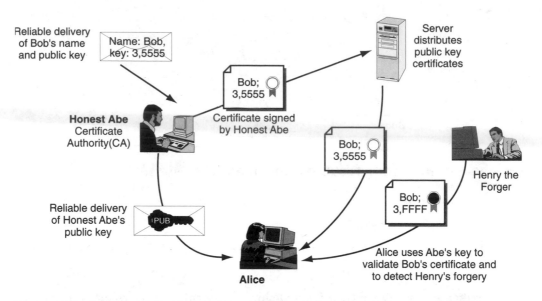

Figure 12-2: CERTIFICATES ARE SIGNED WITH THE PRIVATE KEY AND VALIDATED WITH THE PUBLIC KEY. Alice needs Bob's public key. She has a copy of the CA's public key sent to her safely. The CA has issued a certificate with Bob's public key. Alice retrieves a legitimate copy of Bob's certificate from a server along with a forged certificate from Henry the Forger. The CA public key validates Bob's key.

2. **Hierarchical authority.** The ability to sign certificates is delegated through a bureaucratic hierarchy. At the top of the hierarchy is a "root public key" that signs certificates for all top-level authorities, and these authorities in turn sign certificates for lower level authorities. An individual user's certificate is signed by a local CA. To validate the user's certificate fully we must also validate the local authority's certificate; to validate that certificate we must validate the upper authority's certificate, and so on, back to a key we received through manual distribution. This may be the root key or a subordinate key, depending on how the system is set up. Privacy Enhanced Mail (PEM) and the evolving Defense Message System (DMS) for the U.S. military both use the hierarchical approach.

3. **Web of trust.** Anyone with a certificate may act as a CA by signing another certificate. Individuals who use the system must judge for themselves whether to trust a given certificate based on whether they can validate any of the certifiers' signatures and whether they personally trust any of those certifiers. This is the approach used in Pretty Good Privacy (PGP).

These three choices are also referred to as *trust models*, since signatures imply something different about a certificate's trustworthiness in the different systems. In the centralized system, a signature can mean exactly what the central authority wants it to mean. It can simply provide an identity or it can grant particular access rights and privileges. Hierarchical systems are similar to centralized systems but are more flexible about issuing certificates. They can support many CAs and some may process certificates differently than others. In web-of-trust systems, a certificate may be signed by several different people. Individuals must judge a certificate's meaning based on their personal knowledge of the people who signed it. The three different trust models yield three distinct approaches, which are examined in later sections.

12.3 Technology: Public Key Certificates

A *public key certificate* is a data structure that convincingly identifies the owner of a particular public key. The certificate is a block of digitally signed data that contains a public key and the name of the key's owner (Figure 12-3). The certificate declares that a particular entity with a particular name owns a particular public key. The signature on the certificate verifies that the key and the name go together. Without the signature to check, an attacker could substitute one public key for another and masquerade as one person or another in a data exchange using public keys.

The certificate's digital signature is produced by a CA. Crypto software must have a copy of the CA's public key in order to check a certificate's digital signature.

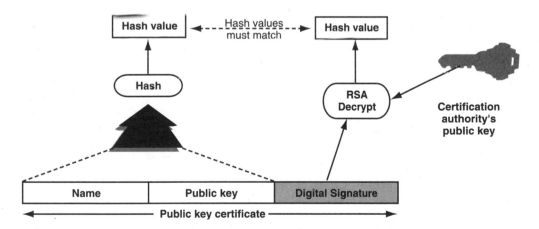

Figure 12-3: VALIDATING A PUBLIC KEY CERTIFICATE. A hash is computed over the name and the public key value. The digital signature is decrypted using the authority's public key, yielding a hash value. The two hash values will match if the certificate is valid.

This public key essentially "trains" the software on how to recognize valid certificates signed by a particular authority.

In the world of paper documents, this is similar to the training of bank tellers to distinguish between genuine and forged currency. The tellers will only take currency they have been trained to recognize and will only take currency they can recognize as genuine. They don't take foreign currency and they don't take bills printed on the wrong paper.

By analogy, properly configured software will reject certificates not issued by the authority it has been trained to recognize. The software will also reject any certificates that claim to be issued by an acceptable authority but are judged to be forgeries. The forgery test consists of verifying the certificate's digital signature by using the authority's public key.

Certificates can use any digital signature mechanism, although most commercial systems use the RSA algorithm. The certificates traditionally handled by Netscape's SSL-based servers and browsers carry an RSA digital signature. Every copy of the Netscape Navigator carries the RSA public key of a specific CA at Verisign, Inc. The latest version of the Navigator allows users to enter additional public keys for other authorities that may in fact use other algorithms. Both PEM and PGP use RSA to sign their certificates. The only well-known exception is perhaps the Fortezza crypto card, which uses the Digital Signature Standard (DSS) to sign its certificates.

Figure 12-4 shows the construction of a public key certificate. Bob generates his public keying material at his host computer. Then he copies his public key and delivers it to the CA, Honest Abe. Bob must choose a reliable means of delivery,

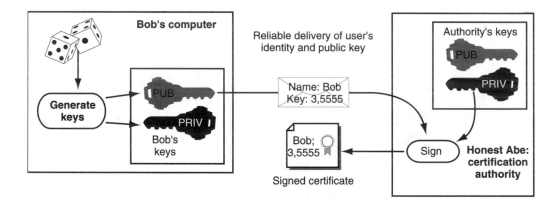

Figure 12-4: THE PUBLIC KEY IS CERTIFIED AFTER IT IS GENERATED. Bob generates his public keying material, consisting of a public key and a private key. He keeps his private key secret and safely delivers a copy of his public key to the CA. The certificate signed by the CA provides a tamperproof report of his identity and his public key.

since someone might substitute a bogus key for his correct private key, or a different name for his own name. Honest Abe should only issue the certificate if he is positive that Bob himself has really delivered the keys and not some imposter. The authority's job is like a notary's, since both must verify a customer's identity before they take action.

12.3.1 Generating Public Key Pairs

There are two approaches to generating public key pairs. Some systems generate them on the host belonging to the key's holder while others generate the keys as part of generating certificates. Figure 12-4 illustrates the first case. The user generates a public key pair, retains the private key, and delivers the public key to the CA to produce the certificate. In the second case, the CA generates the public key pair, produces the signed certificate, and then delivers both to the user who is to receive the key pair. There are a number of trade-offs between these alternatives, and each has its benefits (+) and shortcomings (-):

Keys Generated by Owner	*Keys Generated by Authority*
• Users must deliver public keys to authority. -	• Fewer steps for users to perform. +
• Private key does not need to be copied. +	• Private key can be backed up in case of loss. +/-
• Personal signature keys do not get backed up. +	• Private key must be copied and delivered. --
	• Key generation can be shared among users. +

Generating the keys on the user's own workstation has a number of security benefits. If the key is to be associated with only that individual user, then in essence it should never really reside anywhere except within that user's personal computer. Making copies of such a private key and moving them around simply increases the risk that the key will be leaked, rendering it worthless. In particular, personal keys for digital signatures should never be copied or backed up. They can never be used constructively by others, and they might be used for forgery. The only drawback to this approach is that users must safely deliver their public keys to a CA in order to acquire a certificate. This is less convenient than the alternative approach.

There are a number of interesting procedural and security implications when the CA must generate all keys. This centralized approach imposes simpler procedures on crypto users. If Bob must generate his own keys, the process takes three steps instead of just one—generate keys, deliver them to the CA, and receive his certificate. If the CA generates the keys, then Bob simply waits for a single delivery of keying material that contains both his private key and his public key certificate. This approach also allows the enterprise to keep archival copies of Bob's private keying material. The backup copies will allow the enterprise to retrieve data that Bob has encrypted. This can be used to protect Bob from mishap (such as lost or destroyed keying material) as well as to provide emergency access if Bob is unavailable. Also, there may be security benefits if the CA's host computer has special hardware to generate higher quality random numbers or to validate more effectively prime factors for public keys.

The downside is that Bob's private key gets copied and moved a few extra times. Every time we move it or copy it we increase the risk of improperly disclosing it. If we generate the key on Bob's host, then we never have to move it elsewhere and we reduce the risk of disclosure. If we keep archives of private keys, that archive becomes a very valuable resource and a tempting target to attackers.

12.3.2 Certificate Revocation

The cure for bad speech is more speech.

—Political slogan

If your private key is accidentally disclosed or needs to be changed for any reason, you face a difficult problem. The certificate for the corresponding public key will still look valid even though you may wish otherwise. There is no way to reach out to every computer that may have a copy of your certificate. There's no way to keep track of such things. While various mechanisms have been designed to deal with this problem, few are effective and the mechanisms have not been widely deployed.

Key revocation is less of a problem in secret key systems. Key distribution is so critical that you always know who holds what keys. If you need to revoke a particular key, you inform the systems on either end of the connection. The task is more difficult if you have shared the same secret key between several sites. You must change the key for all of them. In any case we can keep the problem under control even though the procedures may be burdensome.

The typical solution in today's public key systems is the *certificate revocation list*. This is a list of certificates that are no longer valid. The CA collects reports of certificates that are no longer valid. If the system has more than one CA, the authorities share their lists in order to produce a systemwide list of invalid certificates. This is similar to paper lists of revoked credit cards that merchants used to check when processing a credit card purchase (credit card revocation is now usually checked electronically).

For example, imagine what happens if Alice's laptop is stolen along with her private key. She informs her CA, Honest Abe, of the problem and he adds her certificate to the revocation list. As lists are updated and distributed, Alice's old certificate shows up on these lists. If Bob tries to send a message to Alice, his software should automatically check the certificate he uses against the latest revocation list. If he tries to use Alice's old certificate and he has the latest list, his software should warn him about the revoked certificate. If Bob receives a message generated with the revoked certificate, his software should also warn him, since the message might be a forgery.

PGP relics on its users to evaluate certificates individually before deciding to use them. This same philosophy applies to certificate revocation. Users may create PGP revocation certificates that declare their previous certificate is invalid. These certificates are then sent everywhere that the revoked certificates may have gone. However, it is still up to individual PGP users to see and recognize the revocation certificates, and to act on them. There is certainly no guarantee that a PGP revocation message will be seen by everyone who might use the invalid certificate.

Revocation is probably the weakest part of the public key certificate concept. There is not enough practical experience with certificates and revocation to predict how well it will work if widely used and relied on. There are very few programs in use that automatically handle revocation lists. Moreover, there are very few mechanisms to distribute the revocation lists efficiently and effectively to every host that needs them. SSL-based Web browsers have some limited support of revocation lists, but it is not yet automated. Some experts suggest that on-line validity checking is a more realistic approach, given its success in validating credit card purchases.

12.3.3 Certification Authority Workstation

The *certification authority workstation* (CAW) is a special, dedicated system that signs public key certificates. The basic behavior was shown in Figure 12-4. The workstation holds the authority's private keying material plus the hardware and software needed to collect, sign, distribute, and revoke certificates.

The CAW is similar to employee badge-printing equipment in an organization. The certificates identify people and associate them with the entity that owns the CAW, just like employee badges. Forged certificates can pose as big of a problem as forged badges, particularly in modern, "wired" organizations. The security necessary to ensure the integrity of badge-making equipment is similar to that needed for a CAW. It must be physically protected from access by anyone except those who must operate it and it should contain special features to limit the risk of misuse or forgery.

The CAW should be treated as a special device and not as a software utility package that shares a multipurpose host computer. There are too many risks to the certification process that come from sharing the host with other activities. Errors by other software packages could interfere with CAW activities and possibly damage crypto materials or certificates. This would render the certificates and possibly the entire crypto system unusable. The presence of unnecessary software also opens the risk of subverted software tailored to attack the CAW's crypto activities. These risks also make it unwise to connect a CAW to a general-purpose network.

PROTECTING THE CAW PRIVATE KEY

The CAW's private key is a critical piece of information in your key management system. The integrity of the certificates relies entirely on the secrecy of the private key. In previous examples we've talked of it as "Honest Abe's key," but in fact it belongs to the organization. When Honest Abe retires or moves on to something else, we need to continue using that same key. Otherwise we'll need to update the CA's public key in software distributed far and wide, and then reissue all the certificates under the new key. This is not practical.

We want Honest Abe to sign peoples' certificates with the CAW's key as long as he's serving as a CA and to never use it for anything else. If we simply install the private key on a host the way we install any other piece of digital data, then there's nothing to prevent the key from being copied and used elsewhere. We chose Honest Abe because he can be trusted to follow the rules for acting as a CA. But even Honest Abe recognizes that people and even computers make mistakes. Any data on a computer, especially secret data, is at risk of loss or disclosure through several different avenues. Abe himself might be vulnerable to subversion if appropriate personal pressure is applied. We need to protect the keys in order to reduce risks to him as well as to the overall system's integrity.

The solution is to set up the CAW so that Abe never really has access to the private key. The degree to which we enforce this restriction will depend on how much damage we suffer from forged certificates. At one end of the spectrum we can follow PGP's approach and ignore the problem entirely. PGP views every user as a potential CA, so there is no difference between a CAW key and a personal key. A slightly more effective approach is to apply file permissions and perhaps some secondary encryption to the private key so that the operator can't observe it. Ideally the key should be encrypted when not in use so that a thief can't retrieve it from a stolen backup tape. This approach allows the operator to sign certificates without granting direct access to the keys. Without direct access there is no easy way to copy the keys secretly for later misuse.

The most effective approach today is to use hardware crypto modules to contain the keys and crypto algorithms. These crypto modules were noted in Section 10.5.3 as a way of protecting keying material from hostile software. The modules encapsulate the keying material and the crypto algorithms all in a single, relatively tamperproof package. CAW keys can also be kept in the same type of crypto module, and the CAW's module can be kept in a physically secure location. The operator must always enter a pass code to activate the module. The pass code allows the keys to be used with the internal crypto algorithms but will not divulge the module's keys. Similar pass codes in conventional software implementations will not protect the keys from disclosure to a persistent attacker.

If Honest Abe is the CA, we must give him physical access to the crypto card that holds the CAW keys and he must know the pass code to activate it. This allows him to operate the CAW and sign keys. If Abe moves on to a different job, he will no longer have physical access to the crypto card, so he won't be able to sign any more certificates. We can also change the pass code as an additional security measure. The only way Abe could steal the CAW keys is if he steals the crypto card, too. The card serves as tangible evidence that the keys are safe. If the card disappears, the keys may have been compromised. If it disappears while in Abe's custody, we know who is responsible for it. This reduces risk dramatically by making the theft of the CAW keys into the theft of a real object with which only a small number of people could tamper.

12.3.4 Technical Security Requirements

The following requirements for certificate systems are given in priority order with the most important given first. Note that these requirements reflect the assumption that we are performing commercial transactions and using the crypto services to protect them.

1. **Usage of an established system.** Certificate systems have not really seen a lot of use. In order to best benefit from existing lessons, use a system that has been in use and has evolved in response to practical lessons learned.

2. **Effective digital signature implementation.** The client's digital signature software should comply with the requirements given in Section 11.5.3. Note that the signature key size is very important. It is possible to subvert public key certificates if signatures can be forged.

3. **Dedicated, off-line CAW.** The CAW deserves serious protection. Sharing it with other applications or placing it on a general-purpose network will put

the certificate system unnecessarily at risk. It is better to run the CAW on an old, low-performance, dedicated workstation than on a fancier workstation that must pay for itself by doing other duties.

4. **Reliable distribution of the CA's public key.** A legitimate copy of the CA's key must be present in every crypto application that needs to validate certificates. The simplest approach is to configure a standard copy of the applications and to distribute it to users in as safe a manner as practical. Physical delivery is safest.

5. **Generation of keys by the CA.** The increased risk is balanced by simplifying matters for users. Risks are lowest here if the private keys are overwritten after they have been copied for delivery to the key's owner. Distribution should follow the recommendations for secret keys that appear in Section 4.4.

6. **Protection for the CA's private keying material.** There must be special protection in place so that the operator of the CAW cannot extract the CA's private keying material. This may be software protection, but a hardware crypto module provides the best protection.

7. **Protected key backup.** All private keys that are stored on the CAW, including its own, must be protected from disclosure. The best approach is to encrypt them whenever they are stored in files on the system. This ensures that the keys are safe when backed up, so that the loss of a backup tape does not compromise the system. If the keys are not encrypted, then backup tapes must be carefully guarded and strictly accounted for.

8. **Support for key revocation.** There must be a mechanism for revoking public key certificates. Ideally the mechanism should operate automatically.

12.4 Certificate Distribution

Certificates give us a safe method of distributing public keys via electronic media. The next problem is to deliver the certificates to the hosts that need them. If Alice needs to send another message to Bob, she probably already has his key since she used it in a previous message. If she is sending a message to Carl, to whom she rarely talks, she needs a way of retrieving his certificate. The following electronic techniques are often proposed or used in practice:

- Transparent distribution: directory servers, key exchange protocols
- Interactive distribution: e-mail requests, Web sites, finger requests

12.4.1 Transparent Distribution

There are two sets of protocols today that automatically deliver public key certificates: directory protocols and key exchange protocols. The directory protocols evolved from the X.500 directory concept developed to support X.400 e-mail. The key exchange protocols evolved as public key alternatives for the ANSI X9.17 protocols.

DIRECTORY SERVERS

The public key certificates used today largely evolved from specifications for the Consulting Committee, International Telephone and Telegraph (CCITT) X.500 directory server which is an integral part of the X.400-compatible e-mail systems. In X.400, e-mail addresses are so arcane and hard to read that they developed a separate system, the directory, to translate readable names into the unreadable addresses (some say that X.500 names are likewise unreadable, but that's a different issue). To send a message, a user would enter the name of the recipient, and the e-mail client would request the recipient's real e-mail address from a nearby directory.

This same approach is proposed as the general solution for distributing public key certificates. Originally, many people expected X.400 e-mail to replace existing Internet e-mail completely. If this had happened then e-mail recipients' public keys could be retrieved from the directory at the same time their physical e-mail addresses are retrieved. The extra request could in effect be "piggybacked" on an existing part of the e-mail protocol.

However, e-mail service evolved differently, and X.400 is only used by a narrow segment of the Internet community. Different experts may offer differing opinions on why this has happened. In any case, it is worthwhile to note that a fully functional X.400 e-mail system is far more complex than a comparable Internet e-mail service provided by the Simple Mail Transfer Protocol (SMTP). A minimal SMTP e-mail service requires an SMTP server and a small program for editing and retrieving e-mail. A minimal X.400 implementation requires an e-mail client, an X.400 mail server (a "message transfer agent"), and an X.500 directory with associated administrative support. Furthermore, the X.400 and X.500 software relies heavily on arcane and rare software tools for manipulating a special notation that is used to define message formats.

Despite its relative cost and complexity there is still significant interest in X.400 e-mail, and systems using it continue to appear. Microsoft's latest e-mail system, Microsoft Exchange, is built heavily on X.400 and X.500. DMS is also based on X.400 and X.500 protocol specifications. The perceived benefits of X.400

e-mail continue to appeal to some customers, especially those with large-scale e-mail systems.

Regardless of X.400's use in practice, this bit of history shows the origin of certain features appearing in typical certificate systems. The ASN.1 syntax used in PKCS is the same notation used in X.400 and X.500. The standard certificate format is generally based on X.509, part of the X.500 directory specification. Also, the relative immaturity of alternative distribution mechanisms for certificates might be tied to the suspicion among product planners that anything less than an X.500 directory would be a stopgap. Recently, several organizations including Netscape Communications have collaborated on the Lightweight Directory Access Protocol (LDAP) as an alternative to full X.500 protocol support.

KEY EXCHANGE PROTOCOLS

The key exchange protocols proposed or deployed for network and transport encryption all provide facilities to deliver public key certificates to participants in a key exchange. This is seen in the IPSEC key protocols SKIP, ISAKMP, and Photuris. It is also an important element of SSL and its PCT variant.

Figure 9-8 illustrated this process. When Alice initiates a key exchange, Bob's host provides his public key certificate. Alice validates the certificate using the CA public key and then uses Bob's public key to protect the key exchange message. If Bob wants to authenticate Alice, he can query Alice for her own public key certificate. Bob then validates the certificate using the CA's public key and then incorporates Alice's public key in the key exchange process. The IPSEC key exchange protocols handle certificates in a similar fashion when certificates are called for. The public key exchange protocols used with IPSEC typically use certificates to authenticate Diffie-Hellman public key values.

12.4.2 Interactive Distribution

While transparent certificate distribution is usually best, it is not the only approach. Many systems rely on other mechanisms to distribute certificates interactively. When users need certificates they perform their own electronic search for the certificate they need. This may involve one or more e-mail messages to promising sites that may have the certificate, or browsing of Web sites for the right certificate. Such techniques usually yield a certificate encoded in an ASCII format that is then downloaded into the user's crypto software.

Often these systems provide a mechanism to save a collection of certificates that the owner may need to use. This minidirectory can also increase the efficiency of certificate checking. The system can check the certificate's signature once when it is saved, and just use it directly thereafter. This approach leads to problems, however, if a saved certificate becomes invalid. Here are three typical mechanisms used to collect certificates interactively:

- **E-mail**

  E-mail often distributes certificates in two different ways. First, many e-mail systems with crypto support will provide a way to include a certificate with the messages it sends. This simplifies matters if the recipient needs to send a reply, since the certificate is immediately available. However, this can make e-mail messages unnecessarily long. In practice, writers are more likely simply to provide a pointer to where their certificates can be located.

  The second approach is to use a certificate server that accepts e-mail requests. Several systems have been set up to serve PGP certificates in this manner. When users need a particular certificate they send a request to one of the PGP "key server" hosts established in various parts of the world. The same approach can even be applied to X.500-based directories. The *quipu* implementation of X.500 accepts e-mail requests for directory entries.

- **Web sites**

  As Web pages become more and more common, so do personal Web pages. Users can and do publish their certificate either directly on their home page or easily linked to it. They can then easily point to their certificate by providing the URL.

- **Finger requests**

  Many Internet sites support the "finger" protocol, which returns identification information about the owner of an Internet e-mail address. Typically a "finger" request will return the owner's name and contact information along with an ASCII text file that the user can provide. These files serve as a "poor man's Web page," and contain personal information about professional and recreational activities. PGP users also often put a copy of their PGP certificate in that file so that other PGP users can easily retrieve it.

Regardless of how particular certificates are received, keep in mind that they are all equally at risk of attack. You must always check the digital signature on a certificate against a public key you trust before using it. Otherwise an attacker could use weaknesses in the different delivery mechanisms to provide you with a bogus certificate.

Vulnerabilities show up while the certificate traverses the Internet as well as on the key servers themselves. Certificates in transit could be substituted by a sophisticated attacker, or certificates could be fabricated completely and transmitted by a subverted host. X.500 servers are probably vulnerable to sophisticated buffer overrun attacks because of their heavy reliance on variable-length messages. In practice, however, few attacks have been reported against X.500 servers, probably because the technology is still complex and rarely encountered by attackers. Attacks on the other servers are common and well known. Both e-mail and finger servers were attacked by the Internet Worm. Newer attacks have also evolved, as they have against Web servers.

12.5 Centralized Certification Authority

The simplest approach for certification is the centralized authority. This approach relies on a single CA with a single set of keying material to sign all valid certificates in the system (Figure 12-5). All public key software must contain a valid copy of the CA's public key to validate its certificates. Any certificate signed by a different authority will be rejected. This approach has several security advantages, but it lacks the flexibility highly prized among many Internet software developers. A compromise is to provide mechanisms to install public keys for multiple CAs in public key software.

This approach has some appealing features, particularly to security-conscious organizations. It puts the organization in complete control of the certification process. Specifically

1. Certificates are accepted and rejected solely on the basis of whether they were signed by the organization's own authority. Third parties cannot create acceptable certificates that bypass the organization's security measures.

2. The single, centralized certification point makes it easier to enforce specific conditions reliably for issuing certificates. Uniform policies are harder to enforce consistently among multiple authorities, especially if some are in other organizations.

3. The organization can use certificates as credentials to grant access to restricted resources, like dial-in access to their site over encrypted connections, since they fully control the conditions under which they are issued.

4. The organization is solely responsible for the physical security of the private keys used for certification. They are not vulnerable to security breaches or relative carelessness in other participating organizations.

The principal disadvantage of this approach is that it produces a bottleneck in the system. Since every certification operation must go through a single workstation, each must wait its turn. Such clerical activities are costly and lightly staffed,

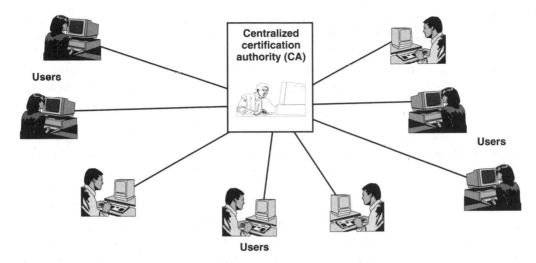

Figure 12-5: CENTRALIZED CERTIFICATION AUTHORITY. All public key users must get their certificates signed by this specific authority. The authority's public key has been distributed to all public key users so that they may validate certificates.

particularly since they require special training and trustworthiness. This approach can also produce political problems if the authority belongs to one organization and issues certificates to others. This caused numerous complaints with the early versions of Netscape's SSL Web security software.

12.5.1 Netscape Server Authentication

Early versions of the Netscape Navigator validated server certificates against a central authority's key. Initially all SSL server certificates were issued by a commercial CA operated by Verisign, Inc. This authority's public key was embedded in every copy of the Netscape Navigator browser. When a copy of the browser set up an SSL session with a server, the server would send its public key certificate (see Figure 9-8). The browser would validate the certificate's digital signature using Verisign's public key. This approach led to operating simplicity and a relatively clear interpretation of certificates.

Operating simplicity came from a reliance on a single public key. Browser users did not need to do anything to set up crypto keys. The Navigator's SSL software would automatically establish a session key and validate the server's certificate. The crypto activities were based entirely on the Verisign CA key and other data embedded in every copy of the Navigator. Servers had no choice in the matter: To interoperate with the Navigator they had to get a certificate from the appropriate Verisign CA.

The clear interpretation of certificates also came from the centralized CA. Certificates were intended to identify Internet hosts reliably in support of commercial transactions. The developers realized that typical users would like a reliable method of confirming the identity of the site with which they communicate, especially if they are planning to buy things. Certificates were formatted to identify the company owning the site as well as to identify the site's Internet host name. Verisign established a set of rules for issuing certificates that required clear, legal documentation that the holder of a particular public key was in fact the entity identified in the certificate. Users could rely on the fact that certificate names would match Internet host names, and that certificates would be issued only to the organization that really owned a given host name.

This rigid approach also had disadvantages. The general approach worked poorly for organizations interested in using the Navigator and SSL for private purposes. Other organizations were operating their own certification systems and did not want to rely on Verisign for that service. Also, the students, researchers, and hobbyists that make up a large and vocal part of the Internet population could not efficiently experiment with these mechanisms since they needed a Verisign server certificate to do so. This led to the support of multiple CAs.

In Netscape Navigator 3.0, the browser allowed public keys for other CAs to be installed and used, and also supported hierarchical CAs as described in Section 12.6.

12.5.2 Handling Multiple Certification Authorities

A single CA makes the software simple if inflexible. The alternative chosen by Netscape for later versions of the Navigator browser is to allow users to install additional public keys for alternative CAs. When so configured, the Navigator will validate certificates signed by any of the authorities in its database of public keys. This provides a useful balance of flexibility, convenience, and risk. The flexibility and convenience mostly appeal to developers who are experimenting with the new capabilities offered by public key crypto techniques. The risk comes from the uncertainty produced by a varying database of acceptable public keys. Microsoft has taken a similar approach with the Internet Explorer browser.

The initial risk posed by these public keys is that of a bogus key being installed along with the legitimate ones. This has always been something of a risk, since an attacker could simply replace the built-in key belonging to the central authority with a bogus key. This attack is somewhat recognizable since it would prevent legitimate certificates from working. The risk changes when we have a list of keys to check. If an attacker inserts a bogus key into the list, the legitimate keys will still work. The bogus key simply means that certificates signed by the bogus authority will also be accepted as legitimate.

Another risk is that a legitimate certificate might be misinterpreted. For example, assume that Alice uses the Web to send various transactions to the home office. The Web server's certificate was issued by the enterprise's central authority and her browser has been configured to contain a copy of the CA's key. The browser also comes configured with keys from several other authorities. If Bailey the Switcher manages to fool one of those CAs into issuing a certificate similar to the one for Alice's enterprise, Bailey can use the spurious certificate to stage a MIM attack against Alice. When Alice connects to her server, Bailey interrupts the certificate transmission to insert her own version of the certificate. Since the certificate was signed by one of the acceptable authorities, Alice's browser will accept it as valid, thus treating Bailey's public key as if it were the server's.

Later versions of the Netscape Navigator try to block such attacks by requiring a match between server host names in Web URLs and in the public key certificate used for the session. This may be sufficient to block such an attack through the Navigator, but it shows that any public key software that accepts multiple authorities must be careful to interpret the different certificates correctly.

12.6 Hierarchical Certification Authority

A major complaint against the centralized CA is that it becomes a system bottleneck. The Netscape experience found many enterprises and activities that wanted server certificates that worked with the Navigator but had no intention of hosting a commercial server on the Internet. One size rarely fits all, particularly with new, evolving technologies. Hierarchical certification was originally developed to blend features of the centralized authority with a more distributed arrangement. PEM and the evolving DMS for the U.S. military both use the hierarchical approach. Netscape's system for authenticating browser users is also hierarchical.

Hierarchical systems start with a root authority with a public key that is usually distributed to all participating hosts. Unlike the centralized systems, the issuing of certificates is delegated to several CAs. The root authority only signs certificates for CAs. Some CAs may only sign certificates for lower level authorities, and so on. At the bottom of the system are authorities that sign certificates for individual entities or users (Figure 12-6).

The series of certificates leading back to the root public key must be retrieved and checked in order to validate a user's certificate. Since a user's certificate is signed by a local CA, we use the public key in the local authority's certificate to validate it. To validate the local authority's certificate we must use the key for the organizational authority that signed it. The process repeats itself as we walk up the hierarchy back to the root key that is manually installed in the software. This may

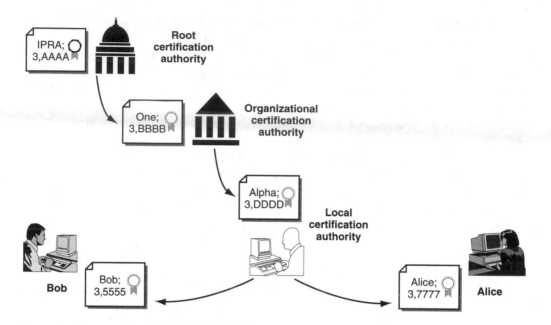

Figure 12-6: SERIES OF AUTHORITIES IN HIERARCHICAL CERTIFICATION. In hierarchical systems, every CA has its own certificate signed by a higher level authority. At the top there is a root authority with a public key that must go into every device that's part of the system.

be the root key of the entire hierarchy or a subordinate key, depending on how the system is set up.

12.6.1 PEM Internet Certification Hierarchy

PEM was the pioneer project for deploying public key cryptography in the Internet community. The specification for PEM certificates (Internet RFC 1422) has served as a model for a variety of hierarchical public key systems, although the PEM hierarchy itself has only been partially implemented. The specification describes a grand scheme that seeks to embrace almost any CA within a single hierarchy (Figure 12-7). In practice, the Internet community has not really embraced this single, comprehensive system. However, the design concepts have borne fruit in other hierarchical systems.

The PEM hierarchy incorporates the notion that different CAs will need to operate under different rules. At the top the hierarchy immediately branches into separate *policy creation authorities* (PCAs), which establish rules for the CAs under them. The next level down issues certificates to authorities operating on behalf of different organizations or geographical location. Beneath that are local CAs for organizational units. The lowest level authorities issue certificates to individual users.

The PCAs establish rules that a particular group of CAs are supposed to follow and then issue certificates for those authorities. For example, there can be a "high-assurance" authority that issues certificates to authorities that enforce a high standard of certificate security and authenticity. These authorities might require background investigations before issuing a user certificate and enforce particularly stringent requirements on CAs. A separate PCA might be a "medium" or even "low" assurance, issuing certificates under more casual constraints. Certificates issued by experimental groups as part of system development and testing may fall in the low-assurance category since operating flexibility is usually more important than certificate assurance.

The PCAs issue certificates to organizations or geographical locations such as local governmental entities. These in turn operate CAs for users under their jurisdiction. Small organizations will use this key to sign users' certificates while larger organizations will use it to sign certificates for lower level CAs. Some organizations could end up with two or more PCA certificates if they need to operate CAs under different policies.

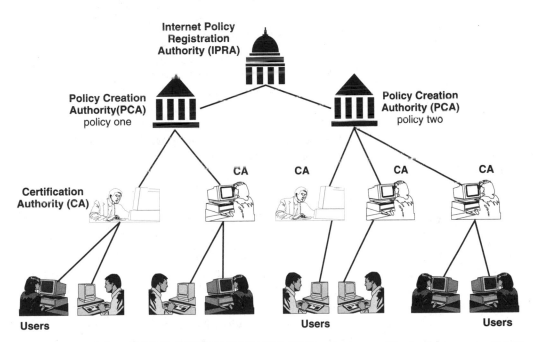

Figure 12-7: HIERARCHICAL CERTIFICATION FOR PEM. CAs sign certificates for lower level CAs in the hierarchy or for individual users. The Policy Creation Authorities (PCAs) sign certificates for CAs in individual enterprises or sites. The PCA certificates are signed by the root key held by the Internet Policy Registration Authority (IPRA).

The actual PEM hierarchy was established but has seen very little use in practice. Several reasons are suggested for this. Some experimenters objected to the amount of paperwork and complexity associated with a reliable certification structure. Others objected to the requirement that everyone register through the root authority, which was established through RSA Data Security, the holder of the RSA patents. Some perceived this as an attempt to collect patent royalties, which caused discomfort in organizations that had already licensed the patents through other channels and overseas, where the patents were not valid. In some cases the integrity requirements grated too strongly on the casual, cut-to-fit, experimental attitudes of the Internet development community.

Today the RFC 1422 architecture is being deployed in the certification architecture established for the Fortezza cards. The system includes PCAs, organizational authorities, and a series of local CAs to issue certificates to individual users.

12.6.2 Private Trees

The failure of the PEM centralized tree to catch on has led to a different evolution of hierarchical certification systems. Many of the features of RFC 1422 remain, but the central root and PCAs have disappeared from many implementations. Instead, a vendor offering public key services defines its own root and installs the corresponding public key in its software. Now we have a "forest" of CAs instead of a single tree.

This is actually somewhat healthy because different certification trees are being developed for different reasons. The Verisign authority continues to sign server certificates for use by the Netscape Navigator, but now other public key vendors also have their authorities' keys installed in the Navigator, including Nortel, GTE, and AT&T. A new hierarchy is also evolving to support the Secure Electronic Transaction (SET) protocol, designed to protect credit card transactions for Visa and Mastercard.

12.7 PGP "Web of Trust"

Of all the certification techniques, PGP embodies the prevailing spirit among Internet system developers: personal authority, flexibility, and personal losses if failures occur. Unfortunately, these are not the best properties for supporting commercial transactions. A commercial transaction typically involves business entities, and only rarely are all of these entities really individuals acting personally. PGP cryptography is designed to let individuals authenticate each other and communicate reliably. Typical implementations don't give us the right tools to associate PGP keys with business roles that are passed safely from one employee to another.

The fundamental feature of PGP certification is that there is no difference between an individual PGP user and a CA. Any user may sign another user's key, acting as a CA when doing so. The convention among PGP users is that certificates are only signed if the signer is reasonably sure the certificate is legitimate. Figure 12-8 shows how this works in practice. Users sign each others' certificates as the opportunity arises, and they judge whether a certificate is genuine according to whether or not it carries the signature of someone they trust. There are two essential criteria for trusting a certificate based on a particular user's signature: You must have a legitimate copy of that user's public key and you must be confident that the user will only sign legitimate certificates.

For example, Alice and Bob both had their certificates signed by Honest Abe. Both have legitimate copies of Honest Abe's public key and both trust Abe. Since they both trust Abe and they can both verify Abe's signature, they believe each others' certificates are genuine. This allows them to communicate with each other since they can use the keys provided in each others' public key certificates. Bob and Alice will also exchange messages with Carl since Abe signed Carl's certificate. Bob can also send messages to Emily. Since Bob signed her certificate he must have a copy of her public key that he trusts. Nobody, except Carl who signed it, will trust

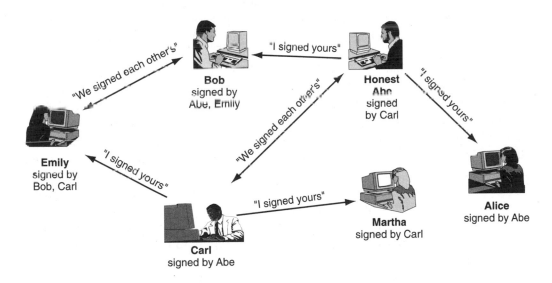

Figure 12-8: WEB-OF-TRUST RELATIONSHIPS BASED ON INDIVIDUAL SIGNATURES. Users can decide for themselves who else they trust to sign certificates reliably. Bob and Alice can trust any capable person to sign their certificates and they both happen to trust Honest Abe. If Alice only trusts Abe, then she won't believe the certificates from Martha or Emily are genuine. If she trusts Bob's judgment about signing certificates, she can trust Emily's certificate; if she trusts Carl, she can trust everyone's certificate.

Martha's certificate unless they also trust Carl, since he's the only one who has signed her certificate.

Both parts of the criteria are important: assessing other users' judgment and having legitimate copies of their public keys. Omitting either step can admit forgeries. Even if Martha trusts Honest Abe completely, she can't trust any certificates he signed unless she has a trustworthy copy of his public key. PGP users can look at a certificate and see names of users that signed it, but neither the number of names nor the names themselves should give us reason to trust the certificate. We must verify the signatures behind the names and only pay attention to verified names that we trust.

If we relax our guard, we open an entering wedge for the industrious attacker. For example, Henry the Forger can construct his own set of certificates that aim at attacking Martha's attempts to send messages to others. Henry gives one of these new certificates the name "Honest Abe," another "Bob," and others get the names "Alice," "Carl," and "Emily." Then Henry constructs exactly the same set of interconnected signatures. When finished, Henry generously transmits this collection of certificates to Martha to "help her get started with PGP." Martha just might be fooled. A superficial glance at PGP's display of these bogus certificates won't look very different from a display of the legitimate ones. However, Martha can easily detect the forgery if she independently fetches a certificate from any of the other users and checks their signature on any of the suspicious certificates. If she fails to do this and simply relies on the unverified names, she will succumb to Henry's trickery.

Another issue that often arises in PGP circles is *transitive trust*. A casual observer might notice that Abe signed Bob's certificate, indicating its validity, and then Bob signed Emily's certificate. People who trust Honest Abe will believe Bob's certificate is legitimate. Should they in turn believe that Emily's certificate is legitimate? Some say yes and some say no. Strictly speaking, all that Abe is certifying is that he signed a certificate he really believes is Bob's. His signature does not mean that he trusts Bob to be equally careful when signing other certificates. Bob might be perfectly capable of keeping his public key associated with his personal identity, but be careless at judging other peoples' identities. Therefore, a strict reading of the certificates won't lead friends of Abe to trust Emily's certificate. They also have to know and trust Bob in order to trust Emily's certificate. In practice, however, many PGP users rely on transitive trust. This is probably acceptable for casual PGP usage. However if trust is spread thinly, you increase the risk of accepting a forged certificate.

SIGNING PGP CERTIFICATES

Some PGP users take certificate signing very seriously, especially if they are using PGP for important applications. Cautious users only sign certificates when they are certain that the certificate is genuine. This is often limited to two situations:

1. **Social contact.** In this situation the PGP users physically meet each other and exchange PGP certificates on diskette or other digital media. If the two users know each other personally and are confident they can spot an impostor, this is the best method of exchanging keys. There are occasionally "PGP signing parties" among groups of PGP users in order to facilitate reliable association of PGP keys with identities.

2. **Fingerprinting.** Many PGP users publish a "fingerprint" of their PGP public key: a 128-bit MD5 hash of the key's value. This is more compact and easier to handle than the entire key, which always contains several hundred bits. For example, Emily could place her key's fingerprint in her outgoing e-mail messages, on her Web home page, and even on her business cards. If Alice doesn't trust Bob's or Carl's signature, she can still validate Emily's certificate by computing the key's fingerprint and checking it against the fingerprint Emily has published. The MD5 hash is secure enough in this application that many users are willing to sign a certificate on the strength of the matching fingerprint.

Less cautious users will accept and sign PGP certificates received in e-mail messages, trading assurance for convenience. This is probably not a problem when the users involved face a limited practical threat. There is little practical benefit in forging e-mail from an arbitrarily chosen Internet user.

12.8 For Further Information

- **CCITT,** *Recommendation X.509: The Directory—Authentication Framework*
  The starting point for most public key certificate designs. Most commercial systems use some variant of the X.509 certificate format.

- **Kent, "Privacy Enhancement for Internet Electronic Mail: Part II: Certificate-Based Key Management," RFC 1422**
  The classic specification of a universal public key infrastructure. It covers a broad range of real and potential issues in certificate system design and management.

- **Schneier,** *E-Mail Security: How to Keep Your Messages Private*
  A useful general reference on e-mail crypto and the certificate systems associated with it. Includes reprints of the basic PEM and PGP documents.

- **RSA Laboratories,** *The Public Key Cryptography Standards (PKCS)*
  The published standards for safe public key crypto. PKCS #7 is the standard for formatting X.509 certificates with RSA public keys.

Appendix
A
Glossary

active attack

an attack in which the attacker must create or modify information. This includes attacks by Henry the Forger, Play-It-Again Sam, and Bailey the Switcher.

Advanced Research Projects Agency (ARPA)

an agency of the U.S. Department of Defense that promotes exploratory research in areas that carry long-term promise for military applications. ARPA funded the major packet switching experiments in the United States that led to the Internet.

algorithm

a procedure; a *crypto algorithm* defines a particular procedure for encrypting or decrypting data. Specific algorithms include DES, IDEA, and RC4.

American National Standards Institute (ANSI)

an organization that endorses and publishes standards for various industries

annual solar limit

the total amount of energy produced by the sun in a year. It is possible to calculate a worst case upper limit for the number of keys that can be tested with that amount of energy: 2^{192} keys. This suggests that a secret key containing 192 bits is impractical to crack using brute force methods.

ANSI X9.17

ANSI standard for secret key exchange using the DES algorithm

application encryption

cryptographic functions built into the communications protocols for a specific application, like e-mail. Examples include PEM, PGP, and SHTTP.

application software

software that provides a service to a user, as opposed to lower level software that makes useful services possible

ARPANET

a pioneering wide area, packet-switched computer network developed by ARPA. The ARPANET was the original backbone for the modern Internet, and many of its protocols were adapted to work on the Internet, including those for e-mail, FTP, and remote terminal connections.

asymmetric algorithm

a crypto algorithm that uses different keys for encryption and decryption; most often a public key algorithm

authentication

the process of verifying that a particular name really belongs to a particular entity. For example, a server will authenticate Alice to ensure that the person at the other end of the network connection isn't Henry the Forger instead.

Authentication Header (AH)

the IPSEC header used to verify that the contents of a packet haven't been modified in transit

authenticity

the ability to ensure that the given information was in fact produced by the entity whose name it carries and that it was not forged or modified

autokey

the block cipher mode in which the cipher is used to generate the key stream. Also called *output feedback (OFB) mode.*

Bailey the Switcher

an attacker who attacks network traffic by modifying the contents of other peoples' messages

block cipher

the cipher that encrypts data in blocks of a fixed size. DES, IDEA, and SKIP-JACK are block ciphers.

browser

client application software for accessing data on the World Wide Web

brute force cracking

the process of trying to recover a crypto key by trying all reasonable possibilities

bucket brigade

an attack against public key exchange in which attackers substitute their own public key for the requested public key; also called a *Man-in-the -Middle attack*

bypass

a flaw in a security device that allows messages to go around the security mechanisms. Crypto bypass refers to flaws that allow plaintext to leak out.

CAPSTONE

an integrated circuit that implements crypto functions for e-mail applications using the SKIPJACK cipher and the Escrowed Encryption Standard

certificate, public key

a specially formatted block of data that contains a public key and the name of its owner. The certificate carries the digital signature of a certification authority in order to authenticate it.

certification authority (CA)

a trusted entity that signs public key certificates

checksum

a numeric value used to verify the integrity of a block of data. The value is computed using a checksum procedure. A crypto checksum incorporates secret information in the checksum procedure so that it can't be reproduced by third parties that don't know the secret information.

cipher

a procedure that transforms data between plaintext and ciphertext; a crypto algorithm

cipher block chaining (CBC)

a block cipher mode that combines the previous block of ciphertext with the current block of plaintext before encrypting it; very widely used

cipher feedback (CFB)

a block cipher mode that feeds previously encrypted ciphertext through the block cipher to generate the key that encrypts the next block of ciphertext; also called *CTAK*

ciphertext

data that has been encrypted with a cipher, as opposed to plaintext

ciphertext autokey (CTAK)

a, block cipher mode that feeds previously encrypted ciphertext through the block cipher to generate the key that encrypts the next block of ciphertext; also called *CFB*

client

the entity in a networking relationship that seeks service from other entities on the network. Client software generally resides on personal workstations and is used to contact network servers to retrieve information and perform other activities.

CLIPPER

an integrated circuit that implements crypto functions for voice and telephone using the SKIPJACK cipher and the Escrowed Encryption Standard

Computer Emergency Response Team (CERT)

an organization that collects and distributes information on computer security incidents and software problems relating to publicly used networks like the Internet

Computer Incident Advisory Capability (CIAC)

an organization established by the U.S. Department of Energy to track and report on computer security events and situations

confidentiality

the ability to ensure that information is not disclosed to people who aren't explicitly intended to receive it

Consulting Committee, International Telephone and Telegraph (CCITT)

the international standards committee for telephone communications systems

cracking

the process of overcoming a security measure. Cracking a key means an attempt to recover the key's value; cracking some ciphertext means an attempt to recover the corresponding plaintext.

critical application

a computing application in which an attacker could cause incredibly serious damage, including loss of life

cryptanalysis

the process of trying to recover crypto keys or plaintext associated with a crypto system

cryptography, crypto

> mechanisms to protect information by applying transformations to it that are hard to reverse without some secret knowledge

cryptoperiod

> the amount of time a particular key has been used; sometimes refers to the amount of data encrypted with it

cut-and-paste attack

> an attack in which pieces of one message are assembled with pieces from other messages to yield a forged message that will be decrypted more or less correctly

Data Encryption Standard (DES)

> a block cipher that is widely used in commercial systems

data key

> a crypto key that encrypts data as opposed to a key that encrypts other keys

data link

> the portion of a system of computers that transfers data between them, including wiring, hardware, interfaces, and device driver software

decipher, decrypt, decode

> the process of converting ciphertext to plaintext

Defense Message System (DMS)

> a system being developed by the U.S. Department of Defense to provide secure e-mail services for critical applications

device driver

> a software component that controls a peripheral device. For data link devices, it manages the process of sending and receiving data across the data link.

device driver interface

> a standard interface used by a host's software to communicate with peripheral devices, including data link devices

differential cryptanalysis

> a technique for attacking a cipher by feeding it chosen plaintext and watching for patterns in the ciphertext

Diffie-Hellman (DH)

> a public key crypto algorithm that generates a shared secret between two entities after they publicly share some randomly generated data

digital signature

a data value generated by a public key algorithm based on the contents of a block of data and a private key, yielding an individualized crypto checksum

Digital Signature Standard (DSS)

a digital signature algorithm developed by the NSA and endorsed by NIST

domain name

the textual name assigned to a host on the Internet. The Domain Name Service (DNS) protocol translates between domain names and numerical IP addresses

electronic codebook (ECB)

a block cipher mode that consists of simply applying the cipher to blocks of data in sequence, one block at a time

electronic mail, e-mail

an application protocol for sending messages between users on a network. Messages may be queued, stored, relayed, or delayed and still be delivered to the intended recipients eventually.

Encapsulating Security Payload (ESP)

an IPSEC header that encrypts the contents of an IP packet

encipher, encrypt, encode

the process of converting plaintext to ciphertext

entering wedge

a weakness in a crypto system or other security system that gives an attacker a way to break down some of the system's protections

Escrowed Encryption Standard (EES)

a standard developed by the NSA and published by NIST for crypto systems, that allows law enforcement and other authorized agencies to tap encrypted communications by providing a method to recover the crypto keys being used

exclusive-or

a computational operation on bits that adds the two bits together and discards the carry; the basis of the Vernam cipher and key splitting

executable contents

data with contents that represent an executable computer program that is capable of modifying persistent data on a host computer

export control
> laws and regulations intended to prevent products from being exported when not in the government's interest. Typically, munitions are placed under export control.

Federal Information Processing Standard (FIPS)
> standards published by NIST with which the U.S. government's computer systems should comply

File Transfer Protocol (FTP)
> an Internet application and network protocol for transferring files between host computers

firewall
> a device, installed at the point where network connections enter a site, that applies rules to control the type of networking traffic that flows in and out. Most commercial firewalls are built to handle Internet protocols.

forgery
> a data item with contents that mislead the recipient to believe the item and its contents were produced by someone other than the actual author

Fortezza
> a PC card (formerly called *PCMCIA cards*) containing a CAPSTONE chip and providing crypto services needed to support e-mail applications

hash
> an improved checksum in which similar data blocks still produce different results

headers
> formatted information attached to the front of data sent through a computer network; contain information used to deliver and process correctly the data being sent

Henry the Forger
> an attacker who generates completely forged network messages to try to fool victims

high risk application
> a computer application in which the enterprise operating it can suffer a significant loss through a computer security incident

hijacking
> an attack in which the attacker takes over a live connection between two entities so that he can masquerade as one of the entities

host
> a computer system that resides on a network and is capable of independently communicating with other systems on the network

host address
> the address used by others on the network to communicate with a particular host

Hypertext Markup Language (HTML)
> the textual format used for pages on the World Wide Web

Hypertext Transfer Protocol (HTTP)
> an application protocol used to carry requests and replies on the World Wide Web

in-line encryptor
> a product that applies encryption automatically to all data passing along a data link

information security (INFOSEC)
> technical security measures that involve communications security, cryptography, and computer security

integrity
> the ability to ensure that information is not modified except by people who are explicitly intended to modify it

International Data Encryption Algorithm (IDEA)
> a block cipher developed in Switzerland and used in PGP

International Standards Organization (ISO)
> an international organization that published a large number of networking standards (the OSI protocols), most of which are incompatible with the Internet protocols.

internet; Internet
> a computer network that uses the internet protocol family; when capitalized, the single, well-known, globally connected network using those protocols

Internet Address and Numbering Authority (IANA)

an administrative organization that assigns host addresses and other numeric constants used in the Internet protocols

Internet Engineering Task Force (IETF)

a technical organization that establishes and maintains Internet protocol standards.

Internet Protocol (IP)

a protocol that carries individual packets between hosts, and allows packets to be automatically routed through multiple networks if the destination host isn't on the same network as the originating host

Internet Security Association Key Management Protocol (ISAKMP)

a key management application protocol for IPSEC that has been endorsed by the IETF as a required part of any complete IPSEC implementation

intranet

a private network, usually within an organization, that uses the Internet protocols but is not directly connected to the global Internet

IP address

the host address used in IP packets

IP Security Protocol (IPSEC)

the network crypto protocol for protecting IP packets

key

information that causes a cipher to encrypt or decrypt information in a distinctive way. Individual keys are usually associated with individual entities, or at most a pair of entities.

key distribution center (KDC)

a device that provides secret keys to allow pairs of hosts to encrypt traffic directly between themselves

key encrypting key (KEK)

a crypto key used to encrypt session or data keys, and never used to encrypt the data itself

key escrow

a mechanism for storing copies of crypto keys so that third parties can recover them if necessary to read information encrypted by others

key recovery
> a mechanism for determining the key used to encrypt some data, usually through the use of an escrowed key

least privilege
> a feature of a system in which operations are granted the fewest permissions possible in order to perform their tasks

lightweight crypto
> a set of crypto capabilities that is as strong as possible but still sufficiently weak to qualify for favorable treatment under U.S. export regulations

link encryption
> crypto services applied to data as it travels on data links

local area network (LAN)
> a network that consists of a single type of data link and can reside entirely within a physically protected area

low risk application
> computer applications that, if penetrated or disrupted, would not cause a serious loss for an enterprise

Man-in-the-Middle (MIM)
> an attack against a public key exchange in which the attacker substitutes his own public key for the requested public key; also called a *bucket brigade attack*.

mandatory protection
> a security mechanism in a computer that unconditionally blocks particular types of activities. For example, most multiuser systems have a "user mode" that unconditionally blocks users from directly accessing shared peripherals. In networking applications, some vendors use mandatory protection to prevent attacks on Internet servers from penetrating other portions of the host system.

masquerade
> an attack in which an entity takes on the identity of a different entity without authorization

medium-risk application
> a computer application in which a disruption or other security problem could cause losses to the enterprise, some of which are an acceptable cost of doing business

medium-strength crypto

a set of crypto capabilities that may qualify for favorable export treatment by the U.S. government if the vendor is actively developing crypto products that contain key escrow features

message

information sent from one entity to another on the network. A single message may be divided into several packets for delivery to the destination and then reassembled by the receiving host.

Message Digest #5 (MD5)

a one-way hash algorithm that is widely used in crypto applications

Message Security Protocol (MSP)

an e-mail crypto protocol developed as part of the Secure Data Network System and used in the Defense Message System

mode

one of several ways to apply a block cipher to a data stream; includes CBC, CFB, and OFB

modulus

in public key crypto, part of the public key

munition

anything that is useful in warfare. Crypto systems are munitions according to U.S. law This is the rationale behind export controls on crypto systems.

National Computer Security Center (NCSC)

a U.S. government organization that evaluates computing equipment for high-security applications

National Institute of Standards and Technology (NIST)

an agency of the U.S. government that establishes national standards

National Security Agency (NSA)

an agency of the U.S. government responsible for intercepting foreign communications for intelligence reasons and for developing crypto systems to protect U.S. government communications

network encryption

crypto services applied to information above the data link level but below the application software level. This allows crypto protections to use existing networking services and existing application software transparently.

network protocol stack

> a software package that provides general-purpose networking services to application software, independent of the particular type of data link being used

nonce

> a random value sent in a communications protocol exchange; often used to detect replay attacks

one time pad

> a Vernam cipher in which one bit of a new, purely random key is used for every bit of data being encrypted

one-time password

> a password that can only be used once; usually produced by special password-generating software or by a hardware token

one-way hash

> a hash function for which it is extremely difficult to construct two blocks of data that yield exactly the same hash result. Ideally it should require a brute force search to find two data blocks that yield the same result.

Open System Interconnection (OSI)

> a family of communications protocols and related abstract model (the *OSI reference model*) developed by the ISO, most of which are incompatible with the Internet protocols.

output feedback (OFB)

> a block cipher mode in which the cipher is used to generate the key stream; also called *autokey mode*.

packet

> a block of data carried by a network. When one host sends a message to another, the message is broken into one or more packets, which are individually sent across the network.

packet switching

> network technology in which data is transmitted in packets. The traditional alternative was to establish a connection between source and destination, and to transmit data as a sequence of bits. Packets travel from source to destination along whatever route is immediately available, and different packets in the same message might take different paths.

passive attack

> an attack in which data is observed but not modified. This is the type of attack performed by Peeping Tom.

password, pass code

a secret data item that is used to authenticate an entity. Passwords are often words that an individual is supposed to memorize. The system authenticates the person on the assumption that the password is only known by the person to whom it belongs.

password sniffing

an attack in which someone examines data traffic that includes secret passwords in order to recover the passwords, presumably to use them later in masquerades

PC card, PCMCIA card

a small, standard, plug-in peripheral card often used in laptops as well as workstation computer systems. Modems are often packaged in PC cards. They are also used to hold crypto facilities and to store keying material safely.

Peeping Tom

an attacker whose attacks are based on examining network data traffic; such as password sniffing

perimeter

the physical boundary between the inside and the outside. Security measures rely on being able to trust individuals within a perimeter, at least to some degree.

physical network address

a host address on a data link

plaintext

data that has not been encrypted or data that was decrypted from ciphertext

Play-It-Again Sam

an attacker whose attacks are based on intercepting legitimate messages and transmitting them over again in order to trick the system or its users somehow

port number

a number carried in internet transport protocols to identify which service or program is supposed to receive an incoming packet. Certain port numbers are permanently assigned to particular protocols by the IANA. For example, e-mail generally uses port 25 and Web services traditionally use port 80.

Post Office Protocol (POP)

an Internet protocol for retrieving e-mail from a server host

Pretty Good Privacy (PGP)

an e-mail crypto protocol that uses RSA and IDEA, implemented in a software package widely distributed on the Internet

Privacy Enhanced Mail (PEM)

an e-mail crypto protocol published by the IETF and provided in some commercial products

private key

a key used in public key crypto that belongs to an individual entity and must be kept secret

programmed attack

an attack on a computer device or protocol that can be embodied in a computer program. Such attacks can be used by attackers with limited expertise.

protocol suite

a collection of communications protocols that work together to provide useful services. There are two widely known protocol suites: the Internet protocols and the ISO/OSI protocols.

proxy

a facility that indirectly provides some service. Proxy crypto applies crypto services to network traffic without individual hosts having to support the services themselves. Firewall proxies provide access to Internet services that are on the other side of the firewall while controlling access to services in either direction.

pseudorandom number generator (PRNG)

a procedure that generates a sequence of numerical values that appear random. *Cryptographic* PRNGs strive to generate sequences that are almost impossible to predict. Most PRNGs in commercial software are *statistical* PRNGs that strive to produce randomly distributed data with a sequence that may in fact be somewhat predictable.

public key

a key used in public key crypto that belongs to an individual entity and is distributed publicly. Others can use the public key to encrypt data that only the key's owner can decrypt.

public key algorithm

a cipher that uses a pair of keys, a public key and private key, for encryption and decryption; also called an *asymmetric algorithm*

Public Key Cryptography Standards (PKCS)

standards published by RSA Data Security that describe how to use public key crypto in a reliable, secure, and interoperable fashion

random number

a number with a value that cannot be predicted. Truly random numbers are often generated by physical events that are believed to occur randomly

red/black separation

a design concept for crypto systems that keeps the portions of the system that handle plaintext rigidly separate from portions that handle ciphertext. Portions that handle both are vigorously minimized and then very carefully implemented.

replay

an attack that attempts to trick the system by retransmitting a legitimate message

reusable password

a password that can be used over and over, as opposed to a one-time password. Most passwords used today are reusable passwords.

rewrite

an attack that modifies an encrypted message's contents without decrypting it first

Rivest Cipher #2 (RC2)

a block cipher sold by RSA Data Security, Inc.; treated as lightweight crypto under older U.S. crypto export rules when used with a 40-bit crypto key.

Rivest Cipher #4 (RC4)

a stream cipher that is widely used in commercial products

Rivest, Shamir, Adelman (RSA)

a public key crypto system that can encrypt or decrypt data and also apply or verify a digital signature

RSA Data Security, Inc. (RSADSI)

the company primarily responsible for selling and licensing public key crypto for commercial purposes

router

a device that carries IP packets between a pair of networks when the packets' destination host is either on the receiving network or nearer to the receiving network; dedicated to this task and rarely provides other services

routing host

a host that routes IP packets between networks as well as provides other services

secret key

a crypto key that is used in a secret key (*symmetric*) algorithm. The secrecy of encrypted data depends solely on the secrecy of the secret key.

secret key algorithm

a crypto algorithm that uses the same key to encrypt data and to decrypt data; also called a *symmetric algorithm*

Secure Hypertext Transfer Protocol (SHTTP)

an extension to HTTP to apply crypto services to Web data and transactions

Secure Multipart Internet Message Extensions (S/MIME)

a proposed protocol for embedding crypto-protected messages in Internet e-mail

Secure Sockets Layer (SSL)

a crypto protocol applied to data at the socket interface; often bundled with applications, and widely used to protect World Wide Web traffic

seed, random

a random data value used when generating a random sequence of data values with a PRNG

server

the entity in a networking relationship that provides service to other entities on the network. Server software generally resides on hosts with constant, well-known network addresses so that clients can reliably contact them. Servers provide information and perform other activities in response to client requests.

session key

a crypto key intended to encrypt data for a limited period of time, typically only for a single communications session between a pair of entities. Once the session is over, the key is discarded and a new one established when a new session takes place.

shim

a software component inserted at a well-known interface between two other software components. Shim versions of IPSEC are often implemented at the device driver interface, below the host's TCP/IP network protocol stack.

Simple Key Interchange Protocol (SKIP)

a protocol that establishes session keys to use with IPSEC protocol headers. SKIP data is carried in packet headers and travels in every IPSEC-protected packet

Simple Mail Transfer Protocol (SMTP)

an Internet protocol for transmitting e-mail between e-mail servers

SKIPJACK

a block cipher developed by the NSA and provided in the CAPSTONE, CLIP-PER, and Fortezza devices

snake oil

a derogatory term applied to a product whose developers describe it with misleading, inconsistent, or incorrect technical statements

sniffing

an attack that collects information from network messages by making copies of their contents. Password sniffing is the most widely publicized example.

socket interface

the software interface between a host's network protocol stack and applications programs that use the network

splitting

the process of dividing a crypto key into two separate keys so that an attacker cannot reconstruct the actual crypto key even if one of the split keys is intercepted

stream cipher

a cipher that operates on a continuous data stream instead of processing a block of data at a time

strong crypto

crypto facilities that exceed the standards for lightweight or medium-strength crypto and therefore face significant restrictions under U.S. export rules

symmetric algorithm

a crypto algorithm that uses the same crypto key for encrypting and decrypting; also called a *secret key algorithm*

TCP/IP

the common acronym for the protocols packaged in a network protocol stack for the Internet protocols

Telnet

the Internet protocol that supports remote terminal connections

token, authentication

a hardware device that generates a one-time password to authenticate its owner; also sometimes applied to software programs that generate one-time passwords

token, e-mail

a data item in the header of an encrypted e-mail message that holds an encrypted copy of the secret key used to encrypt the message; usually encrypted with the recipient's public key so that only the recipient can decrypt it

Transmission Control Protocol (TCP)

the Internet protocol that provides a reliable connection between a server and a client

transport encryption

crypto services applied to information above the network level but below the application software level. This allows crypto protections to be applied to an existing application protocol and also use the existing network protocol stack and underlying networking services. Transport encryption is typically packaged with the application that it is protecting.

transport mode

an ESP mode that encrypts the data contents of a packet and leaves the original IP addresses in plaintext

triple DES (3DES)

Cipher that applies the DES cipher three times with either two or three different DES keys

Trojan horse

a program with secret functions that surreptitiously access information without the operator's knowledge, usually to circumvent security protections

tunnel mode

an ESP mode that encrypts an entire IP packet, including the IP header

VENONA

a U.S. military project to cryptanalyze Soviet one time pad ciphertext from the 1940s

Vernam cipher

a cipher developed for encrypting teletype traffic by computing the exclusive-or of the data bits and the key bits

virtual private network (VPN)

a private network built atop a public network. Hosts within the private network use encryption to talk to other hosts. The encryption excludes hosts from outside the private network even if they are on the public network.

virus

a small program that attaches itself to a legitimate program. When the legitimate program runs, the virus copies itself onto other legitimate programs in a form of reproduction

wide area network (WAN)

a network that connects host computers and sites across a wide geographical area

work factor

the amount of work an attacker must perform to overcome security measures

World Wide Web (WWW)

an international information network using HTTP and HTML residing on Internet host computers

worm

a computer program that copies itself into other host computers across a network. In 1988 the Internet Worm infected several thousand hosts.

X.400

an e-mail protocol developed by the CCITT and endorsed by the ISO as part of the OSI protocol family

X.500

a specification of the directory service required to support X.400 e-mail

X.509

a public key certificate specification developed as part of the X.500 directory specification, often used in public key systems

Appendix
B
Bibliography

Abrams, Marshall D., and Harold J. Podell, eds. *Tutorial: Computer and Network Security.* Los Angeles, CA: IEEE Computer Society Press, 1986.

Anderson, Ross J. "Why Cryptosystems Fail." *Communications of the ACM* November 1994: Reprinted in William Stallings ed., *Practical Cryptography for Data Internetworks.* Los Angeles, CA: IEEE Press, 1996.

ANSI Standard X9.17, Financial Institution Key Management (Wholesale). Washington, DC: American Bankers Association, 1985.

Atkinson, R. "Security Architecture for the Internet Protocol." *Internet RFC 1825.* August 1995.
ftp://ftp.internic.net/rfc/rfc1825.txt

Atkinson, R. "IP Authentication Header." *Internet RFC 1826.* August 1995.
ftp://ftp.internic.net/rfc/rfc1826.txt

Atkinson, R. "IP Encapsulating Security Payload (ESP)." *Internet RFC 1827.* August 1995.
ftp://ftp.internic.net/rfc/rfc1827.txt

Bellovin, Steven M. *Problem Areas for the IP Security Protocols.* AT&T Research, working draft, 1997.
ftp://ftp.research.att.com/dist/smb/badesp.ps

Brickell, Ernest F., Dorothy E. Denning, Stephen T. Kent, David P. Maher, and Walter Tuchman. *SKIPJACK Review Interim Report: The SKIPJACK Algorithm.* Posted to sci.crypt, July 28, 1993.
http://www.cosc.georgetown.edu/~denning/SKIPJACK.txt

CCITT. *Recommendation X.509: The Directory—Authentication Framework.* CCITT, 1988.

Chapman, D. Brent, and Elizabeth D. Zwicky. *Building Internet Firewalls.* Sebastapol, CA: O'Reilly & Associates, 1995.

Cheswick, William R., and Steven M. Bellovin. *Firewalls and Internet Security: Repelling the Wily Hacker.* Reading, MA: Addison Wesley, 1994.

Cohen, Frederick B. *A Short Course on Computer Viruses.* New York, NY: John Wiley & Sons, 1994.

Comer, Douglas E. *Internetworking with TCP/IP, Volume 1: Principles, Protocols, and Architecture*. Englewood Cliffs, NJ: Prentice Hall, 1991.

Computer Emergency Response Team. *CERT Advisories*. 1997.
ftp://info.cert.org/pubs/advisories/

Davis, Peter T., ed. *Securing Client/Server Computer Networks*. New York, NY: McGraw-Hill, 1996.

FIPS. "Security Requirements for Cryptographic Modules: FIPS-140-1." *Federal Information Processing Standard*. Washington, DC: NIST, 1994.

FIPS. "Escrowed Encryption Standard: FIPS-185." *Federal Information Processing Standard*. Washington, DC: NIST, 1994.

Garfinkel, Simson. *PGP: Pretty Good Privacy*. Sebastapol, CA: O'Reilly & Associates, 1995.

Garfinkel, Simson, and Gene Spafford. *Practical Unix and Internet Security*. Sebastapol, CA: O'Reilly & Associates, 1996.

Greenlee, M. Blake. "Requirements for Key Management Protocols in the Wholesale Financial Industry." In Marshall D. Abrams and Harold J. Podell, eds. *Tutorial: Computer and Network Security*. Los Angeles, CA: IEEE Computer Society Press, 1986.

Holbrook, R., and J. Reynolds. "Site Security Handbook." *Internet RFC 1244,* July 1991.
ftp://ftp.internic.net/rfc/rfc1244.txt

Kahn, David. *The Codebreakers: The Story of Secret Writing*. New York, NY: Macmillan, 1967.

Kalakota, Ravi, and Andrew B. Whinston. *Frontiers of Electronic Commerce*. Reading, MA: Addison Wesley, 1996.

Kaufman, Charlie, Radia Perlman, and Mike Speciner. *Network Security: PRIVATE Communication in a PUBLIC World*. Englewood Cliffs, NJ: Prentice Hall, 1995.

Kent, Steve. "Privacy Enhancement for Internet Electronic Mail: Part II: Certificate-Based Key Management." *Internet RFC 1422,* February 1993.
ftp://ftp.internic.net/rfc/rfc1422.txt

Knuth, Donald E. *The Art of Computer Programming, Vol. 2: Seminumerical Algorithms*. Reading, MA: Addison Wesley, 1969.

Koops, Bert-Jaap. *Crypto Law Survey,* Version 6.0. January 1997.
http://cwis.kub.nl/~frw/people/koops/lawsurvy.htm

Linn, John, Steve Kent, D. Balenson, and B. Kaliski. "Privacy Enhancement for Internet Electronic Mail: Parts I-IV." *Internet RFCs 1421-4,* February 1993.
ftp://ftp.internic.net/rfc/rfc142[1-4].txt

Metzger, P., and W. Simpson. "IP Authentication using Keyed MD5." *Internet RFC 1828,* August 1995.
ftp://ftp.internic.net/rfc/rfc1828.txt

Metzger, P., P. Karn, and W. Simpson. "The ESP DES-CBC Transform." *Internet RFC 1829.* August 1995.
ftp://ftp.internic.net/rfc/rfc1829.txt

National Computer Security Association. *NCSA Firewall Certification Program.* Web pages.
http://www.ncsa.com/fpfs/fwindex.html

National Computer Security Association. *Certified Secure Web Site Certification Program.*
http://www.ncsa.com/webcom/webcert.html

National Computer Security Center. *Trusted Computer Systems Evaluation Criteria.* DOD 5200.28-STD. Washington, DC: Department of Defense, December 1985.

National Research Council. *Cryptography's Role in Securing the Information Society.* Washington, DC: National Academy Press, 1996.

National Security Agency. *The VENONA Translations.* Web pages.
http://www.nsa.org:8080/museum/venona

Netscape Communications. *SSL 3.0 Specification.* Web pages.
http://www.netscape.com/libr/ssl/ssl3/index.html

Pekelney, Rich. *Electronic Cipher Machine (ECM) Mark II.* Web pages.
http://www.maritime.org/ecm2.shtml

Rivest, Ron. "On the Difficulty of Factoring." *RSA Newsletter* Fall 1993: 361–364. Reprinted in Garfinkel, Simpson. *PGP: Pretty Good Privacy.* Sebastapol, CA: O'Reilly & Associates, 1995.

RSA Data Security. *S / WAN Interoperability Testing.* Web pages.
http://www.rsadsi.com/swan/

RSA Laboratories. *The Public Key Cryptography Standards (PKCS).* RSA Data Security, Inc., 1993.
http://www.rsadsi.com/pubs/pkcs/

Schneier, Bruce. *E-Mail Security: How to Keep Your Electronic Messages Private.* New York, NY: John Wiley & Sons, 1995.

Schneier, Bruce. *Applied Cryptography: Protocol, Algorithms, and Source Code in C*, 2nd ed. New York, NY: John Wiley & Sons, 1996.

Sheymov, Victor. *Tower of Secrets.* Annapolis, MD: Naval Institute Press, 1993.

Simmons, Gustavus J. "Cryptanalysis and Protocol Failures." *Communications of the ACM:* November 1994, 56–65. Reprinted in Stallings, W. *Practical Cryptography for Data Internetworks.* Los Angeles, CA: IEEE Press, 1996.

Smith, Richard E. "Securing Client/Server TCP/IP." In Davis, Peter T., ed. *Securing Client / Server Computer Networks.* New York NY: McGraw-Hill, 1996.

Stallings, William. *Practical Cryptography for Data Internetworks.* Los Angeles, CA: IEEE Press, 1996

Stein, Lincoln D. *How to Set Up and Maintain a Web Site*. Reading, MA: Addison Wesley, 1997.

Stein, Lincoln D. *World Wide Web Security FAQ*. Web pages.
http://www.genome.mit.edu/WWW/faqs/www-security-faq.html

Stevens, W. Richard. *TCP/IP Illustrated, Volume 1: The Protocols*. Reading, MA: Addison Wesley, 1994.

Stoll, Clifford. *The Cuckoo's Egg*, New York, NY: Doubleday, 1989.

Voydock, Victor L., and Stephen T. Kent. "Security Mechanisms in High-Level Network Protocols." *ACM Computing Surveys* June 1983: 135–171. A shorter version is reprinted in Marshall D. Abrams and Harold J. Podell, eds., *Tutorial: Computer and Network Security*. Los Angeles, CA: IEEE Computer Society Press, 1986.

Wagner, David A., and Steven M. Bellovin. *Bump in the Stack Encryptor for MSDOS Systems. Symposium on Network and Distributed System Security*, San Diego, CA: February 1996.

Weiner, Michael J. "Efficient DES Key Search." *Report TR-244,* CA: Carlton University, 1994. Reprinted in Stallings W. *Practical Cryptography for Data Internetworks*. Los Angeles, CA: IEEE Press, 1996.

Wright, Peter, with Paul Greengrass. *Spycatcher: The Candid Autobiography of a Senior Intelligence Officer*. New York, NY: Viking Penguin, 1987.

Index